No Bath But Plenty of Bubbles

The Colville commune also put together Come Together 15 *in early 1973 . . . In the commune's history, 'Happy Families', there is an invitation to visit them. 'Come up and see us sometime. We are squatting in a disused film studio with no bath but plenty of bubbles.'*

– from chapter sixteen, p. 229

No Bath But Plenty of Bubbles

An Oral History
of the
Gay Liberation Front,
1970–73

Lisa Power

CASSELL

For J

For a catalogue of related titles in our
Sexual Politics list please
write to us at the address below:

Cassell plc
Wellington House
125 Strand
London
WC2R 0BB

215 Park Avenue South
New York
NY 10003

First published 1995

British Library Cataloguing-in-Publication Data
A catalogue record for this book is available from the British Library.

ISBN   0-304-33195-3
       0-304- 33205-4

Typeset by Ben Cracknell
Printed and bound in Great Britain by Biddles Ltd, Guildford and King's Lynn

Contents

Acknowledgements

I would like to thank:

Steve Cook at Cassell for buying me lunch and saying 'Have you ever thought about writing a book?' and not gulping too hard when I told him I'd doubled the length of it, and Liz Gibbs for generally being sunny whenever I rang with another problem. Rictor Norton for his tactful editing and Douglas Slater and Helen Sandler for their determined proofing.

Sue Donnelly, keeper of much buried treasure at the Hall Carpenter Archives (where all material gifted to me has gone) and the Archive, staff at the London School of Economics.

Time Out who (via Tim Clark) let me rifle through their archives and rearrange their photo library, and all the photographers – I have done my best to trace you!

Everyone from the Gay Liberation Front who put up with my stupid questions and my lengthy borrowing of their precious mementoes – Nettie Pollard, Elizabeth Wilson, Angela Mason, Julia L, Sue Winter, Jane Winter, Annie Brackx, Martin Corbett, Peter Tatchell, Carl Hill, Bette Bourne, Aubrey Walter, David Fernbach, Michael Mason, Alaric Sumner, Cloud Downey, Micky Burbidge, Ted Walker Brown, Tony Halliday, Tim Clark, Antony Grey, Harry Beck, Simon Watney, Jim Fouratt. In addition to the above thanks, Mary McIntosh, Sarah Grimes, Max McLellan, Alan Wakeman, Jeffrey Weeks and above all John Chesterman lent me vast amounts of materials for months at a time. Steven Bradbury, before his death, told me the stories that reawakened my determination to do this book. I apologize to all those people I didn't manage to speak to and hope I have not wronged anyone, or spelt too many of your names wrongly. Thank you for opening up your heads, your homes and in some cases your wounds. You were all very kind to me.

In particular Carla Toney, Stuart Feather, Paul Theobald, Michael James and Andrew Lumsden of GLF for their support and friendship, not to mention the drinks, walking tours, postcards and endless phone calls.

And Julian Hows for an abundance of all the things that I have thanked other GLF people for, and also for his computer when my machine gave out, and his typing chair when my back did. That's what I call real support. For once, it is true to say of someone that I could not have written this book without them – literally.

Preface

THIS book was written out of love and irritation. Love for the people who told me wonderful stories and for the memory of others who could have told me more. Love for the flame that still flares up in their eyes and animates their voices as they tell them. Love for the strength of characters which were forged by street action and absurd but beautiful hopes and ideals.

Love and irritation. Irritation at the dismissive male verdicts upon the women and queens of GLF which have persisted without their voices being heard for themselves. Irritation at the way that current gay politicians remake our history to suit their goals. Irritation – no – anger at the waste of lives told here but lost in the later epidemic of AIDS amongst gay men.

The lives are not reclaimable but the memories are and that is what this book is about. Although it follows a rough chronological progress, it tries to tell the stories as much as possible through the memories and documents of the London Gay Liberation Front and its contemporaries. It tries to show the traces of GLF thought and organization which have subtly affected the lives of every person who has come out since 1970. It tries, on the whole, not to comment too much upon them in the light of the 1990s except to sometimes marvel at their audacity, or where GLF people themselves have made such comments.

The language is often that of the 1970s and thus uses, for instance, 'gay' for both lesbians and gay men. The people who told me their stories often slipped not only into the language but the mannerisms and attitudes of the period. Many of them have changed their lives since then and I have tried to respect that. I have called them by the names that they asked me to, whether these were the ones they used then or the ones they use now.

I was not able to talk to every London GLF person (they were always people, not members, because GLF was a movement and not an organization – something the reformist groups could never quite grasp) but I have tried to talk to at least a couple of people from each area of it. I chose to concentrate upon London not because it is intrinsically more important but because it was the first and the biggest in the UK. If you have a story or your town has a history which is not here then tell it or get it told, somehow. This part of our history should not be lost or ignored, as it nearly has been.

I do not think that GLF can come again, but I think that there are things to learn from it. At a time of extreme consumerism, when the lesbian and gay scene is once again at a great distance from the youth culture and most political hopes for change, when Freedom is a cafe, Heaven a disco and Attitude a style magazine, there are two things homosexuals still can't buy – ideals and self-respect. The Gay Liberation Front, for all its faults, had both in abundance.

Lisa Power, London, July 1995

(NOTE: As a general rule, I have quoted from GLF and related documents without amending original spelling, punctuation or typographical features.)

Chapter one

To *the Revolutionary Brothers and Sisters*

We must relate to the homosexual movement because it's a real thing. –Huey Newton, Supreme Commander, Black Panthers

THE Gay Liberation Front, like so many other aspects of the modern lesbian and gay movement, started in the United States of America. And, again like so many other aspects, it has subsequently been sanitized, simplified and revised to fit the interests and prejudices of activists who want their history to echo and validate their current preoccupations. Popular historical accounts have an organization apparently springing full blown from the forehead of a brave drag queen (bar dyke/transsexual/rent boy, depending on your political affiliations and current fashion) at a spontaneous riot in New York City which may or may not have had something to do with the death of their icon Judy Garland that week (depending on whether she was yours too). But life is always messier than history.

The Gay Liberation Front was waiting to happen in 1969. The bar queens who rioted so angrily in New York were not the people who actually started it, though some of them like Marsha Johnson joined GLF later. It was started by the radicals and hippies who had mostly stood on the fringes of the crowd that night and who had been trying to get something together for a while. People who were sick of having to put on a suit to fit in with gay activism as it was then; people who were sick of hiding their gayness in order to be able to articulate their other political views. The Stonewall riots on 27 June 1969 and subsequent nights were just the wind that carried gay liberation to the homosexual population of the United States and allowed it the toe-hold it needed in the

2: No Bath But Plenty of Bubbles

popular imagination to sprout and grow into hundreds of groups, many thousands of people across the continent in a few short months.

The Gay Liberation Front, according to eye witnesses, was technically born at a meeting of the Mattachine Society, a gay campaigning group, in New York. On 4 July that year a group of young, politically experienced gays of both sexes walked out of a discussion about the riots of the previous week because the line being taken by Mattachine leaders was too apologist. The story of that night and all that led up to it are best told by Martin Duberman in his book *Stonewall*, unless you can get one of the ringleaders of the walkout (like Jim Fouratt, who still lives a stone's throw from the Stonewall) to make you a cup of coffee and explain it all. The story has led many people to vilify the Mattachine Society as the ultimate gay appeasers though it is worth remembering that previously they had a good track record in protesting police brutality. But the sight of a riot by a bunch of working-class drag queens who don't give a shit is apt to upset many a person aspiring to respectability.

Realistically, the seeds of GLF had already existed for some time. Younger gay activists were already showing their dissatisfaction with traditional campaigning. West Coast groups in particular were refusing to accept the hierarchy and rules imposed by older Eastern organizers and looking to the new liberation movements for their inspiration. Leo Laurence, editor of *Vector*, the magazine of the Society for Individual Rights (SIR) in California, had begun to call for an alliance with black and anti-Vietnam groups, and gays in San Francisco had demonstrated outside the offices of a company which sacked Laurence's lover Gale Whittington. Ironically, Laurence himself was subsequently sacked by SIR for his attitudes. 'Gay Is Good' was already an accepted slogan on the West Coast.

As in England the following year, the majority of young people who became central GLF activists in New York and many other cities already had a history of radical activism. Jim Fouratt, Martha Shelley and others had worked against the Vietnam war. Martha and others had been active in the feminist movement which was then entirely heterosexual (on the surface). Others were in a variety of leftist groups. Some had been involved with Timothy Leary and other gurus and Jim himself had been a leading 'yippie' – one of the politicized hippies who had rioted at the Republican Convention in Chicago and zapped many institutions. The only thing they had in common was that they were believers in some sort of social revolution and the practice of those beliefs had hitherto meant that they had to hide their homosexuality to some degree. As Duberman puts it, 'They had learned much in making everybody else's revolution; now they would apply that learning to making their own.'

What marked out GLF from the start within the gay movement were two things: their new style of unashamed assertiveness and their determination to make links with other movements for social revolution such as the Black Panthers and Women's Liberation. The style was adopted to varying degrees by many other gay groups, but the rainbow philosophy remained distinctive to GLF in the organization's lifetime. Indeed, within months there had already been a split within the GLF ranks with gay (mostly male, mostly white) activists who liked the new style but did not see why they should spend their energies in collaboration with other movements. In New York, these people left to start the single-issue Gay Activists Alliance which, with its combination of an in-your-face manner and acceptance of male-identified formal organizing, was soon far more visibly successful than GLF. In many ways, they were similar to the group of gay men in GLF London who formed one side of the arguments in its last year – more interested in rights than revolutions.

GLF in New York started to meet at Alternative University, a radical meeting place. They produced a newspaper, *Come Out!* and promoted consciousness-raising, a form of encounter group whereby people shared their personal experiences to learn more about themselves and each other and to inform their political actions. They took action in support of women and black people and rapidly came into conflict with other gay groups with more traditional approaches by trying to introduce ideas to their memberships in what was often seen as an aggressive recruiting campaign. Some existing activists, like Craig Rodwell of the Oscar Wilde Memorial Bookshop in Greenwich Village (an open gay community resource predating GLF), sought to work with them. It was Rodwell who first proposed a commemorative march on the anniversary of the New York riots. Many others found their introduction of race, sex and class issues terrifying, subversive and diversionary – a reaction repeated in every gay movement touched by GLF.

GLF pioneered the formation of communes, a hippy concept of alternative family living, within the gay movement across

America. Their activists travelled the country starting groups. Jim Fouratt helped organize the Venceremos Brigade, volunteer workers for Cuba's revolution in defiance of the US government, and was then barred from travelling with it because of his sexuality – an oppressive act which sounded a warning note for gay leftists throughout the US and Europe. Through this and similar activities, GLF was soon a target for the Federal Bureau of Investigation, and was infiltrated and investigated as GLF London would be.

Because so many of its people had training as organizers within the radical movements or student backgrounds which left them highly articulate, GLF philosophy developed fast. By the summer of 1970, not only were there groups all over the country but there were newspapers, pamphlets, developed views on how to live and on the pride that gay people should feel in defiance of religious ministers, politicians and psychotherapists. Drag was an issue on the East Coast and a valued weapon on the West. Martha Shelley and other GLF lesbians were challenging the women's movement and Jim Fouratt and others were beginning to criticize the Black Panthers and the left for their reactionary attitudes to gays. GLF was in its full glory and ready to conquer the hearts of others who had begun to hear of it from overseas.

> I left home at eighteen. I was going to gay clubs and in the Communist Party, the Young Communist League. I did a Sociology degree at West Ham College and read about the Stonewall riots as part of being a politically aware student. I had been the person who took the hammer in to break the gates down at the London School of Economics [during student riots there]. I and David Fernbach helped to found the Revolutionary Socialist Student Federation . . . I read about Gay Liberation in the States in *The Times* and after my degree exams I went over there, doing sales stuff for the *New Left Review*, going round towns and meeting the underground newspapers in each of them and the Gay Liberation people at the same time. I saw the Cockettes who broke down gender roles and which Sylvester was a member of. I met Bob Mellors [another LSE student] at a meeting and demos outside the Women's House of Correction in New York. With Sylvia, the drag queen, and Martha Shelley and others, I went along to the Philadelphia meeting organized by the Black Panthers, who were highly

respected by the rest of the left at that point. I remember
the Black Panthers having machine guns. And gay
liberation ideas were on the agenda. (*Aubrey Walter*)

It is at the Revolutionary People's Constitutional Convention in Philadelphia, a meeting called by the Black Panthers to draft
a new constitution for the American revolution, that Jim Fouratt
remembers Aubrey standing out amongst the crowds. 'He was
golden, this gorgeous young man with a halo of curls who sat and
drank everything in. He was fascinated by it and he was really
together.' The Panther Supreme Commander, Huey Newton, had
responded to Jim's public criticism of the group's sexism in a speech
at a Panther rally – an act of considerable courage – by issuing 'A
Letter From Huey To The Revolutionary Brothers And Sisters
About The Women's Liberation And Gay Liberation' and inviting
Jim and other gay revolutionaries to the Convention. This letter
was long quoted by gays seeking legitimacy with black activists or
remonstrating with black homophobia and it bears repeating.
Given that some Panther leaders, such as Eldridge Cleaver, were
deeply and proudly sexist and homophobic, it is a remarkable
document and was instrumental in changing attitudes throughout
the revolutionary left.

> Whatever your personal opinions and your insecurities
> about homosexuality and the various liberation movements
> among homosexuals and women (and I speak of the
> homosexuals and women as oppressed groups), we should
> try to unite with them in a revolutionary fashion . . . We
> must gain security in ourselves and therefore have respect
> and feelings for all oppressed people . . . we must relate to
> the homosexual movement because it's a real thing. And I
> know through reading and through my life experience, my
> observations, that homosexuals are not given freedom and
> liberty by anyone in the society. Maybe they might be the
> most oppressed people in the society.

The letter went on to confront and reject the common leftist
view that homosexuality was a product of capitalist decadence, to
admonish revolutionaries to take each gay person and group on
their own merits and not react to a stereotype, to admit to and
confront straight male fears about male homosexuality and to
criticize anti-gay language and its use as an insult to establishment

enemies such as President Nixon. 'Homosexuals are not enemies of the people. We should try to form a working coalition with the Gay liberation and Women's liberation groups . . . All Power To The People!' The statement was published in the Black Panther newspaper on 21 August 1970, ready for the Convention which took place in the first week of September.

Although the GLF lesbians, along with most other women outside the Panthers, had walked out on the Convention immediately after discovering that they were only to be allowed one heavily Panther-controlled workshop, the 'Male Homosexual Workshop' suffered less interference and was able to make a statement to the plenary. After defining and rejecting sexism and acknowledging Huey Newton's letter, they listed eighteen demands. Duberman claims that it was met with snickering as well as applause, but still, it was made. The demands were:

- The right to be gay anytime, anyplace
- The right to free physiological change and modification of sex
- The right of free dress and adornment
- That all modes of human sexual self-expression deserve protection of the law and social sanction
- Every child's right to develop in a non-sexist, non-possessive atmosphere which it is the responsibility of all people to create
- That a free educational system present the entire range of human sexuality, without advocating any one form or style; that sex roles and sex-determined skills be not fostered by the schools
- That language be modified so that no gender take priority
- That the judicial system be run by the people through the peoples' courts; that all people be tried by members of their peer group
- That gays be represented in all governmental and community institutions
- That organized religions be condemned for aiding in the genocide of gay people and be enjoined from teaching hatred and superstition
- That psychiatry and psychology be enjoined from advocating a preference for any form of sexuality and from enforcing that preference by means of shock treatment, brainwashing, imprisonment, etc.

7: Revolutionary Brothers and Sisters

- The abolition of the nuclear family because it perpetuates the false categories of homosexuality and heterosexuality
- The immediate release of and reparations for gay and other political prisoners from prisons and mental institutions; the support of gay political prisoners by all other political prisoners
- That gays determine the destiny of their own communities
- That all people share equally the labour and products of society regardless of sex or sexual orientation
- That technology be used to liberate all peoples of the world from drudgery
- The full participation of gays in the peoples' revolutionary army
- Finally, the end of domination of one person by another
- No Revolution Without Us! An Army Of Lovers Cannot Lose! All Power To The People!

Aubrey travelled across America and was able to see the varieties of gay liberation springing up in different cities. In particular, he remembers the West Coast GLFs, with their emphasis on personal as well as social revolution and their dynamic opposition to psychiatric treatment of gays. He was able to witness another historic event in American gay history, the disruption of the American Psychiatrists Convention by GLF drag queens protesting at their diagnosis of gays as needing psychiatric help. This was at a time when homosexuality was still formally classified as an illness in international guidance.

> In San Francisco I met Konstantin Berlant, who had dragged up to disrupt the American Psychiatrists Convention and I stayed in their commune. The stuff around the Convention was seminal and it's important to remember that most of the ideology of GLF came from the West Coast groups, not from New York. The think-ins were a very simple structure: agree a topic, split into small groups, report back to the rest. It seemed very revolutionary at the time. It really tapped in to the more rebellious people in the gay world, the queens and the butch dykes, who really took to it and fed into the campaigns. Coming from the Communist Party, it hadn't related to issues about gender and sex roles. (*Aubrey Walter*)

8: No Bath But Plenty of Bubbles

Meeting up with Bob Mellors, who had been hanging out with GLF in New York, the two student activists were able to compare their observations and to contrast them with the very different scene they had left back in London – a scene perhaps not so far removed, in its smaller way, from that of the USA before the spark of the Stonewall riots.

Chapter two

Covert and Neurotic vs. the Counterculture

GLF was . . . a new stage of gay consciousness and organization. But it was not the beginning of the gay movement. –David Fernbach, *The Rise and Fall of the Gay Liberation Front*, Gay Culture Pamphlets, LSE

WHILE Aubrey Walter and Bob Mellors were hanging out with the new revolutionary movement in America, others were trying to improve the lives of British lesbians and gay men in a more traditional fashion. The Sexual Offences Act of 1967, passed by Harold Wilson's Labour government along with abortion and sex equality laws in a sudden rush of liberalism, had produced a limited decriminalization of male homosexual acts in England and Wales. Masterminded by Antony Grey and the Homosexual Law Reform Society, a small band of dedicated lobbyists without any allied popular campaign, it had been greeted as a huge advance, although many of the politicians supporting it saw it primarily as a humanitarian attempt to minimize blackmail against homosexuals and were horrified at the growth in gay visibility which followed. Limited change having been achieved by being good and quiet and allowing heterosexuals to speak for them, British gay campaigners were reluctant to push too far too fast.

Things went rather quiet after 1967, as the existing organizations tried to work out what had changed and how it would affect the lives of gay people. 'The Manchester people thought that everything would be better after the '67 Act but it wasn't. The Albany Trust gave up campaigning and just did counselling and there was effectively no leadership for three years' (*Michael Brown*). Most people continued to live the same kind of lives as they had before the Act, and things were no better for lesbians than they ever had been, though quite how bad often depended upon class and urban proximity. 'We had been Gateways lesbians till then. I was involved in the Minorities Research Group a little – I wrote letters, spoke at a meeting in the 1960s and was also involved in the beginning of Kenric, which was some time before 1968. We were part of a loose network of lesbians, mostly middle-class, mostly academic' (*Mary McIntosh*). For most working-class, or apolitical gays, or those under twenty-one, the outlets were limited if enjoyable. 'What I did was to play truant, going along and spending my whole day at Waterloo cottage. A fabulous place, Waterloo or Clapham Common cottage, I used to go along with my duffel bag, change out of my school clothes and into something more appropriate and cottage for the whole day' (*Julian Hows*).

It is understandable that it should take a while for gay men to come to terms with their legality. 'Changing the law, which we had done in 1967, was an essential prelude to even being able to meet and organize openly' (*Antony Grey*). It was far more common then for people to be sacked immediately their homosexuality became known, to be driven from their homes and often to commit suicide rather than let people know. Although this still happens, then it was close to the norm. Homosexuals were universally portrayed, if at all, as sick, sad people. The newspapers, having joined gleefully in various witch-hunts against homosexual spies, ran articles such as 'Ten ways to spot a homosexual' (suede shoes, for some reason, were considered a give-away). The most enlightened attitude that could be hoped for was that homosexuality was a pathological sickness rather than an evil; that, being 'born that way' we couldn't help ourselves and were more to be pitied than condemned. Consequently, most campaigning was around a medical model of homosexuality acceptable to liberal straights.

Within this framework, the two most active organizations were the Albany Society, a counselling charity which worked in conjunction with a political arm, the Homosexual Law Reform Society (responsible for the 1967 Act), and the Committee for Homosexual Equality, formed in the North West but soon to spread nationally on a 'club' format. The latter, which eventually renamed itself the Campaign for Homosexual Equality (CHE) to reflect the greater air of militancy after the founding of GLF, was then the more radical in that it encouraged homosexuals to meet with each other and not just to integrate discreetly with a hostile society. Where the Albany Trust organized research and seminars and trained psychiatrists and other professionals to be more 'sympathetic', the Committee for Homosexual Equality produced plans for gay social clubs and declared that homosexuality was not a medical condition. The Albany Trust were hesitant even to allow the formation of a small support group which came to be known as the St Katherine's Group for their clients. Correspondence in the Hall Carpenter Archives shows a frosty but impeccably polite series of attempts to keep therapeutic control of the group, whose caretaker committee (including Andrew Henderson and Christopher Spence, who went on to found London Lighthouse in the 1980s) were more disposed to allow the members to determine their own organization.

Plans for a series of 'Esquire Clubs' from the North Western Committee for Homosexual Equality in order to encourage social contact were roundly condemned by both the Albany Trust and the politicians responsible for the 1967 Act, on the grounds that this would encourage a 'ghetto' mentality. This attempt to control the growing socio-political scene for gays led to great suspicion of Antony Grey when he attempted, on a personal level, to assist in the founding months of the Gay Liberation Front.

> The trustees of the Albany Trust had refused to support the formation of social clubs – Esquire Clubs – by CHE, so they would not have supported GLF at all. I went along as an individual, having just left the Trust, but I was still seen as representing the Albany Trust. What troubled me about it was . . . people don't appreciate what it was like for earlier generations. For me, the big problem was the closeted gays who felt threatened by the behaviour of GLF and with our straight supporters who were afraid that what we were doing might encourage more people to be gay. The GLF people looked on the past period of gentle law reform as Uncle Tom-ism. I feel that I was Stalinized, treated like Trotsky, because the past history wasn't popular.
> (*Antony Grey*)

At the end of the 1960s there was no gay press as we would recognize it, only a couple of heavily discreet magazines with clothed pin-ups, such as *Jeremy* and *Spartacus*. If they had any politics at all, it tended to be of the 'don't rock the boat' variety. Nor was there any explicitly gay culture, though there was an incredibly large gay subculture within the entertainment industry which defied censorship by being incomprehensible to outsiders.

12: No Bath But Plenty of Bubbles

From Julian and Sandy in *Round the Horne*, a popular radio show listened to by many families on Sunday lunchtimes after *Family Favourites*, to the plays of Joe Orton, all was innuendo. Even *The Killing of Sister George*, which created a huge scandal at the time, showed nothing except that some women were too attached to each other and very unhappy. Any book or film storyline which admitted homosexuality had to end unhappily. So it was in the straight press, alongside the sniggering reports of court cases and scoutmasters inexplicably too fond of their charges, that alert lesbians and gays heard something of the new militancy in gay rights groups in America. Academics and students of left leanings, such as Aubrey and Bob, might read something in revolutionary literature imported from the US or even have access to the newly-founded *Advocate* or other US publications, but this was unusual.

The bars were no better. At the time of the founding of GLF *Time Out*, the underground-affiliated new listings magazine, listed no bars as 'gay'. It offered a small handful of drag pubs scattered across the capital, as much for the voyeurism of straight tourists as gay men. They included the Black Cap in Camden and the Royal Vauxhall Tavern. Other than this, there were a few known gay pubs in Earls Court, the Salisbury in central London (featured in *Victim*, the Dirk Bogarde film about blackmail which gave support to the 1967 Act) and a few members-only drinking clubs in Soho. In any of these, you could be ejected for the slightest sign of affection towards another person of the same sex. Time and again, GLF people speak of the unfriendliness of the bars, their 'meat-market' quality. Sex was hard to get, but easier than conversation with another homosexual.

Larry Kramer, the US AIDS activist and writer, lived in London in the late 1960s and has clear, if rather grim, memories of what then passed for 'the scene'.

> It was bleak. It was covert and you felt slightly as if you were slinking around back alleys. To go for a drink you had to be a member of a club and they were always up three flights or down three flights and the sun never entered. I'm sure that some people thought it was all wonderful and better then, but it was very covert and social life existed mainly by going to people's houses and meeting there for dinner, or cruising and there was a bathhouse over at Edgware Road which was awful with mould on the walls. Everybody always would fly off to Amsterdam to

have a decent time, you weren't allowed to dance together
here as I recall. Everybody was just in the closet as a matter
of course.

On the other hand, from the day I arrived I couldn't
escape a sense that there wasn't an Englishman that I
couldn't get into bed, whether he was married or no matter
how many kids he had. So I thought, I'm in the gayest
country in the entire world and nobody here will admit it. I
remember one day I went to Fortnums for tea and sat
down at the table with a very nice guy and he was British
and we went back to my house and it was just like these
books you read – he was married and had kids and he
wanted me to take him across my lap and spank him.
Which is what had happened at his public school or
whatever. (*Larry Kramer*)

And 'homosexual' was what most respectable people called
themselves. 'Gay' was the up-and-coming term, for both men and
women ('gay girls' more often than lesbians), and 'queer' was a
deadly insult, embodying the heterosexual assumption that something was wrong with you if you loved your own sex. In inter-
viewing people for this book, I found only two GLF members,
Peter Tatchell and Nettie Pollard, able to use that new fashion
phrase of the 1990s without flinching or audibly putting it in
quotes. 'Dyke' was similarly a taboo word. Most interviewees slipped seamlessly back into using the term 'gay' for both sexes, as has
this book largely. At the turn of the 1970s, the most recently
minted term was 'homophile', used to indicate that there was more
than mere sex involved in same-sex emotional attachments. It was
with the rise of women's liberation during the course of GLF that
most lesbians (a word which had run in tandem with gay for the
more daring) began customarily to call themselves such rather than
gay girls or gay women.

Returning from their adventures in the US, Bob and Aubrey
might have read the bulletins of the Committee for Homosexual
Equality, the cutting edge of gay rights in England in 1970. The
bulletin failed to appear, though, in September or October due to
(among other reasons) shortage of notepaper, holidays and the lack
of an addressing machine which was vital to cope with the increase
to more than six hundred members across the country – until now,
envelopes had been addressed by hand. The November bulletin,
published as the first members of GLF were gathering in the small

lecture room at the LSE, boasted that there were now four active groups in London. Roger Baker, London Organizer, wrote 'It is clear that CHE makes its appeal on two levels. First there is a definite response to the implied militancy of the organization's title with its suggestion of education of the public . . . leading to the creation of a good image and an increase in personal confidence . . . second . . . CHE is obviously going to fulfil a desperately needed social function in establishing a comfortable, relaxed climate in which people can meet and talk.'

CHE groups also existed in Bristol, Birmingham, Wolverhampton, Liverpool, Nottingham and in Cambridge, Oxford and Sheffield Universities, and a steering committee was setting up a constitutional structure. The bulletin wished Antony Grey well in his retirement from the Albany Trust and reported on the work of the Scottish Minorities Group; in fact, there were plans afoot for a federation of homophile organizations bringing all the relevant groups together. A large chunk of the paper was taken up with the press letters of J. Martin Stafford, Counselling Secretary of CHE, an eccentric right-winger who two years later reported the fledgling *Gay News* to the Director of Public Prosecutions for their publication of personal adverts.

The most interesting item, with hindsight, is a piece by R. J. Elbert on 'The American Homophile Movement':

> It is noteworthy that the serious consideration given by the media to homosexual organizations has increased in direct proportion to the latter's militancy. In keeping with that country's contradictory traditions of a puritanical and often crude conservatism and a freedom loving individualism, American homosexuals, while suffering from more archaic laws than Britain's, have been building organizations to promote their interests for some twenty years, so that now more than fifty exist across the country. In the past, the most impressive of these has been the Society for Individual Rights, which runs a social centre in San Francisco and publishes a monthly magazine, *Vector* . . . The SIR has aimed to conciliate the local political establishment and the police force . . . In the past it has aimed to include all shades of homosexual opinion, to be 'a family based on a sense of togetherness' as a former editor of *Vector* would have it.

Recent developments in the homophile movement have damaged this cosy ideal. This summer's 'Gay Pride Week', which brought out large demonstrations by homosexuals across America, commemorated last year's riot in New York provoked by police efforts to close a gay bar. Since then a new revolutionary wing of the homophile movement, best represented by the 'Gay Liberation Front' and 'Radicalesbians', has rejected the efforts of established bodies to achieve integration into society, aligning itself instead with 'all oppressed peoples' in a struggle to overthrow the oppressive conventional order. A casualty of this ferment has been the liberalism advocated by such organizations as SIR, which recently sacked an editor of *Vector* who wrote in favour of Gay Revolution. But the resulting debate on the homosexual's situation and on his relationship with society has achieved a depth and urgency lacking in this country. For the demonstrators a vocal pride and sense of solidarity has been born, contrasting with the homosexual's usual covert and neurotic situation.

It may be that these developments will encourage those in Britain who have been fearful or apathetic to claim their right to free expression as homosexual citizens and some to present a fundamental challenge to a society whose ideals exclude and oppress them. An energetic promotion of their cause would benefit all homosexuals, while even moderates need militants to make them appear moderate!

Such a measured response was not to last, as GLF exploded into the comfortable, friendly structures that CHE was busy weaving. As in America, the gay movement had somehow been left in a timewarp, previously untouched by the revolutionary liberation movements setting up around it and out of touch with youth culture and popular politics. It was about to be brought into the 1970s with a bump; a rude unsettling that put many existing activist noses out of joint. The countercultural wolf was at the homophile door.

'[GLF] recruited support mainly from that section of the gay population that had already been touched, to some extent at least, by either the "new left" or the counterculture' (*David Fernbach, The Rise and Fall of GLF*).

The counterculture was about dropping out, drugs, free sexuality, hippiedom, flower power and that was still part of the heady atmosphere that was behind it but I think by 1970 it had become much more hard edged and political. There was this sense of, the Americans used the term more than us, 'The Movement', a sense that it was not just about personal lifestyles, it was also about much wider social change. All the rhetoric of GLF was about revolution and there was a real confusion between revolutionizing one's lifestyle and revolutionizing society. A belief, which I think came through in lots of GLF's concerns, that if you changed your head and changed your lifestyle then somehow the edifice of militaristic capitalism would all come crumbling down. So it was about lifestyle, but it was about that lifestyle being a precursor almost of a better society, but also the means by which that better society would come about. (*Jeffrey Weeks*)

My and David's political background was in the anti-Vietnam movement, we had been in the Vietnam Solidarity Campaign and I was at Grosvenor Square. The spirit to fight back came from the Vietnam struggle and the cultural revolution in China, the idea that it was right to make a revolution. Other people's struggles, black people, women, had shown the intelligentsia that you should fight from where you were oppressed yourself. (*Aubrey Walter*)

As in America, many of the young activists who flocked to GLF had found their training and philosophy, not in the old-fashioned and out-of-touch gay rights movement but in the new left or the many variations of a revolutionary movement; others were simply hippies and 'heads' (short for dopeheads). GLF London attracted, amongst others, people with a background in resistance to the Vietnam war, black rights, women's liberation, the underground press, the White Panthers (a support group to the Black Panthers), the International Marxist Group, the Communist Party, a wide variety of other leftist groups including Maoists, the drugs culture, transsexuals and rent boys – none of whom would have felt happy in (or indeed been welcome in) existing gay organizations.

All of them to some extent reflected the general youth culture of the time, 'sex, drugs and fucking in the streets' as it was frequently characterized both by its proponents and a scandalized media. Much of the revolutionary rhetoric and concepts which defined the difference of GLF came from this cultural mix, from the frequent references to 'oppression' of various kinds to the rejection of the nuclear family and the emphasis on 'peace and love', 'sisters and brothers' and 'power to the people', all dressed in acid-influenced graphics and bright, flowing clothes. At its most extreme, there was also a belief in a kind of Armageddon – the 'Helter Skelter' in which Charles Manson and his murderous followers believed, that revolutionary forces would rise up and overthrow society and that this could be brought on by acts of terrorism or anarchy. As appendix one illustrates, bombings of a variety of social and political targets were frequent throughout 1970 and 1971, although in Britain these were seldom fatal.

Other people drawn to GLF had done the hippie trail or 'dropped out' in a variety of ways. 'I was a real hippie and I'd spent a year in Crete just before GLF. I went to Greece in early 1970 with a woman that I'd fallen in love with, we were trying to go to India but we never got there. My sister had been sending copies of *IT* [*International Times*] to me, so I was keeping in touch with the counterculture. I wrote to tell my parents that I was gay and they said that they'd always known' (*Carl Hill*). Others were heavily involved in the underground culture and media of London. 'I hung out at *Frendz*, the magazine, and did stuff for them. I knew about the black power movement in the US, I had been involved in getting Cleaver and Davis published. I was even briefly allowed into the Black Panthers in London, which I left to start the White Panthers who were groupies to the Black Panthers. I was involved in the Mangrove defence work. I was a Trotskyite and I wanted to relate the movements to each other' (*John Chesterman*).

Gay hippies were not a new phenomenon, though the intense sexism of much of the hippie movement had suppressed them publicly. Just as hippie women were drawn to women's liberation because of the atrocious way that hippie society treated them as earth-mother cooks and cleaners, always ready to 'put out' for their menfolk and preferably their menfolk's friends, gay hippies were alienated by the frequent and casual heterosexism of role models such as Abbie Hoffman and its uncritical acceptance by his followers. *Radical Arts*, a British magazine of 1970, full of rhetoric about challenging society and supporting the oppressed, approvingly quoted him on how to talk to the police at demonstrations. 'When I get pissed at cops it goes something like this: "You fuckin' fag-ass cocksuckers! you commie pimps! you Jew-bastard fags! . . . I'll bet you fuck each other up the ass . . ."

That spooks 'em. You can hurt their feelings . . . psychic ju-jitsu always has its risks but you always get the message through.' The message gay hippies got was that they should keep their mouths shut if they wanted to keep their street cred.

But in the summer of 1970, with the example of America before them, Aubrey and Bob were not the only people to be thinking of making waves. A couple of GLF people vaguely remember groups of male hippies getting together that summer in an informal way, talking about the importance of doing something but being too stoned or too untogether to actually get a meeting organized. The furthest they seem to have got was a letter, published in several of the underground newspapers around the same time that GLF began to meet.

> To All Gay Heads Everywhere
> We are a minority within a minority subculture and it is time for us to get an alternative thing to the straight gay scene – Earls Court is a far cry from Phun City. We have read all the articles about gayness and how there are no homosexuals in the Underground. Well, this means fuck all to us as we still have to use the straight gay scene for our basic needs.
> We don't accept the straight gay scene because it is just a fool copy of the straight system. It's a drag having to categorise but for a while it is necessary so that we can get together as brothers and sisters and work out an alternative scene.
> If you are a bi/gay head, please write to me and send me your ideas, scenes and if the response is big enough then we can work towards something real.
> Peace and love, David, Park Hill Road, London NW3

'Aubrey and Bob had been round the US and at the same time, some heads and anarchists had been getting together in the summer and talking about doing something. The latter people were very condemnatory about "straight gays"' (*David Fernbach*).

Gay men had also become visible through the trial of *International Times*, the most famous (to some, infamous) of the underground press. The paper had published pretty well every kind of sexual material, a great deal of which was crude and sexist, but when the police finally decided to prosecute it was the gay contact advertisements that were made the most of in court, bringing up a number of concerns which gay men felt about the limitations of the

1967 Act. Briefly, the prosecution was based upon the assumption that while certain homosexual acts between adult gay men had been decriminalized, the basic criminality of homosexuality had not been removed. This meant that encouragement of homosexual acts, whether they were legal or not, was still immoral and those publishing such advertisements were liable to prosecution. The prosecution made a farce of the recent Act – a feeling that was returned by some of the gay people forced into court.

'Tarsus Sutton was a witness at the *IT* trial. He was advertising for a partner, they were the only people who accepted gay ads. There were covert ones elsewhere, seeking people to go to the cinema or opera, and in *Exchange & Mart*, black leather jacket for sale, things like that. But *IT* were quite upfront and Tarsus, being Tarsus, put in an upfront ad. *IT* were busted and they took all the papers and got his name' (*Michael James*). Tarsus was cross-examined about a personal advert he had placed in *IT*. 'When asked by the judge what "well-hung" meant, he replied without any hesitation, "it means I have no hang-ups, M'lud"' (*John Chesterman*).

The *IT* trial, increasing debate about censorship and sexuality, the growth of women's liberation and the growing understanding of alliances against what was seen to be an increasingly repressive state all conspired together to create a situation in which many gay people were ready for a more revolutionary stance in their politics. All that they needed was someone with a background of organizing to provide them with an outlet.

'I came back to the UK and it all seemed flat. Bob had gone back to college at the LSE and we spoke on the phone. Bob booked a room and we held a meeting' (*Aubrey Walter*).

Chapter three

Power to the People

David Fernbach was the brains and Aubrey the networker in the early days. –Micky Burbidge

(GLF) consisted of confronting the society around us with the fact of our proclaimed homosexuality, struggling for simple but basic demands for acceptance . . . developing a new gay pride and defending the gains we had made. –David Fernbach, *The Rise and Fall of GLF*

LSE at this point, at least the student body, was still a radical school. There were sit-ins going on all the time at the LSE. I was influenced by the leftist tendencies of the time; the Heath government had come to power, there was the campaign against the Industrial Relations Act and here was a body that was gay, that was countercultural, it was heady in its personal atmosphere and it was leftist and all those things were really intoxicating. –Jeffrey Weeks

FEELING the lack of a radical alternative to the 'straight gay' organizations, Bob Mellors agreed with Aubrey to hold a meeting to test the water. The London School of Economics (LSE) was known for its support of countercultural activities and there were a number of gay students there including Bob so, on Wednesday 13 October 1970 and with the minimum of publicity and fuss, the London Gay Liberation Front met for the first time in a basement classroom in the Clare Market building. Published estimates of the number present run from nine to nineteen, with the latter being the more likely according to survivors. Among those present were Aubrey Walter and Bob Mellors as the instigators, David Fernbach (Aubrey's partner), Richard Dipple (a friend of Aubrey and David who had been involved in the Albany Trust), Bill Halstead (like Richard, an LSE student) and one woman, Bev Jackson, a prominent student activist at LSE who later ran for college office under the arresting slogan 'Bev the Lez for Prez'.

There was no chairing or formal organization because of the small size of the meeting, and most of what was discussed was the news from America and the possibilities of a London equivalent to GLF.

Almost everyone I spoke to who arrived over the course of the next two months assumed that what they attended was the second meeting or so, but in fact the big increase in attendance did not take place until early in November. Those who arrived before then were mainly other students and people such as new research graduate Jeffrey Weeks, sociologist Mary McIntosh and psychiatric social worker Elizabeth Wilson, who heard about it from other gay academics. The distinctive style of GLF was already evident.

> I got in about the third week of GLF meeting at LSE, simply because I was working at LSE. I'd just started working there on the third of October and about two weeks after I saw this leaflet in the refectory at the LSE and picked it up. There was a meeting a few days later, which I couldn't make because I was doing something else and I was a bit nervous as well, I suppose. It must have been the third or fourth meeting, right at the end of October. It was just amazing. I'd never been in a room with so many flamboyantly gay people ever before. It was an overwhelming experience. I'd met gay people before, I'd been to gay bars but this was quite different. The room was absolutely jam-packed. There was also the hippiness of it, I'd been on the fringes of hippiedom but never been involved and everyone looked outsiders. And there was also the faint hint of drugs and sex in the air, which was very exciting. Again, I'd been on the fringes of the counterculture but here was the counterculture manifest and a gay counterculture, because what had put me off the counterculture really, except to dabble occasionally, was that my sexuality wasn't validated. And here was a coming together of the counterculture and my sexuality. And there was this heady political rhetoric.
>
> At the bar afterwards in the LSE I met some of the people I am still in touch with. I met Barry Davis there and Ken Plummer and Mary McIntosh, who are people I've had strong political and intellectual engagements with ever since, for the past twenty-five years, I met on that first occasion. And two weeks later I saw Angus (Suttie), and

we became lovers within a couple of weeks and that transformed my personal life. That was one of the major personal things for me. It was bringing together the different parts of my life, because I was a young academic researcher doing my postgraduate research in my first academic job at LSE and that was completely separate from my personal life, my sex life was self-contained, occasional forays into bars or cottaging. The thing about GLF was, its ideology was very much about linking those parts of your life. Angus and I started a really intense emotional and largely monogamous relationship and that was the first time in my life I'd had such a relationship. So sex became a mainstream part of my life and not a peripheral part, which was really quite transforming. (*Jeffrey Weeks*)

I had an academic interest in the movement, I had collected stuff on the US movement in the fifties and sixties. I had seen that there was a gap, a need for a liberation type movement for homosexuals and I heard GLF was starting so I went along. I can't remember wanting to get involved. I was with Elizabeth at the time, and I remember thinking well, women's liberation is a funny enough idea, but gay liberation . . . [a friend] said would we like to go to a meeting with him, I think he didn't want to go on his own. We probably wouldn't have wanted to go on our own. But we went along and never looked back. We found ourselves discussing the demands, that list that got circulated which included the right to hold hands on the street and so forth. And we were discussing it as 'we should say this' and 'we should say that' in the way you sometimes do. We came to scoff and stayed to pray. That's the first thing I remember, discussing the demands. The others I remember were Bob and Aubrey at the front of the room. There were twenty to thirty people that week, but the next meeting was much bigger. There was Pat Arrowsmith, lots of others checking it out. I remember Pat Arrowsmith arguing that gayness was good for keeping the population down.
(*Mary McIntosh*)

I think Mary must have heard about it from Ken Plummer, she certainly heard about it from some sociologist mate, he's the most likely. It was in one of the small rooms in LSE, it hadn't got big then and it was in the same room

that I'd had seminars with Donald Winnicott in when I was training to be a social worker there, so it was a very meaningful but strange coincidence because Winnicott, in the nicest and most genteel way, was very homophobic. I don't remember much about the meeting. There weren't very many women, there was all this buzz. David and Aubrey were making most of the running, they were Maoists. It was an exciting feeling and within a couple of weeks the meetings had grown absolutely huge.
(*Elizabeth Wilson*)

'Elizabeth and Mary arrived at the third or fourth meeting, in S101 upstairs. The leafleting was done in Earls Court just after that, and that's when most people started to arrive' (*Aubrey Walter*). The handwriting on the first leaflet is definitely Aubrey's, but nobody can remember whose the demands were. David is credited by Aubrey with realizing how important it was to get some down on record, but he himself has no memory of it. 'The demands were adopted very early. I don't know who wrote them. The US GLF had some and we needed something to focus on' (*David Fernbach*). A number of other people remember having some hand in the demands and they are a remarkably practical set of reformist issues to a modern eye. The most striking thing about them on first reading, and certainly the most depressing, is that not a single one of them has been wholly realized twenty-five years on and they could almost pass for the shopping list for Stonewall or OutRage!

THE GAY LIBERATION FRONT DEMANDS . . .
– that all discrimination against gay people, male and female, by the law, by employers, and by society at large, should end
– that all people who feel attracted to a member of their own sex be taught that such feelings are perfectly normal
– that sex education in schools stop being exclusively heterosexual
– that psychiatrists stop treating homosexuality as though it were a problem or sickness, thereby giving gay people senseless guilt complexes
– that gay people be as legally free to contact other gay people through newspaper ads, on the streets and by any other means they may want, as are heterosexuals, and that police harassment should cease right now
– that employers should no longer be allowed to

discriminate against anyone on account of their sexual preferences
– that the age of consent for gay males be reduced to the same as for straights
– that gay people be free to hold hands and kiss in public, as are heterosexuals

GAY IS GOOD!
ALL POWER TO OPPRESSED PEOPLE!
COME OUT – JOIN GAY LIBERATION FRONT!

The leaflet stated that meetings were being held by now in Room 101 of the St Clement's Building at the London School of Economics, at 7.30 p.m. every Wednesday. The publisher's address was given as GLF, c/o 160 North Gower Street, London NW1. This was the address for Agitprop Bookshop, a popular revolutionary centre, and indicates that either or both of the gay workers there who were to become central figures in GLF, Andy Elsmore and Tony Reynolds, were already attending. Leaflets were pinned up there and at Compendium in Camden Town, where a gay Canadian hippie already heavily involved in politics called Warren Haig worked, and at Housmans in Kings Cross, where another gay man, David McLellan, worked. These brought in others, as did the Earls Court and scene leafletting.

> I knew some other gays through cottaging. People I met this way would ask 'are you active or passive' and there were a lot of self-denigrating attitudes. I was very relieved when I finally found out that you didn't have to be one or the other. I saw a poster in Compendium for the first meeting and I thought that it was incredible, I wanted to go but I was afraid to walk into a room full of openly gay people. It was Jeffrey [Weeks] who insisted I go to GLF, we were friends. (*Micky Burbidge*)

> I heard about the meetings at the LSE and went to about the third or fourth one. I was a dentist with a practice in St Johns Wood, a very straight law reform campaigner and had never thought of anything else. At GLF I saw lots of new, different people. I was exhilarated and shocked at the odd clothes, the hippies, hard left people, students, many different people. There was no chairman and the leading figures were mobile from week to week. I felt envious of it.

Someone asked me early on if I was in the Communist Party and I was shocked. At the Balls, I envied their freedom and the way that people bounced around, it made me feel I was uptight. It was a nice sort of envy. After a couple of weeks, we talked about leafleting for more people.

I met others at Queensway tube and we did the Bayswater Road crowds on a Sunday, where the artists display their stuff on the railings. I wanted to do it but I was scared to be recognized as gay – I was shoving the leaflet into people's hands and running off. I didn't feel able to stop and talk to people the way that some of the others did. There were about four of us. I was hungry for action after three years of nothing and I found it exhilarating. It felt like a boiler, with the pressure building up and up for years and then suddenly released. I was angry, I was thrilled, we thought we could change the world, change the sexuality of everyone and not just homosexuals. (*Michael Brown*)

The first known public action of London GLF certainly showed that they held a wider concern about sexism than a purely gay angle. *Time Out* reported in its last issue of October 1970 that the young organization had invaded the offices of *Sennet*, the London School of Economics student newspaper, in protest at an offensive article. The piece, supposedly on students and sex, was said to have denigrated 'queers', as it called them, but also women in general. The invaders sprayed slogans around the office and served notice to all the underground press, *IT*, *Oz* and *Friends* (later *Frendz*) that the same would happen to them if they persisted in operating on what was characterized as a 'tits and arse' basis. This willingness to stand up to the countercultural press, rather than slavishly courting them, seems to have done GLF little harm.

The meetings soon began to need more organization as the numbers attending rose. 'When we first met, we just organized it between us. Then when we went into the bigger room we had a rotating chair but they weren't elected as such. Then when we got bigger, we had a steering committee that was elected and that happened for the first time at the New Theatre at the LSE. If it wasn't chaired, Warren tended to dominate it by making people feel stupid' (*Aubrey Walter*). But to be fair, Warren Haig was not the only person who flowered in the heady atmosphere of the early days at the LSE. Even previously reticent people sometimes found their voice there and are remembered as making regular contributions to the debate. 'I think one reason GLF was important to me was because it did release something. I was terribly inhibited and never spoke at anything ever at all before that. It obviously unleashed something' (*Elizabeth Wilson*). And thanks to the leafleting, the people attending were soon not only greater in numbers but from a wider variety of backgrounds.

I knew I was gay before GLF. I was adopted as a child into a very poor and dysfunctional family and went into the army at seventeen to get away from home. I bought myself out after four years because I was beginning to accept that I was gay, having realized I was 'queer' years before. This was in 1967 and I went to India and Morocco and became a hippie. I was very politically unaware and I hated myself. Warren Haig was the first man I kissed in public. I already knew a small group of gay people that I used to do acid with. Some of them ended up in GLF too, people like Mitch and Angus and Jeff Marsh who lived on Portobello Road. When I walked into the LSE, I saw lots of gay men and women who actually looked like me, not like the stereotype I had of mincing limp-wristed men. There was a real glow of being together, like I hadn't expected. I'd never even been into a gay bar by this stage. I remember Sue Winter being very forward. The most vocal people at those early meetings, the most memorable ones, were Warren, Aubrey, David Fernbach, Richard Dipple, Mary, Elizabeth and Sue Winter. (*Paul Theobald*)

I was in GLF from the start because two friends were given a leaflet by a hippie in Oxford Street and they told me about it. I went and I was fascinated and I got very involved, which cost me my boyfriend because I got so into all the meetings. I was working at the time managing an employment agency in the City, which was pretty ironic. I was attracted to GLF by a general feeling of dissatisfaction with the world and the problems of being gay and people there were prepared to talk. There was only the cruising scene in the bars or private socializing – no gay debate whatsoever. It was Aubrey, Bob and co. that put gay sexuality into a political context and made sense of it in alliance with women and race. (*Stuart Feather*)

I was mainly involved in GLF from 1970 to 1972. I
identified as straight at the time, because you were only
given two choices in those days. Now people understand
that it's much more complicated. I came along to the
second or third meeting. Paul Theobald's lover Trevor had
brought Howard [Wakeling] home and I fell in love with
him immediately, so I went along with them. (*Sue Winter*)

In the early days, there were very few women around. At
that time there was so much pressure on all of us – people
had been beaten up, aversion therapy, people in prison for
being gay – Mick Belsten had spent time in prison. I
know of several men who had had aversion therapy, and
been beaten up all sorts of places and the only place for
lesbians to meet was the Gateways, only one place in all of
London. Sometimes there were only a dozen (women),
sometimes fifty – it grew fairly rapidly but there were very
few at first. The belief that women would go off with men
if offered that choice, that lesbians didn't exist – in the
initial phase it was very important to identify as a lesbian
or as gay, homosexual . . . It was really important. Now,
twenty-five years on with thousands of people on Pride
demonstrations what's important is choice for women. It's
definitely a different kind of time now. I didn't know many
women there. I was at the Gateways with Rosie, and
Beverley handed us a leaflet, so we went together.
(*Carla Toney*)

Rumours about the growing crowds at the LSE attracted not
only women from the bars and men from the streets, but also some
experienced gay activists, curious to see what the fuss was about.

They were the first really big gatherings of gays that I'd
been to that weren't primarily a meat market. GLF
meetings were very friendly. Since people didn't assume
that you were trying to pick them up, they didn't feel the
need to put you down or reject you. When GLF started I
was not involved in much, so I went along as an individual
but all sorts of things got read into it. Aubrey made odd
comments. My emotional allegiance in a way was with
GLF and that sort of thing rather than CHE, but I know

that the political analysis is needed. It was unimaginable before it happened. (*Antony Grey*)

The arrival of what were seen by some of the founders as dangerously moderate traditional organizers was not the only subject of controversy. As Sue Winter soon noticed, the rhetoric about sexual freedom for all and the destruction of sexual categories foundered rapidly when power was at issue within the organization. This was not due to hypocrisy so much as the legacy from previous organizing, in which heterosexuals had often spoken for gay people or gay people themselves had posed as straight or at least sexually ambiguous on the assumption that this would be more palatable to the general public. So, while heterosexuals were welcome at GLF, they were not welcome to take positions of authority. 'Having straight people around was a very big issue at the start, over the elections to the Steering Committee. There were some straight women friends who came and a few hippies who wanted to be thought of as "humansexuals", but there was a clear consensus amongst most people that gays needed to run GLF for themselves' (*David Fernbach*). And that was not all. 'Cottaging was an issue very early on at the LSE. Andy Elsmore got up and spoke as someone who cottaged, which was felt to be quite radical and daring. There were a number of people who took the view that people who cottaged were in need of help' (*David Fernbach*).

But mostly the early days of the organization were taken up in planning the growth and activities of the new group and finding ways of bringing it to the attention of more gays and the general public. 'We used to pore over all the American publications – *Come Together* (the GLF paper) was based around *Come Out!*, which was the name of a New York paper put together by Steve Dansky, which only lasted a few months. Steve Dansky's piece "Hey Man" was reprinted in *Come Together 5* and was very influential over here' (*David Fernbach*).

But before the first edition of *Come Together* was, as it were, got together, the meetings began to discuss the need for an action which would put them on the public map. 'We debated what the first demo should be, we knew we ought to have one but we weren't sure what. There was a proposal to go to the American Embassy about their visa restrictions on homosexuals and then there was the proposal about the Louis Eakes case, which was what we took up. He was this supposedly wrongfully arrested heterosexual – I always had my doubts about that' (*Stuart Feather*). 'The Louis Eakes issue was a very recent incident, a matter of weeks before, and was something useful to latch onto' (*David Fernbach*).

The Eakes case was publicly prominent at the time, because Eakes was a Young Liberal organizer arrested on Highbury Fields during a police entrapment exercise. It was alleged that he had approached several men in front of police witnesses, but Eakes maintained that all he had been doing was asking for a light for his cigarette. The point was not his guilt or otherwise, but to protest the police action in seeking to arrest people for attempting to procure an act which was not in itself illegal, and when heterosexual men were free to approach women in public without fear of arrest.

Chapter four

Making Our Presence Felt

THE most ironic part about the first openly gay demonstration in Britain, apart from the small fact that the avowedly heterosexual Louis Eakes was rearrested and successfully convicted a few months later for a similar incident in another park, was that it was suggested by someone from the deeply disliked Albany Trust. 'I felt that there was a lot of paranoia and misconceptions about me. I did suggest a couple of lobbying things early on at meetings, including the protest march to Highbury Fields' (*Antony Grey*). This is corroborated by others who were there (although one suspects that many who hadn't noticed where the suggestion came from at the time might well have rejected it out of hand if they had). But the Eakes case it was and on 27 November 1970, the Gay Liberation Front gathered to make history on Highbury Fields in the then working-class district of Islington.

> I went on the Highbury Fields demo. It was all a bit bizarre really because it was suggested by Antony Grey, who used to come to those early meetings and was rather marginalized really because he was seen as the remnant of the old homophile movement. People used to think he was a CIA agent, it was all stupid because in his own solid way he'd done very good work. He and his partner suggested it and people jumped at it because we were really looking for an excuse to do something public. The Louis Eakes case had been in the press.
>
> I went along, it was a Friday night and we were given candles and we marched around the Fields several times and I talked to Angus for the first time and David Fernbach

and various other people, and then we went to the pub across the road, which was called the Cock. I always thought that was very apt. And then we dispersed and I got on the tube back home. And on the tube, there was an atmosphere of outness, people were hugging on the tube carriages and so on and that was a real first for me. I'd been on anti-apartheid demos and so on, but it was an abstract thing. This was the first time that I'd been on a demo that was about me. Even if the reason was a bit false, it was an artificial occasion in many ways, manufactured, it wasn't really about Louis Eakes, but we wanted to go out on the streets to make a public presence. That was the main reason why we did it. It was a very affirming experience because it was the first time, apart from those meetings at LSE, that most of us had ever openly declared our gayness. The fact that we were watched only by a handful of people and by a journalist from *The Times*, if I remember rightly, didn't matter because we were making our presence felt. (*Jeffrey Weeks*)

'It was dark and there was no enemy target, which was different from my experiences at anti Vietnam demos – and it felt very weird. It didn't have much dash compared to the later demonstrations but there were torches and people milling around' (*David Fernbach*). 'It was dark and we all wandered around lighting each other's cigarettes which was the action given in police evidence against Eakes and then we kissed openly, which was extraordinary. It was an enormous release to be able to kiss and carry on. And then we went to the pub for a drink. I've never been back there since. I remember that someone read the Demands out' (*Stuart Feather*). 'It was at the south end near the tube, people were carrying torches and walked about stopping each other and asking for a light. There were a couple of speeches and police hung about the edge on motor bikes. There were about fifty people, it didn't go on long' (*Michael Brown*).

At least one person did not go to the historic demonstration because he had tickets for Bertolucci's *The Conformist* at the London Film Festival – a rare showing of a gay film. But others attended who had little previous contact with GLF.

I heard about the Highbury Fields demo through a friend and I went along on my own. I was very impressed by the togetherness of everybody and thought it was really nice. I didn't really understand the political importance of it at that time. I had a couple of close women friends who were getting involved in the women's movement and it was actually through them that I first learnt about this organization called GLF. I was fascinated by what was going on around me and looking at people. I was dazzled by the fact that these people had actually got together to make a stand about their own lives. At Highbury Fields there were men, particularly, in very colourful outfits which were costumes really, they weren't just dressed in the way men usually dressed. It was partly the hippie era as well, so there had been flower power, I knew all about that but this was something else. I remember people openly smoking dope, which I'd never ever seen before. I remember some people playing instruments and a lot of shouting, chanting . . . I didn't know anybody so I was hesitant and once it was over I just went home. (*Cloud Downey*)

This was the first gay demonstration in London but there was little coverage in the press despite attendance by several journalists. Only *The Times* had the foresight to give it a few paragraphs the next morning.

HOMOSEXUALS DEMONSTRATE FOR EQUAL RIGHTS
By Geoffrey Wansell

The first public demonstration in Britain by the Gay Liberation Front, a movement dedicated to altering public attitudes towards homosexuals, whether men or women, was held last night on Highbury Fields, London.

Some 80 members of the front gathered to hear the aims of the movement read out at the scene of the arrest of a man for gross indecency.

They ask that homosexuals should be allowed to kiss and hold hands in public, just as heterosexuals are; that all discrimination against 'gay people, male and female, by the law, by employers and by society at large should end'; and that they should be allowed to contact each other through newspaper advertisements or on the streets in exactly the same way as heterosexuals.

Miss Bev Jackson, aged 19, a member of the steering committee of five, said 'It is important to know that we are not ashamed to be homosexual.' She explained that the front had been organized in Britain for six weeks and had about 250 members, although it was a large organization in the United States.

Mr. John Breslin, aged 41, an actor, said that he felt the acting profession was one of the few in which homo-sexuality was tolerated.

At the peaceful meeting members of the front criticized the public attitude to homosexuals. As one said: 'We don't want to be a freak show. We just want to be the same as everyone else.'

At the end of the 90-minute torchlight demonstration members of the front emphasized that their membership included ordinary people. One said: 'There are straight people, lesbians and male homosexuals in the front.'

The small piece in the news pages reached more people who had not yet heard of GLF, including one person on *The Times*' own staff who was to become a central figure. 'I was a journalist, had been for about seven years. I read a tiny item in *The Times* about how there had been a demonstration somewhere and also there was something in *Time Out* in the same few days. I gathered that this was happening. I can't really say why I was so determined to go. I suppose it was something to do with how we all felt at the time, the mood of the time and the name of the thing' (*Andrew Lumsden*).

The only other coverage was in GLF's new paper, *Come Together*, which stated 'We're Coming Out Proud' and said that a Wednesday meeting of 200 people on the 25th had decided, whether or not Eakes was straight, to hold a 'gay-in' at 10 p.m. on the Friday and that '150 beautiful gay people' had assembled at the tube at 9 p.m., talked to reporters and then walked to the scene of the 'crime' carrying balloons and shouting gay power slogans. At the far end of the field, they lit candles and torches and 'a brother read out our list of demands. After each demand we all responded with "RIGHT ON" which echoed round the fields.' Then people held and kissed each other and some challenged a group of journalists who had been heard to refer to them as 'pooves'. The issue also contained an article on being a gay local government officer and a declaration by Media Workshop, the group publishing *Come Together*, that 'we would just like to say right now, that all the so-called gay mags . . . are just a load of absolute bullshit and an outright insult to gay people. They just try to foist a "closet queen" mentality on us; they think that all we are interested in are the secret life of closeted pseudostars and the latest in rip-off bourgeois fashions . . . NO MORE. From now on gay people in Britain are going to write their own history.'

'The very first edition of *Come Together* was put together in the flat of a friend of Lindsay Kemp's, Lindsay Levy on Colville Terrace off the Portobello Road' (*Paul Theobald*). 'Stuart Feather brought us a load of duplicating paper from his office which was used for the first edition. The Media Workshop used to have discussions and act as a collective, meeting in each other's flats' (*Aubrey Walter*). The paper also advertised another pair of historic events; the first openly gay dance, at the LSE on 4 December and a much more ambitious event, a GLF People's Dance at Kensington Town Hall on the 22nd (tickets six shillings, which would be 30p in the new decimal currency to be introduced the next year).

> The Kensington Town Hall dance was the first of its kind, the first gay dance in England openly advertised as such. I was a steward with Mary McIntosh and we were quite apprehensive. We hung about not knowing what to expect. In the end there wasn't any hassle except that people complained about the band for being excessively straight and sexist, so the band got hassled. People were not used to being able to dance together in public and they wouldn't get up and dance even though they'd braved coming to the event. They just waited and waited to see what would happen when someone did. (*Tony Halliday*)

My memory is that nobody could manage to take the floor and eventually I took the floor with Tony Halliday! So it's extremely ironic . . .' (*Elizabeth Wilson*). 'I helped with organizing the first dance at Kensington Town Hall. The band was supposed to be straight, but I got off with one of the guys in it so they can't have been all that straight' (*Paul Theobald*). 'I remember there was an article in the *People* which described the variety of different people there, people in hippie clothes, jeans, suits . . . I wore a suit and it was wonderful because we were all just there together and it didn't matter how you looked. It was just a wild feeling, bopping away. I just remember an incredibly heady atmosphere, it was packed' (*Jeffrey Weeks*).

> I went with my women's group and it was preceded by an incident in a pub in [Kensington] Church Street. In those

days it was very unusual for a crowd of women in short hair and trousers to be together in any numbers and men would scream at you and pick fights and so on. That happened all the time, constantly. You went out with women who were harassed. These men started having a go at us and ended up pouring their beer all over us and the police were called and that's how it started. These incidents were absolutely commonplace, they seemed to happen all the time. You were attacked with impunity by men, by police, you could be arrested and tried and put in prison, it's hard to imagine that it would cause such a furore but I suppose it was radical for the time. (*Angie Weir*)

The dance, advertised in *Time Out* and around lesbian and gay clubs, attracted such huge crowds that many had to be turned away. The most common estimate is that around 750 got in and 500 were left outside. The next Sunday, the *People* ran a very good-humoured article, 'It's All Happening At The Old Town Hall' with a photograph of dancers, featuring a man thought to be Chris Blaby waving his arms about and captioned 'The one in the chain is not a mayor'. The report referred to GLF as 'Britain's youngest civil rights group' and noted the range of people. An extensive quote from an architect using a false name said 'Our main target is to change social attitudes simply by announcing that we are homosexual and showing that, apart from that, we are ordinary people . . . About one person in ten is gay . . . there are homosexual policemen, homosexual MPs – even homosexual newspapermen.' The new purple GLF badge, copied from a Philadelphia GLF design which would have been brought back by Aubrey or Bob, with the name of the group around a fist enclosing a flower with male and female symbols (see appendix three), was on sale alongside the second edition of *Come Together*. Badges were to become a central part of the GLF ideology, since wearing one meant that you were automatically out and proud, and some 8,000 were sold in the first year. According to the *People*, dancers were demanding to be photographed – a far cry from the decades of hiding many of them had experienced.

The second edition of *Come Together* carried the new Principles of GLF, which had been agreed at the meeting on 9 December. These were written by David Fernbach and contain the genuine core of London GLF's beliefs. Where the Demands had been reformist and could have been espoused by CHE and some traditional activists, the Principles clearly spelled out that the need for gay liberation was sited within a wider social context of oppression based on the nuclear family and traditional Judaeo-Christian beliefs and that GLF was part of a wider movement including women's liberation, black people, the working classes and youth. But while speaking the language of revolutionary theory, it also roundly declared its independence from any specific revolutionary group and stated clearly that the interests of gay people would come first for GLF. The Principles form a remarkably coherent and cogent statement of values and are worth quoting in full.

(i) GLF's first priority is to defend the immediate interests of gay people against discrimination and all forms of social oppression.

(ii) However, the roots of the oppressions that gay people suffer run deep in our society, in particular to the structure of the family, patterns of socialisation, and the Judaeo-Christian culture. Legal reform and education against prejudice, though possible and necessary, cannot be a permanent solution. While existing social structures remain, social prejudice and overt repression can always re-emerge.

(iii) GLF therefore sees itself as part of the wider movement aiming to abolish all forms of social oppression. It will work to ally itself with other oppressed groups, while preserving its organisational independence.

(iv) In particular, we see these groups as including:

(a) the women's liberation movement. The roots of women's oppression are in many ways close to our own (see ii above).

(b) black people and other national minorities. The racism that these peoples are affected by is a similar structure of prejudice to our own, but on the basis of racial instead of sexual difference. They are socially and economically the most oppressed group in our society.

(c) the working class, i.e. all productive manual and mental workers. Their labour is what the whole of society lives off, but their skills are misused by a profit-oriented economy, and their right to organise and defend their interests is under increasing attack.

(d) young people who are rejecting the bourgeois family and the roles and lifestyles offered them by this society, and attempting to create a non-exploitative counterculture.

(e) peoples oppressed by imperialism, who lack the national political and economic independence which is a precondition for all other social change.

(vi) We don't believe that any existing revolutionary theory has all the answers to the problems facing us. GLF will therefore study and discuss all relevant critical theories of society and the individual being, to measure them against the test of our own and historical experience.

The original paper put by David and Aubrey to the meeting included the following additional suggestions, many of which eventually came to pass.

Organisational suggestions

(i) fortnightly general meetings

(ii) Groups based on particular types of work. E.g.

- community work
- anti-psychiatry
- anti-repression and legal defence
- media workshop
- street theatre
- office and organisation
- education group

(iii) groups based on locality or occupation. Every GLF member should belong to at least one of the groups (locality, occupation, or task groups).

For some reason this document, as circulated to the meeting, is signed 'Jonathon Wilde', which was a common pseudonym used by a number of people early on, but not usually David or Aubrey.

One further section, (v), was voted down by the meeting. Contemporaneous notes made by Mary McIntosh on the back of her copy show that two thirds of the speakers were opposed to it, on a variety of grounds. It read:

Gay people cannot be indifferent to the worldwide struggle against capitalism and imperialism. This whole system is in an ever more acute state of crisis and all signs are that the capitalist ruling class will resort to any means necessary to preserve their power, including wholesale repression against all 'deviant' minorities. In Britain the failure of capitalism to serve the people's needs (housing, education, social services etc.) has already led to black people being used as a scapegoat, with racist demagogues such as Powell playing on reactionary popular prejudices, and both Tory and Labour governments willingly conceding to racist demands (immigration laws etc.) Now the ruling class is moving to legal repression against working-class militants with the I.R.B. (Industrial Relations Bill). Every historic example shows that repression of the working-class, racism and attacks on gay people go together. They are all components of authoritarian capitalism or fascism (e.g. Nazi Germany, Spain, Brazil, Greece etc.) In Britain, gay people may well be the next victims of the policy of 'law and order'.

'We didn't dig our heels in over the part of the principles that was voted down. It wasn't felt by people to be clearly enough connected to gay issues' (*David Fernbach*). The paragraph does not sit well with the rest of the document, reading more like a section from a speech illustrating the earlier abstract principles. Some at the meeting may have been negatively influenced by a piece in *IT*, published shortly beforehand, which stated:

A split has developed in the Gay Liberation Front between the revolutionaries and the chickenshit liberals. David Burke explains 'If we are to smash oppression of both us and the straight people, then we have to get up off our asses and show a real alternative, not just dream about one. We are part of the underground subculture and therefore we are White Panthers, Yippies, Weathermen and all other anarchistic groups who are bringing on the change. We base our policy on the only true revolutionary policy of dope, rock'n'roll and fucking in the streets; power to ALL oppressed people.' Accordingly, the revolutionaries are to propose a series of principles to the GLF, the most important of which reads: [the article then quotes part (v)].

This was responded to in the next issue of *IT* by Tony Salvis, a South African gay man popularly rumoured to have been either a gun runner or a member of the South African army, who was to become central to later GLF. 'I think that David Burke should get his facts right before pontificating on GLF. The Gay Liberation Front does not advocate a policy of "dope, rock'n'roll and fucking in the streets", although I don't see why people shouldn't do these things, if that's what they want (but that's just my opinion). What GLF says is "If you dig it, do it – but make it a gay scene".' The letter went on to deny any split between factions. But it was the first serious political argument within London GLF and the score was clear: revolutionaries nil – chickenshit liberals one.

The day after the Kensington Town Hall Dance, the meetings moved to a new venue at the Camden Arts Lab while the LSE was closed for its Christmas break. The few short weeks in which they were there saw a large number of significant developments and it is at this time that a film, *Come Together*, was made of the meeting and of leading members such as Warren, Mary, Aubrey and Bob. The grainy, amateur feel of the film goes well with the emerging philosophy of GLF and shows something of the diversity already present, politically and sexually, within the organization. There is an air of self-discovery alongside an almost missionary zeal. 'GLF was the first time I'd had to think about things like racism and sexism and homophobia. Most gay people in those days had very low opinions of themselves and GLF boosted their self esteem hugely' (*Paul Theobald*).

The news about this rapidly growing new movement had spread to other groups in the left and women's liberation. In particular, GLF soon started to forge strong links with the London women's liberation groups who were similarly into public action, having just crashed the public consciousness with a highly-visible action against the Miss World competition, in which they invaded the stage and disrupted the event extensively. A BBC van at the event had been blown up. Women's liberationists came to check GLF out – and sometimes to stay.

> I can't remember where I heard about GLF, possibly from a friend of mine called Pauline Conroy who was a feminist. I was already involved in the women's movement, which was just getting going. The women's movement started from the first Oxford conference in 1970 at Ruskin College. I remember the Miss World demo that year, that was the invasion of the stage.
>
> I came by myself I think, under the guise of being an emissary from women's liberation. The meetings were still

at LSE, in a room off the student union building and then they transferred to a lecture theatre in the main building over the road. And the first women's meeting was in the bar of the student union, in the meeting room there. I remember the meeting at which I came out, which I think was the second meeting I attended. I was announcing a demonstration, some women's liberation one that we were doing. So I stood up to give this announcement in the middle of a rather packed meeting and explained about women's liberation and solidarity between the two struggles and so on. That meeting was chaired by Warren Haig. I was about to sit down and Warren said, 'We have a rule here and anyone who speaks has to declare whether they're straight or gay' . . . and I thought, I can't walk away from this moment so I staggered out 'I think I'm gay' and sat down and collapsed. That's how I came out.

I was particularly involved in trying to set up a women's group and argued that it would be useful if the women met separately. Which happened with the opposition of Elizabeth [Wilson] and Mary [McIntosh], I remember. They were very doubtful about it and they were very doubtful about feminism, which they saw as a movement of heterosexual women which was not necessarily very sympathetic to lesbians and gay men. There was a sense in which that was true, that women's liberation only challenged the position of heterosexual women by focusing so much on experiences of being wives and mothers and also in a sense endorsed those lives . . . Mary, Elizabeth and I became friends eventually because I considered myself, like most people at the time, to be a socialist and they were socialists, so that was something that drew us together. (*Angie Weir*)

The arrests at the Miss World event led to a series of trials in which an unusual style of defence was used which was later to become a defining feature of GLF's court appearances.

We practically invented the use of Mackenzie lawyers and speaking for yourself in court – it was all about making your voice heard and deconstructing the relationships and the organization of the trial within the courtroom. I was a Mackenzie in the Miss World trial, several people had been arrested in the Albert Hall and we decided to confront the courts so we challenged everything and people represented themselves, except for Sally Alexander who was represented by a feminist lawyer, so then you also got the development of radical lawyers and there were excellent solidarity demonstrations outside the Old Bailey from GLF. It was the period of the Upper Clyde and the workers' takeover as well.

I remember that at the meeting when we moved into the large lecture theatre with tiered seats I was amazed to see people like David Fernbach there. He may well have been at those earlier meetings and I hadn't seen him. I knew him from the LSE and radical student politics and I thought, oh my god, it's the left come to infiltrate this new organization. It didn't dawn on me for a moment that he might be gay himself. He presumably thought exactly the same about me. So there very much wasn't that factional sense in the early days, it was very unfactional compared to student politics and left politics. And that was true in the early days of both GLF and the women's movement, it was in a sense a casting aside of all the political clothes that people normally wore and getting in touch with aspects of their sexuality which were completely denied by those politics. (*Angie Weir*)

'There was a party in South London and Angie and Mary O'Shea came along together from a women's liberation group to try and get us to join women's liberation which in the end we did, but the men kicked us out really. That was around Christmas time and then women's meetings started' (*Elizabeth Wilson*). 'It was from a feeling that women wanted to meet separately. Carla didn't speak much at meetings but was much more significant among the women. That was true of Angie too, to some extent and Marion and some others. Bev was quite significant in the big meetings, but I don't remember her at the women's meetings at all, or Sue Winter. She and her sister Jane were seen as heterosexual' (*Mary McIntosh*).

The period at the Arts Lab was short but highly productive for all of GLF, not only the women.

The Steering Group began to be formed there and Street Theatre was formed there. I got very involved straight away. Our very first meeting was in Derek Jarman's flat at Bankside one Sunday afternoon, though he wasn't there. We had no regular place to meet so I opened up my office on Sunday afternoons, there were two big empty rooms upstairs. We planned our demos there. The first was quite simple. Howard Wakeling was a director and had a show on at the Aldwych. Somebody who worked at Berman's 'borrowed' the costumes from Fellini's *Satyricon*. We dressed up and walked down the Strand with banners to his show at the Aldwych, just a gentle stroll in costume. (*Stuart Feather*)

The Counter-Psychiatry Group also began to meet. This group, which is the subject of chapter eight, was intended to oppose psychiatric practices which addressed homosexuality as a disease, in a way similar to the US West Coast groups that Aubrey had visited. In London the group formed around Elizabeth Wilson, herself a psychiatric social worker with previous experience of the anti-psychiatry theories and writings of R. D. Laing. The original lists of GLF members interested in the group survive and show twenty-eight names including Elizabeth, Mary, Jeffrey Weeks, Micky Burbidge and David Hutter, all of whom were to be centrally involved in its writings, actions and spin-off groups.

The meetings continued to evolve in style and a number of issues started to come to the fore.

You weren't supposed to cruise at meetings, but people did. I did. You weren't supposed to be ageist and there was lots of talk about children's rights, like in the *Oz* schoolkids issue. Some people I'd known for a while turned up at one meeting, but they were very disapproving about the lack of formal organization. They were upset that nobody asked them to help, they thought it rude and it never occurred to them that it was up to them to offer to help. They never came back. (*Michael Brown*)

The biggest debate in the LSE meetings was about the presence of straights in GLF. The argument about heterosexual involvement was very decisive early on in the direction that we took, not allowing heterosexuals onto the steering group. Up till then we had always had a straight public image for pro-gay activism, whereby gays pretended to be sympathetic straights to gain public sympathy. (*Tony Halliday*)

I stood for the Steering Committee but I was seen as straight, so I didn't get on. I'd had more sex with men than with women up until then and the complexity of it just wasn't seen. I only just missed being elected and Carla came over to me and told me that it had been because I was considered to be straight. I never got involved in any of the arguments about whether straight people should be allowed into GLF, I felt that it was all much too cut and dried. (*Sue Winter*)

There was a Steering Committee right from the start of my involvement. Going to the meetings in the lecture theatre at the LSE, there on a platform would be a group of people and we were told that they were the Steering Committee. They were people like Aubrey and Bob and David Fernbach, I really don't remember, there were so many bewildering people to see and know. The Steering Committee kind of chaired the sessions. In a way I have no memory of, they started to rotate the members of it. And somebody just proposed my name without me having anything to do with it. I remember the moment when I thought, I don't want to do this sort of thing at all, I'd better say no, but then I thought, I can't, that's rather nice that somebody's suggested it and so I was voted on. We used to meet in people's flats and if we did anything I have no memory of it at all, I can't imagine what we did.

At meeting after meeting at the beginning, people would come up then with 'I know how to organize teas' which was Michael James, or 'I know how to book a town hall for a dance'. I was always most impressed by these people who knew the practical side of life rather than just being able to make a political remark, I loved people who knew how to make something work. And week after week, people were effervescent with things they could contribute or suggest, or set up a group. People were always saying in the early meetings, can't we have a membership list or membership fees to raise money or something like that. And week after week, somebody would leap to their feet and say 'This is not an organization, we don't want to be an institution of any sort.' So many things did come out of the ideas put forward, people concentrated on what suited them the most. (*Andrew Lumsden*)

I was a very besuited young actor with quite a nice comfortable career going along, doing lots of parts in theatre and telly and so on. I left drama school in the early sixties and worked as an actor right through the sixties into 1970. Then I met a young art student called Rex Lay and we became lovers for two or three years. He came back one night and said, 'I've been to this Gay Liberation meeting' and I said, 'What?' I didn't have anything to do with politics, especially something that was radical . . . in those days you didn't let it get out that you were at all political and certainly not gay, it was a no-no, so anything like that would frighten me. Having forgotten of course that my father was a lifelong member of the Socialist Party and my mother had worked for the World Congress of Mothers. I said, 'I can't go to that' and he said, 'Well, there's all these sexy blokes there.' Sex dragged me into the revolution screaming . . . well, I started screaming once I got there. But I was this butch little East End number, I was brought up in Stepney so I kept it carefully guarded. I think I thought of myself as being the John Gielgud of the times, doing a lot of Shakespeare and all that.

So I went to this meeting at the Arts Lab at Kings Cross. I didn't know anybody but I think Graham Chapman was there and this gorgeous fifteen-year-old number. The next week, they'd moved to the LSE and I met a lot of other people there. But I went to this meeting wearing a suit and soon realized that it was not that scene. Next week I was there in my green velvet flared bottoms, T-shirt and a huge Afghan coat. My hair got longer and I had a beard like Che Guevara. Rex said 'Oh well, at least you've got the right gear.' It was a very exciting time. That's when I met Mary and Elizabeth and Angie Weir. They were all pretty young gels at the time, in their early twenties I think, not much more. A lot of friendships came out of it. There was a feeling of euphoria, like on the stage when you get a job, if it goes well. You would meet people and think, I want to know you for the rest of my life. Of course, it didn't always turn out like that. But there was a strong fusion of things. (*Bette Bourne*)

I attended the first few meetings with Mark Rowlands, but then we set up a GLF in Brighton where we were living. I found the meetings quite querulous and violent . . . it could be quite frightening, especially some people like the

hardline Maoists. There were lots of links to anarchist and peace movements, especially through the office being in the basement of Housmans Bookshop in Kings Cross – there were a lot of other anarchist groups based around there at the bottom of Pentonville Road at that time.
(*Simon Watney*)

The theoretical basis of GLF was strengthened by the use of 'think-ins', mass meetings of the membership which would break into small discussion groups so that everyone could contribute – a strange concept to activists for whom Roberts' Rules, by which motions and points of order and formal chairing were used to keep large meetings rigidly in order, was the norm to show serious respectability. 'The think-ins were a very simple structure; agree a topic, split into small groups, report back to the rest. It seemed very revolutionary at the time' (*Aubrey Walter*).

At the first GLF think-in on Saturday 16 January 1971 there was a very clear decision by the mass of people present to reject the rigid membership structures and organization favoured by those traditional gay activists present. 'All of us saw CHE as too respectable. The first think-in at the LSE made that clear. Antony Grey came in with lots of "be respectable" ideas and they were automatically opposed by people. If you were in GLF you had to be in an awareness group, which was basically consciousness-raising techniques. I was in one with Bette Bourne which met for about a year weekly' (*Aubrey Walter*).

CR (consciousness-raising) or awareness groups as they were usually called in London were another import from America and were used extensively in the gay and women's movements, in both of which many people felt the need to explore what their true feelings were as opposed to those which society had imposed upon them. A discussion paper, thought to have been written by David or Aubrey, suggested to London GLF at one point that attendance at awareness groups should be mandatory for all new members, but like any attempt to make any action compulsory in GLF it fizzled out.

> I was in a CR group with Micky Burbidge and others. We met once a week for nine months in someone's home in the evenings. You could crash there if you needed to, which was very alien to me, being able to turn up and just stay overnight. You brought food to share and sat in a circle on

the floor. Sometimes there was a topic but we also talked about what we had done in the week and people would ask questions. We talked about self-oppression, zaps, politics, lifestyles, communes and how to change society. (*Michael Brown*)

Our awareness group was me, Luke Fitzgerald, Michael Mason, Jane Winter, Micky Sequeira. We called it a be-wareness group. We used to go into the country for weekends and we went to Salisbury in Michael's brother's Land Rover. We sat and smoked a joint in the Cathedral cloisters and I remember that the man sweeping up the leaves came and sat down and shared it with us and then took us all home to his cottage. I dropped some acid without telling anyone, which was strictly against the rules, and I had to confess to Jane when we went into town to eat, because I didn't want to face any mirrors. Everybody very politely pretended not to know, while manoeuvring me into the right position in the cafe. (*Carl Hill*)

A number of characters were coming to the fore in GLF, both male and female. While David and Aubrey were seen as the driving force behind the development of GLF, others such as Warren Haig, Tony Reynolds, Andy Elsmore, Mary McIntosh and Elizabeth Wilson were making themselves heard too. An abiding memory for several people interviewed was that of Elizabeth Wilson sitting on the platform or in the crowd, knitting or crocheting placidly through a furious debate and producing spidery, rainbow coloured waistcoats for friends. 'The thing about me knitting waistcoats for my favourites is complete legend. People would pay me £2.50 or whatever for them, but I suppose there's a sense in which it is true inasmuch as I would be more likely to be asked to make one by somebody I knew rather than someone I didn't' (*Elizabeth Wilson*). The habit of crocheting was taken up by a number of the radical queens and eventually became something of a hallmark of the feminist men.

Soon after moving back into the LSE in January, it became clear that GLF needed some sort of central office base, rather than just an accommodation address at Agitprop. 'I got involved because I was working at Housmans and we had a lot of contact with Agitprop, where early GLF was based. Housmans had space in the rear of their basement and there was a general meeting at which Roger Moody and I proposed they should move into it. Early on, the main people in the office were me, Stuart Feather, Tony Salvis, Michael James and Michel who became treasurer eventually' (*Max McLellan*). Shortly afterwards there was a joint Housmans and GLF party in the new office which was disrupted by a group of straight men who, saying that they were police cadets from Hendon, first tried to gatecrash and then to disrupt the party. They were unceremoniously ejected by the gay liberationists – a suitable housewarming. The move to Housmans, a bookshop with strong links with pacifist and anarchist causes and owned by *Peace News*, confirmed the philosophical difference of GLF to other gay groups.

The disruption was not the first time that a GLF social had been invaded. Despite the peaceful reception of GLF's first discos at the LSE and their People's Dance at Kensington Town Hall – or possibly because of the coverage of the latter – GLF's first attempt to hold a disco in an ordinary pub attracted an unpleasant show of force from the Metropolitan Police which was chronicled by Paul (possibly Theobald) in an article in *Come Together* 4, 'Bust to Show The Flag':

> I was out of love that night. Well, fuck it, if it's a drag I can always get pissed or maybe even high. That was the state my head was in when I arrived at the Prince of Wales in Hampstead Road where the GLF disco was being held on Friday 22nd January. I don't go to pubs very often, and rarely can I get into dancing, so I wasn't too keen on this idea of a disco as the only alternative scene that GLF (i.e. WE) had managed to come up with. But it was really nice to walk into the pub and be confronted with a few friendly, familiar faces, and the offer of a drink from a guy who wasn't trying to pick me up. This was a Gay pub for the night, but happily without the hallmarks of the gay pubs and clubs that I've been into before. Here were PEOPLE. Happy, smiling, touching, talking and not walking away with the impression of having talked to just 'nice fitting pants' or 'pretty face'. I saw them. But I could also feel the nice vibes that came from these people. So together we danced, we talked, we touched, and we DUG IT. We were digging it . . .
> KNOCK KNOCK who's there
> KNOCK KNOCK who's there
> ME that's who ME
> oh well you'd better come in then

Evening all, we have reason to believe that there are drugs
on the premises. Who's in charge?
No-one's in charge. We're a group of people who've come
together TOGETHER.
Alright, men over there, women over here. And they went
through our pockets, and they went into our bags, and into
our hair, and la la la was there anywhere they didn't look?
Well, it seemed that everyone was clean . . . not a nasty
reefer in sight. One thing though, I and several other people
who were there have been searched for drugs several times
before, and they were always very much more thorough
than that. I don't think that's why they were there at all do
you? They didn't even bring any lady policemen with them,
so the sisters underwent an extremely tepid handbag
search. But I did hear a policeman say something about
'showing the flag' . . . don't know what he could have been
talking about, the only flag I could see was ours . . . we're
homosexuals and proud to be so.
During the search the policemen asked some sisters and
brothers for their names and addresses . . .
After the raid the police had a little chat with the landlord,
intimidating him to the extent that we can no longer hold
any functions at his pub. Up until this point the landlord,
who was a really nice guy, had been very keen that we
continued to use his pub. So we find another place . . .
POWER TO ALL OPPRESSED PEOPLE – RIGHT ON!

From here on, GLF came increasingly into conflict with the
Met, culminating in their targeting as part of the Special Branch
operation against the Angry Brigade, dealt with in chapter fourteen. The Front's confidence in public actions was growing,
primarily through the actions of the Street Theatre group, and they
soon came into conflict with the police again at the February trials
of the women arrested at the Miss World contest, which they
picketed in support of women's liberation. But it was a picket with
a difference.

I got involved because I was a flatmate of Mitch and
Angus, they enthused about it. I didn't think I ought to go
because I was straight, but they said it wasn't like that and
I was welcome. I got involved in Street Theatre. We devised
the 'Miss Trial' show for Bow Street, mainly to take the

piss out of Bob Hope the compere. Nobody was very
confident about it, we were all new to Street Theatre and
we didn't know how to make an entrance so we dressed up
at someone's house and acted all the way there on the tube,
which was a bit of a shock to all the other people on it. We
had a basic outline for most Street Theatre shows but then
would ad lib over the top of it. There were a lot of men in
drag as the contestants and we tried to auction them to the
passers by in a Dutch auction and I was the auctioneer in
male drag. You can imagine how the Covent Garden
market people took to that, we got a lot of fruit thrown at
us. Prominent people in early Street Theatre were Sue
[Winter], Mitch and Angus, Paul Theobald, Michael
Mason and Carl Hill, Janet P, someone called David, Stuart
Feather, Luke Fitzgerald, Tarsus, Philip Want and Charlie
Pig who was an extraordinary character. He did wear
women's clothes without it ever being drag and often used
to paint his face very creatively. (*Jane Winter*)

The second [Street Theatre action] was more to my taste. It
was at Bow Street in support of women's lib after the
arrests at Miss World in the November before . . . I
remember the Covent Garden porters hurling abuse at us.
There was Tarsus, Paul Theobald, Edsel (who ended up
going religious but who was a proto-punk in 1971, he had
pink hair well ahead of his time), Marion Prince and some
others I can't remember. Bette came along to watch. BBC2
came along and filmed us, which was a tremendous boost
that we could get media attention, but then we got knocked
off the news by the financial collapse of Rolls Royce. But it
was a turning point – the press started taking a lot of
interest in us after that, cartoons and things started
appearing. (*Stuart Feather*)

We lived in Wicklow Street in Kings Cross and would get
dressed there and parade through Kings Cross. The first
time that I wore a frock was doing the Miss Trial demo, I
borrowed a black and silver lamé number from Sue Winter.
It was really hard to find shoes to fit, I had to use sandals
or sneakers. (*Paul Theobald*)

The growing interest of the press was a hard-fought battle
for one new GLF attender with an insight into their workings.

I tried to get the straight press to do a bit, because that was the world that I lived in and it was natural for me to do so. I tried to get the editor of the *Daily Mirror*, which then had the largest circulation – the *Sun* existed, but it hadn't become what it has since. The *Mirror* was a middle of the road, leftish paper. It seemed a natural subject for them to do something on and I knew the editor himself was in no way prejudiced about gays, there were gays on his staff, lesbians on the staff and he was a friend of mine. I knew he had no personal difficulties at all. And to my shock he said, 'No, I won't have a piece in the *Daily Mirror.*' He said he wouldn't send anyone along to GLF because it was only a London thing and was of no interest nationally.

The Times refused to run an article that I wrote about the Gay Liberation Front – William Rees-Mogg himself barred it – so then I asked a weekly, the *Spectator*, to run it and they did, at the start of 1971. The *Spectator* was then run by George Gale, who was immortalized by *Private Eye* as Lunchtime O'Booze. I came out with the article, which attacked the lack of media interest in GLF. And then Jill Tweedie met me at a House of Lords lunch and we talked about the article and GLF, as a result of which I took her to a meeting and she wrote about us. Through *The Times*, I had an Aston Martin and we painted a big GLF sign on the back of it.

There was also at the same time a programme called *Panorama*. My general attitude, working as I did in a newspaper that was 'the top people's newspaper', was to try to get flagship programmes to do something. *The Times* was one, the *Mirror* another and *Panorama* a third and a very famous current affairs programme, far more so than now. After a lot of support from Julian Pettifer, they did a short interview with three people from GLF and then they kept deferring the broadcast of it. We got very suspicious about this, but then they did, in the end, broadcast it. And it broke my oldest friendship because my oldest friend didn't at that time know I was gay, I hadn't seen him for quite a long time, a friend from earliest schooldays. He was sitting at home with his parents in Sussex and suddenly there was this oldest friend of his talking about being gay. He rang up a few days later and said, he was in a terrible state, he said 'Everybody I know knows that you have been my closest friend for most of my life, they'll all think that I am homosexual as well.' So though he didn't quarrel with me, it broke the friendship. That was a price I was very sorry about. (*Andrew Lumsden*)

The difficulties that he had experienced in getting coverage, while they might seem routine to current activists, were a shock to an idealistic journalist in the early 1970s. They set him thinking along an entirely new line which was eventually to bear important fruit.

And I thought that it wouldn't do for us just to have quality papers and *Panorama* and the *Mirror* writing the occasional bit. I was so angry that the principal Labour Party supporting paper and the principal top paper both refused in the space of a fortnight to carry a description of what the Gay Liberation Front was in the simplest terms, just that it existed and a little information . . . it seemed to me that there was only one thing to do and that was to have a newspaper of our own. (*Andrew Lumsden*)

Chapter five

Coming Out Proud

We have been meeting now for close on six months and . . . we have achieved none of our demands. –Anonymous contributor to *Come Together 5*

THE attendance of the BBC at the Bow Street 'Miss Trial' demonstration marked the start of a visible, though not always serious, level of media and public attention to the Gay Liberation Front. With their bold behaviour, hippy appearance and revolutionary stance, they were a godsend to cartoonists and columnists, always good for a paragraph from someone wanting to show that they were 'with it'. Groups within GLF took on a distinctive character, and that spring a number of campaigns were begun which were to have repercussions for many years after the demise of the Front. Externally, relations with the Campaign for Homosexual Equality and other gay groups became strained as GLF London stole their thunder and their audience, while other GLF groups began to spring up across the country and in other parts of Europe.

The state of GLF is best summed up by an article written by them for *Time Out*, the London listings magazine for their edition of 21 February 1971.

Gay Liberation Front has been going in London for around 3 months. Our members number around 500. We haven't been that active yet – we've done a lot of leafletting, we've had a torchlight protest against police harassment of homosexual people on Highbury Fields, we had a very nice dance in Kensington Town Hall in December, and our Street Theatre group have done some great imaginative things. But already we're having an effect upon people.

The aims of the Gay Liberation Front are to let gay people know that we're not 'queers' or 'perverts' or 'unnatural' or 'wicked' and to encourage us to set ourselves free and just be ourselves. The other part of our action is to attack the psychiatrists, newspapers and public figures who've been putting us down for years. Gay people are getting themselves together and we're coming out proud.

It is one of our basic principles that we realise that gay people cannot be totally free until everyone in this society is free and so we support other oppressed groups who are fighting for their own liberation. We demonstrated with our sisters from Womens Liberation outside the Miss World Trial, we have marched with other workers and Trade Unionists against the Industrial Relations Bill. There is an alarming increase in repression on all fronts and gay people, women, black people, workers, old people and freaks must stick together.

We have weekly meetings on Wednesday nights, at the moment, in the London School of Economics at 7.30pm, but these meetings are too large and cumbersome and most of the work gets done in smaller groups where people have more of a chance to get to know each other. We have a Counter-Psychiatry Group, a Schools Group, a Trade Union Group, a workshop which produces our journal 'Come Together', a Street Theatre Group, Research and Education Groups, an Action Group and several Awareness Groups.

GLF hopes to provide a desperately-needed escape for people who are tired of the alienated and exploitative 'gay' world, furtive sex in public loos, and dangerous excursions to Hampstead Heath. We want to provide a better scene for gay people. But we know that the very distinction between homosexual and heterosexual is part of oppression; that we're all just people and we shouldn't allow ourselves to be divided and oppressed in any way. So we're setting up an alternative gay ghetto. Our dances are People's Dances and everyone who digs the music should come along and do their thing.

We are also aware that merely providing an escape, a social alternative, is not enough. If we ask why gay people are oppressed, why so many people put us down we can only answer by looking at the general distortion of all sexuality in this society. This society creates and exploits people's sexual anxieties for the purpose of social control, and to sell the surfeit of consumer goods the economic system grinds out. It's not enough for us to have a groovy time, there are important questions that need to be answered, there are revolutionary changes we will have to make before we can be really free.

If you're gay come to GLF, if you're heterosexual – there's more than one front for fighting for the revolution.

All Power to the Oppressed People!

The greatest aid to visibility was the newly formed Street Theatre Group. 'The *Daily Mirror* at one point had a full-page spread about the Street Theatre people, with a picture of them in black leotards including Edsel and Barbara Klecki' (*David Fernbach*).

The whole thing about radical drag came out of Street Theatre, who began to dress up without using false tits and leaving beards on. In the early days, we used whiteface make-up as a defence against hostility, we were trying to indicate that we were actors in the hope of not getting hit. One of the early actions was to make up placards with a question mark on a black background, wearing head to toe black clothes and on the other side of the placard would be a question like 'How dare you presume I'm heterosexual?' and other similar slogans. We all just got on the Central Line tube with some others who were in drag and pretended to be outraged housewives. We did some same-sex kissing and then held up the placards while the 'housewives' complained about us to the other people on the tube and got them into conversation about us. Then when most people had got off or changed over, we'd repeat it again – round and round the Circle Line. It acted as recruitment, publicity and confrontation. We didn't call the press because it wasn't some publicity stunt, it was meant to reach people and get them into really serious one-to-one conversation and it worked. (*Sue Winter*)

At Alexandra Palace [Easter Sunday 1971] Street Theatre was doing our stuff and having a good time and then this policewoman started taking pictures of us, she'd obviously decided we were subversives – so we started taking pictures of her, which she didn't like very much and went away. But it was "a downer" as we would have said then.
(*Jane Winter*)

The next demo was an internal one when there were elections for the Steering Committee, which changed over regularly, maybe it was every three months. Four of us became this character Doris Haversham and stood as one person for the SC. It must have been the first manifestation of drag in GLF. People were shocked and surprised, but they laughed. Just before the vote, Andrew Lumsden came up to me and asked me quietly if we were serious.
(*Stuart Feather*)

A guy called David used to get the costumes from Bermans for us. He invented Doris Haversham, who was wonderful – Street Theatre always reported back to the general meetings as Doris, whoever it was doing the report. Most of the Dorises were men in drag and if it was someone like me who didn't want to do Doris, we would stand up and give her apologies. Loads of people found being her a liberating experience, most of them weren't used to standing up and talking to hundreds of people and it was easier as Doris. We used to make things up and lie outrageously about what Street Theatre had been up to, people thought it was funny. I'm sure we were frowned upon by some of the more solemn element, but most people accepted us. We were taking the piss out of being structured. (*Jane Winter*)

There were all these educated types there and they were doing all the yapping so the queens got stroppy. A few of the queens got up and did a drag act at one meeting in the LSE, that was very funny. They all came as Miss Haversham. (*Bette Bourne*)

Street Theatre also devised a trial show based on *Alice Through the Looking Glass* with playing card court attendants and a lot of jokey contemporary references. There was a point when there was a version of the Speaker's processional walk to the Commons and then the attendants broke out into 'Here Come De Judge' which was from a popular television programme, *Rowan and Martin's Laugh-In*. And there had been a famous case, the Challoner case, of a policeman who fitted up a defendant with half a brick, so our defendant was fitted up with half a prick. (*Jane Winter*)

Street Theatre had it all – it was a focal point at all the demonstrations; a CR group came from it and it was generally a very close group. (*Michael Mason*)

I went to the Street Theatre do at Alexandra Palace against the Festival of Light, everyone was dressed in gear from Bermans. I saw my history teacher, Brian Burt, dressed as Cleopatra. Then I went to Cavendish Avenue, the Astor place [where rehearsals were being held], where Princess Obolensky let me in. I had been a paying guest of her grandmother in the 1960s, so I felt less isolated. She and her brother owned the house and lived at the top of it. I was in yellow dungarees and I had long red hair. That was where the Theatre Group was, but I was much more interested in the Street Theatre Group. (*Carl Hill*)

Theatre Group was effectively an offshoot of the Street Theatre Group which flourished briefly in early 1971 under the direction of John Chesterman.

The Theatre Group tried to get together a deconstructed, transsexual production of *Measure for Measure*, with rehearsals at the Astor family home next to Paul McCartney's place in St Johns Wood. Thelma Holt came to see us in rehearsal one day to consider putting it on, but that day we were so bad that she walked out. At the next rehearsal, everyone gave a blazing performance, but it was too late. I felt I had blown it and the cast deconstructed shortly afterwards. (*John Chesterman*)

Others in GLF criticized the Theatre Group for its 'straight' ambitions and its adherence to hierarchical and disciplinary theatrical norms.

The Theatre Group came out of Street Theatre but was very different. It was John Chesterman's idea to put on *Measure for Measure*, hopefully at The Open Space. He had a wonderful script which used bits from a lot of other Shakespeare plays, so you had all these other resonances, and the sex of some of the central characters was changed to give it a gay slant. It took a lot of people away from Street Theatre for a while and took a lot of energy rehearsing and learning lines. I was Isabella and it became clear to me I wasn't very good, unlike Lala who turned out to have a real natural talent. Then Thelma Holt and a big shot theatre man came to see it and were very unimpressed with it and with me, so I decided to stop. John was a very good director, very supportive and inventive, but we'd bitten off far more than we could chew and people just gave up on it around that time. (*Jane Winter*)

But if this group failed, the Counter-Psychiatry Group was just getting into its stride. After a couple of months of discussion in which those less familiar with the anti-psychiatry movement were able to learn the principles and jargon, they set their sights on a target which became a unifying struggle for many others in GLF, bringing together various groups in a couple of huge set-piece demos later in 1971. A book had recently been imported from the US and published by W. H. Allen, written by a popular American psychiatrist called Dr David Reuben and purporting to tell the plain truth about a variety of sexual issues and problems. It was called *Everything You Always Wanted To Know About Sex – but were afraid to ask* and large sections of it, particularly those relating to women and homosexuals, were complete and utter rubbish.

The campaign against it started quietly enough on 12 February 1971 with a small deputation which took a letter with 158 signatures on it to explain to the publishers what the problem was. The text, with its measured language and polite tone, gives the lie to those who felt that GLF was an organization incapable of civilized debate with the straight world. At least as far as the Counter-Psychiatry Group was concerned, it was willing to ask nicely; if the straight world chose to ignore such a polite request, only then would they learn the difference between GLF and CHE.

Mr. Simmons,

On behalf of the Gay Liberation Front we protest against the publication by you of Dr David Reuben's book "Everything You Always Wanted To Know About Sex – but were afraid to ask", and specifically against the chapter on male homosexuality and the reference to female homosexuality.

According to your blurb this book purports to be an 'utterly candid' guide to the facts of life. You claim that 'avoiding any moral judgement (it) fills a dangerous educational void by leaving no sexual activity unexplored'.

These claims are unfounded. Dr Reuben reinforces society's most vicious prejudices, and elaborates them in a quite hysterical way. Much of what he says about homosexuality can only frighten those, especially young people, who turn to this book for help and enlightenment.

We do not say that some of the phenomena described in this book never occur, but refute the claim that they are typical and representative. The author confirms and reinforces general preconceptions and stereotypes and his writings will lead many people to feel that contempt of the homosexual is justified.

What is so dangerous about this book is that one man has used his medical status to give his private prejudices the appearance of scientific fact. Throughout, Dr Reuben sensationalises homosexuality, confusing it with transvestism and transsexuality in a way we would have thought no responsible psychiatrist could possible do.

His only remarks about female homosexuality are under the chapter heading of 'Prostitution'.

He untruly asserts that male homosexual relationships are almost invariably short term and impersonal. 'A masturbation machine might do it better' he says at one point.

In fact, many homosexuals live together for years in relationships that manifestly offer their partners companionship and affection within a sexual relationship – but Dr Reuben devotes only one disparaging paragraph to such people. He simply uses the unscientific methods of denial and assertion to 'prove' that such relationships cannot be happy.

We are shocked to see a reputable publisher printing such pernicious and dangerous rubbish. The tone throughout is one of leering innuendo, the very tone of the 'locker room whispers' and sniggers you claim this book will end. We feel revulsion at Dr Reuben's obvious contempt for those he claims he wishes to help.

W. H. Allen are mistaken if they imagine that homosexuals are any longer a disorganised minority who can be insulted and vilified with impunity. We demand that this book be withdrawn from circulation immediately.

GLF people also leafleted W. H. Smiths branches in central London the next day. They got coverage in the *Guardian* and the *Evening Standard* and received an offer from the publishers not only to forward their critique to Dr Reuben in the States, but also to publish a GLF book putting forward their views on homosexuality.

No sooner was this over than GLF was in the news again for 'zapping' the Gateways, the only lesbian drinking club in London. The full story of this is told in chapter ten, but it resulted in further press coverage and thirteen arrests – two of them of total strangers who got caught up in the running mêlée outside the club after GLF leafleters were ejected and police called. It is an indication of the expectation of justice from a magistrates court in those days that these were the only two arrested who pleaded guilty, on the grounds that they were bound to be convicted on police evidence and hoped for a smaller fine that way.

The very day after this demonstration, GLF attended the giant protest against the Industrial Relations Bill. It was not the first such demonstration they had attended, but this time they came with a banner and many placards reading 'Homosexuals Oppose The Bill', 'Poof To The Bill' and so on. They also distributed a leaflet to tell the others on the March why they were joining them. Headed 'Homosexuals Are On The March', it listed fourteen unions from which GLF people came and said:

> The threat to Trade Unions is only one part of the
> continuing oppression of working people. Homosexual
> people are demanding an end to our oppression in society.
> We know that homosexuality is just as valid an expression
> of human feeling as heterosexuality. The whole of sexuality
> in this society has been messed around . . . nearly one
> million trade unionists are homosexual people. One of the
> most direct forms of our oppression is in employment –
> people either lose their jobs because they become known as
> gay, or we are too scared to be honest and are compelled to
> lead alienated double-lives. Trade Unionists must join the
> fight against ALL prejudiced discrimination at work.

It went on to discuss the ways in which prejudice was also used against the working class and racial minorities and to draw a comparison between biased media representation of unions and gays, and finished 'United We Stand!'

The presence of GLF caused a considerable stir amongst other marchers as well as the media. As a non-union organization, they were due to march in the last section and were firmly relegated to last because nobody else wanted to march with them. This was greeted with different levels of acceptance from GLF people, some of whom saw it as an act of discrimination in itself. Certainly it set a pattern which has been regularly repeated, right up to the leftist marches against the British National Party in the 1990s; gays always come last.

'There were always terrible rows (over GLF at other demos). I started off with the Claimants Union, we all had letters spelling it out and then I went off and marched with GLF, with my U or whatever. People probably thought it was some cryptic sexual message' (*Angie Weir*).

'There's a photo of me on the IRB march in the *Come Together* book. I remember when they made us go to the rear. I was carrying a placard that said "Homosexuals Oppose The Bill" (*Paul Theobald*).

The GLF group trailed along at the rear, chanting gay slogans and generally making their presence very thoroughly felt. John Phillips, in *Radical Records,* recounts how their numbers swelled: 'We made our way through central London. Marching down the Haymarket I became aware of the ever-increasing amount of noise we were making and, looking behind, I realized our numbers had increased to nearly two hundred. Gay men and women, sympathizers from other groups and onlookers from the pavement had joined us.' 'The Industrial Relations Bill demonstration in February 1971 had hundreds of GLF people on it, not just the regulars from the meetings. It was the Socialist Worker people who forced us to the very back of the march, I think they were worried that GLF would get more media attention than other people' (*David Fernbach*).

The left were, of course, quite right that the presence of GLF would 'distract' the media from the rest of the message they were trying to put across, to stop the passage of repressive legislation which would restrict trade union practices. Several cartoonists took advantage of the presence of their latest hobby horse, as did sketch writers. Jak, in the *Evening Standard*, portrayed a TUC official reading the different papers' accounts of numbers at the rally and saying to Vic Feather, leader of the Congress, 'Well, Vic, I make it eighty to one hundred and fifty thousand, depending on whether you include the "Gay Liberation Front" or not!' But there was also an entirely justified suspicion from many left wing activists that some GLF people failed to treat their gods with sufficient reverence. 'One action we always meant to do and never did, which I regret, was that we were going to go up to Highgate Cemetery and put some make-up on Karl Marx's face, but somehow we never got around to that one' (*Andrew Lumsden*).

Not all GLF activists understood the practical implications, rather than the theory, of workers' rights.

> There was another [dance] in Camden Town Hall in 1971 and I remember vividly at that one at midnight, all the lights went on and a number of people started protesting about the place being shut down and started calling the attendants, who after all were working overtime, 'fascist pigs' and shouting 'Revolution now!' as if attacking the poor attendants was somehow going to bring on the revolution. That actually made me aware that there were different strands of GLF, there was the strand that supported trade union rights, that supported the workers – they had rights as well and they wanted to go home, why should they stay after midnight? And there was also a streak in Gay Liberation of pure individualism, whatever the language of 'revolution now', it was actually 'I want it and if so, I must have it.' I think those two strands are still with us in the sexual culture, between 'sexual' being about my right to do whatever I want, regardless of the consequences, and those who believe that my right to do something must always be tempered by the rights of others. That divide was there right from the beginning, between extreme libertarianism and a sort of liberationism which stressed solidarity and community and involvement with others. (*Jeffrey Weeks*)

Class was itself an issue within GLF at times, though it was noticed more by the women.

> It's been a very different kettle of fish for the middle-class women and the working class women . . . I don't question their commitment and it wasn't any unkindness on their part – it's English society and its divisions . . . but they became the spokeswomen not the working-class women. I remember an early meeting of the Women's Group at my flat . . . Max and Libby were there and Mary and

Elizabeth. They were talking about the difficulties of coming out in their profession and Max said 'Me and Libby don't have any trouble coming out in our profession' and Elizabeth said 'What is your profession?' and Max replied 'Industrial cleaners.' You could have heard a pin drop. The gay liberation movement, unlike the women's liberation movement at that time, was not solidly middle-class. Of course a lot of people were, but there was everyone from Lady Rose to Max and Libby. The mixture was much greater and in that sense it was far more exciting – all these different perspectives, there were black people in gay liberation but not much in women's liberation at that time. (*Carla Toney*)

There continued to be noticeable differences in how much and in what way people of different sexes contributed to debates. 'Warren was a big talker. He was only like lots of men in lots of movements. He was a natural leader but people weren't into it and they did take the piss out of him. Lala was very conciliatory and sensible whenever people got into heavy argument. It was always a place of lively debate. Michael Mason would chip in, too. I wasn't into that side of it' (*Jane Winter*).

The GLF philosophy was making an impact, not only on the media and the left, but also in other countries. Just as Bob and Aubrey had visited the American groups, activists from other European countries came to London for a while and then returned to form revolutionary gay movements in their own countries. 'London GLF was a training ground for many people who went on to start gay movements in other countries – Mario Mieli from Italy, lots of Latin Americans, and the people who set up FHAR in France' (*Peter Tatchell*). FHAR (the Homosexual Front for Revolutionary Action) was founded in March 1971. FUORI (United Front for Revolutionary Homosexuals), an acronym meaning 'Out', took a little longer in Italy but was all the more militant for it. As Mario Mieli announced in their first communication back to London 'Its political line is very close to that of the French organization FAHR [*sic*]. FUORI has also expressed criticism of the GLF's policies which it feels to be too reformist and at times too sectarian in relation to the revolutionary movement.' They nevertheless asked for GLF's help in contacting Italian brothers in London, though no mention was made of Italian sisters.

While FUORI was complaining that GLF was not revolutionary enough, CHE was taking the opposite tack – very loudly
and in public. 'CHE disassociated themselves from GLF publicly in
the spring of 1971. They were also a young group, but a very
different one. They were very rude to GLF, they thought that they
were the only pebbles on the beach. They modelled themselves on
the National Council for Civil Liberties and had good conferences,
but they failed because they couldn't grasp the challenge of being a
developed political movement' (*Antony Grey*). It was in April that
a series of press interventions were made by CHE attacking GLF,
first in the *New Statesman* by ex-MP Ian Harvey, a leading light
and later in the *Guardian* by Paul Temperton, their employee.

Harvey, who was writing to publicize his forthcoming
autobiography *To Fall Like Lucifer* said, in an article titled 'The
Homosexual Plight', 'the arrival on the scene of the Gay Liberation
Front . . . has not been helpful. Its members, who include both
sexes, incline to display a neurotic state of emotionalism which is
out of date in the light of recent reforms . . . The organisation has
associated itself with Marxism, although Marx had no homosexual
tendencies and has demanded "all power to the oppressed people".
A great deal of this oppression is now more imaginary than real.'
GLF reacted angrily, pointing out that it was Harvey's own
apologist 'sit tight and wait for people to be reasonable' attitude
which was outdated.

The Temperton outburst was in response to a stunning piece
of propaganda for GLF from Jill Tweedie, the highly regarded
Guardian columnist who had taken to Andrew Lumsden over
dinner at the Lords and visited a meeting with him. The article,
'Gay's The Word', contrasts the 'healthy', outgoing attitude of GLF
to the closetry of older generations of homosexuals, as characterized by the expatriate upper-class homosexuals of Tangier. It details
the demands, the working groups and the philosophy of GLF in
linking with women's liberation and other groups in near-romantic
language:

> They have come together because, as homosexuals, they
> refuse any longer to stay in the zoo, to be labelled medical
> or psychiatric problems, to feel guilty as humans for what
> is natural to animals . . . though they want legislative
> changes . . . these young homosexuals, by their very
> acceptance of the normality of homosexuality, challenge the
> status quo, the dedicated heterosexuality of the normal

man and woman which creates the family unit, foundation stone of the capitalist system. Gay Lib does not plead for the right of homosexuals to marry. Gay Lib questions marriage . . . And they are beautiful to see. It is lovely to be with men and women who are not ashamed to express their affection openly . . . Suddenly, watching them, the whole evil squalid image of homosexuality crumbles – are these bright faces corrupters of children, lavatory solicitor, the something nasty in all our woodsheds? Is that young lawyer over there, proud of his Gay Liberation badge, a lurker behind bushes, a pouncer on little boys?

The whole article is a public relations dream. No wonder CHE was stung, rather than rejoicing virtuously in any good coverage for gays. In six short months they had gone from vanguard to back seat.

And the meetings continued to grow, until there were people spilling out of even the largest room (E71) that the LSE could provide, until the Steering Committee system was creaking at the seams and people started to fall off the edges, to come to one meeting and be so confused by the lack of coordination that they did not return. By April 1971, people were predicting the end of GLF if it did not change; but change was the only constant in GLF and things were on the move already. At the start of that month, the Front was finally forced to leave the LSE for good and it was up to the Steering Committee to find new premises.

I was on the Steering Committee, which we called the 'queering committee'. It was so self-driving a political enterprise, it didn't need people to organize it. The only thing I can remember having to do was find new premises, others might remember more. It was me that suggested we move to Middle Earth in Covent Garden when the LSE got too small, but I announced it before getting the agreement of the owner. As I remember it, the LSE said they had had enough of having these meetings, they were getting larger and larger. In some way I'd come to know the publisher of Jean Genet's books in England, Anthony Blond. He was a person who knew everything that was going on. I must have said to him that we were looking for somewhere and he had either rented, or had access to, what should have been a nightclub called Middle Earth in Covent Garden with endless, cavernous rooms, much bigger than anything

we had met in before. He said he thought he could swing it for us to use those, and so we came to the last meeting at LSE and I had to say something about where we would go next and so I just said, we shall meet at Middle Earth in Covent Garden. But we hadn't got the go ahead, so I had a vision of some three or four hundred queens and dykes turning up and not being allowed in. In a way, it wouldn't have mattered much because everybody was so self-motivating that we would all have done something, I don't know what, all gone to St Paul's churchyard or something, a pub. But a couple of hours before we were due to meet, the keys turned up and we duly met there.
(*Andrew Lumsden*)

Chapter six

Early Christians and the Road to Damascus

We didn't know whether it was a revolution or a party.
–John Chesterman

All our lives changed. Friendships were very close and strong, you'd abandoned your old friends to get into it and demonstrating together forged bonds and made changes that others couldn't understand. Nothing is ever different to those who sit in their armchairs – it's going out and meeting circumstances that change your point of view. –Stuart Feather

MIDDLE Earth, as it is usually known, was a huge basement premises at 43 King Street in the heart of Covent Garden, then undergoing a huge redevelopment. As property values rose in central London, a number of old London markets began to be moved out to the East and South; Billingsgate to the Isle of Dogs, Spitalfields to Poplar and Covent Garden to Vauxhall. In 1971 the market was still in Covent Garden, as GLF people had found to their cost at the Miss Trial demonstration, when stallholders pelted them with fruit. The best record of Covent Garden before the redevelopment is in Hitchcock's *Frenzy*, filmed around this time. Consequently, tenure of any building in the area was insecure.

Middle Earth had been a famous gathering place for the counterculture as an Arts Lab, where performances, concerts and experimental theatre were put on. The building was bought by a consortium of London arts figures including Anthony Blond and the intention was originally to ensure its continuation as a performance space; but plans for the area changed again and after a few short months the building was put up for sale again. It was in that interval that GLF found its most bizarre home. The new premises, with their huge, gloomy, interconnecting rooms and sense of space, brought a new freedom. 'The early LSE meetings in the lecture theatre cramped the style of the meetings. They developed better when people could sit in a circle' (*John Chesterman*). 'We moved to Middle Earth. That was exciting because it was the real world, not just the university and it felt more accessible to other sorts of people' (*Mary McIntosh*).

> You went downstairs and there seemed to be room after room with large pillars supporting the ceiling, it was all underground with no natural light. I didn't like it as much as LSE or All Saints Hall because there was an air of a nightclub. And it came to me – we were temporarily holding meetings that seemed to me identical with what I'd heard about the early Christians in Rome, who met in the Catacombs and had their own language, their own signs. I only knew a few words of polari before this and now I was meeting people who could speak it all the time, knew a lot of gay slang. All around us were plenty of Christian right wingers and politicians denouncing homosexuals and denouncing, when they came to hear of it, the Gay Liberation Front. The feeling was amazing – we were meeting in something like a catacomb, using coded language (gay slang) and symbols, we were anti-authority and had to cope with police interference. It really was like the early Christians. (*Andrew Lumsden*)

New members were still arriving all the time, some of them quickly becoming central.

> I first got involved about six months in. The previous September I'd been arrested for importuning in the West End and it had shattered me and I'd spent a horrible autumn. I had an antiques stall in Shepherd Market in Mayfair and a Saturday cafe in Portobello Road, at the Red Lion. With the arrest, I became terrified to walk down the street in case a policeman looked at me. I guess this all built up and festered over the months and just before Easter I was really low. A friend of mine, Basil, came to see me and I broke down, he was only the second person I'd told after Terry Madeley who lived downstairs from me. He told me about GLF and took me to the meeting the following week.

I turned up in a three piece suit, looking very smart but my friend met me and said he couldn't come because he had a late audition. He told me the new address at Middle Earth, so I went the first week it was there. Middle Earth was this hole in the ground, all dark, no light. I thought it was the wrong place but people kept dashing in, all these hippies and things like that. I didn't see anyone who looked gay in the same sense of the word that I knew and then I saw Bette Bourne, who I'd seen about, dressed in green velvet. So I followed Bette in.

It was quite a silly evening, going into this place with no light that was like a gloomy cave. It was all pillars and things and there was some sort of meeting being convened down the end, it was like a set for *Phantom of the Opera* really. There was a little blue light down the end and there was Carla and Warren Haig and someone else, Aubrey probably. I lurked behind a pillar and then at one stage they said 'We're going to have a newcomers meeting, so anybody that's here for the first time, come along' so I went into this other room. The place was like a big room with coal bunkers, but divided by very wide [half] walls. There was Warren Haig standing in the middle of this maze-like pattern of coal bunkers and we were all standing with this big gulf in between us. He gave us this political harangue and I guess with everything that I had gone through, the arrest and everything, it just all fell into place.

It was the road to Damascus experience. I just saw it in my head, I'd never had drugs or anything, but I was so excited and so attracted by this . . . I couldn't wait for the following week, to see all these wonderful lesbians and gay men again. And the following week I didn't wear a suit, I wore some jeans . . . it was obvious it was a whole new fashion look. They asked for volunteers to do the teas in meetings so, as I had a cafe, it was straight up my street and I volunteered. And then when I ended up closing the cafe down I sold all my equipment to GLF. But I guess I didn't want to be a tea lady all my life and I got into the Media Workshop which produced *Come Together*. (*Michael James*)

The growing fame of GLF attracted a number of celebrity visits to Middle Earth. Those of Kate Millett and Jill Johnson are dealt with in chapter ten, but others remembered for their attendance include Quentin Crisp, David Hockney and Duncan Grant. Among the more regular attenders or supporters were Derek Jarman, Jim Anderson of *Oz* magazine and Graham Chapman of *Monty Python's Flying Circus*. 'I took Duncan Grant along to one of the meetings at Middle Earth in Covent Garden. He was eighty-five at the time, but he wasn't the oldest person at the meeting, which pleased him. Dennis Altman also turned up there around that time' (*Simon Watney*). The meetings, if fragmented, were certainly welcoming to anyone who could cope with the chaos.

> My best friend who was called Jake read about it in the
> *Daily Mirror* in April 1971 and we went along. It was in
> Middle Earth. I was straight then. Bruce Wood was there
> and Ted Brown, Micky Burbidge. Elizabeth Wilson got up
> and told everybody about the Women's Group and what
> they were doing . . . The second week I went, there was an
> argument about intergenerational issues. It was seen as an
> issue of solidarity – people wanted to help anyone
> oppressed by the state. I felt that I could identify with it
> even as straight, because it was about sexual liberation and
> not gay rights, it was involved with women's liberation and
> gender roles and so on. There was lots of debate about
> what gay meant – did it include transvestites and
> transsexuals, anyone who didn't fit in. It was just like the
> queer debates. (*Nettie Pollard*)

> I only came out through GLF . . . my memories of all of it –
> the mass meetings, the Media Workshop, the actions, the
> groups – was that all of it was incredibly warm. When I
> first went, to Covent Garden, the visual impression was of
> a great seething mass of people in this cavern, it was very
> dramatic, there were people milling around and gossiping
> and then most of the people sitting in a circle and people
> would just speak in it, so there was a focal point but no
> platform, you'd just go up and speak. I used to speak quite
> frequently from Media Workshop, say, and I didn't find it
> intimidating, it was very warm and the warmth between
> the women was particularly heartening, and while there
> was obviously chauvinism, I was blind to it. Women were
> strong in the organization, they were strong in the Media
> Workshop and they were strong in the Manifesto Group,

with Mary Mac [McIntosh] and so on. Elizabeth and Mary were very central figures, and Angela for defining the ideology, which was unspoken. The Manifesto represents some of it. (*Sarah Grimes*)

The meetings were beginning to be too large and the organization too diverse in its actions to manage under the existing system, whereby a small Steering Committee simply organized the running of the meeting and any emergencies in between. Now, they had a dozen working groups and an office in Kings Cross to manage. The second London GLF think-in on 8 May decided on a new system, which effectively lasted for the rest of the active life of the all-London meetings. Each working group sent representatives to a weekly coordinating committee, which met on the Monday night before the Wednesday meeting and decided on business. Anyone was welcome to come along and the meeting was apparently held in the office, although anyone who has ever been into the tiny space at the rear of the basement of Housmans might think this was the greatest GLF miracle of all. It also eventually became the base for the office's collation of information for a weekly news sheet which started up that summer to provide better circulation of information in between the monthly or bi-monthly issues of *Come Together*. The coordinating committee was also partly responsible for ensuring the fair running of what was always a fairly chaotic office, although this was not yet an issue at dispute.

We had the basement [of Housmans] as an office, the first real physical centre that GLF had and the Office Collective operated from there, about six to eight people – Denis Lemon, Martin Corbett, Stuart Feather, Tony Salvis and others. The office was open fairly normal hours, about 10 a.m. to 10 p.m. and we operated a rota. If the phone rang, whoever was there answered it, there was no central committee or delegated authority, no hierarchy – it was one of the things that people couldn't understand, they would ring up and say 'What does Gay Liberation think of such and such' and whoever was on the phone would say 'Well, I can tell you what I think' and then you'd find yourself in the *News of the World* as a spokesman for GLF, which was outrageous. (*Alan Wakeman*)

I think that was one of the nicest things about [GLF], it worked cheaply and sold the magazines cheaply and had a scruffy little office. It helped people informally – rent boys came down to the office for a chat and you could always get a coffee, there was a nice atmosphere. Maybe people ripped the money off, I didn't see any of what I would call really nasty types . . . They weren't just people on the make. I think the office did have to tighten up eventually or close down. I went and was part of the office collective for one half day and answered the phone to a few people. One man said 'What colour underwear do you have on?' And there was a letter from a woman saying 'I am a student doing a project on male homosexuality, please send me all your information.' And at the time my girlfriend and I thought the best way to answer – remember, they were writing to GLF and not to Stonewall or whatever, it was a different thing – was to reply 'You're a woman, you should be writing about yourself, why have you chosen male homosexuality? I'm sending you some information about lesbianism because that's a bit nearer to your experience.' I mean, in some ways you might say that was a bit oppressive but on the other hand, maybe it made her think. It's probably not something that would be done today. The idea was to confront people and make them think and in a way we didn't like people who weren't part of an oppressed group studying them. There was something very un-GLF about that. Maybe she was a closet lesbian and really pleased to get it. (*Nettie Pollard*)

Some dozen different working groups were operating by this stage. The process for starting one was simple. You just stood up at a Wednesday general meeting and announced that you had an idea for one, and did anyone want to meet you at the back to discuss it? And if they did, you had a new working group. Some, like Media Workshop, had become a strong and efficient machine with a definite central core of regulars.

Media Workshop had a weekly meeting and there were usually about half a dozen people there. Mick Belsten, Bill Halstead, Aubrey Walter, Annie Brackx – she and I were the only two women who stayed, other women used to come and go, and that very sinister man in black, John Chesterman, was around sometimes . . . Mostly we'd write a lot of the articles ourselves and we'd agree what would go in the issue and each article would be read out to us for discussion. We put it together ourselves as well, it was all a bit *ad hoc*. We started hanging out in various lefty publications like *Time Out* and *IT* and places. We'd go in at night and use their equipment, so it got slightly smarter as it went along. It was all real amateur stuff, but they look quite good really when you pull them out now, all the illustrations and the care and things. Not so much the design and typography, but the imagery.

Mick Belsten was particularly warm. It wasn't until I read his obituaries that I realized his background, with the merchant navy and everything, so he was a bit older than most of us, most of the Media Workshop were in their early twenties. We would meet in his flat in Barnes, it was a lovely place. I don't think he did an awful lot of the writing but he was a great facilitator, he could put people at their ease and get discussion going. He had a great kindness, he never got overwrought so he could sort things out, with the printers and so on. We used a socialist printers in Hackney, they used to charge us commercial rates.

We got people writing things, like for instance from the Youth Group, the declaration of rights, and there was quite a lot of submitted stuff. The Cuban stuff was John Chesterman. There was one article, called 'Why Fear' (*Come Together* 9) by Ramsay, he was a black guy and came along but didn't stay in Media Workshop, and that piece was quite academic, the language was rather off-putting. I think there probably was quite a lot of political censorship, I can't think what issues it came out in. I don't remember the argument over 'Shirley Temple Knows' [an article about cottaging], but I'm sure it's true that there would have been a problem over cottaging. There was a sort of puritanism, there was one article I really hated which criticized something Pat Arrowsmith had written in the women's issue about butch and femme roles. This was another article saying how awful that was. So there was a sort of hidden political right-on-ness that certain gay lifestyles were out of the question. (*Sarah Grimes*)

'I was very involved with *Come Together* in the early days, it was me that did the illustration of Che Guevara turning into a woman (*Come Together* 8). It was Rex Lay who wrote "Shirley Temple Knows". Aubrey didn't want to print it and I did. Tarsus and I also suggested using the pink triangle as the GLF symbol at one meeting, but we were shouted down because it was too depressing' (*John Chesterman*). Although most people involved in Media Workshop were well aware that they occasionally edited and refused pieces, or at least put them back in the Media Workshop folder in the office indefinitely, this was a surprise to others and led to a considerable row, detailed in chapter fourteen.

Another important piece of work was being done in the Manifesto Group. Having agreed the Principles, many people felt it would be useful to have a more expansive and explanatory document which gave more background to the philosophy behind gay liberation. A group started to work on what immediately became known as the *Manifesto* (see appendix two). Not surprisingly, it contained some of the intellectual heavyweights of GLF, the moving forces behind the Counter-Psychiatry Group and those most concerned with its political direction, which made for some interesting disputes.

> The *Manifesto* was done by a group, not in the big meeting. I think it was one of those things where a time was announced and people who wanted to be involved went along. In the end, it was Aubrey, David, Jeffrey, me, Elizabeth, a chap called Paul [Bunting] and others, Bob Mellors. One person talked about children's rights and adult–child sex and he wanted us to put much more in than we wanted to about paedophilia. That was an issue in dispute. I seem to remember six or more meetings, quite a long-lasting group for that time. We were worried about what the rest of GLF would think about it.
>
> We worked from the Principles. Aubrey wanted to put much more in about what our ideal world would look like, about cloning and futuristic ideas about how society could be run without sex differentiations. He seemed to think you'd have to end sex reproduction. I was rather dismissive of that and didn't want to put in anything like it, I don't think it got in. We didn't see it as a political dispute, we were all in GLF, we just thought of it as Aubrey's personality rather than a political difference and it was the same with [other disputes]. (*Mary McIntosh*)

The Manifesto Group was myself, Elizabeth Wilson, Mary McIntosh, Tony Halliday, Bill Halstead, Paul Bunting mostly. Michael Mason came along sometimes. It was a

productive group and experience, meeting weekly for
several months in the spring and summer of 1971. There
were tensions there that widened afterwards; the *Manifesto*
held together people from very different backgrounds.
The majority came from a Marxist background, though
not Tony Halliday or Paul Bunting. Different sections have
different styles; the Youth Cult bit is very much Elizabeth.
(*David Fernbach*)

'The Manifesto Group could get very heated in negotiation,
but it was never handbags at twenty paces' (*Michael Mason*).

Not all the groups were so successful. One, the Book Group,
was formed in response to the suggestion from W. H. Allen after
the first demonstration against Reuben's book and met for a couple
of months but got nowhere. A leaflet distributed at one of the
March 1971 meetings refers to it as 'Putting The Record Bent' and
says that Anthony Blond was also interested in publishing it. It was
extremely ambitious; a list of proposed contents covers everything
from the *Manifesto*, through personal accounts and information on
'the gay life-style' to explanations of a whole range of oppressions,
a complete history of Western homosexuality and its cultural
expressions, a guide to coming out, a health manual and legal
rights advisory and a complete gay guide to the UK.

'I was in the Manifesto Group. That's Sarah Grimes' hand
on the cover of the *Manifesto*. And there was a Book Group, which
was where I met Michael Mason. Everything was very *ad hoc*, the
book never happened. We just followed ideas' (*Tony Halliday*).
'The Youth Group, run by Tony Reynolds, more or less operated
from the Muswell Hill commune. He was in the Book Group too.
They did some work, but you can't write a book by committee – it
didn't gel' (*Michael Mason*).

The office volunteers soon formed a collective of their own,
and there were strict rules for volunteering in the office. Although
anybody could offer, they were theoretically supposed to be
approved by the collective and the Wednesday meetings and not
supposed to work there for more than four months at a time,
followed by a two-month rest. They met immediately before the
coordinating committee each week. The use of rules in what was
generally one of the least restrictive of organizations shows an
understanding of the potential abuses of power that were possible
within that part of the organization which controlled image,
information flow and finances. All mail and calls came through the

office and were distributed by the volunteers, with each group having a large envelope. The same basic system, including the names of working groups and coordinating committee, is used to this day by London Lesbian and Gay Switchboard, an organization born of GLF which eventually inherited the office.

> The Action Group seemed to merge with the office collective sometimes, it was many of the same people, but I didn't go very often. There were John Chesterman and John Church and Denis Lemon and Martin Corbett definitely. People did tend to come and go. There was Robin Farquarson who was a rather strange South African man who wrote a book. He died. He had used the phone to phone South Africa, which caused a bit of a stir at the time. But what was nice about GLF was that it didn't have flash offices and security systems. So people ripped it off, so? We would just try and get some more money somehow, we would never have considered going to the police.
> (*Nettie Pollard*)

The Action Group met on Tuesday nights. They organized some of the involvement in demonstrations, although many of the working groups, particularly Counter-Psychiatry and Street Theatre, organized their own and Action Group merely made sure that others knew and could help out. They were responsible for the Gay Days and support for other groups' demonstrations and also organized the early GLF dances. As they put it in a leaflet to the general meeting about their work, 'the dances perform three functions – they are a political act against the repressive society, they are part of our liberation, an atmosphere where we talk and dance and enjoy being with people, and they raise money for GLF, which is very important'. GLF was an entirely self-financing organization and although there were occasional discreet donations from richer homosexuals – people credit David Hockney, Graham Chapman and Jim Anderson with support – most of the funds came from teas at the meeting, badge sales, newspaper sales and the dances.

> I helped with the dances, I remember when we tried to book Hammersmith Town Hall they were worried about whether the lesbians would start a fight. We drank the bar dry and made the barman, who was called Terry, very happy. When we booked Porchester Hall, they were used to

drag balls and gave us champagne but no beer – we had to get hold of some barrels of beer and a trestle table quickly. (*Martin Corbett*)

The Communes Group began to meet in May, usually on a Thursday night in Penge, where Tony Salvis and Max McLellan and others lived. Communal living was another imported aspect of GLF and a general feature of the counterculture; the idea was that by living with a number of others who shared everything, the barriers of capitalist society would be broken and new forms of social structure would emerge. It was a brave ideal which found a variety of manifestations, some of which are covered in chapter sixteen. 'I remember the commune in Penge and David McClellan, Tim Clark and a drag queen from Glasgow called Claudia' (*Martin Corbett*). The Youth Group, as has already been noted, met mostly in the Bounds Green commune and had a nifty line in poetic slogans. One of their earliest was 'Remember – how can love corrupt when there are as many sexes as there are people!'

A later addition to the group structure was the International Group, which eventually produced its own newspaper, *Gay International News* (GIN). There were also at various times a Trade Unions Group, a Night Workers Group which met in the afternoon, a Premises Group which hoped to found a proper centre for GLF, a Jewish Group because of the anti-Semitism of many members, a Church Research Group, a TV/TS Group and a number of groups set up for special purposes, like the Christmas Party Group which organized a party for children in Notting Hill. Added to this were the Women's Group and the many Awareness Groups, all of which met on a Friday night. As Jeffrey Weeks said and many others echoed, 'I had a meeting every night for the first eighteen months of GLF.'

Chapter seven

Frenetic Faggots Frolicking through the Streets

One sort of politics ran into another sort of politics, there was a sense of constant activism. –Angie Weir

Their nose for social hypocrisy is as gratifyingly keen as their readiness to do something about it. –Bob Sturgess, *Lunch* Issue 6

GLF people were not only busy with internal groups and gay actions. One of the basic tenets of their philosophy was the interconnectedness of gay oppression with women's oppression, black oppression and working-class oppression. Accordingly, for many people in GLF these were also issues about which to protest, agitate and demonstrate.

The biggest single connection through sexism, of which heterosexism was considered to be a subdivision (or would have been if the word was in common use then), was with women's liberation. A large number of the women in GLF, particularly the lesbians, had strong links with the women's movement although they could not yet feel at home in it. Angie Weir, Mary O'Shea and others kept up their friendship with the women of the London Women's Liberation Workshop, and both the women and men of GLF attended women's pickets and events. The Wimpy Houses demonstrations against clear sexual discrimination are a good example, as a cutting from *Time Out* at the end of July 1971 shows.

Last Friday night more than 150 Women's Lib supporters including members of the Gay Liberation Front staged their tenth and, to date, most successful sit-in and picket of Wimpy Houses.

The demonstration against Wimpy Houses policy of refusing to serve unaccompanied women after midnight started outside the Marble Arch Wimpy at around 11.30 with picketing and leafleting of passers by. At midnight they started filing into the 60 seat Wimpy and taking available seating. About 20 got inside the restaurant including women dressed as men and vice versa (amongst them a GLF member wearing a stunning red wig, lace blouse and maxi skirt) and a woman in a nun's habit, who asked for a glass of water but was refused.

After about twenty minutes the pickets started demanding service and the management of the bar called the police.

Because the premises are private property the police had to ask each demonstrator to leave personally. Several were ejected though. Outside the bar enormous picket lines were formed and the management decided to shut the place at 1.30am.

After this move by the Wimpy management, about 20 of the demonstrators went on to the Praed Street (Paddington) Wimpy Bar. Around ten of them got inside (including the GLF member in the red wig) before the management locked the door.

The waiters were willing to serve the group, but the management was adamant in their refusal.

The situation got tenser when the others outside the door tried to get in. Led by the 'nun' they attempted to get through the revolving door. The manager of the bar immediately shut it.

The police arrived and freed the nun whose leg was trapped inside the door, but did not make any arrests. Everyone left at around 2.30am . . .

The stand taken by Empire (owners of Wimpy) is on the grounds that they can be prosecuted for 'knowingly permitting prostitutes, thieves or drunken and disorderly persons to use their premises under the Late Night Refreshment Houses Act 1969'. Women's Lib justifiably say that this is a curious interpretation of the law. 'They imply that men are never thieves, prostitutes or drunken and disorderly.'

General street-theatre type interventions about the consumer society and capitalism were also popular activities amongst anyone who considered themselves part of the revolution and shoppers or passers-by were liable to get swept up into actions that must have seemed to some of them like an extract from *Candid Camera*.

> We did an action in Carnaby Street to protest about commodity fetishism and we handed out leaflets to people walking down Oxford Street which said that John Lennon and Yoko Ono were going to make an appearance in Carnaby Street at two o'clock or something, so come along. We got great crowds at Carnaby Street and then we got up on soapboxes and gave these little lectures about commodity fetishism and how we'd been duped by consumer society. And then we ran through the shops and knocked clothes off rails and so on. So there were all those sorts of actions happening at the same time. (*Angie Weir*)

> I remember being in Marks and Spencer with Angie, both of us with megaphones and trying to get the shoppers out. We were determined to get them out and we did. (*Julia L*)

'There was quite a good amount of activity in support of black liberation, especially after we moved to Notting Hill Gate, like the Metro campaign' (*Sarah Grimes*). The Metro campaign was one of a number of incidents in the early 1970s when the Metropolitan Police, often in Notting Hill but also in other areas, raided a black event or club in the hope of drug and other criminal charges and ended up charging people with assault or other offences which related far more to the way in which such raids were handled and the poor relations between the Met and the local black community. GLF supported those arrested in this manner, having some experience of heavy-handed policing themselves. They also produced leaflets for the local black community in Notting Hill explaining this and asking for reciprocal support and understanding. After the general meetings moved to Notting Hill in the summer of 1971, they also participated in the Notting Hill Carnival.

The involvement of GLF in activities in support of other causes often also provided a useful vehicle for bringing gay issues to the notice of other rights movements.

I was involved in the Troops Out movement. In January 1972 when the Paratroop Regiment shot dead thirteen peaceful Republican protesters in Derry, there was a huge march the following Sunday through London. There were four feeder marches and most of the GLF people went on the West London one. We met at Roger Belsten's [Mick Belsten's brother] flat in Barnes and joined the march at Hammersmith. We carried the GLF banner – Gay Solidarity with the Irish Liberation Struggle, and we chanted 'Police out of gay bars – Troops out of Ireland'.

The march was attended by lots of left wing groups and trades unions. There were lots of Irish people, often from very conservative homophobic Catholic backgrounds. We saw this as an opportunity to shame them into realizing that our struggle for gay emancipation was a valid and legitimate one . . . A lot of people came up and talked to us . . . In the four or five hours of that demonstration we must have talked to hundreds of people. We got our share of abuse but we also won over quite a few hearts and minds. (*Peter Tatchell*)

Many on the 'straight left' were not entirely pleased to be thought the natural allies of homosexual rights, though it was the International Socialists' printing press that usually produced *Come Together*.

Rooted in the Stalinist witchhunts of the 1930s, the dominant view on the left was that homosexuality was a bourgeois perversion. I can remember going on a demonstration against the Greek junta where left wing students surrounded the Greek embassy chanting the Greek for 'One who gets fucked in the arse'. They were using homophobia as a weapon to attack the dictatorship. When we turned up they went berserk. They couldn't cope with gay people being there. As soon as they started the chant we demanded they stop. We put them on the defensive, nobody had challenged them before. (*Peter Tatchell*)

Not all people in GLF, especially those with strong leftist backgrounds themselves, viewed the left with such optimism.

The left wouldn't touch GLF with a barge pole, except for the Angry Brigade people. We were approached to get involved in a 'gay wing' of that – but the respectable

Marxists didn't want to know us for the first couple of years at least. The left were into everybody else's meetings. Just before GLF started, we went to a Maoist meeting on women at the LSE which was led by a man, Harpul Brah, who was giving us a lecture on women's rights. But they only began to relate to GLF when it had become calm and almost reformist. (*David Fernbach*)

A lot of people brought baggage with them to GLF of their earlier political involvements such as the peace movement or the International Marxist Group, etc. The straight left had condemned them as deviationist. And GLF also had people who tried to set up norms and conditions, who were more exclusive and vanguardist and felt they were the elite of the sexual revolution. These people, for the most part, had themselves had earlier political involvements from which their vanguardist habits derived – chiefly Maoist, I think. I think it was the facility which some of these people had for articulating and imposing a 'party line' which later led to radical effeminism with people like Phil Powell. In retrospect it appears like a prefiguration of political correctness. (*Tony Halliday*)

There is little doubt, though, that the presence of GLF people and their sympathizers did start debate about homosexuality amongst people who might otherwise have unthinkingly bought into the tabloid view of 'queers'.

There was a demonstration that GLF joined in when the dockers were imprisoned in Pentonville and GLF office collective used to come along with the banner and support things. At a point when we were trying to stop buses, there was this man called Julie who was a transvestite and he was holding a banner and fell over his dress and the bus got through and someone said 'Oh, for heavens sake, these gays can all bugger off!' or something like that. My father was there, not being GLF but being a union demonstrator and he just said 'This man is giving us his support and that's all that is important.' I was really impressed, I thought well, I didn't think you understood, that's great, standing up for a man in a dress to all these butch trade unionists. We did lots of little demonstrations like that, with perhaps ten people there. (*Nettie Pollard*)

There were occasions on which the GLF commitment to alternative lifestyles must have come as something of a shock to those who came into contact with them through more orthodox political affiliations.

I first took acid with someone after we'd gone to the Royal Court Theatre to see a play and we were in a taxi going back to Barnes where Peter Flannery and Mick Belsten lived. He said, try this. We got back to the flat in Barnes which was like a first little salvo of what became 7a [the radical drag commune], it was very similar inside in atmosphere.

So everybody was lying around and then a French deserter came to the house, just when everybody was simultaneously peaking. I don't know the ins and outs of it – I was told there was an underground railway for deserters from various armies and this was one of the safe houses. And that evening, Peter Flannery had decided that if he took some shaving foam and piled it on the top of his head, he could shape it like Marie Antoinette's hairdo. He'd got it about a foot in the air and spectacularly shaped – he was a big man, anyway – and we suddenly became conscious that the doorbell was going.

As anyone who's been in the middle of an acid party knows, getting to a front door downstairs is a tremendous difficulty. Peter finally managed to get a dressing gown, some flamboyant silk thing, round him and got down the stairs and even remembered, when he got to the bottom of the stairs, why he was going to the bottom of the stairs, which was also often a problem. And he opened the door. And this French deserter, who did spend the evening with us, who was a little late adolescent with no English, was confronted on the doorstep by an enormous drag queen in a Chinese silk dressing gown and a high coiffure of shaving foam.

Also, of course, when you're on acid if you do manage to get something together you're very punctilious about it. I could just make out Peter saying to this young man as he walked him up the stairs, 'Mind your footing, that stair there isn't all that good. Have I asked you if you'd like a cup of tea? Oh no, you can't speak any English, can you?' and so it went on. And I had enough French to have been able to say something to him, only I found that I couldn't remember any French at that particular point, at all. So this unfortunate man spent the evening with a lot of people tripping. Maybe he knew, but if he didn't he must have thought the English were just as eccentric as all the French had always said we were. (*Andrew Lumsden*)

John Chesterman was one of the GLF people with a long history of involvement in other countercultural causes and with strong links to the underground press. This connection was exploited to obtain material and logistic support for GLF actions, and could lead to some interesting meetings. He and Warren Haig obtained an introduction, through Bob Brown at *Time Out*, to John Lennon and Yoko Ono who were major financial and political supporters of a range of activities and groups.

> Copying was much more laborious in those days – you had to type a stencil as neatly as possible and crank it out, usually by hand. John Lennon had brought in this revolutionary cyclostyling machine which printed in three colours, he'd brought it back from America and Bob Brown of *Time Out* used to take people down to his house to see it. I learnt how to use it and that's what the coloured Miss World leaflet [November 1971] was done on. John Lennon was quite keen on GLF but I only met him once. I was down using the cottage that the machine was kept in, across the lake from the big house, and he came in and said 'I've just finished recording this new song, have a listen', and it turned out to be the newly pressed 'Imagine'. John Lennon was obsessed with white. There was a white Land Rover that used to pick me and Warren up to go down there each week. I don't know whose it was.
> (*John Chesterman*)

The most important underground press event, and one that had a profound effect upon the sense of persecution that the counterculture felt in Britain in the early 1970s, was the *Oz* trial in the summer of 1971. *Oz* was an underground magazine with relatively high production values and a popular following, run by three men, Richard Neville, Jim Anderson and Felix Dennis. It was called *Oz* both because Richard Neville, the founder, was Australian, and after the magical city in the Judy Garland musical. *Oz* had a habit of sailing close to the wind on British obscenity legislation, but it was finally prosecuted for its Schoolkids Issue, which was primarily put together by a group of schoolchildren and which contained, among other things, a cartoon of a schoolteacher suggesting sexual overtones to corporal punishment and a rather accomplished cartoon of Rupert Bear having sex with a grannie.

This coincided with a furore over another publication, *The Little Red Schoolbook*, which also accepted that people under eighteen were liable to have sex, take drugs and want not to be pushed around by teachers and other adults. As *The Little Red Schoolbook*'s introduction put it, 'All grownups are paper tigers. Tigers are frightening. But if they're made of paper they can't eat anyone. You believe too much in the power of grownups and not enough in your own capabilities. Even if you're at a particularly progressive school you should find a lot of ideas in this book for improving things.' Both publications encouraged young people to demand their rights and enjoy their bodies, and both caused a furore in a repressive British society which entertained alternating fantasies that either nobody under eighteen ever did anything sexual and had no independent thought, or that the youth of Britain were about to rise up in revolution as had the Paris students in 1968. Both publications were successfully prosecuted, in the case of *Oz* despite a mass of prominent defence witnesses including parents of some of the children involved in the publication, who declared that they were perfectly happy with it.

GLF was linked to *Oz* through Jim Anderson, an occasional attender at meetings and a friend and supporter of the Front. Many GLF people attended the demonstrations outside the trial and the parade to the Old Bailey, where it was held, on the opening day. The defendants themselves appeared in shorts and school caps and carrying satchels. On the day they were sentenced, eleven people were arrested including Jeff Marsh of GLF, and Street Theatre performed their celebrated 'The Courtroom Charade' piece outside the Magistrates Court where those arrested were tried. GLF's support for *Oz* was questioned by some of the lesbians, notably Carla, who felt that the magazine was too sexist to deserve support, and there was debate within the Media Workshop and the general meeting about the tensions between the support of free speech and the offensiveness of some of what was expressed thereby.

The arguments were covered in *Come Together* 8 by Mick Belsten:

The objections . . . sprang from what many of us thought was the blatant 'sexism' in *Oz* magazine's treatment of women (and also Gay people) as sex objects, subject to male superiority . . . others in GLF either could not see the sexism in *Oz*, or felt that if it was sexist, it was something which GLF should deal with at a later date. GLF support for *Oz* had already been published, which rankled many sisters and brothers . . . although the general feeling was probably sympathetic to *Oz*. This sympathy . . . came principally from the men in GLF, not generally from the women, who were the most critical . . . In the event, the sentences were announced and the reverberations of shock hit GLF immediately. It seemed to come together in its true proportions. We did feel attacked, we did feel victimised and our intelligence was insulted . . . we are angry.

On at least one occasion, some of the GLF women did something concrete about these feelings in collaboration with women's liberationists.

We did a women's issue of *Come Together* and also one of *Frendz*, one of those underground magazines. That was really Angie and I and her friend Pauline Conroy, who wasn't lesbian. We did that together and at about the same time as the *Come Together*. That was fun. It was run by this old Etonian who was wreathed in clouds of dope smoke, some super-hippie who took one look at us and said 'Oh, wow, heavy women.' I thought that was wonderful. I'm not sure if he knew it was a compliment or not really. Anyway, he was completely unable to withstand us, we just walked in and said, we're going to do a women's issue of *Frendz*. He didn't invite us. We just said we were going to do it. I remember the flyover [the Westway] hadn't long been built and I was late so I had to get a taxi and the driver refused to take me by the flyover because he was frightened of it, so we had to go all the way round. (*Elizabeth Wilson*)

This type of action and John's involvement, in particular with *Frendz* magazine, ensured that some of the underground stayed in touch with GLF and its activities despite the over-whelming sexism and chauvinism of much of the rest of what was published. Their support eventually extended to more than just coverage. 'I was always keen to get representation of gay issues in the media. I was involved with *Frendz*, one of the underground newspapers, so I made sure it had the best Festival of Light coverage. *Frendz* was at 305 Portobello Road and I did *Gay International News* from the back room there. I painted the whole room red in a revolutionary fervour' (*John Chesterman*). *Gay International News* was an offshoot of the International Support group of GLF and each issue chronicled developments in gay liberation around the world, carrying information from the most developed sections of US West Coast GLF to the most repressive regimes in Asia or Eastern Europe. The history of international gay activism in the UK is usually dated from the first International Congress in Edinburgh, several years later, but GIN shows that GLF at least was interested well before that.

The coverage of some supposed socialist paradises opened a few of the more idealistic eyes in the movement. '*Gay International News* meant that we started to correspond with the existing groups in North West Europe and the new groups that were starting up in many countries. We started to investigate the treatment of gays in Cuba. We started to think in a grown-up way about politics instead of just the slogans' (*John Chesterman*). There was little practical that GLF could do except alert the left to this repression, but they had some impact in this, if the front page of *International Times* shortly afterwards is anything to go by. It carried a full-page head of that hero of the Cuban revolution, Che Guevara, wearing blue eye shadow and bright red lipstick.

GLF London did not only reach out to other gays abroad. Many of its members have vivid memories of weekends spent in transit vans on their way to and from conferences, speeches, debates and zaps around Britain. 'We used to go round the country talking to other groups. I remember going in various vans and cars with mainly men to Preston and Bradford, sometimes to quite large meetings of people wanting to set up a GLF, or debates between gay people and homophobes and they just used to shout and rant and rave and we'd try to explain what GLF was about and try to encourage people to take part' (*Angie Weir*).

> There was a lot of importance attached to having other groups outside London, to show that we were a grass-roots, mass movement. We spent lots of time bombing up and down the motorways doing speaking engagements. I went to Keele, Leeds . . . I remember a van breaking down

in Northampton, which was my home town, with a driver
in total drag, probably Stuart Feather, who just carried on
and dealt with the mechanics as if there was nothing going
on out of the ordinary at all, which of course they
responded to. (*Tony Halliday*)

Postlip Hall was a nice interlude in all this. It was a Hall
somewhere near Cheltenham, I think a Jacobean house and
they had a weekend festival that we were invited to with
private grounds, three or four bands, dance groups, films –
it was some West Country group that had organized it. The
Street Theatre group even went to the Bath Festival to
perform that year. There was always lots of moving around
the country to think-ins and other meetings.
(*Stuart Feather*)

I was mainly in Street Theatre and I was one of the people
who went to Bath with them. Michael Mason was with us
too, and he got beaten up for walking hand in hand with
me. (*Carl Hill*)

Starting with a very successful meeting in Leeds on Saturday
19 June 1971, GLF groups from all over the country agreed to meet
regularly for national think-ins. This was a useful exercise in cross-
fertilization, because the groups could vary quite a lot from town
to town depending upon the people that had set them up. 'I
remember at the Birmingham think-in, the left was giving us all
grief about how people outside London couldn't possibly come out
like we had – and then a six-foot-tall transvestite got up and told
them that he worked in drag as a petrol pump attendant down
the road' (*Stuart Feather*). The Leeds meeting, of which a John
Chesterman photograph survives showing Warren holding the floor
while Bette Bourne, Mick Belsten, Luke Fitzgerald, Bill Halstead,
Andrew Lumsden and others look on, was only half of an extraordinary trip which took some of the central core of GLF men on
to Edinburgh to meet up with Scottish activists for a Traverse Trial.
    Traverse Trials were debates organized at the Traverse
Theatre in Edinburgh on fashionably controversial issues. For each
side an advocate would introduce three witnesses, who could be
cross-examined by the other side's advocate, followed by a vote
and general questions and debate. On the motion 'All discrimination against homosexuals by law, by employers and by society at
large, should end' the three witnesses for were Ian Dunn of the

Scottish Minorities Group (SMG), Tony Hughes of Edinburgh GLF and Louisa Hunt of London GLF. There is a transcript of large sections of the trial in the Chesterman section of the Hall-Carpenter Archives which gives the flavour of bigotry in the early 1970s. Councillor Lester of Edinburgh accused one witness of saying that he 'had intercourse with a small boy', when in fact he had clearly meant a youth. The councillor also said 'Prejudice after all is a basic emotion given to civilized people who rise above the beast. And it is by this emotion that we enjoy a higher standard of civilization', and referred to a GLF man as 'this so-called human being'.

Both Lala and Andrew Lumsden thoroughly lost their tempers with him and Andrew threw out a challenge to the meeting. 'We don't like this attitude of having a nice little liberal discussion and going away thinking, it's all right, we voted in favour of it. Get on with it. Do something. Welcome homosexuality. It's not much in the population. Love it when it comes, look at it, have homosexual children.' When the audience laughed at the councillor, a GLF voice called out to them 'It's funny if you don't have to live with it. None of you have tasted bitterness.'

Relations with SMG were clearly better than with CHE, although the London CHE activists seem to have been the most rigidly against GLF. Immediately after the Leeds think-in, which some Northern CHE members attended, their National Secretary Paul Temperton in Manchester wrote to Nick Stanley, a leading CHE activist:

> The GLF conference was quite good towards the end as the more hostile people on both sides cooled down a bit and some of the rest of us managed to put more emphasis on the common ground between CHE and GLF rather than the differences, and it is proposed to form a steering committee of 4 GLF people and 4 members of the CHE executive . . . there has obviously been a breakdown in communications between CHE people in London, on the one hand, and GLF on the other, because it became clear to me on Saturday that contrary to everything I had heard from our London people there are some GLF people (one or two, anyway) who are at least prepared to discuss possible areas of cooperation with us.

CHE archives within Hall-Carpenter show that, although little came of the proposed committee, Paul Temperton continued to occasionally correspond with GLF via Bob Mellors, correcting mistakes in *Come Together* and trying to be friendly, asking for 'a supply of your excellent warning stickers for the Reuben book' and gently chiding GLF for publishing a list of CHE convenors of local groups. It is illustrative of the fundamental differences between the two that it had probably never occurred to anyone in GLF, who were trying to be helpful by publicizing both types of group, that a person running a gay campaign might be in the closet.

But in London there was little common ground. As Laurence Collinson, the poet, wrote in CHE's magazine *Lunch* in early 1972, 'there seems to be a considerable lack of understanding if not downright ignorance amongst many CHE members as to what GLF is and does . . . could it be that GLF is to CHE what homosexuals are to 'straights'? . . . perhaps GLF makes your sense of security wobble?' (*Lunch* 5). It certainly had that effect upon one CHE member, Hugh Corbett, who wrote in Issue 8, of GLF, that 'the vulgarity of frenetic faggots frolicking through the streets demonstrating defiance, bad taste, disregard for the susceptibilities of others and adherence to the bogus and the base can only provoke dismay and disgust'. He goes on to say that homosexuals have no rights because they are a minority: 'clamour about discrimination, equal rights . . . is not only moronic but destructive'.

Chapter eight

'A Brief Analysis of Oppression'

To you, our gay sisters and brothers, we say that you are oppressed; we intend to show you examples of the hatred and fear with which straight society relegates us to the position and treatment of sub-humans, and to explain their basis. We will show you . . . how we, together with other oppressed groups, can start to form a new order, and a liberated life-style, from the alternatives which we offer. –London GLF Manifesto

THE Counter-Psychiatry Group was one of the very early groups formed within London GLF. It became one of the most influential in the development of gay politics and gay pride. It sprang from the twin forces of the general anti-psychiatry movement of the 1960s and the gay political rejection of the theory of homosexuality as a mental disease. The anti-psychiatry movement, headed in the UK by R. D. Laing, himself a psychiatrist, argued that much 'mental illness' was the result of the stresses imposed by the way in which people lived, and in particular by the nuclear family. In other words, they argued that in many cases it was society rather than the individual that was sick and that behaviour diagnosed as mentally disturbed was often a reasonable response to an unreasonable situation. Given the number of abused women who were put away as mentally ill and the racist imbalance in diagnosis by which black people were far more likely to be diagnosed as, for instance, schizophrenic, this seemed a pretty sound theory to anyone not overly attached to the current social system.

The gay rejection of the popular psychiatric diagnosis of homosexuals as sick rather than criminal marked a break with the homophile movement, many of whose adherents had been happy to accept a medical pronouncement that they were unable to help themselves and therefore more to be pitied than condemned. This diagnosis had led to a series of appalling medical experiments on homosexuals in the 1950s and 1960s reminiscent of Nazi concentration camp experiments on prisoners. Gay men (mostly) had been electrocuted, experimentally drugged, their brains had been surgically altered and in the most extreme instances, they had been castrated. The endless and expensive psychoanalysis undergone by many, designed to wake their latent heterosexual impulses, was a minor offence compared to these. Countless undoubted homosexuals married and lived in misery, making whole families unhappy, in the belief that this would cure their homosexual impulses – a belief held to this day by some. Psychiatric treatment, up to and including chemical castration, could be part of the sentence for men convicted of victimless homosexual sex offences.

The Counter-Psychiatry Group of London GLF was an echo of groups, mainly in the US West Coast, which had protested this diagnosis by disrupting events and conferences, most notably those of the American Psychiatric Association who at that time listed homosexuality as a mental disorder in their *Diagnostic and Statistical Manual of Mental Disorders*. But the London group was given a particularly practical and populist slant, partly by the general ethos of London GLF and partly by the combination of experience within the group of people who had received treatment and those who were employed within the psychiatric system. Of the latter, the leading character (though she herself plays down her importance) was undoubtedly Elizabeth Wilson, now a leading academic and writer but then a very unhappy psychiatric social worker. It was she and Mary McIntosh who called the first meeting at their house in Haverstock Street, Islington. 'Elizabeth knew most about psychiatric practice, because she was a psychiatric social worker and knew at first hand how heterosexist all that line of work is. There were other people who knew it as patients, and she complemented that' (*Mary McIntosh*).

> I was feeling particularly interested in that issue because I was so fed up with my job. [It] was very fraught for me because I was working in a child guidance clinic housed in the Tavistock at the time and that was very problematic. I wasn't happy with being a social worker anyway, but I was particularly unhappy because of the atmosphere there. It was the women issue more than the gay issue, I mean you

assumed they didn't like gay people, that went without
question, but they were so awful about women, so
paternalistic and didn't think women should work. So
perhaps for me it felt particularly transgressive and wicked
and amusing to be involved in this gay liberation and then
in the daytime trot off to the Tav. (*Elizabeth Wilson*)

The list of attendance at the first few meetings, in December
1970 and the following January, survives and shows a cross-section
of GLF people from different backgrounds – Elizabeth Wilson,
Mary McIntosh, Jeffrey Weeks, Angus Suttie, Micky Burbidge,
David Hutter, Hugh Gaw, Tony Halliday, Simon Benson, Andrew
Lumsden, Paul Jessep, Flora Langford, Angus Goldie, Peter
Moloney, Barry Davis, John Man, Patrick Pollard, Bill Poole,
Richard Poore, Sue Winter, Andrew Higgott, Huw Rowlands,
Martyn Jones, Frances Burchnall, Marshall Weekes, Peter
McInally, Jacqueline Horesh, Juan Tosco. 'The group was a mixture
of academics and activists' (Micky Burbidge).

Of course the whole argument about homosexuality was
the same, that originally it had appeared to be a move
forward, that it was a product of your childhood rather
than horribly sinful, but then the debate moved on to say
it's not a sickness. So that was the central plank of the
Counter-Psychiatry Group – that it was worse for people to
be sentenced to some sort of treatment rather than just to
be treated as a criminal, and in particular, there were
horror stories about people being treated with shocks in
aversion therapy. Someone came along who had had
aversion therapy and it was still quite respectable and one
had to make an argument against it. I'll never forget
Richard Dipple used to come and somebody had once said
to him, 'Oh yes, I agree with you, there's nothing wrong
with being homosexual, it's just like having green hair or
seven legs.' (*Elizabeth Wilson*)

Aversion therapy (usually electric shock treatment) was
such a major issue because it was the publicly accepted way
of dealing with homosexuality. I knew that I was gay in
1962 and decided that I didn't want to be. I read an article
about a man who did aversion therapy for homosexuals
and I wrote to him asking for therapy. He had a long
waiting list, so nothing happened. Then I read a story in

the paper about a man who had aversion therapy to make him fall out of love with the wrong woman and I suddenly realized that it was awful to think of switching off loving feelings by shock treatment. There had to be another way of dealing with it. That totally changed my mind and I decided that I wanted to be what I was, after all.
(*Micky Burbidge*)

I got involved fairly early on with what became known as the Counter-Psychiatry Group and I used to go to Mary and Elizabeth's house. This was, if you like, at that stage the more intellectual part of GLF. Mary was a sociologist and Elizabeth was a social worker who had got very much involved in the whole counter-psychiatry movement. I was very impressed by their cool lifestyle. I was slightly nervous because both of them had already made their presence felt as the two leading dykes in GLF, they were very articulate. Mary was a well-known sociologist already. I think I'd already read her article on the homosexual role, which has played an enormous part in my own intellectual life since.

We sat around and talked about the whole counter-psychiatry movement, which had been going on through the 1960s, the whole critique of psychiatric practices, the idea that it wasn't so much the individual who was sick and to be treated by objective science but that society itself fucked you up and that you needed ways to deal with that. And what became central to it was the idea that we were not sick, it was a sick society that made us believe that we were sick. Many of those early discussions were a mixture of familiarizing ourselves with the jargon and trying to find ways of being practical. (*Jeffrey Weeks*)

One of the earliest pieces of work for the group was to get an understanding of the issues across to the rest of GLF. A copy survives of the earliest leaflet distributed internally, giving Haverstock Street as the contact for the group.

INTERIM STATEMENT – COUNTER-PSYCHIATRY GROUP
The Counter-Psychiatry Group of the Gay Liberation Front. Why its name . . . why it exists . . .
WHO writes books about male and female homosexuals?
WHOSE authority is sought when schools plan sex education programmes?

WHO decides whether homosexual behaviour is
'pathological' or 'normal'?
TO WHOM are young people sent when their natural sex
feelings are condemned by family, church and society?
TO WHOM does the law refer convicted homosexuals?
TO WHOM do doctors, ministers, parents and counsellors
turn when people seek their advice about sexual problems?
WHO has a vested interest in maintaining the fiction that
homosexuality requires 'professional' treatment?
THE ANSWER IN EACH CASE IS THE PSYCHIATRISTS – AND NOT
THE MEN AND WOMEN WHO ARE THEMSELVES HOMOSEXUAL.
THE PSYCHIATRISTS HAVE BECOME THE HIGH PRIESTS OF
MODERN SOCIETY.
But have psychiatrists really got specialist knowledge about
homosexuality? The Counter-Psychiatry Group does not
believe that they have. But it does believe that homosexuals
have a better understanding of their own situation than
these theoreticians.
What is the basis of the Psychiatrists' claim to expertise?
Only a number of questionable assumptions, such as:
Homosexuality is a sickness
Homosexuality is a form of immaturity
Homosexuality is a result of family conditioning
Homosexuality is a result of hormonal imbalance
Homosexuality is a freak genetic condition
Each of these assumptions (and each psychiatrist has his
own favourite) implies that homosexuality is a clinical
condition that requires treatment; that the homosexual
needs to adjust to society; that society does not need to
adjust to the homosexual.
Psychiatrists themselves may not be aware that all their
attempts to theorise about homosexuality are merely
rationalisations; that they are simply reinforcing, under the
guise of scientific objectivity, primitive Judaeo-Christian
morality. The only difference between now and then is that
what was once regarded as a sin is today regarded as a
sickness.
The Counter-Psychiatry Group is not interested in
providing alternative theories. We do not believe that
theories are needed about why men and women are
homosexual.
Homosexuality is a form of sexual expression that comes

naturally and is satisfying to many millions of men and women. It is as fundamental a way of life to the homosexual as heterosexuality is to the heterosexual. Its potential for love, joy and creativity is as great as that of heterosexuality.
The functions of the Counter-Psychiatry Group include: Countering the above mentioned assumptions.
Forcing psychiatrists to recognise that homosexuality can be a happy and satisfying way of life.
The broad aim of these functions is to make society recognise the right of homosexual men and women to fulfilment as human beings.

The primary campaign for which the group became known was one against the David Reuben book, *Everything You Always Wanted To Know About Sex – but were afraid to ask*. It was Andrew Lumsden, ever aware of the media and its influence, who brought the book to that attention of the group originally. 'There was this silly book written by this silly psychiatrist and then it became a rather good film, actually. But people rushed down Charing Cross Road and hurled the books out into the road and there were demonstrations' (*Elizabeth Wilson*). The main campaign against the Reuben book, imported from the US, will be covered in chapter twelve, but it was started as early as February when leaflets were distributed and a letter was delivered to the publishers of the hardback version. 'I was also on the campaign against Reuben's book which the Counter-Psychiatry Group played a part in, that was the first half of 1971. Mary had a major part in the whole campaign because I remember when we did the bookshops in Charing Cross Road Mary was interviewed by someone from the *Sunday Times*. I was standing by her as she was interviewed. She was probably our most articulate spokesperson' (*Jeffrey Weeks*).

But it was in the summer of 1971 that the Group officially ventured onto the streets for the first time, assisted by Street Theatre. The event was a well-attended demonstration in Harley Street itself, the London address associated with doctors and particularly psychiatrists. It was publicized in a news-sheet of GLF – the earliest extant that I could find – as 'Harley St demo meet 12.30 on Friday 25th June 1971 outside Coutts Bank in Cavendish Square – Please try and make it in your lunch hour if you are working that day. Support essential in our first demonstration against psychiatrists' attitudes to homosexuals. Street Theatre will be there, WILL YOU??????' The intention, as discussed in the group and general meeting, was to distribute leaflets and do some street theatre based on scenarios of gays and psychiatrists, but a few of the more adventurous souls decided on an impromptu addition which was not universally approved of.

> I had already been in Freudian analysis by this time. I found that GLF helped with my emotional problems and I went along to the Counter-Psychiatry Group. On the Harley Street demo, I had written a leaflet and Street Theatre people had arranged to act out various psychiatric scenarios, but when we got down there we found that two people had gone down the night before and spray painted GLF slogans around the street. I was very upset because I thought it was disruptive and spoiled the message; I was very straight still then. I never did know who it was who did that. (*Michael Brown*)

> I went on the Harley Street demo. It was me and Aubrey Walter and possibly Mick Belsten who went down at midnight the night before and spray painted slogans like 'people not psychiatry' on walls and doorsteps. We had to take a few drinks before we could get up the nerve to do it, but it was worth it, it made a real difference to see it there the next day. I was on the first big demo for GLF in August 1971 and I can tell you it was a demonstration, not a parade because of all the shit that you got from people on the sidewalk . . . It wasn't like it is now. (*Paul Theobald*)

'We spray painted it the night before the demonstration, "gay is good", whatever you could write quickly' (*Aubrey Walter*). The demonstration achieved press coverage for the issue, as well as startling a good number of eminent doctors. One leaflet handed out there, written by Mary McIntosh (or at least with draft amendments in her handwriting) demands:

> 1. Check whether your own attitudes to homosexuality are rational
> 2. Stop treating homosexuality with drugs, hormones, aversion therapy or analysis; stop treating homosexuality at all
> 3. Campaign for sex education that deals truthfully with homosexuality

4. Inform the public that homosexuality is as basic and as healthy a condition of existence for homosexuals as heterosexuality is for heterosexuals
5. Send homosexuals to gay lib, stop growing rich out of their way of life

Spray painting became a feature of the Counter-Psychiatry demonstrations, whatever some members might have though of it. That summer, there were 'zaps' (hit and run demonstrations) at a number of psychiatric institutions in London, including the Maudsley Hospital and the Tavistock itself. 'We did go to the Maudsley, I remember we were stopped by the police because we were in this terrible rackety old van which wasn't really road-worthy but of course they didn't notice the spray paint, they probably weren't terribly attuned to it then. They just waved us on' (*Elizabeth Wilson*).

Not all the group's actions were quite so risky, though they were constantly challenging to the authorities. They also forged alliances with others.

> We discussed things a lot and had a critique of the 'not bad but mad' attitude, you know, sickness not sin. I remember a whole load of us going to a television programme, Mary had been invited because Jock Young was a panel speaker, so we were invited as audience to talk if asked to. The debate was between Jock Young, who was a radical criminologist, and the police, who were a scary bunch. The police all thought that Jock's argument would be that crime is a kind of sickness, including homosexuality, that it's because you had a bad childhood and you need a therapist and all this. But the criminologists had moved from that position to that of 'these people are perfectly *compos mentis* and it's a form of rebellion' so the police were unprepared for that. (*Elizabeth Wilson*)

> I was in the Counter-Psychiatry Group with Micky and others. I helped to organize a conference at the London School of Economics in Autumn 1971 – Homosexual Oppression? Freedom? Mary McIntosh spoke on abolishing the age of consent and people from outside, like doctors, came along. (*Nettie Pollard*)

We zapped psychiatrists' meetings. I remember one on aversion therapy where people got very badly rattled. And there was a Granada documentary which I was in by accident. I was up in Liverpool on work and I went to see Liverpool Friend for Icebreakers. They invited me in to the office while the programme was being filmed there. The coordinator was Alan Swerdlow and the television crew were actually filming a woman there in his office who practised aversion therapy. She was doing the therapy in an old X-ray van in the grounds of a Liverpool hospital. I was so outraged at the nonsense she was spouting that I just started arguing with her right in the middle of her doing the interview.

I had a blazing row with her. I'd never felt so high in all my life. We must have argued for half an hour – I remember the film people asked me to stop and wait for a minute while they reloaded the camera so that they could carry on filming us! Some of it got used in the final documentary, and later I ran into the man from Granada and found out that she'd given up aversion therapy. The programme questioned her approach and the reviews agreed with Granada. I think aversion therapy may still even go on today. It wasn't a common treatment even then but it was high profile. I met some people who'd been through it and only yesterday I was asked to talk to some researcher about it. (*Micky Burbidge*)

Micky Burbidge I remember well because he was the person at whose house Counter-Psychiatry met. He's quiet and unassuming but very radical on some issues. Sadly, I wasn't involved in writing *Psychiatry and the Homosexual*, I don't know why not. I did have something to do with the title though, because I remember saying that I thought a fairly low key title rather than 'Smash Psychiatry' or something like that might be a wise thing to do. Because you look at that, it had a very low key cover, it looks respectable and it's actually extraordinary radical on things like the position of children. In some ways, it's more radical than the *Manifesto*. (*Nettie Pollard*)

Psychiatry and the Homosexual was a pamphlet written by members of the Group, subtitled 'A brief analysis of oppression' which dealt with the treatment of gays by the medical and psychiatric professions. Under chapter titles such as 'The Homosexual in a Hostile Society', 'The General Practitioner', 'The Myth of Voluntary Treatment' and 'Run, The Past Is Behind You' it covered Freudian and behavioural theories, hormone and aversion therapies, psychotherapeutic techniques, the sexuality of children and young people and self-oppression and illustrated these with case histories.

> Counter-Psychiatry Group later after long vicissitudes went in different directions. Mary got involved in the Manifesto Group, so that was like the theoretical bit of the group. Some of us, myself, David Hutter, set up a small group who produced the pamphlets. *Psychiatry and the Homosexual* was my suggestion and David Hutter, Andrew Hodges, Paul Bunting and myself drafted it. The first two went on to do *With Downcast Gays*. Another wing moved in to what became Icebreakers. We worked on *Psychiatry and the Homosexual* from September 1971 into 1972. The group moved around and part of the rota was Ivor Street where Micky, Angus and I lived at the time. One particular meeting, I remember, we discussed the way forward and I suggested the pamphlet. One subgroup formed to do that, another talked about the helpline which became Icebreakers and we just evolved in different directions and went on meeting separately. The group as such faded away and its energies went into the subgroups. (*Jeffrey Weeks*)

The Counter-Psychiatry Group survived into 1972 with changing membership. Its last known action would not have happened if it had not been for one young GLF person whose determined heckling single-handedly disrupted a talk by Hans Eysenck, an internationally respected authority whose expertise was in need of challenging when he claimed that electric shock therapy was effective as a treatment for homosexuality.

> The Counter-Psychiatry Group were supposed to turn up to the Eysenck zap but for whatever reason, I was the only person. I hovered around by the entrance to the lecture theatre and when a big group of medical people went in I mingled with them and got inside. As far as I know, Eysenck has never retracted what he said there. As I was being dragged out by my arms and legs I was given a few elbows and fists in the ribs . . . I had thought everybody

else from GLF was already inside, having gone in without me, so I went in and then realized . . . (*Peter Tatchell*)

Apart from the pamphlets, the other major document produced by the London Gay Liberation Front was the *Manifesto*. The early history of the group set up to write it is covered in the previous chapter; the *Manifesto* itself is reproduced as an appendix. The *Manifesto* has been reprinted previously, but in a bowdlerized version which omitted all mention of communes and the destruction of the family because the group reproducing it, the GLF Information Service, disagreed with those sections.

Certainly Elizabeth's style is visible in sections of the *Manifesto*, as is that of David Fernbach and Aubrey Walter. Many of the ideas that Aubrey and Bob Mellors brought back from the US movement are there, expanded and adapted to British issues. The document defines the movement succinctly and is easily readable, so I am loath to try to encapsulate it in a few phrases, but Peter Tatchell attempted to put it into 1990s gay political language.

> GLF's critique of straight society amounted to more than condemning violations of gay civil rights and campaigning for equal treatment. Revolutionary not reformist, our ultimate goal was an end to 'male chauvinism' and the 'gender system'. There was a sense that some aspects of gay lifestyle and culture could teach heterosexuals a thing or two, in particular GLF argued that in a sexist, patriarchal culture it was almost impossible for heterosexual men and women to have egalitarian, mutual relationships. For those gay people who could step outside the copycatting of butch and femme roles, GLF felt they were creating the seeds of new more equitable relationships. In the GLF *Manifesto*, it argues that at this time, because gay men do not need to oppress women to achieve sexual and emotional fulfilment, and because lesbians do not need to relate sexually and emotionally to their oppressor, relationships between people of the same sex are probably the most free and egalitarian.
>
> In the GLF *Manifesto*, law reform is a small section at the back headed 'Our immediate demands'. GLF saw the gender system as the key institution and located the oppression of women and gays in the oppressive nature of it. The family was the way in which it was organized and reproduced. The gender system was seen as assigning

particular roles to men and women . . . Straight masculinity is what oppresses both women and gay men, our common enemy is straight male machismo. GLF saw a very clear link between patriarchy and what we now call homophobia. Both are about the maintenance of a privileged social status for heterosexual men. The gender system dictates certain types of acceptable behaviour for men and women . . . We said that the right to be gay includes the right to disobey straight gender norms. In particular, we singled out hetero masculinity, with its inclination to aggression and violence, as the number one enemy of queers and women. The dissolution of straight male machismo was, we argued, the key to ending homo oppression. In other words, the essence of the GLF strategy for queer emancipation was changing society, rather than adapting to it. We understood the need for a cultural revolution. (*Peter Tatchell*)

Chapter nine

Pickin' the Chicken

I want to be a lesbian when I grow up. –Teenage passer-by at a
GLF demonstration

AT the end of July 1971, after only a few short months in
Middle Earth, GLF was forced to move premises once again. The
King Street premises had been bought with the idea of turning them
into an Arts Centre and this had failed to materialize. With the
development of the Covent Garden area, which was then being
turned from a giant market area with warehouses into a consumer
paradise, pressure led the consortium of owners to sell off the
property and gay liberation was on the move again. Nobody
remembers how, but on 28 July London GLF moved to their best-
remembered meeting place at All Saints Hall in Powis Square,
Notting Hill. The new premises, a community hall attached to a
fairly liberal church, allowed even greater expansion in numbers
and finally provided a local community willing to interact with the
group.

'I was rather glad when we moved on to All Saints Hall. We
were shoved on, and that began the move West, which changed the
character of GLF' (*Andrew Lumsden*). Notting Hill was a melting
pot; with one of the best-established black communities in London,
it had also attracted artists, hippies and a strong drug culture.
Many of the queens already lived in the area, which was home to
many countercultural activities such as the drugs legal advice
service Release, hippy information service BIT and *Frendz*
magazine. 'David Hockney came to Powis Square in a snakeskin
jumpsuit' (*John Chesterman*). The artist and a friend lived nearby;
after the establishment of the Colville Terrace squat the next year,
people remember food parcels coming from them.

As their fame spread, another wave of GLF activists arrived
at All Saints. 'The general meetings also had newcomers meetings

in a separate area at All Saints Hall, but mostly people couldn't wait to get into the main meeting' (*David Fernbach*).

I arrived in Britain off the boat at Southampton in August 1971, having left Australia because I refused to be conscripted . . . to fight in Vietnam, which I regarded as an immoral and unjust war. The following day I was walking in central London and saw a GLF sticker on a lamp post near Oxford Circus . . . Four days later I was at my first GLF meeting in All Saints Hall. It was an incredibly exciting experience . . . When I left Melbourne there were two gay bars, no clubs or social centres and not a single gay organization. (*Peter Tatchell*)

I heard of GLF as a student outside London. I rang *Private Eye* and asked how to find them, that's where I'd read about it, but they hung up on me! Later on I moved to London, to Kings Cross and found them there. I went into the basement at Housmans, where the GLF office was. It was basically one phone and a lot of demented queens. They were meeting at Powis Square by then. The meetings were fabulously shambolic. It was my introduction to crime, drugs, promiscuous sex and political awareness all together. Magic Michael would get up and take his clothes off. There was Jesus, who believed in himself and used to turn up to try and spread the gospel. People just got up and blathered. There were a lot of students, you could say it was a 'nicer class of homosexual' at GLF, lots of hippies who didn't really mix with straight gays. There weren't a lot of black people, but a few, I remember Ted Brown. Warren Haig was more focused and sounded like an authority on libertarianism. I particularly remember Bette Bourne, Paul Theobald and John Chesterman. I went to everything, because it was unmissable, you never knew what was going to happen. (*Tim Clark*)

Notting Hill Gate was a very strange experience. It was a very long way from Brixton in more ways than one. It required a certain amount of subterfuge and pecuniary embarrassment for me to actually get there [as a fifteen-year-old], all the way on the tube. I got lost twice. And then getting out at Notting Hill tube station and trying to find where Powis Square was from there, even with an A–Z, was a difficult experience. And All Saints Church Hall was even more difficult, but I got to about fifty yards from it by following whoever looked strangest – long hair, Afghan coats, beads, earrings, *et cetera* because I thought you had to suss it out by nose. I got to the railings of All Saints and there were people overflowing into the streets. I just hung around, thinking to myself, everybody here is looking at me as if I'm one of the local kids. I hung around for about an hour and a half and then I thought, I'd better go home, it's half past nine, so I did. (*Julian Hows*)

Each week more people turned up until it was packed – five or six hundred people, it was a big hall and for someone coming to their first gay event it must have been very intimidating. There was everything from fourteen-year-olds, who must have been attending without telling their parents, right through to seventy-year-olds. Everything from long haired hippies in embroidered jeans, like me, through to smart business men. At least a third were women and I remember them making an equal amount of valid contributions. The trouble is, if you're talking about something that's a vital part of your life and you're in a room with 400 other people, it takes a lot of nerve to get up and speak at all and most people don't have that nerve. Even quite eloquent people would feel intimidated. The only reason I could speak was that I'd just done eight years teaching English as a foreign language. I'd given a lecture to 500 sleeping professors in Japan and if you can cope with that you can cope with a GLF meeting.
(*Alan Wakeman*)

At the church hall, the speakers would be up one end of the room . . . there were the superstars like Warren who would generate a certain amount of hostility because people felt they were trying to take over. Then there were the queens, like Stuart or Michael, who weren't quite like the superstars, they were different because you didn't sense they had an agenda behind it, they weren't manipulating to get us to agree to something. (*Sarah Grimes*)

'Superstars' was the slightly pejorative term for those who spoke too often and too well for public approbation in an age when 'ego-tripping' was a social crime. It was at Powis Square that the dominance in meetings of some of the more experienced members began to be remarked upon, despite the use of Chairs and the coordinating committee structure.

> Superstars? Warren, though I didn't know him very well. He was the most obvious. Andy Elsmore perhaps as well. I think that the most dominant people were David and Aubrey in my time, but they did tend to be the people who'd stand up and talk to the room. They usually said things at most meetings and had very strong views. Mary McIntosh spoke a lot and so did Elizabeth Wilson. Peter Bourne spoke quite a lot as well. He wasn't called Bette then. It may well be true that he only started to speak up when he got into frocks. I never spoke at any time at one of those main meetings. I remember Michael [James] very well, I felt I had an affinity with him, he was very sweet and very passionate and I think he really really wanted to change things, but I also felt he was very sympathetic to women, in the nicest possible way. (*Nettie Pollard*)

Demonstrations continued throughout the summer, including a successful zap of Fleet Street. Photographs show dozens of protesters using the newspapers' own hoarding placards with gay slogans superimposed to get their message across that the tabloid press was sexist and anti-gay and contributed to prejudice. 'There was a picket of Fleet Street, there were quite a lot of people there. We organized it because of the general way that the tabloids were treating gays, it wasn't sparked off by any particular article. We went to the *Sun* and the *Daily Mirror* and along to the *Daily Express*, giving out leaflets on the way. Some of the men were carrying placards saying "Give Us Our Daily Male", of course (a current slogan)' (*Sarah Grimes*). As a journalist himself, it left Andrew Lumsden in something of a quandary.

> I was all in favour of it, but talking with the group who were organizing it I said, I hope you don't mind but I'm not actually going to walk along Fleet Street itself, I'm just going to meet up beforehand, because it seemed hypocritical to me to take the Fleet Street shilling and at the same time be carrying a placard outside, but I made sure everybody in the buildings knew what was going on. So I wasn't on the entire route of the protest itself . . . but I was there for part of it.

But increasingly, GLF was far more than the general meetings and the satellite working groups. The membership was growing and bonding.

> There were quite a lot of young gay men who'd had the
> most deprived childhoods in terms of their homosexuality
> and they lived like a sort of courageous flame for a few
> moments at these meetings, and they were inspiring and
> uplifting. Two things were inspiring; those individuals and
> their sort of flamboyance and courage and defiance and
> also the collective actions . . . when we came together in
> parks, on demonstrations, there was a wonderful sense of
> energy and togetherness. (*Angie Weir*)

One of the basic tenets of GLF, and what made it very different from other, more discreet, more apologist gay groups such as CHE, was its determination to confront the general public. One way to do this, comprehensively explored by summer 1971, was by the demonstration and its smaller relation, the zap. But these were traditional leftist weapons, if given a distinctive GLF twist by Street Theatre. Out of GLF's other parent, the counterculture, came another tactic still remembered with great pleasure – the Gay Day, a phrase which, bastardized by comedian Larry Grayson, eventually entered the English language. Gay Days had a triple purpose: to show the public that gays could, indeed, be gay in public; to recruit others by appearing in a positive and playful light; and to have a good time together as a 'tribe'.

> It was really good when everyone sat around in hippie
> clothes and danced around and played games. There was
> often quite a good mixture of men and women together
> there. It was relaxed and such a different thing. That was
> one of the nicest things about GLF, that it understood that
> play was political and that it was important to play as part
> of your politics. And it's deeply subversive . . . it's a way of
> getting through to people you can't get through to by
> intellectual or confrontational methods. People were
> generally very friendly and on the whole I think in many
> ways things were less homophobic than they are now.
> Although unions have adopted formal policies for gay
> rights and all that sort of thing, I think the general public
> were more friendly then. Also GLF was part of the general
> progressive movement, therefore although we did have

some hostility, you also had a lot of people who thought of us as the gay brothers and sisters. (*Nettie Pollard*)

Street Theatre was a leading element in the Gay Days because we organized games for everyone. They were trust games, things that we practised in our meetings, touching people while blindfolded and having to guess who they were, throwing the ball to someone who then had to kiss you and throw it in turn. (*Stuart Feather*)

The first Gay Day was in Holland Park. I remember walking around hand in hand with my lover, Trevor, and there were lots of older gay men who were hanging about the edges, acting like spectators and not participants. Then I saw a man I knew, who'd sexually abused me years before when I was fifteen. I pointed him out to Trevor and we went over. I talked to him and reminded him of what he'd done. He got embarrassed, so we walked off. It was a completion. (*Paul Theobald*)

Early Gay Days were in safe, solidly middle-class areas like Holland Park or Hyde Park, but after an article in the first women's issue of *Come Together* urging that working-class areas be targeted they sometimes moved east.

I was at the Gay Day in Victoria Park. It was rather wonderful. I thought they were splendid occasions. We were all sitting in a circle and played that game where someone in the middle threw the ball and whoever caught it had to come up and kiss the thrower. There were a group of Hackney girls behind us who had come along to watch the fun. They were really interested in this game and thought it was a happening of some sort. That was the whole point about happenings, life had been so boring . . . The ball kept going man, woman, man, woman, so they didn't think there was anything peculiar about it. Then it went man, man and the first gay kiss and then there were some more, and I remember one turning around and saying, "Cor, some of them are queer" and then they looked around at this great big crowd and said, "'Ere, they're all fucking queer!" We talked to them about it all – it was a great belief you know, that you just went out onto the streets and collared the nearest person and explained your theory of life and revolution. We were very keen on doing that. And I remember that time because it was a lovely day and afterwards the women went up to swim at the women's pond. We were all slightly high. (*Angie Weir*)

I remember the Gay Day in Victoria Park very well. It was a sunny day and Gay Days were well established by then. There were lots of East End families in the park and I got talking to a local vicar who turned out to be Malcolm Johnson of St Botolphs, who was so supportive to the Gay Christian Movement later. We had arrived very noisily, with a drum, and were quite noticeable. We were sat in a big circle several people deep and playing games in the middle. We had this game where the person in the middle would throw a ball to someone else, who had to enter the circle and kiss them and then take their place. Suddenly some policemen and women arrived and forced their way into the heart of the circle, where they saw two people kissing and started to make a fuss – except that when they separated them , one of the 'men' turned out to be a woman and they looked very silly and there was nothing they could do about it. (*Michael Brown*)

Apart from the games, people brought food and drink to share, talked with the other people out in the sunshine and generally got their message across. It was not always subtle – for the *Oz* Festival in Hyde Park, Aubrey Walter devised a bunch of letters spelling GAY LIBERATION out of large paper bags upended with holes for peoples' heads, which they ran around wearing. This created its own problems. 'I mean, this was GLF. It was hell trying to get people to stay in line so that they spelt the right thing. We weren't big on discipline' (*John Chesterman*). However, it was enough of a success to warrant a repeat performance, this time spelling out COME TOGETHER in Trafalgar Square at an unknown event.

Things just suddenly escalated that year and we had Gay Days in various parks, the biggest one was in Victoria Park. We were having dances on about a monthly basis at various Town Halls, Chelsea, Hampstead, Kensington . . . We had a huge social round and within about three months I'd given all my suits away to the lesbians in Faraday Road and I was into thirties frocks for everyday wear. I took to

frocks in a big way, I'd done drag professionally, which was
an exception in GLF, and it was a great leap for me to
come from trying to achieve a bust and cleavage with a
Wonderbra, which did actually give you cleavage – so the
whole sexual liberation thing with men in drag not having
to have tits was a wonderful liberation for me because it
opened up a whole new area of dressing up which was not
bound up in cleavages and things like that. I took to it like
a duck to water. (*Michael James*)

It was that first summer at Powis Square that drag fused
with fashionable unisex dressing, beginning in Street Theatre, to
create the unique 'radical drag' style that emerged amongst the men
of later GLF. Charlie Pig is credited with the first 'politicized'
wearing of a dress simply because he felt like it and it would be
sexist not to wear what he felt like just because it pertained to the
wrong role; but it was a habit that soon spread and liberated the
tongues of a number of previously shy, less macho gay men.

The 1969 Stonewall riot in New York was already
commemorated there by a summer march through major cities. In
1971 London, as usual a year or two behind, also decided to have
a major summer march. The GLF Youth Group took over the
organization and gave it a specifically British angle – a Gay Day in
Hyde Park, followed by a march to Trafalgar Square and a rally
there against the unequal age of consent. The Youth Group, along
with Street Theatre, was one of the more together and visible
elements of GLF, possibly because of the strength at the time of
youth culture and the move towards empowerment of young
people – the *Oz* Schoolkids Issue, *The Little Red Schoolbook* and
so on. But in an atmosphere when all gay activity was subject to
violent prejudice at every turn, with no gay youth organizations or
even sympathetic general ones, it was even harder to be a teenager
and gay.

I was very aware that I was illegal until I was twenty-one.
I was involved in the youth group and it was constantly in
our minds. Not from the point of view of getting caught,
but simply that it put us in a different relation to the law
than most of the other men. It also meant we were in a
different relation to our lovers than 'legal' partners. In
other words, every time we did something we were being
illegal. (*Alaric Sumner*)

I was nineteen. Illegal, which I knew. It was a problem,
when I first met Noel we were extremely cautious.
I remember a number of occasions when ages were
discussed and we were very careful about whether we let
people know, because we could have got into trouble.
(*Ted Walker Brown*)

Tony Reynolds was probably the prime mover in it. He had
a lot of ideas well worked out and was able to put them
into practice, he was very organized. I remember his
insistence that different types of sexual behaviour were as
much part of GLF as same-sex sex, things like SM and so
on. It may have been him that made me take more notice of
drag and got me into it. I remember him being very
involved in the youth group demo organization and the
Youth Group issue of *Come Together* and constantly
pushing the sexual side. That it was a sexual liberation,
pro-pornography, pro-cruising and so on. There were big
arguments about cruising and I probably had a slightly
moralistic streak, but I was led to an understanding of it by
Tony who argued for it coherently. (*Alaric Sumner*)

Because of their feminist concerns about sexism and objectification, many members of GLF took a rather moralistic line over
certain forms of sexual behaviour. One of the first things I came
across during research was a rather good fake Metropolitan Police
sticker (another John Chesterman and co. production, I suspect)
which said 'Police Entrapment Practiced Here' and I assumed that
it was part of a pro-cottaging warning campaign. Not so. 'The
police entrapment sticker was produced with the idea of deterring
cottagers, not protecting them. Cottaging was objected to because
objectification was a big sin, as was 'owning' someone, i.e. monogamy or coupledom' (*Michael Mason*). A leaflet from that time
suggests this sticker was part of a campaign also involving the
burning of physique magazines, and a special edition of *Come
Together* 'to attack those elements in homosexual life which above
all create and sustain the "role playing" that cripples the ability to
form balanced relationships and that destroy the emotions in
wasteful fantasy'. 'My first brush with GLF was through my new
school teachers. I had just been expelled from a Catholic grammar
school and Trevor gave me my first RE lesson (at the new school)
by opening up page three of the *Sun* and saying we would talk
about charity and objectification. I thought, this is not the sort of

religious education I got in the last place!' (*Julian Hows*) But the Youth Group, at least, was having none of it.

I remember one occasion on a tube when a guy called Ellis who was on the tube with me said, "Look at that gorgeous man, oh, he's absolutely wonderful" and I said "Where?", not seeing anyone exciting, and finally he said "That one there, the balding one with the paunch." To me that was just the opposite of my own desires at the time. And because this was before I got fully involved in GLF, it was one of the first hints that the range of different sexualities was quite so bizarre, in other words that my desire wasn't the same as other people's who would identify themselves in the same way (*Alaric Sumner*).

Tim Clark, however, remembers that others in the Youth Group thought that Alaric was terrifically cool because his mother had sent him to GLF in the first place and the group was sometimes allowed to meet in her house.

The demo and the *Come Together* were being done at the time when I arrived, so there was a time when I was being assessed if you like to see if I would become part of the inner circle, but not in an organizational way – Youth Group people were working out what I would do in relation to them. I was at the front of the Youth Group demo but I don't recall doing much organizing for it, though I did do leafleting. On one occasion at a meeting they all started smoking dope and then I put on a record, which was Terry Riley's *Rainbow In Curved Air* and everybody just flaked out and were lying around in ecstasy, a dream state, and after it finished they just lay absolutely still on the carpet. About half an hour afterwards, they were all saying what marvellous music it was. So the next time, I put on the same record but without any cannabis and they all said 'Take that awful noise off!'
The Youth Group always had its lighter side. It wasn't an organization where you did business and then you got onto the other things. The business was part of the socializing and being involved. There was no separation. Because the things we were organizing were utterly integral to our everyday living. There weren't any women in the Youth Group at that point that I remember, and I think I would.

Obviously there were others around and I think they went to the women's group because the youth group mainly campaigned on the age of consent and was partly set up to be protective of us against the chicken hunters as well. And those two things were seen as specifically male. Not that there was any suggestion that we shouldn't sleep with older men, but that it should be our choice and we shouldn't feel hassled . . . The Youth Group did quite a lot about the way that even in the general meetings we were being harassed. It ranged from being chatted up to enticement and we found it very ageist and offensive. It wasn't a simple outrage, there was quite a lot of pleasure at being found attractive. (*Alaric Sumner*)

Women had been in the group at the start, according to Ted Walker Brown of the Bounds Green commune.

I remember there was a certain amount of unfair resentment towards the few young lesbians in the group because lesbian sexuality wasn't illegal and a lot of the men's attitude was, we're more oppressed than you . . . The women's attitude wasn't reciprocated back, because at the time women weren't talking much about women's oppression so they didn't have a rejoinder to that. There was a lot of nervousness about some of the older men who used to hang out around us and be rather predatory.

Following the example set by *Oz* and other radicals of handing power to their youth, the Youth Group of GLF was put in charge of a demonstration and a special issue (8) of *Come Together* that August. The Group did their best to involve more than just GLF, but were not always welcomed with open arms in the scene pubs.

Leafleting the Boltons was just before the age of consent demo. I don't remember much except that one of the people we leafleted kept on telling us that he knew what we really needed, which was to go to bed with him. The whole youth group had gone to do Earls Court, we were trying to get the scene people out and we did that at the William IV too. There were people in there who said, we don't want the age of consent lowered because then the older men will go for you lot instead of for us. Which made me feel a bit disgusted. (*Alaric Sumner*)

The demonstration attracted more interest from the straight press than from straight gays. *The Times*, possibly under Andrew Lumsden's influence, assigned columnist Victoria Brittain to do a major article for that day which gave highly favourable coverage to GLF. The next day, the *Sunday Times* ran a piece across four columns titled 'A gay day camping in the park' which said that around 500 people had attended. It mistakenly assumed that GLF were calling for an age of consent of eighteen and described the march as 'orderly if exotic', claiming that a Nigerian drum band played while transvestites handed out leaflets.

Street Theatre also devised a special piece for the demonstration, of which there is a photograph.

> Street Theatre devised a game called Pickin' the Chicken. As far as I can remember it consisted of a number of different couples and the idea was that looking at them, you just saw couples of people kissing and there was nothing really to distinguish them except, of course, that one of them contained an under-age male kissing another man, so that arbitrarily – and it was to show the arbitrariness of the law – this one couple was a criminal act. And to confuse the issue, in one of them you had two gay men over the age of consent but one was a drag queen. You had two dykes and you had a man and a woman and you had an under-age gay man kissing another, that was the set-up. And I was the compere, in a plum-coloured Biba suit. What we did I have no idea except that it was probably pretty bad. Carl Hill and Jane Winter played the heterosexuals, though Carl wasn't all that heterosexual at the time – Jane was. Luke Fitzgerald was part of it. I don't remember who played the under-age youth, there were so many of us . . . (*Michael Mason*)

Street Theatre even devised a questionnaire for bystanders watching the show, asking if they understood what it had been about and whether they were sympathetic to the issue; possibly the earliest piece of gay consumer research in the UK. It would be fascinating to know, though, what casual passers-by thought of one of the leaflets for the occasion, written by Youth Group members, which is one of the clearest illustrations of the gulf between GLF and more 'respectable groups' and the gulf between the early 1970s and now. Try to imagine what would happen if a leaflet like this were handed out on Pride nowadays . . .

We are stardust – we are golden. We are fifty million year old children. And we've got to get ourselves back to the garden.

Love is eternal. Love is natural. Love is golden. Love is God. God is homosexual. God is negro. God is a Jew. God rapes children. God is the Archbishop of Canterbury, the Pope, Edward Heath, the Queen and you all rolled into a ball. A cosmic ball. Essence of porphyry. Magic mushrooms, LSD, pot, cocaine, heroin and Tia Maria. These things too are part of our natural environment. As are homosexuals under the age of 21 who want to make love to each other. What difference does it make to you, Mrs Smith, if two boys make it in a room? Does it offend you while you sit watching Coronation Street to think that somewhere somehow two males under 21 are screwing the daylight/moonlight/love/fuck/ass/cocksuck/want it want it want it out of each other while the world outside continues unperturbed. Do you really believe that it does the world harm when two people make love. Or when three people make love. Do you really believe that it harms the people who make love. Do you make love?

When my son asked me what homosexuality was, I made love to him.

If your son was homosexual wouldn't you prefer him to know where homosexuals met rather than hide away, ashamed of his supposed guilt, mentally dented, incapable of decision, afraid of love. Homosexuality is natural. And Love is the greatest force for Good. In the present conditions of social unrest we need all the love we can get. So do you. So does the world. Turn on, tune in, turn over. Make this Help a Homosexual week. Give your bedroom to two guys for a night. Preferably two guys under 21. Then walk the streets and see the ways that society forces gays to meet – in public lavatories, in bushes, in shady groves. Then decide which way you would like your son to make it if he were a homosexual.

COME OUT
SUPPORT YOUR GAY HUMAN COMMUNITY
WE WILL NOT CORRUPT YOUR CHILDREN
BUT THEY'LL BE DAMNED GLAD WE'RE HERE IF THEY'RE HOMOSEXUAL
AND STATISTICS PROVE THAT THEY MIGHT BE

Gay Liberation Front Demonstration. August 28th.
Lower the Age of Consent. Lower your threshold of
prejudice. We love you.

Although it was a male theme, lesbians from GLF turned
out in support.

> The first Trafalgar Square demonstration I was wearing a
> T-shirt that said 'Lesbian' that Sarah Grimes had made. I
> remember walking through the street with Tarsus and Paul
> Theobald. Some old woman came up and said 'You can't
> possibly be a lesbian, you're too pretty.' We got to
> Trafalgar Square, and remember that at that time a lot of
> people were still scared to come out – all the middle-class
> women were terrified, afraid to lose their jobs, none of
> them wanted to speak and the working-class women were
> afraid to get their pictures in the newspapers, so that left
> me and Rosie. I was six thousand miles from home and
> she'd been raised in care. Her father was Nigerian, her
> mother Scots and she had on a purple wig that day. All of
> the other women refused because they were chickenshit,
> they didn't want the comeback on their jobs and being
> threatened. Of course the men hadn't even planned for one
> of the women to speak, they hadn't thought this far ahead.
> They said 'We need one of the sisters to speak' and I started
> hearing 'Where's Carla, where's Carla' and I turned to a
> friend and said 'I can't go up there alone' . . . I grabbed
> Rosie's hand and dragged her up to the plinth with me and
> we stood there holding hands, and all I could think of to
> say was 'I'm gay and I'm proud' or something and Rosie
> and I put our fists in the air and I heard this cheer from the
> crowd, and when I got down there was this young girl just
> in her teens who said 'I want to be a lesbian when I grow
> up' and I said 'Well, you just need courage.' (*Carla Toney*)

Issue 8 of *Come Together* contains a cogent Declaration of
Youth Group Rights, mainly written by Tony Reynolds, which
echoes the *Manifesto* (then about to be published) and says plainly,
'We believe that the nuclear family is not in the best interests of
women or gays.' However, most of the issue is filled with more
general articles and debate and a number of hefty clues to the growing dissent within GLF. There are articles with clear sympathies for
the revolutionary left (John Chesterman, Angie Weir), an attack on

politically incorrect expressions of lesbian sexuality (an unknown Sarah), an attack on masculinity (Aubrey Walter), a plea for collective working across what is characterized as a political divide (Sarah Grimes, Bill Halstead, Tim Bolingbroke) and a painfully honest examination of the rights and wrongs of political censorship within GLF (Mick Belsten). But the issue also lists fifteen working groups, awareness groups throughout London, a plan to fund proper premises and the first warning note about the Festival of Light, the battle which was to become GLF's greatest triumph. If the growing cracks went unnoticed, it is hardly surprising.

Chapter ten

Sisterhood Is Powerful

It is not difficult to understand why GLF split between women and men. Instead of the usual question: why did the women split from the men?, it might be more profitable to ask: why did lesbians find themselves in GLF in the first place, rather than in the women's movement? –David Fernbach, *The Rise and Fall of the Gay Liberation Front*

ANGIE Weir recalls, 'When the GLF Women's Group first formed we tried to join women's liberation. We sent a letter to the secretary of women's liberation, who was this Maoist called Maysel Brah, with a postal order for 7/6d and she wrote me back a letter saying that lesbians couldn't be part of women's liberation and returned my postal order.' The women's movement already existed and was beginning to be highly vocal, but sexism was something thought to be primarily of concern to heterosexual women who had to live with men. Lesbians had nothing to do with the women's movement – indeed, were barely thought of as women and often referred to as a separate sex, even by enlightened liberals like Jill Tweedie. When the women of Gay Liberation began to think about the women's movement, the response was unequivocal.

There were even fewer avenues in social or political life for lesbian expression than for gay men. If you didn't want to spend your life in the Gateways and you hadn't already found a partner to retire to Hastings and breed dogs, what could you do? But women were not in GLF simply because they had nothing better to do with their Wednesday evenings. Lesbians – and heterosexual women – joined GLF because they believed it could make a difference to their lives and because at least some of the men were as convinced as they were of the need to work together. Women as much as men speak of the transformatory effect it had upon them. 'I think one reason GLF was important to me was because it did release something. I was terribly inhibited and never spoke at anything ever at all before that. It obviously unleashed something' (*Elizabeth Wilson*).

Women were involved in the Gay Liberation Front from the first meeting and there is hardly an aspect of its work in which they are not apparent. Although often in a minority and not on the whole a very vocal one at the general meetings, women were central to many actions and projects – Street Theatre, Counter-Psychiatry, the *Manifesto* and many of the demonstrations. Their lack of involvement in the Youth Group seems to have been mainly due to its overwhelming emphasis on male law reform and sexuality, and their low level of input to the main meetings was due to female training (or lack of it) in public speaking. But, given their disadvantage in both numbers and social training, it's not surprising that from quite early on, the women of GLF carved out their own group and actions. What is more interesting is that both men and transgender people were present throughout. Separatism, as opposed to self-determination, was largely a post-GLF concept.

Anti-sexist and pro-feminist politics were present throughout GLF. The last October 1970 issue of *Time Out* reported that the London Gay Liberation Front had invaded the office of the LSE student magazine, *Sennet*, to protest about an article which denigrated both homosexuals and women and had issued a warning to *IT*, *Oz* and *Friends* that they would do the same to them if they operated on a 'tits and arse' basis. When Angie Weir arrived some time towards the end of the year saying that she was a delegate from Women's Liberation, she was given a warm welcome and listened to by the meeting as she told them information on women's actions. There was also informal contact. 'There was a party in South London and Angie and Mary O'Shea came along together from a women's liberation group to try and get us to join women's liberation. That was around Christmas time' (*Elizabeth Wilson*).

It was at the meeting of 30 December 1970 in the Arts Lab, where GLF had been banished for the holidays from the LSE, that the idea of a separate women's meeting was first publicly raised. Most women remember it as Angie's idea, but a welcome one. The men were less sure, and a perceptive article by Tony Reynolds in *Come Together* 3 confronted the problem:

> At the last meeting . . . there was a lot of discussion on
> whether there should be a separate women's caucus and

'The one in the chain is not a mayor' – The *People* comment on
the first GLF dance at Kensington Town Hall
(© The Mirror Group)

"Well, Vic, I make it eighty to one hundred and fifty thousand, depending on whether you include the 'Gay Liberation Front,' or not!"

above: 22 February 1971 – *Evening Standard* comment on GLF's presence at the Industrial Relations Bill march (© *London Evening Standard*/Solo)

right: Charlie Pig challenges the patriarchy, Alexandra Palace, Easter Sunday 1971 (© *John Chesterman/HCA*)

below left: Paul Theobald and Jane Winter with others at the 'Miss Trial' demo, Bow Street (© *Stuart Feather*)

below right: Stuart Feather and Edsel as 'Miss Trial' contestants at Bow Street (© *Stuart Feather*)

above: Street Theatre at Alexandra Palace, Easter Sunday 1971 (© *John Chesterman/HCA*)

below: First National think-in, Leeds, 19 June 1971. Warren speaks, Bette Bourne (centre) and others listen (© *John Chesterman/HCA*)

POLICE

ENTRAPMENT

PRACTICED HERE

G L F L O N D O N

above: Gay Liberation at the *OZ* Freak Festival, 4 July 1971: first use of sack letters *(© John Chesterman/HCA)*

left: GLF sticker intended to deter cottagers, spring 1971

above: GLF demonstrate against sexism in Fleet Street, 17 August 1971

below: Carla and Rosie (centre right) address the crowds, Age of Consent rally in Trafalgar Square 28 August 1971

above: 'Pickin' the Chicken', Trafalgar Square, 28 August 1971 – Michael Mason compering *(© Peter Boll)*

left: Manifesto compilation shot of Age of Consent demo, 28 August 1971 – Simon Watney and Mark Rowlands (bottom right)

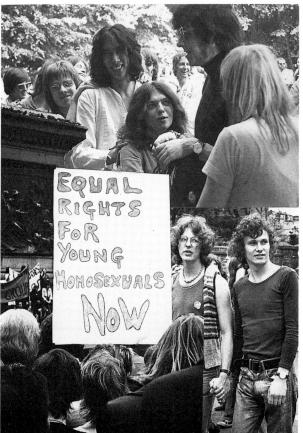

top: Stuart Feather conducts the Festival Choir on the steps of St Martin-in-the-Fields, 25 September 1971

above left: Tony Salvis preaches to the Hyde Park crowd, 25 September 1971
(© Martin Corbett)

right: The countercultural response to the Festival of Light – the Festival of Life

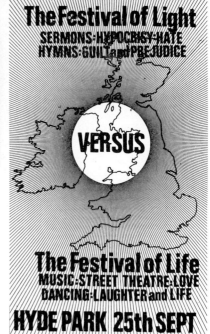

whether they should meet. As I felt the women in the meeting were yet again dominated by the men in the debate on whether the men should be in on their discussions, I think that that example is in itself a good reason for the women talking on their own . . . I feel bad about the fact that I'm a man putting forward a point that should be made by the women, but as was shown in the last meeting the women didn't get very far and I think the point should be made pretty soon.

The lesbians began to meet separately on a Friday night from then on, whatever men thought of it. Some women didn't participate. 'There were women in GLF who never came to the Women's Group and I don't know why – either they didn't agree with it or they saw it as a clique. Those who came included Angela, Mary McIntosh, Mary O'Shea, Carla, Barbara, I think there were two Barbaras, Annie Bracxz. October was a bit later. The early discussions were about behaviour, heterosexual behaviour, role playing. We never talked about sadomasochism in those days.' (*Sarah Grimes*). 'Bev was quite significant in the big meetings, but I don't remember her at the women's meetings at all, or Sue Winter' (*Mary McIntosh*). Other women, like Angie and Carla and Marion, blossomed there. But the first big 'women's demonstration', while the result of a Women's Group action, was decided on by the whole meeting and was very much a shared piece of work.

The Gateways thing came about because we were having a Ball in a Town Hall. The boys had sold tickets in Earls Court, so of course we went to do the same at the Gateways. Elizabeth and I hadn't been for a while, but we were Gateways people and so were a few of the others. We had this thing that we were supposed to involve the gay community, we were very anti the commercial scene and wanted to get through to the people on the commercial scene and show them something better. One of the things we wanted to show them was a Ball, so we went there selling tickets. We were having a hard time getting any interest and of course they didn't want us selling tickets to something else. Smithy [one of the owners] told us to stop and Elizabeth and I got into a discussion with her on the door as she was throwing us out. (*Mary McIntosh*)

I remember her saying, 'I'd like to kick your bum up Bramerton Street, Elizabeth.' I don't think she'd ever addressed me by my name before, I didn't even know that she knew it. She said, 'I wouldn't want my sister to be a lesbian', she revealed this horrific ideology.
(*Elizabeth Wilson*)

It was a fascinating discussion in which she said, 'You don't have to hold hands on the street.' She went through the demands one by one and said they were completely unnecessary, 'You've got this nice scene here, you don't need to do things on the street, you can come here and be yourselves in peace and you don't have to tell the public and children what you're doing, it's much better to be discreet and it's nothing to be proud of, there's nothing wrong with your lives as long as the Gateways is here.' You know the sort of thing. We were just fascinated by it because it seemed to articulate everything, it made it clear to us what GLF was about because we were opposed to all of that, in ways that we hadn't questioned before.

So Elizabeth wrote it up for *Come Together*, because it seemed to be such a good way of stating the difference between us and a certain position out there. And of course, the Gateways was absolutely outraged. After Elizabeth's article about it came out, the Gateways banned us – so the big meeting decided to have a demonstration against the Gateways. It was a build-up of confrontation. So we had a demonstration outside and some people had to go inside to tell people what was happening and explain it to them.
(*Mary McIntosh*)

I was a member at the Gateways. I remember the demonstration vividly. There was Angela Weir and Elizabeth Wilson, Mary McIntosh, Barbara Klecki, Barbara Cooper and Beverley and Marion Prince I think. There were a dozen women and we left the brothers, as we called them, outside the club to go down and leaflet and talk to women. The leaflet said 'Out of the closet and into the street' and we went in and did a spiel, talked to different women at tables and asked if they were out and why not, and of course the women in the Gateways were horrified at all these dykes coming in and telling them to come out. Somebody at some point had asked me to dance and said 'I can't tell by the way you're dressed whether you're a butch or femme.' So people were handing out leaflets and mostly talking to people about coming to the next meeting. Barbara Klecki at some point pulled the plug out on the juke box and screamed something like 'We're gay and we're proud.' (*Carla Toney*)

[Pulling the plug] was a terrible thing to do. The Gateways depended on the juke box and everyone was very fond of it. (*Mary McIntosh*)

There may have been a secondary reason for the management's objections. The GLF women had produced a special version of the Ball flyer for the Gateways demonstration. On one side is a simple advert for the event, with the addition of the stirring 'Do come – and remember . . . Sappho was a right-on woman!' But on the other, alongside an invitation to the dance, are the lines 'The Gateways has made thousands of pounds out of women who come to the club (precisely how much money and publicity was gained from *The Killing Of Sister George?*) yet the management of the Gateways considers lesbians to be sick. We are not sick and don't like people who condescendingly treat us as such – especially when they are making a living off us.' As one GLF woman said, seeing it for the first time in twenty-four years, 'Oh, well, I don't suppose that would have endeared us to them, would it?'

Gina used to have policemen come and drink in the club regularly, treat them to a drink, so she got on the phone to the police and they came promptly. In the meantime Gina dragged Marion Prince up the stairs by the hair and some of us fled as fast as we could. On the street, Mary O'Shea was there and Marshall Weekes and Pete McInally. The police told us to move along and Mary, who was lovers with Lady Rose, told them to bugger off, so they snatched her and put her in the van. Marshall or someone screeched 'Don't let our sister be taken away alone' so about ten people leapt into the van to go with her. In the meantime, she'd crawled out over the front seat and disappeared down the Kings Road . . . and then they just started grabbing us and shoving us into the vans. By the time we got to the police station there were eleven of us plus they'd accidentally picked up two passers-by from the bus stop who had never heard of GLF in their life.

In the police station Charlie Pig, who used to paint a pig over his eye, went 'Oooh!' when they went to search him, like it really gave him a thrill. They really hated that so they locked him up in solitary. They slowly released us over the night. Mary had disappeared and in court the people from the bus stop pleaded guilty and got a £1 fine, because their solicitor had advised them that if they pleaded not guilty the magistrate would assume they were with us and come down really heavy on them. All the people from Gay Liberation pleaded not guilty and the two people who'd never heard of it pleaded guilty. We were fined much more for pleading not guilty. (*Carla Toney*)

The event did achieve coverage from an increasingly aware press, who reported that those arrested were: David Leach and Greg Honey (innocent bystanders), Louisa Hunt, Hugh Gaw, Tarsus Sutton, Bob Mellors, Sue Finch, Hazel Twort, Marshall Weekes, Robert Lengside, Charles Garner, Vernon Page and Carla Hughes. Most were charged with obstruction. Marshall Weekes was found to have overstayed his visa and was deported after telling the court that he had stayed 'because he had formed a strong attachment towards another man' – probably the first time such an explanation had been given in a British court and certainly a headline-making one.

The London Gay Liberation Front had begun to make quite a splash by the spring of 1971, not only within Britain but on the international revolutionary and feminist circuit. The Women's Group, now officially occupying a Friday night slot alongside the consciousness raising groups of GLF (which may indicate how people thought of it) started to receive a stream of feminist and lesbian visitors.

In the summer a whole series of Americans came over to tell us what to do, that was really quite annoying. Somebody from the American Socialist Worker Party, who are part of the Fourth International and Trots, came and told us what to do about the class struggle and everything. Then Jill Johnston came over and told us what to do, which was rather different, and then Kate Millett came over and told us to do something else. She came when the meetings were at Middle Earth. She was friendly with someone who had an autistic child whose therapy involved people doing things to it all the time. Kate Millett told us

our revolutionary task was to help this autistic child and a
lot of people did for a time. I didn't see quite what it had to
do with gay liberation except that it was kind of people to
go. I remember feeling that she wasn't really talking as a
lesbian and it was very top down, shall we say.
(*Elizabeth Wilson*)

The women's meetings began during the main meeting or
just after it, and then they moved to our house for a time.
Being involved in that had been a very intense experience
and that confirmed lots of women's interest in women's
liberation. There was a woman called Suki who floated in
and out of all these things and Pam Thompson, who was a
black lesbian. There was this extraordinary period when
we had all these visiting Americans. Jill Johnston was
terrible. She was extremely dogmatic. Kate Millett was
pretty dogmatic on the first occasion though she mellowed.
I think what happened was that women's liberation at the
time was also very exciting and the women in the women's
group wanted to explore that side of themselves and the
men were largely unreconstructed and not at all used to
feminist ideas. And I think at the beginning there was a
very strong feeling of all being together and supporting
each other and perhaps after the initial high, differences
that were there emerged more clearly. (*Angie Weir*)

As the summer progressed, women increasingly felt that the
group should do some actions in the manner of other GLF groups.
To add emphasis, they decided to take a new name. After discussing
several suggestions, including 'Daughters Of The Manifesto' (rather
optimistic, given that the *Manifesto* was not yet published), they
settled on one.

I remember Angie Weir suggesting that we called ourselves
the Red Lesbian Brigade and I was a bit shocked, it was a
bit close to 'Angry Brigade'. The group met in my flat in
Arundel Square. It was very short-lived. It was just a
meeting of the Women's Group which decided to do some
spray painting because we thought we should have some
actions. We picked the name just in order to have a name
and something challenging. I remember spray painting the
Maudsley Hospital over psychiatric treatment of gays.
(*Mary McIntosh*)

The leaflet for this event survives, although its wording suggests it came with a packet of information:

> Dear Madam/Sir (are you sure?)
> Further to our slogans painted outside, the enclosed explanatory material may be of interest to you.
> WE ARE NOT SICK
> WE ARE NOT ABNORMAL
> WE ARE NOT IMMATURE
> Stop making a fat living out of saying we are
> WE ARE STRONG
> WE ARE BEAUTIFUL
> Power to the patients, we don't need you!
> In anger,
> Red Lesbian Brigade

The Red Lesbian Group wasn't, really! Someone gave me a badge that said Red Lesbian. I remember there was a certain amount of spray painting. I realized when I was delivering a letter to the Tavistock about Socarides recently that I remember spray painting the Tavistock with anti-psychiatry slogans. (*Angie Weir*)

Elizabeth Wilson, with her background in psychiatric social work, chose a number of the targets for these campaigns; the Tavistock was where she worked at that time. But the action which gained public notoriety for the Group was something of a set-up, with repercussions far beyond what they might have expected.

> OBSCENE SLOGANS
> **Stock Exchange:** There were fears today for security after a militant group daubed obscene slogans on the walls – under the noses of security guards.
>   Two men and a woman – thought to be members of a group called Red Lesbians – drove past the guards in a green Morris Minor convertible.
>   Then they walked past the main door of the building and sprayed slogans on the walls in three foot high red letters. They then painted an inverted sex symbol in black paint.
>   Security forces at the centre of Britain's financial world were checking to see if any attempt had been made to get into the building.
>   The Red Lesbians are a militant breakaway group from

the Gay Liberation Front – an organization which wants social acceptance for homosexuals.

[*Evening News*, 10 June 1971, underneath a report on a women's liberation demonstration against Wimpy Bars refusing to serve unaccompanied women between midnight and six a.m.]

I always felt rather annoyed about the Stock Exchange zap because this woman turned up who was a journalist, a lesbian, and she really inveigled people into going and doing that, and of course it got into the papers whereas we went off into Hackney to spray paint. And times have changed, not that I go spray painting any more, because I remember a police car coming along when we were actually spray painting something and we weren't quite caught in the act, but we must have been looking terribly suspicious and they just slowed down and passed by.
(*Elizabeth Wilson*)

We painted the Stock Exchange or as we called it the Cock Exchange, that was what we picked. Which was rather unfortunate, because at the time it was in temporary buildings with hoardings up outside. We hadn't quite realized this, but hoardings were very easy to spray on. I was doing the driving rather than the painting and we were pretty terrified. (*Mary McIntosh*)

Despite the report, only one man was involved in this action, Tarsus Sutton. As at a number of other events, guards and police were confused about the sex of GLF members because of their failure to observe the dress codes of the times. Despite their nerves, the raiders managed to spray 'Sod The Cock Brokers' across the front of the building along with lesbian symbols. The Morris Minor belonged to Marion Prince, who was Mary McIntosh's girlfriend at the time.

Although the intention of this action was a fairly innocent one, it came less than three weeks after the bombing of New Scotland Yard's computer room by the real Angry Brigade. Paranoia amongst the security forces was running very high, especially about the safety of government buildings, and it must have been particularly humiliating to have security breached so easily by what was, despite any amount of tabloid hype, a blatantly amateur outfit. With Special Branch already mindful of the Gay

Liberation Front in their trawl for evidence through the liberation movements and regularly raiding both Agitprop and women's liberation addresses, this must have been provocation.

A photograph of the graffiti was published in *Come Together* 7, next to a quote from Rosa Luxemburg, 'The dialectic is not through a majority to revolution, but through revolutionary tactics to a majority', and above an article titled 'Catch The Oppression', remembered as Angie Weir's, which was a prophetic and scathing attack on identity politics and political lesbianism. Altogether, Issue 7 was one of the most thought provoking and accessible issues of *Come Together*. It was written by the Women's Group that early summer of 1971.

> I remember doing the first women's issue, the one with photos of us in drag. It wasn't anti-men, we just wanted to do something on our own and didn't feel we had much influence on the regular issues. And we wanted to have some fun together, which we did. We did it in Sarah Grimes' flat. You can tell who did it by the pictures. Carla, Annie Brackx, me, Elizabeth, Angie, Barbara, Sarah Grimes . . . (*Mary McIntosh*)

> The handwriting is all mine, I did the layout and graphics. I wrote 'Hold Your Head Up High, Love' which was a personal confessional piece. I was thinking about why it had been so hard to come out before GLF and it was to do with the image of lesbians, of not having any charisma, any glamour, any creative ability or genius. Lesbians were silly, crass. There wasn't a role model equivalent to Oscar Wilde. There were two counterposed articles – 'Revolution In The Head – Or In The World'. That was two different points of view which we allowed to coexist, individualism and internal revolution versus seeing that as just the first step to external revolution. We didn't try to assimilate the views or allow one to overcome the other, there was no power struggle over it. I don't know who wrote 'In The Head' – I think Mary McIntosh and Elizabeth wrote 'In The World' together. Carla wrote 'To my sister and her husband', and there was the dressing up, which was great fun.

> It was at my flat in Notting Hill, and my brother lived upstairs and we raided his wardrobe. I don't know who

had the idea of dressing up but it was a very good tactic because it brought us together as a group, like one of those exercises at a strategy group to put people at their ease. (*Sarah Grimes*)

The photographs of GLF women playing with male drag, including guns and stubble and, for Mary McIntosh, a black eye, bring to mind nothing so much as the US 'drag king' workshops promoted as the last word in female queerdom in the 1990s.

Issue 7 is both more blatantly socialist–political and more encouraging of differing viewpoints than many others. Apart from openly exploring the incipient political split in GLF as described above by Sarah Grimes, it urged that Gay Days be widened out from middle-class areas to the East End, which led to the successful Gay Days in Victoria Park. There was also an article about life in Holloway prison by Pat Arrowsmith which was attacked in a later issue for its portrayal of butch/femme life there. 'There was one article I really hated which criticized something Pat Arrowsmith had written in the women's issue about butch and femme roles. This was another article saying how awful that was. So there was a sort of hidden political right-on-ness that certain gay lifestyles were out of the question' (*Sarah Grimes*). But in the heady summer of 1971, there had been few splits amongst the women despite tensions around class, sexuality and politics. These became apparent as the autumn progressed and arguments elsewhere about political direction were mirrored amongst the women. But when the rows came, the lesbians of GLF had an escape route denied to the men, as a result of their most successful and most celebrated action – an event which drastically altered the history of feminist politics in Britain.

It began with a letter of invitation:

Dear Sisters & Brothers at Gay Lib,
At the N.W.C.C. (National Women's Coordinating
Committee) Nottingham meeting last Sat. – a women's lib
conference was set for October 15th in Skegness
(Lincolnshire) – there are official accommodation
arrangements for 500 – but many more are expected. Just
bring a sleeping bag I guess and friends!
It's a drag but so few women from Workshops were there –
a motion was passed to allow men. By the Maoists &

Socialist Women (consciousness raising has been
denounced as a false channel for hostility against
capitalism!) mainly.
Well, so I thought why not have Gay Lib come and say do
whatever you want! Perhaps gather all the super-male
lefties into a Workshop on Male Chauvinism. Something
really revolutionary in an active way – not just stale rhetoric.
I talked this over with members of the Nottingham group
and you can say we asked you. Friday night it all begins,
and you all are very welcome.
Write: Barbara Yates . . . Roslyn Smythe . . . or anyone you
know in W.L.!

Skegness was a meeting of the Women's Liberation
National Coordinating Committee and we were
approached by Roz Delmar, who was a friend of Angie's.
She said they really needed women to come to this meeting,
which the Maoists were attempting to take over and run in
a centralized way. We wanted it to be more open.
(*Mary McIntosh*)

There was enormous rage because they (the Maoists) were
a mixed group, Harpul Brah and his wife Maysel and their
friends, two officious men who kept trying to interfere with
everything. They organized the whole conference in this
incredibly bureaucratic and repressive way.
(*Elizabeth Wilson*)

We questioned their organization of it and were largely
instrumental in stopping the conference from going along
that road. That was the conference that really got the
women's liberation movement going. We had a stall and it
was a very zappy and exciting time. (*Angie Weir*)

A minibus went up with GLF women and the Grosvenor
Avenue women. There'd been some sort of strategy worked
out, obviously, among some of the women, the Grosvenor
Avenue women and Angela and the others who knew how
the women's movement had been developing before
Skegness. (*Sarah Grimes*)

I imagine we thought there would be a bit of a ruckus
really and we were prepared for that. The Maoists were a
caricature of themselves. We all slept in this church hall

and we found ourselves in this hall with the Maoists. There was a dais at the end of the room with a red curtain and they created this *cordon sanitaire* with the red curtain. And when we woke up in the morning there they all were, sitting up and reading stuff out of '*The Little Red Book*', I couldn't believe it! They were slightly mad. (*Elizabeth Wilson*)

It was non-stop agitation at the conference and there was a great deal of dissatisfaction being voiced throughout the morning. We were sat in these workshops discussing socialist texts and people were absolutely pissed off, so after lunch we just decided that we would appeal to the conference to split up and reorganize itself. (*Angie Weir*)

The first day was the Maoists, including men, trying to take over. They were all arguing over process and over the control of the movement and whether men should be involved. Their argument was that you had to have a properly elected committee and they were it and so forth. This Maoist line was being put out – as soon as the lesbians came out, we were told we were a bourgeois deviation and that we would disappear under socialism. (*Mary McIntosh*)

I was the one who got up on the platform! What happened in the first session was very much dictated from the platform, pseudo-Marxist papers being read out and there was a great deal of regulation. There was a terrific sense of alienation amongst a lot of the women, a reaction against the leadership and I guess what the Maoist women were positing was part of an economic analysis. Men were allowed in and were on the platform. So in the break there was a little caucusing going on with the GLF women and a few other groups about what we should do, how to deal with this . . . we knew we had to go up and stop it and I think I was just chosen as someone with a new face, who could go up to the platform and get the microphone because they had control of it and were deciding who to give it to. They wouldn't be suspicious of me. So I went up and said, 'I think we should all go outside and discuss things in small groups, I don't think this is the way it should be, we should be talking about our lives', and they said, 'You can't do this', but we did and people just moved out, it was what they wanted. (*Sarah Grimes*)

I was with her but it was her who spoke first into the microphone and urged everybody to stop the conference and split up into small discussion groups. Harpul Brah was extremely aggressive and there was a great row.
(*Angie Weir*)

She grasped the mike and did a long and very telling speech. She said basically, this is a movement for all women. We found ourselves articulating the basic premise of women's liberation. It was a huge learning experience for us. Eventually there was just a mega-row which ended in fighting over microphones. Harpul Brah had to be bodily thrown out by other male security guards in the end, and his wife was the leading light left on the platform. It was taken extremely well by the rest of the women, who were relieved. People just couldn't bear it, and we were much more bold and activist than a lot of the others. So we ended up taking the initiative and doing what the rest of the room wanted and we were lionized after that. I remember that heaps of women wanted to talk to us about sexuality, wherever we sat down in the hall.
(*Mary McIntosh*)

It all got a lot more clear after that. It was discussion about women's experience, talking from the heart about the basic situation of, for instance, women with children. It was still the economic situation, but more related to people's lives. And of course it was at this point that GLF women were able to raise the point of lesbianism. I think we were a bit cocky about being the sexual vanguard and there were some tensions with other women feeling threatened, as if they were afraid we might be saying that lesbianism is the only way, which we weren't saying. So then people started coming up with their own deep personal feelings and angst.
(*Sarah Grimes*)

It was a very important meeting for the women's liberation movement, it was the first of the big conferences. And of the big interest in lesbianism. There was a lot of interest in it at the time in the women's movement. Lots of them played with lesbian relationships in the seventies. We didn't want to be anti-straight though, we weren't separatists. Our motivation for being gay was not a feminist motivation, we just were and then we came to feminism. 'Any woman can be a lesbian' became a popular view in the women's movement, but I remember Sheila Rowbotham about that time talking about trying to come to terms with the fact that she loved her man but was nevertheless a feminist. That was the sort of thing that you couldn't talk about by the mid-seventies in a feminist meeting. But we were very supportive of that and I remember saying 'We mustn't be anti-heterosexual, those women's bed is the front line of battle with men and we must admire them for that struggle in their private lives that we've escaped.' We definitely were supportive of straight women at Skegness. We weren't trying to win them over, but we wanted to be able to talk about our sexuality and lives. (*Mary McIntosh*)

We had a stall there and lots and lots of miners came up and talked to us and had interesting discussions. In fact it was quite funny because the Socialist Workers Party were also having some sort of do there at the same time, they were the International Socialists then. (*Angie Weir*)

So popular were the lesbians at the conference that women remember the IS paper sellers deliberately placing themselves near the GLF stall for maximum audience. However, with the miners' conference sitting next door and behaving in a rather more traditional and macho manner, the GLF women also found themselves confronting other issues – and being confronted in their turn.

We were rather inveigled into disrupting the miners' conference that was going on at the same time there. They had a striptease as part of their socializing so we zapped that and had discussions with the miners. We did stop the strippers, I don't think they were very happy about it. I just remember getting on to the stage when they were on and then being hustled off. I think it raised the issue very sharply, but I don't suppose it convinced anybody very much. (*Angie Weir*)

I think we did a conga across the stage chanting something – we were conscious that we shouldn't put the women doing the striptease down, only the men for watching them, but the women turned on us and told us to go away. (*Mary McIntosh*)

Then it ended with a plenary session which was basically just trying to cobble together some organization. It had no structure . . . Some women from Bristol took it on until the next conference and that's how the structure arose which worked quite well for several years, of groups taking on coordination between one conference and the next. It was all good fun. (*Sarah Grimes*)

And then we went back to GLF. I don't think they were terribly interested. They liked the idea that there was a big movement out there that was being influenced by us, but it wasn't deeply interesting. Skegness was a turning point. We could go on to the women's movement, but the men had to form other gay groups, like the local meetings, to have another home than the big GLF meetings. (*Mary McIntosh*)

It was after Skegness that some divisions began to become apparent between the lesbians of GLF. It is ironic that the lesbians most concerned with the class struggle and the wider revolution, as illustrated in *Come Together* Issue 7, and those who brought women's liberation into GLF, came into conflict over class and feminism with a younger generation of lesbian activists. These women were rapidly coming to embrace separatism, as illustrated in *Come Together* 11, also produced by 'the women' but in fact by a totally different group (dealt with more in chapter seventeen). However, in some aspects the division was clearly a reflection of the arguments surfacing elsewhere about revolutionary issues.

The earlier women in GLF had lots of experience, they were a few years older than us and were middle-class with good jobs. In fact, they were doing a good job of motivating people and getting things together, but of course, in comes the influx of the young ones and we're going to change this and we don't like that, this can't happen, we don't like the way it's run. We were like a bull in a china shop, going for it straight out with this motivation to change the world. And we can do it better than you started. (*Julia L*)

Points of difference? Well, there was the Marxists and the non-Marxists, there were people who saw GLF as more of a social club and a way for women to come out. I don't remember, but I think there might have been class issues in there but they might not have been recognized as such. (*Sarah Grimes*)

We'd all gone over to Elizabeth's house and they explained
how we should be more committed politically, and the issue
of Rachel [a transsexual] came up and while the meeting
was focused on Rachel it was also a working-class rebellion
against indoctrination by the middle class – we walked out.
It split on class lines over whether Rachel could join the
group – the middle-class women didn't want her to join but
the working-class women were tired of being lectured. At
one meeting I was tired of hearing about Marx and I said
'Marx, who's Marx, the only Marx I've ever heard of is
Groucho.' We kept getting these lectures and the issue over
Rachel was also a spit in their eye. (*Carla Toney*)

The essential debate which spilled over into everything was
the *Come Together* collective. There was this ongoing
ideological debate between Marxism and radical feminism
and Carla was very influenced by David and Aubrey, so
there were disagreements within the women's group and
disagreements in GLF as a whole, which rather exacerbated
the tensions between the men and the women.
(*Elizabeth Wilson*)

But despite these differences, the group continued to work
together on actions, often in collaboration with women's liberation. A typical example of such shared protest and its spin-offs was
one action at Holloway prison shortly after the Skegness conference.

I went to the Pauline Jones demonstration at Holloway,
about a young woman who'd been imprisoned for stealing
a child. It appeared that she had a fair number of problems
and prison really wasn't appropriate. I'd stayed the
previous night at Faraday Road after the Women's Group
and we went along as a group. (*Nettie Pollard*)

I don't remember how much it was GLF and how much the
women's movement, but I remember crowds gathering to
shout at the back of the old prison. We were shouting to
and fro with women at the windows of their cells. It was
about conditions, they were being banged up for twenty-
three out of twenty-four hours and there were a huge
amount of drugs being prescribed. Pat Arrowsmith's book
had come out, so every dyke felt they had something in
common about it. (*Mary McIntosh*)

I got arrested outside Holloway prison. We'd gone along and were standing there. Barbara picked up a stone, there were a lot of gay women there and she started throwing it. I took it away from her and I said, I'll never forget, 'Don't throw those, we're not here to be violent', and this bugger behind me grabbed my hand with the stone in it and said 'I'm busting you for having an offensive weapon.' I said 'But hang on, you've just heard me tell her to put it down.' He said 'I know' and laughed, 'but it's in your hands, isn't it?' It was an Inspector in plain clothes. You know how you don't know how you're going to react to things? Well, I grabbed this lamp post, wound myself round it and screamed to the women across the road, 'I'm being busted!' whereupon a tidal wave came running across Holloway Road and all hell let loose. (*Julia L*)

It was amazing how everyone stuck together. Because if you held on to her, then the police couldn't get her into the police van and it soon became a real incident and photographers were there. She started screaming, 'You're hurting me!', which apparently wasn't entirely true but every time they tried to yank her away she started screaming in a feminine way. They just didn't know how to cope with all these women together, they expected to be able to isolate people. Eventually they did get her but it was hardly worth their while. The whole thing went on for about half an hour and made the demonstration far more noticeable than it would have been. (*Nettie Pollard*)

As soon as they got one hand off the lamp post I got my leg round it. I struggled, I lost a shoe and my bag. They got me to the police van and you know how a cat is when it doesn't want to go? I was like that. And as they got me in one side, the other people they'd arrested ran out the front door of it. Anyway, they bundled me in there and I said, 'Where's my shoe, where's my handbag?' and I tried to get out but they bundled me back in. Then the doors opened and someone else was chucked in, I can't remember who and away we went. (*Julia L*)

One woman remembers vividly trying to stop the traffic in the road outside the prison with other women as a body-barrier. The next morning, she got a call from her father asking her what she was doing standing in the middle of some road in his newspaper.

So we got to the police station and there were people from Radical Alternatives to Prison there, somebody from an old theatre group I used to be in who was older and middle-class, and a middle-class woman who was going out with a working-class man. A black guy was arrested too, and an Indian bloke had been pushed through a window and they had him up for GBH [grievous bodily harm]. I was in a cell with another white girl and the police put a black woman in with us and I'll never forget, the policeman said, 'I'm sorry girls, I've got to lock the door now.' (*Julia L*)

The Holloway prison thing led to a very long-running trial where I was a Mackenzie. It was at Old Street, where there was a stipendiary magistrate and he remanded it from Saturday to Saturday over what seemed like a very long period. He would come in his tweeds because it was Saturday and he was going off to his country seat as stipendiaries will. He sat there in his tweeds and clearly enjoyed the whole thing. We did this elaborate questioning, very respectful. Every question was done by consultation between the Mackenzies and the accused. Mackenzies were named after this case where a judge had agreed that if somebody didn't have a lawyer that they could have a friend sitting beside them to consult with. We took notes on the answers and suggested questions and ways of formulating a point as a question. But we had a Mackenzie for each of the accused and there were five or six of them. We had a bench, we weren't in the dock. People with cool heads got chosen as Mackenzies, like me, though I wasn't combative enough. Some of them were brilliant. And of course you were always liable to get more arrests at the demonstrations outside the court, so they piled up one on top of another. It was one of our theatres, the court room. (*Mary McIntosh*)

We had a group trial with Mackenzies because that was politically right on. I told my school and the headmaster was marvellous, he said 'Never mind.' So every Saturday I went off to this court. I had this spell from Lyndsay and you had to stare at the magistrate and sprinkle it on the

floor and concentrate on being found not guilty and it
always worked. So I was staring at this red-faced chap.
And as it all went on, the first person to be let off was the
white middle-class man. I went in a skirt and twin-set and
crucifix, I told them I was a teacher. The white middle-class
girl was cautioned, her boyfriend was fined heavily, the
black bloke was held over for owing maintenance and the
Indian bloke was sent off to High Court . . . My case was
dismissed after five weeks. (*Julia L*)

Chapter eleven

Of Mice and Nuns

Please wear informal dress – the more informal the better.
–Henry W. Hole, Festival of Light Chief Steward, in a briefing
note to stewards for the Festival's Trafalgar Square rally

DURING the summer of 1971, while the Gay Liberation Front was blossoming in Notting Hill, another organization was also coming into flower which hoped to change the face of Britain in a rather different way. Founded by two Christian missionaries upon their return to England, the Festival of Light, as it was named in May 1971, was a campaign to alert society to moral pollution, to act upon that concern to raise moral standards, to influence government to act for them and to spread evangelical Christianity.

It rapidly became identified in the liberal imagination with censorship and sexual repression, but managed to get on board a number of popular celebrities and figures of authority: Bishop Trevor Huddleston, broadcaster Malcolm Muggeridge, Lord Longford who had recently published a report on pornography, singer Cliff Richard and Mary Whitehouse. If some of those people are now considered figures of fun to a large degree, this is at least partly due to 'Operation Rupert' as the opening blast of the anti-Festival of Light campaign became known. But at the time they carried enormous public weight and the first three were seen as liberal or having liberal pasts.

The Festival organized a national movement from scratch in a few short months, with growing support from Church organizations such as the Salvation Army. Flushed with success, they announced a nationwide event for three weeks in September 1971, starting with a rally in London, involving the lighting of a chain of beacons across the country and many local meetings, and finishing with a proposed huge national demonstration of support through the streets of London to force the government to act against 'moral pollution'. They cited events such as the *Oz* trial, Ken Russell's film *The Devils* and the growth of open homosexuality and sex outside marriage as evidence of the degeneration of British life, to try to generate a moral panic and a return to 'Christian values'.

To their credit, many in the Church and the Establishment hung back, perturbed by the hysterical fervour of much of the campaign and concerned by some of the more obviously right-wing hangers-on it attracted. But few people were willing to come out into the open against the Festival; most waited in the wings to see if the public would buy it. Only the counterculture, led very much from the front by GLF, moved against it throughout the country and most strongly in London. Their campaign, shot through with wit and sheer insanity, tipped the scales against the Festival by its own admission.

There was concern throughout the counterculture about the Festival, but it was GLF who sent an undercover volunteer into Festival headquarters. They stole, forged, obstructed and satirized. They organized the single most stunning set-piece disruption of a political rally ever seen in Britain. They obtained a certain amount of public notoriety and a good deal of sneaking sympathy from Fleet Street journalists covering the event, to whom they were, so to speak, a godsend.

> The Festival of Light was put to us in the middle of the summer and we were told it was this group of League of Empire Loyalists and all sorts of strange people and anti-gay. All the information was got for us by people from the Monty Python team and it was funded by Graham Chapman and others via Denis Lemon. Janet went to work in the Festival office and she got tickets and things so that more could be forged. (*Michael James*)

> We would spend whole weekends talking about ways of furthering gay liberation and countering our opponents. John Chesterman had the kind of mind that could work out plans like kidnapping a statue or subverting a book. The Festival action was much more than just Street Theatre people. They were there from other hippie groups and from the underground press. (*Stuart Feather*)

> 'Networking' as a word didn't really exist then but it's what we did over the Festival of Light. We started to put word out through the underground press. I persuaded Janet

to volunteer for the Festival, in their main office, so we had access to all the literature and even the mailing list. We sent out fake mailings on it. For the big final rally, we sent out false parking plans for the coaches, which gave people real hassle. (*John Chesterman*)

The Festival was scheduled to begin with a prestigious rally on 9 September in Central Hall at Westminster. It was seen as their big chance to get the campaign across to a largely sceptical media and gain sympathetic coverage for the following three weeks. So GLF, women's liberation and the hippie underground, coordinated by John Chesterman, went to work. It was not an 'official' GLF action, discussed and sanctioned by the general meeting, because of its urgency. What follows is an account of 'Operation Rupert' as it came to be known and of the final rally in the words of the demonstrators themselves, in a written account by John Chesterman, contemporary documents and extracts from the official story of the Festival of Light, *And There Was Light* by John Capon.

> John Chesterman . . . asked us in advance to think of ideas for something to do, but not to tell anyone what our idea was. We met in the office, identified who our groups were and he gave us a number each. I was number seven and I knew who number six was. He said that once number six was finished, you won't know what they're doing, but you then take off from there in your own time. (*Michael James*)

John handed round a note:

Festival Of Blight – opening ceremony . . . Enter the hall in small groups. Ones or twos. Act unobtrusively. Dress conservatively. Act cool. Make no sign of protest until it is your turn. Do not speak to each other. Sit as close to the centre of your row as possible. Let the previous demonstration finish completely before you start yours. Let everyone settle down and the speeches start again. Part of the purpose is to slow down and delay proceedings. Stick to the agreed form of protest and/or slogans and do so clearly and loudly. Offer passive resistance only. Do not fight back. A general brawl will only confuse the media image. If there is any aggression, let them look like the villains in the press reports. Do not carry anything that could be construed as an offensive weapon. Do not carry dope or anything else illegal. You may be arrested so make any arrangements . . . beforehand. Make no statements to the police until you have legal assistance. They cannot force you to do so. Do not speak to the press or TV.

The Festival of Light demonstration was the most enjoyable one because it was perfectly orchestrated. All the libertarian left groups collaborated and nobody leaked it, which was amazing. We were divided into groups, told what to do and told what our trigger was. (*Tim Clark*)

Because of the skills in forgery displayed by some members of GLF, there were more than enough tickets for anybody who wanted them. Almost the whole organization and many others from Women's Liberation and the counterculture, including a number of street theatre groups, had them.

We all met at Cleopatra's Needle beforehand. Underneath a suit I had a beige lace dress with pearl buttons all the way down the front, long sleeves and a full circle lace skirt. I don't know how I'd managed to crush it all up and get it into my trousers, but they weren't looking for things like that. Peter Flannery and I got there early with our tickets and came in and I chose this space right at the back of the Central Hall in Westminster. It has this incredibly steep rake, so we sat against the back wall in the middle of the row. Gradually, the hall filled up and we saw various people sitting around the hall in various spots. (*Michael James*)

Because of the level of security, many at the protest, even within GLF, were unaware of the degree to which it had been orchestrated.

At Central Hall, I was with a group of people from the Youth Group who were up in the balcony . . . It was left to everybody's common sense and judgement about when to erupt and what to do. All we did have worked out was that different people were assigned different things . . . the group I was in was assigned to erupt and express same-sex affection at a relevant moment. (*Peter Tatchell*)

It had taken just over ten days to organize. Fifteen independently operating but coordinated groups. GLF,

Womens Lib, *IT*, *Oz*, *Frendz* and others. But mainly GLF. Phone calls; meetings; leaflets to be written, printed and distributed; costumes; banners; all the last minute panic, hustle and briefings. About 150 people from almost all the radical groups in London. That was probably the most important thing of all. NCCL came along as observers. Many individuals came on their own and stood on their own in that huge audience. (*John Chesterman's notes*)

The organizers were not taken completely by surprise, although it is possible that there is a certain amount of hindsight in their later remarks.

To cope with any disruptive tactics or opposition within the hall a strong body of marshals was recruited. It could hardly have been visualized how necessary they were going to be . . . Stewards had noticed several members of the audience who, to say the least, looked unlikely to be supporters of the Festival. Among the characters regarded with suspicion were half a dozen young 'nuns'. Stewards quickly spotted that some of them were young men in disguise. To minimize trouble a steward was stationed behind each of the 'nuns' in the audience! (*Capon*)

If this were true, it is unlikely that their later action would have been as successful as it was.

Janet and I had the white mice and Mary Whitehouse recognized Janet. She said, 'Don't I know you?' but she couldn't quite make the connection, and when the disruption was at its height, she turned and gave Janet a very hard look. People did see us release the mice and this woman started hitting me over the head in a frenzied manner with her handbag, yelling 'Jesus loves you' again and again. (*Jane Winter*)

I can remember a woman coming up to Tony Salvis, who was dressed as a bishop. She made some remark about how we were living in a very sinful world, none of us is without sin. Tony turned to her and said 'Don't worry sister, keep right on sinning.' The woman stood there frozen for several seconds with her mouth ajar and looked Tony up and down and just walked off in utter bewilderment. (*Peter Tatchell*)

Where the hell were the others? Had they got past the
heavies on the door? The faces more than fifteen feet away
ran into a blur. Nuns. There should be nuns. One group,
yes, two, three. Were they ours? They looked too genuine.
Jesus, they were actually praying. Damn this sweat. The
stewards at the end of the row were looking this way. The
one with glasses had been down on the Embankment when
we were assembling. Cameras, microphones, choirs,
people. Hundreds, thousands of them. All the galleries full
and more coming in. Somewhere out there were the groups.
They had to be. Waiting for the signal. Had they got the
right positions? How many of the props had they got in?
Stop trembling, it must be a dead give-away. Smile.
Suddenly, a couple of yards away, a small white mouse ran
like slow clockwork across the aisle. They were there.
(*John Chesterman's notes*)

The choir was up on stage in plum velvet cloaks. The first
thing that happened was the applause – we just went on
applauding, loud and slow, which has a certain menace.
(*Bette Bourne*)

Things started and there was clapping going on too long – I
think that was John Chesterman – and so they eventually
twigged and asked him to leave. (*Michael James*)

The objectors who had revealed themselves during the
address by occasional bursts of ill-timed clapping had
nevertheless given Huddleston a hearing . . . Many in the
crowd began to sense that a conflict was taking place.
(*Capon*)

I didn't get slung out because I wasn't disruptive. One of
the things I thought was impressive about it was that when
Trevor Huddleston spoke, nobody interrupted him because
we did all respect him and we thought that he'd made a
mistake. Michael Brown and I wrote him a letter with our
awareness group, asking him not to be part of it and he
actually went and met with this group and eventually
withdrew from the Festival of Light. And I think that's
partially because we didn't just abuse him, didn't throw
things at him but tried to talk with him. Because we knew
in a way that he was more misguided. I remember various
folk groups and then people coming and talking about

sodomy and unchristian marriage and abortion, those were the kind of people who got interrupted. (*Nettie Pollard*)

We got everyone spaced round the hall and then I noticed that opposite the front row where I was sitting there was a row of plugs. I managed to pull two out but it wasn't enough. I kept going back in after being thrown out. The only trouble that we had was pacing people; everybody wanted to do their bit straight away. (*John Chesterman*)

Judy Mackenzie, a folk singer, came in for some extensive heckling, but the protestors really got into their stride with an evangelist called Joan Gibbons, who made the mistake of trying to interact with them. But there was a lot more than talk going on by now.

I remember all the mice being released. Two elderly women holding on to each other suddenly unfurled a banner from the balcony saying 'Cliff For Queen'. It became total mayhem as the incidents started to pile up into each other. We deposited fake religious literature around which had religious covers, so they would be picked up and taken away to read later – only inside it was porn. (*Tim Clark*)

The speakers struggled on. Next was a Danish evangelist, Johannus Facius, brought in to warn the audience of the dreadful things that had befallen his home country after liberalization of the censorship laws.

Facius tried to complete his address but the opposition was making his task impossible . . . Muriel Shepherd, conductor of the London Emmanuel Choir, strode to the rostrum and led choir and audience in a warrior-like rendition of the hymn 'How Great Thou Art' which more than drowned out the protestors' chants. (*Capon*)

Every so often, this choir would get up and sing the same hymn all over again until we quietened down again. They really didn't know what had hit them. There had never been a demo like that. (*Michael James*)

What was most bewildering to the Festival goers was the range of tactics used and the layers of reality abused. People were blowing bubbles peacefully alongside displays of same-sex affection, suddenly disrupted by respectable-looking people erupting into obscenity or arguing with the speakers while mice scuttled around the hall. Talcum powder and pornography inside Christian texts showered down from the balcony. Worst of all, you couldn't trust even the Church.

> Tony Salvis was going round (as a vicar) going 'Bless you, my son.' He did look absolutely right for the part. All these Christians were coming up very worried about these dreadful homosexuals and then eventually he revealed himself in some way and it was 'Oh, no, not another one!' Because he looked so respectable. (*Nettie Pollard*)

And then Malcolm Muggeridge came forward to speak. Because of his thorough recantation of his earlier liberal views he, like Cliff Richard, was a particular target for the demonstrators and he compounded their feelings almost immediately. 'Malcolm Muggeridge was vile. He was the one who said he disliked homosexuals or something like that' (*Nettie Pollard*).

> When Muggeridge made a statement about hating gays, that was when our youth group got up and started kissing. Lesbian couples and gay couples started kissing. We got jeered and abused by the Festival of Light people in the seats around us. Some of them tried to push us and shove us out of the way but we just carried on kissing for about ten minutes. (*Peter Tatchell*)

> When Malcolm Muggeridge started to attack homosexuals, Simon (Benson) stood up a few rows in front of him and said, 'If that is so, then you must really dislike someone who is both homosexual AND Jewish.'
> (*John Chesterman's notes*)

Malcolm Muggeridge was so badly heckled that the choir was brought back on to sing 'How Sweet The Name Of Jesus Sounds' while attempts were made to restore order by the stewards. '[E]ven though the stewards were escorting many demonstrators from the hall (working to a careful and firmly courteous code), it was obvious that the battle would recommence after the last verse' (*Capon*).

> Plainclothes men were practically carrying me down the corridor. 'Think yourself bloody lucky. We want a word with you outside.' Suddenly the corridor was blocked by a large bald-headed man waving a bible. 'You homosexuals

are SCUM. You're nothing but BESTIAL FILTH.' He was
breathing into my face, shaking with rage and hysteria.
'Read this and find out what subversive MUCK you are.'
(*John Chesterman's notes*)

It was round that time that the nuns acted. I was just by
them and I remember someone saying to them 'Pray for us,
sisters' and I couldn't believe they honestly thought they
were nuns. They were a mixture of men and women
including Sue Gilmore. As far as I remember, they started
walking towards the front and then started running and
whooping and about then the mice were released. I don't
know who did that. But they got right up the front and
people were absolutely staggered, they couldn't believe it.
Somehow it hadn't occurred to them that people would
dress as nuns. They thought they were real nuns and they
couldn't cope – it was incomprehensible, these people had
gone mad suddenly. It was the first time we had used nuns
on a gay demonstration in Britain. (*Nettie Pollard*)

Nuns were a borrowing from women's liberation, who had
used them to throw police into confusion at demonstrations such
as those against Wimpy Bars.

Apparently the GLF nuns had originally been part of a
grander plan which had not come to fruition. John Chesterman
tells a story of sitting in the GLF office one day trying to organize
the event when Graham Chapman of Monty Python's Flying Circus
stuck his head round the door.

He was always the sort of person who wouldn't come right
into the room, he just hovered in and out. He said 'D'you
want any camels?' and there was a sort of stunned silence
and someone said 'Yes'. Then, after a few seconds pause,
someone else said, probably joking, 'And nuns.' 'Camels
and nuns' he said, 'Okay.' But there were all sorts of
regulations and licenses, we were supposed to find camel
handlers, for God's sake. So in the end we just had the
nuns.

I was dressed up as an American evangelist's wife with
some bloke from round here, it drew in all sorts of people.
We had football rattles and we were supposed to run up
and down the aisle shouting. It was co-ordinated really well
and so it was triggered. You would have mice and then

stink bombs and snow and the football rattles. Anyway, we got thrown out and I went 'Oh my God, this is terrible, they've just thrown me out and I'm an innocent woman going to the toilet!' Then this husband and I ran down the middle shouting 'Fuck for Jesus' in front of Cliff Richard. Anyhow we got thrown out again. Meanwhile the nuns came out, and all the audience was going 'Yes, sisters!' and then they turned round and started doing the cancan and people realized they were men. (*Julia L*)

The nuns took off in a flying phalanx, down the aisles towards the platform. A banner unravelled with a personal invitation to Cliff Richard to take over the monarchy. On the platform, he had the grace to blush.
(*John Chesterman*)

A mouse, sailing through the air, landed on a lap full of hymn sheets. A section of the audience erupted. Peter (Bette Bourn), unstoppable, was loudly complaining of the atmosphere of violence, the disturbing vibrations and how could he concentrate on God? A woman turned around in front of him. 'There you are' he said, 'I can see the violence in your eyes.' 'No, no, it's the Light of Jesus.'
(*John Chesterman's notes*)

I was eventually thrown out, I was shouting out 'There is violence in this room, there is violence' and me and John Church, who were two trained actors, gave it lots of *voce*.
(*Bette Bourne*)

My cue was Bette Bourne because I knew Bette. Bette was sat across the other side of the hall in the front row dressed as Colonel Blimp, tweeds and things. The demo previous had been a 'Cliff For Queen' banner which had suddenly been unfolded over the front of the balustrade. They had been hustled out with a great noise and pushing and shoving and ranting and raving. Bette started in this wonderful county voice, going 'There is violence going on here, these men are being beaten up, there's no reason for physical violence.' He shocked everyone because it was quite true and it freaked the stewards, who were kicking people, to have it brought to everyone's attention.

They sussed that Bette was part and parcel of the demo and he was asked to leave, but during this time I'd transformed myself from the three-piece suit, slipped out of that, given it to Peter next to me, who'd put it into a carrier bag, plumped out this lovely coffee lace dress, put the shoes and a little bit of eye shadow and lipstick on and a wig. Nobody noticed – we were at the very back of the hall and people were standing up to sing every time there was a demonstration and I was sat down getting ready behind them. The people next to me didn't notice, they were too busy looking to see what was happening around the rest of the room.

It was in the middle of Malcolm Muggeridge's speech. He must have paused and I shot up in the back of this row and screamed out 'I've been saved! I believe! I see the Lord!' just doing this terrible cod impression of a Southern belle who's suddenly seen the light. Being where we were, in the middle of a row with that steep rake, they had to be very gentle getting us out. We didn't fight, Peter and I came quietly but we made sure they came to us first. So they had to get everybody out the first half of the row and shuffle in to us and then we came out with them. There was massive disruption and I had this wonderful huge steep staircase to the exit in full view of everybody in the hall. I came down very slowly with this beautiful dress wafting the lace all over people's heads and continuing on in the same vein 'I believe! I've seen the Lord! I've been saved! Glory Hallelujah!' all the way down these stairs. (*Michael James*)

I remember when Michael [James] said 'I've been saved!' people went 'Hallelujah!' thinking that somebody really had found Christ. I think these Christians were extremely naive really, because I don't think any of us looked right, I mean, this extraordinarily over made-up man dressed as a woman . . . and he was right at the back, up against the wall and stood on his seat or something. I didn't actually know who it was at the time, then gradually he was revealed as a man. (*Nettie Pollard*)

He came down all the steps in full drag with all these people cheering, they didn't know whether to take it seriously. The meeting was totally disrupted, people were taking out the nuns and the elderly because they thought it was going to get violent, but it wasn't violent at all, it was harmless apart from the stewards, but it was extremely powerful in terms of disruption. (*Bette Bourne*)

As if all that was happening within the hall wasn't enough, a small squad from the office collective, led by Martin Corbett, had managed to get into the basement below and interrupted part of the electricity, causing problems for people trying to film and adding to the air of general anarchy. 'Mine was one of the last actions of the day. We just put on Ku Klux Klan drag and stood there demanding that perverts be burnt at the stake . . . we all got thrown out by stewards wearing crosses, who got quite a few thumps in to prove to us that they were the church militant, I suppose' (*Stuart Feather*). Capon's book claims that after Muggeridge, most of the protestors had been cleared from the hall and people coming after, such as Cliff Richard, were able to speak in peace, but this is not the memory of any of the GLF people left. Although the majority of specific 'zap' style actions were over, heckling and small local discussion continued, both inside and outside the Hall.

Even during the course of the meeting while people were being escorted out, Sister Doreen Gemmel (famed for her Church Army work amongst alcoholic women) had slipped away from her seat to talk with the demonstrators outside . . . the opposition . . .was apparently sponsored by the Gay Liberation Front (a group which seeks to promote complete freedom for homosexuals). (*Capon*)

Outside, a nearby pub was crowded with post-mortems and high spirits. Check leaflets for distribution. 'Is someone outside to direct the groups in here? When does the audience come out? Hey, the BBC TV news cameras are out there.' Tony being interviewed. 'Are you a Roman Catholic or Protestant?' 'I'm a priest of the liberation.' Crowds sweeping out. Leaflets. 'Read our side of the story.' The leaflet with crosses on it is easiest to give away. They take them as a reflex action.

The bald headed steward is there again. 'Get out of here. You are ANIMALS. You are intruding on our privacy.' 'It's a public meeting.' 'Only if you have tickets.' I give him a handful. Eleven or twelve. He tears them in two and throws them on the floor.

'Litter.' I remind him gently, and dodge.
(*John Chesterman's notes*)

I don't think anyone got arrested, which is fairly amazing.
There was an attempt to arrest somebody outside for
kissing a policeman, but it didn't work. There was this
enormous sea of lesbians and gay men suddenly around the
policeman and I remember him looking round and
thinking, I don't think this is worth it, and he shuffled off.
It was very, very funny indeed. You often saw the police at
a disadvantage because they didn't know how to handle us.
I remember there was a stall with Christian books and
people from GLF started stealing them. I got one of Trevor
Huddleston's books that someone gave me and I said to
Paul Theobald, 'I don't think we should be stealing these
books' and he said, 'Of course we should.' He believed it
was right but I'm not sure.

There was a definite decision to try and talk to people as
they came out. It was a really nice atmosphere and I
genuinely think that talking to some of those people did
have an effect and they did think twice about whether or
not they should be involved. Because they weren't just
being shouted at. Although we did such outrageous things
we were real people prepared to talk with them about it. I
went to the thing OutRage! disrupted in Brighton, the
Christian family thing about three years ago, and what
happened there was that they rushed the stage and got
dragged out and then as everybody was leaving they went
through a cordon of angry lesbians and gay men shouting
abuse at them. I just thought, what is the point of this?
Because we're neither preventing them from doing this nor
are we making them think. All we're doing is making them
think we're rabble. (*Nettie Pollard*)

The whole area of pavement outside the entrance is covered
with arguing groups as a public discussion gets under way
with the Children of God. Inside there is a confrontation
with those of the organizers and speakers who are prepared
to talk. The Jesus-freak, the beautiful one with long blond
hair and flowing beard, the one with pale blue eyes,
screams, 'You people are an abomination.'
(*John Chesterman's notes*)

The *Daily Mirror* the next morning dwelt heavily upon the
'five bogus nuns muscle in on anti-porn rally' line. 'They astonished
the three thousand people in the hall by fending off hefty stewards

who tried to stop them.' The *Guardian* on the following day, in humorous coverage, spoke of a dozen specific incidents which they estimated used about 150 protesters and gave special mention to the nuns, Michael's Southern belle and Bette's county colonel. 'Everyone got into a discussion and that was good. We were making everyone aware of this thing called gay liberation and we were rather scoffed at at the time by the *Guardian* and the *Standard*' (*Bette Bourne*).

But although the coverage over the next few days must have looked to some gay liberationists as if it were trivializing events, this was probably the best thing that could have happened. Instead of feeling forced to take the Festival seriously, ordinary people were effectively being given permission to laugh at them. If they can't stand up to a bunch of poofs, the underlying message went, they can't be that powerful. And news of the opposition spread and encouraged others to attempt disruptions at events organized locally. Even the official history is forced to admit that opposition reared its head in unlikely ways and places. 'At Rochdale, the White Panthers, a hippy group, caused some trouble . . .' (*Capon*). The core of national action was the lighting of a series of beacons, to symbolize the alerting of the country to sin, the bringing of light and fire to cleanse it. In at least one place, the beacon was mysteriously burnt down the night before the planned ceremony. People with no connections whatsoever with gay rights or the counterculture began to oppose the evangelical tactics of the Festival and discuss its implications for censorship and repression. Obscure bye-laws were called into play to stop rallies and early environmentalists found very good reasons against huge bonfires in nature spots.

The Festival ploughed on towards its climactic day of events in London on 25 September. A Mass Rally in Trafalgar Square was planned (co-ordinated by the Rev. Eddy Stride, who later caused concern amongst gay activists with long memories when he turned up on the board of Mildmay Mission Hospital, one of the first AIDS hospices). This was to be followed by a march reversing the route taken by GLF's own march against the age of consent less than a month earlier, to Hyde Park where there would be an even huger rally and series of events. Stickers went out advertising an alternative 'Festival of Life', to also take place in the Park at the same time. Official Festival of Light T-shirts, bearing their logo of a crucible of flames (much of the imagery used by the Festival had disturbing echoes of fascism) had been stolen and then copied by

GLF people, who wore them with gay badges for maximum confusion.

With Janet in the Festival office and John and others behind the scenes, fake parking plans in mailings in the name of Henry Hole, the Chief Steward for the rally, persuaded delegations heading for Trafalgar Square to park illegally, or miles away. 'Many letters were sent on Wednesday or Thursday to some who were organizing coach parties . . . saying that due to overcrowding in the Square, their group should bypass the first rally and go straight to the Hyde Park rally which would not now start until 6pm' (*Capon*).

The Festival of Life was advertised throughout the underground press, and most of the opposition went straight to Hyde Park for it, but a hard core of GLF and Women's Liberation decided first to visit Trafalgar Square.

> Michael [James] was a lady schoolteacher with a cane, Nicholas Bramble was the Spirit of Porn, Paul Theobald and Carla and others were dressed as riot police carrying the coffin of freedom, Mary McIntosh and others as choirboys, Michael Redding, Chris Blaby and Douglas MacDougall as nuns, me as Mary Whitehouse. We all met in Covent Garden, in Henrietta Street because we knew there would be heavy security nearer the Square, and we changed into our costumes in shop doorways. We got as far as the steps of St Martins, where I conducted the choir in 'All Things Bright And Beautiful'. We had planned to join the crowd and process to the rally in Hyde Park but we got as far as the south of the Square and we were blocked by the police. (*Stuart Feather*)

> I was in the choir singing at Trafalgar Square. We knew the bit about the rich man in his castle, the poor man at his gate . . . that may have been the only verse we sung. We had to repeat it over and over. (*Mary McIntosh*)

> I was part of a little Street Theatre and we all organized ourselves into heterosexual couples and were chained together as heterosexual couples. There was a sort of sex symbol and a business man and I think I was a down-trodden housewife, and we had discussions with the people around us. So we formed this straggling little procession and we did manage to get to the base of the column . . . it

was a pretty effective protest because people couldn't quite suss whether we were hostile or not. We came up the back of the plinth and generally infiltrated into the crowd and the mass of Christians were basically confused as to whether this was just some odd bit of the entertainment or not. (*Sarah Grimes*)

Richard Dipple was carrying a cross and there were thousands in Trafalgar Square, it was jammed to the gills. There was another group singing hymns and carols, I never knew who they were. Stuart stopped to conduct them. Then there were Womens Lib, they had a demo with prams and dolls and things. They were going across the top of the Square in front of the National Gallery. We slipped down by South Africa House and sidled up to the back of the column, no problem. I was a schoolteacher and I had all my kids in school costume, roped together and I was the oppressive schoolmarm with the cane and an earphone type wig. We had no intention of disturbing the rally itself at all. We were grossly outnumbered. What we were going to do was march with them or beside them. Mary Whitehouse and people were at the front. The police got freaked out – we were outside the railings on the pavement away from the Square itself, looking down towards Whitehall and they told us to stand there and we said, 'We want to stand here, we're not going anywhere else,' and this police inspector or sergeant or something freaked out and they started pushing us and pushing us until they hemmed us in to that little space between two of the lions. Well, we had nowhere to go but up, because they were getting heavy, so up we went and we were quite happy there, we'd said do not go round the front – I think somebody might have done.
(*Michael James*)

They invaded the rostrum and the fake Mary Whitehouse, Stuart, was up there with the proper one. There were several Mary Whitehouses and very funny they looked.
(*John Chesterman*)

We were gathering a crowd at the back, we had no microphones, so we were quite happy to have our little discourse. But of course then the police got up and of

course we could only go higher and they got very rough and grabbed hold of me by the arms and legs and I was hauled to the ground. I was terrified I was going to be thrown down another six feet from the plinth.
(*Michael James*)

There were police chasing transvestites in all directions, smoke bombs going off . . . it looked like a revolution.
(*John Chesterman*)

About two-thirds of the way through the rally, a procession entered the Square and marched along the pavement in front of the National Gallery. Led by a mock Christ carrying a cross they paraded round the Square with banners containing four letter words and other slogans bearing a casket labelled 'Coffin of Liberty'. They were preceded by some women chained together and dressed as, amongst other things, schoolgirls and young children. They made their way to the south side of the Square where the column and plinth are nearest to the road . . . [they] got hemmed in and jumped up on to the plinth to continue their demonstration. At a given signal the police moved in on the plinth and man-handled the demonstrators from their lofty perch. Some were brought to the ground and a struggle ensued before they were taken away in a police van. Several of the Festival of Light supporters who were watching the incident felt that the police had over-reacted to the situation. (*Capon*)

I saw this police inspector who'd started it all coming towards me. I was laying down with one leg free and I just gathered that leg up and shot for his balls. And I hit him, right in the balls. But he never knew it was me, because there were so many people there, all around us. But I got him. Then the next thing I knew, I was being see-sawed off the edge of this plinth. Two policemen had me, one round the neck and one round my legs and they were sawing me backwards and forwards on the edge of the plinth. Then they dropped to the ground and I was being carried by the arms and legs, looking up through all these Christians who'd started marching off. They were screaming 'Hang him! Birch him!' I thought, 'Yeah, that's exactly where you're at, isn't that exactly it.' I felt quite good about that, 'I've dug you out now, you've said what you really believe, we've got the truth.' Once you get that, you know what you're dealing with. (*Michael James*)

The officer in charge who authorized the heavy tactics also levelled an interesting accusation against GLF during verbal exchanges. As the *Sunday Times* reported the next morning, 'Police warned them that they were suspected of being associated with the Angry Brigade.'

They accused us of being the Angry Brigade, that was what some Assistant Chief Constable said to us. We were pushed back against Nelson's Column and our only way of escape was to get up on to it, so we did. The 'choirboys' were at the bottom of the plinth, so we all started singing 'All Things Bright And Beautiful' again. The police were chasing us all over the plinth and they arrested some people. And on the north side of the plinth were Mary Whitehouse, Lord Longford, Cliff Richard and Malcolm Muggeridge and so on. Michael Redding was accused of waving a cucumber obscenely while dressed as a nun. Some people escaped and made it to Hyde Park, but the police swooped on them and arrested them there. (*Stuart Feather*)

I was the only GLF woman arrested in the Square. Mary O'Shea heard a senior officer point at me and say 'Get that one.' Richard [Dipple], who was Jesus, took off his robe and crown and disappeared into the crowd. I was taken to Bow Street and put into a cell with the women from Women's Street Theatre who'd come as the nuclear family. Michele Roberts was dressed as the vicar's wife, Alison Fell was the vicar's son. They had come as a family and chained themselves together, so when the police picked up one of them they got the lot. (*Carla Toney*)

A few of us decided to use the occasion to try to expose the perverse morality of the Festival organizers. On the one hand they condemned lesbian and gay people for victimless consenting relationships, yet on the other hand they were totally silent about the war in Bangladesh which was resulting in the death and displacement of millions of people. We got some collecting tins from the organization that was fundraising to help refugees in Bangladesh and went amongst the crowd in Trafalgar Square, soliciting donations. We challenged them over their concern about homosexuality and their apparent disinterest in the starvation and murder of people in Bangladesh. It very successfully put them on the spot over their distorted sense of moral priorities. They found it very embarrassing. (*Peter Tatchell*)

I remember people shouting 'Jesus was gay!' and the Christians going 'No he wasn't' and me thinking actually I think that was a stupid thing to shout. And there was a lot of shouting at Cliff Richard, I remember. (*Nettie Pollard*)

I was slung into the van. They'd got Michael Redding previously because he was a nun. I don't know how they'd managed to get him. Douglas MacDougall was also a nun, I think there were three nuns and I think one of them escaped. Whoever got into the green van – the women were already there, they'd already picked the women up from the top and they'd done nothing. So it was clear that we were not going to be allowed to express our opinions at all. We were taken down to Cannon Row police station, just by Old Scotland Yard and there were more women there when we arrived, they'd got the singers and the dykes, they'd picked them off first. They knew what to look for, they knew who to go for. We were eventually bailed about nine or ten o'clock that night. (*Michael James*)

The Festival continued on its way to Hyde Park, dogged by the Youth Group and others. A group of several hundred demonstrators had gathered at Marble Arch to jeer and throw stink bombs as they passed. Although the Festival of Life organizers blamed this on GLF, it seems to have been mainly straight hippie protesters. At the Park, there was an enormous police presence. Those there for the Festival of Life, rather than Light, were prone to sudden arrest for little more than sneezing. The most beautiful of the GLF banners, with three interlocking circles, in red, purple and white, was confiscated by police as an offensive weapon and never returned; it is thought to have been destroyed at a later date. Paul Theobald, who was marched off and charged with insulting behaviour, can remember no reason at all for his arrest. Someone from the office collective, probably Martin Corbett, took a number of photographs of the day and they show Tony Salvis, once again a vicar, preaching beside a small gay placard and the performance of a piece of street theatre, both of which played to a large and appreciative-looking audience. Though possibly not as appreciative as the audience for another character, Father Fuck of Tooting, who later distributed his story to a GLF meeting:

> We always have cannabis in the Church of Aphrodite at Elmbourne Road in Tooting . . . we keep it in the chalice on the altar. We . . . said that our Church's contribution to the Festival of Light will be a sacrificial cake baked in the shape of a phallus with half an ounce of cannabis as one of the ingredients, that we'll take it to Hyde Park and share it with the people as the sacrament of our Church . . . three of us took it to Hyde Park . . . I got up on our sacrificial altar and a crowd of about 100 heads gathered round me.
>
> I told my listeners that the prick is the symbol of our Church because the prick with a lovely pair of balls is the symbol of life and the cross is the symbol of death. The heads were saying 'Let's have the sacrament now' . . . I performed the religious ceremony: I broke off the knob of the prick, crushed it in my fingers and as the crumbs were falling to the ground I was praying aloud For Peace, For Love, For Freedom. Having thus prayed I broke off another piece of it for myself and handed the rest to the people to be shared as the sacrament of our Church.
>
> Man, you've never seen a faster castration of the prick. It just disappeared in ten seconds . . . great happiness all round! . . . Later I got a bit closer to the Jesus people, put up our altar, got on it and started to indoctrinate my listeners . . . about 100 people were listening to me, some Jesus people, some heads . . . I was grabbed by a bobby and about six of them started to drag me to the waiting police van . . . A girl, a psychologist, walks beside us and keeps asking the policeman 'Why are you arresting this man?' . . . she too is pulled into the van. Then they drive us to Hyde Park police station. A bobby says to me 'What's your name?' 'Reverend Father Fuck' says I. 'Occupation?' 'Minister of religion' says I. 'Will you sign for bail?' 'Yes' says I. 'In what name?' 'Reverend Father Fuck' says I. 'I can't accept that name' says he and they lock me up in the cell till Monday. (*Father Fuck*)

Everyone was charged with breach of the peace and put in
the cells, but Nicholas Bramble got charged with assault,
which was much more serious. I was opposite him in the
line when they charged him and all it was, was that a
policeman had cut his little finger on Nicholas Bramble's
diamante bracelet while arresting him. Nicholas was a
trained dancer and when the policeman grabbed him, he'd
locked his arms and the policeman's hand had slipped. He
ended up having a separate trial from the rest of us, but he
was found not guilty. We went to court in the drag we were
arrested in. I was Mary Whitehouse, in the dock with Paul
Theobald and Chris Blaby. We used friends as Mackenzie
lawyers and a Catholic priest gave evidence to say that he
hadn't been offended, but wherever nuns appeared they
were found guilty even though the rest of us weren't.
Nicholas Bramble felt that there was very little support
within GLF for the people who'd been arrested and he said
so at a meeting. That was when we began to separate from
the Marxist elements – it became the theoretical and
practical wings, if you like, of gay liberation.
(*Stuart Feather*)

We came up at Bow Street and we all had Mackenzie
lawyers, defending ourselves. Michael Redding appeared
first, not in a frock I think. He was done for being a nun,
they accused him of masturbating with a cucumber. I had
big floppy trousers, a wrapover dress and a long maxi-coat
and an Indian headscarf wound round. I don't think I was
wearing make-up. My nails were painted though. Michael
was found guilty. I went in and the magistrate screamed at
me straight away, 'Take that hat off!' I thought, what on
earth's he talking about? He said to me, 'You take that hat
off!' and I said 'but I'm not wearing a hat.' I wasn't, I was
wearing a scarf, not a hat. He said 'Take that thing off your
head' and I said 'Excuse me, I'm coming here to be tried on
a charge, what I wear is entirely up to me, it's not up to
you, you don't buy my clothes, you've got no say over what
I wear.' 'I'll also charge you with contempt of court.' I said
'I'm not in contempt of court, I'm in contempt of you.' 'Get
out of here and don't come back while you've got the hat
on!' So I'm led from the well of the court by two detectives,
but just as I'm leaving Douglas [MacDougall] is coming in

with a full circle skirt and a broderie anglaise blouse.
And I thought, go on girl, you deal with that now.

Douglas came out and I was called back into court and
the magistrate said to me 'I see you still intend to remain
contemptuous of this court' and I said 'I'm not
contemptuous, but as I pointed out to you, you do not buy
my clothes and you've got no right to tell me what to wear.
This is a free country.' He went 'Hmph! lets get on with it
then.' So we got on with the case and the policeman who
arrested me was lying his head off and I cross-examined
him. He accused me of shouting this obscene rhyme, it was
very bad and I thought 'what!' and said something very
dismissive like 'If I'm going to make up rhymes I'm sure I
can do better than that.' I said 'That was made up in a
police canteen and it sounds like it.' We hadn't been
shouting anything obscene at all, not as far as I was aware.

The dock was actually about a foot away from the
magistrate, I could reach over and touch him. He said 'Tell
me what happened' and I said 'Can I start from the
beginning?' I went into the background of the demonstration
and my part in it. He said 'What were you?' and I
explained I was meant to represent a repressive
schoolmarm. He said 'Did you have button boots?' and I
said 'Oh yes, I did.' And he said 'I think I'll dismiss this
case' and he did. Obviously a shoe fetishist.
(*Michael James*)

The elements of camp and theatricality gave a lot of the
actions a strong humorous edge which police officers often
found hard to deal with. They were used to responding to
belligerent macho left-wing demonstrations, but because
GLF didn't fit that traditional pattern they found it a bit
unnerving. If we had followed the orthodox leftist way of
doing things with the clenched fist, all very serious and
quite threatening, the police would have come down on us
heavier and quicker. Because some officers could see the
amusing side to what we were doing it was psychologically
disarming for them . . . The GLF style of protest was
political jujitsu – we threw the police off balance by not
conforming to their expectations. (*Peter Tatchell*)

It was interesting to contrast it with the peace movement
[demonstration] later in the seventies in Trafalgar Square;

we felt that what was being proposed in Ireland wasn't
peace but surrender, and when we tried to argue with
people in the Square those times we were nearly lynched.
We were hit and poked with umbrellas and things and
threatened. It was a relief to get arrested. There was a lot
more violence there, but maybe that was partly our tactics
because we were being disruptive and heckling whereas
with the Festival of Light we were being festive. We had a
lot of debate about the Festival, how it was moral
rearmament and fundamentalist. We did see it as very
dangerous. It might have developed as something rather
unpleasant and I think it was one of those rare events that
[the opposition] succeeded in its objectives. Everyone loved
putting energy into doing it, it was a target made for us.
(*Sarah Grimes*)

Thank God for Mary Whitehouse. She was a gift, she
turned herself into a caricature. She could have been much
worse. It was humour that really worked for us. My main
complaint about OutRage! is that they are far too serious.
It was very much a youth thing, young people were coming
out and most of GLF was very young. I wish there had
been more good writers, what we needed was a Jane
Austen because it was a social comedy more than anything
else. (*John Chesterman*)

Organizers of the Festival of Light had confidently predicted
100,000 people would attend their final event. They themselves
estimated that 60,000 attended but most independent observers
put the figure at nearer 35,000. The balloon had burst, and from
then on the Festival confined itself to a more nebulous campaign
against moral degeneracy which did not rely on wider public
support, burning beacons or mass rallies.

But the last word on the Festival of Light should really go to
its official historian, explaining why it was not the expected
success: 'the media in general and the national newspapers in
particular must stand condemned for their inadequate reporting of
the Festival. When asked by one of the Festival organizers what he
knew about the Festival of Light, an ordinary man in the street
replied, "Isn't it something to do with mice and people dressed up
as nuns?"' (*Capon*).

Chapter twelve

Everything You Always Wanted

The key to the protests was the participation and empowerment of members and the imparting of a message to those who witnessed what we did. –Peter Tatchell

FROM August to October of 1971 was the heyday of London GLF, when it must have seemed that they could do no wrong. *Come Together* was appearing regularly and growing ever more packed. Their demonstrations and campaigns were the envy of the rest of the underground. Their *Manifesto* was written and published and GLF was spreading throughout Britain. Media coverage overall was remarkably positive – more so than for many years to come for the gay movement. Meetings in Notting Hill were attracting upwards of 400 to 500 people each week. There were more than a dozen working groups and rival meetings every night of the week – something for everyone, whatever their interest.

I immediately gravitated to the Action Group. I was nineteen. A lot of the people in and around the Manifesto Group were university graduates, lecturers – I'd left school at the age of sixteen and felt a bit out of my depth – it was a bit difficult to relate to initially. Also I wasn't so interested in the abstract theoretical debates, I wanted to relate ideas to action. My first impression of GLF was of a glorious chaotic enthusiasm. There was a heady mix of idealism, adventure, humour and daring. We were taking on the straight world, challenging assumptions in a way that no lesbian and gay people had done before. That was both a profound personal liberation and a very exciting political experience as well.

GLF always had a very clever way of using theatricality and humour to defuse hostility and generate interest in what we were doing, whereas the traditional left wing had always focused its efforts around a march from Hyde Park to Trafalgar Square followed by set-piece speeches by celebrities. GLF got away from that boring routine by doing actions which enabled everyone to participate and which also were fun to be part of. The thinking was that if you can make a zap interesting and exciting then it's much easier to impart your message . . . so that passers-by would want to stop and listen to what we had to say. I don't think GLF was particularly media aware. There wasn't such a sophisticated understanding about the way in which the media could be used for political communication.

As with any leaderless organization, GLF had moments of absurd chaos and disorganization. But this . . . also made the organization very accessible. No-one had to sign a membership form or pay a subscription to get involved. By coming along to the meetings people were automatically members with a right to speak, vote, decide policy . . . People literally came to a meeting and got involved . . . The meetings were often fraught with angry scenes over questions of politics. When things were going fine, they were wonderful. When things were going wrong, they were a sheer nightmare. Despite the anarchic mess, meetings sometimes flowed very smoothly and with great energy and enthusiasm. At other times there were incredible political and personal disputes which got very angry and bitter. Yet somehow we managed to surmount the disagreements and antagonisms to go on month after month organizing successful protests. (*Peter Tatchell*)

One series of actions were a particularly smooth collaboration between Counter-Psychiatry, Action and Street Theatre. The campaign against David Reuben's offensive pop-sexology manual, *Everything You Always Wanted To Know About Sex – but were afraid to ask*, begun in February against the hardback publishers W. H. Allen, was renewed with vigour in October 1971 upon the announcement of the paperback reissue by Pan Books, a highly respected 'popular' publisher. The book came out on Friday 8 October and on the following Monday an emergency meeting at the office in Caledonian Road came up with a variety of strategies, both overt and covert.

> It wasn't just demos, we also approached University College who were going to have it as a textbook for students and I think we succeeded in getting that dropped. The Action Group did the very naughty thing that was done, printing the little card saying Pan would give a refund which went inside the book and the publishers, I gather, did get quantities of them back. (*Nettie Pollard*)

'The sticker in the Reuben book was one of John Chesterman's ideas' (*Stuart Feather*). The insert, reproduced in the plate section is a sly little masterpiece of disruption. Purporting to be from Pan Books themselves, it simply offers a full refund to anyone not satisfied with the book provided that they write in with their reasons. Other, less subtle, stickers merely carried a health warning and were obviously from GLF.

> I think the stickers were absolutely wonderful because they were completely illegal and very GLF and great. I thought the demonstrations were good. I thought it was very funny when Peter Tatchell went into Foyles or wherever, getting a whole stand and throwing the books into the street. I saw him do that and it was just superb. It was at the demonstration in Charing Cross Road, we'd had the Street Theatre with Barbara Klecki and the liver and Lyndsay Levy [a demonstration of the abortion section]. If you read that bit, about the coat hanger, it's just so repulsive. I don't use the word pornographic because I reserve it for things that are nice, but it was lurid and sort of cheaply titillating detail giving terrible information to someone who might then try it out themselves. Completely repugnant, I don't know how it got published. Well, I do . . . (*Nettie Pollard*)

The Street Theatre Group acted out some of the recommendations in Dr Reuben's book, using a coat hanger and a lump of raw liver. As so often happens on these occasions, huge crowds of bystanders gathered around them with a mixture of shock, bewilderment, confusion and amusement. It was mostly Street Theatre in Charing Cross Road. There were a couple of small raiding parties which went into Foyles and a couple of other bookshops to put stickers on the covers. (*Peter Tatchell*)

I remember going down Charing Cross Road and zapping all the stands, I remember throwing them over with Annie Brackx. (*Angie Weir*)

Although this demonstration on 30 October gained national press coverage (and several arrests as police chased people in and out of the various entrances of Foyles), the campaign was pursued on many other fronts.

Some of us did bookshop raids damaging the copies of the book and stickering them with warnings. I was travelling all over the country doing store design and window display for Richards [the dress shops]. My job involved me travelling to branches all over the country. Every lunchtime I'd make a point of going out to the local W. H. Smith's or John Menzies and inserting leaflets into every available copy of Dr Reuben's book. I must have distributed a couple of thousand over several weeks.

[On] repeat visits, rather than just reinsert the leaflets I decided to be a bit more confrontational. I remember walking into W. H. Smith's in St Albans and going up to the main counter where they had a huge display showcase of Reuben's book. I lifted it off its pedestal and demanded to see the manager and as he came towards me I walked straight up to him holding this huge showcase of books and said 'Excuse me, sir, I cannot understand why you are carrying such an unscientific and prejudiced book. This book is very damaging to lesbian and gay people, it's just promoting intolerance.' He looked at me speechless. I said 'Are you going to give me your assurance that these books will be removed from display?' and he said, 'I can't give you that assurance.' I said, 'I'm asking you once more, are you going to give me your assurance?' He waffled on. So I lifted the whole thing above my head and threw all the books onto the other display mountings which collapsed all over the place. He just stood there in disbelief and I turned round and walked out of the shop. (*Peter Tatchell*)

I did things like go into shops and tear the covers slightly, so that they couldn't sell them. I don't really support doing that sort of thing now because I think it's more important to let people read things like that and then put the counter arguments, but at the time we were all so horrified and my idea particularly was, imagine some very shy gay person or anyone else, because it was so awful about women and everyone, getting hold of that and then being completely suicidal. I just thought, it would have such a terrible effect on an isolated person. We got quite a few places to withdraw them. I went to Highgate Books near where I lived and I said you should withdraw this because it's terrible. They said, we don't believe in censorship and I thought well, I don't really either . . . (*Nettie Pollard*)

The climax of the campaign was a demonstration on 10 December outside the offices of Pan themselves near St James Park. This time, the theatricals involved quite complex props in order to illustrate the book's contention that gay men used vegetables and light bulbs for sexual pleasure and women used coat hangers for abortions.

For weeks before the zap I collected dead lightbulbs from every Richards shop I visited. On the day I turned up with a couple of sacks full, probably about 200 light bulbs. As we stormed into the head office I dumped them in the foyer, across the carpet. Other people threw piles of coat hangers, cucumbers, carrots and other phallic type vegetables. We met at St James Park tube station and walked along to Pan books headquarters trying to be discreet carrying this huge, gigantic fifteen-foot cucumber made out of chicken wire and papier mache. All the time we were expecting some casually passing policeman to notice us and call for assistance. We did get inside the head office and this huge cucumber was duly presented to the staff. When the police arrived their reaction was a mixture of belligerence and amusement. They knew what we were doing was illegal but they didn't quite know how to handle a fifteen-foot cucumber. So to speak. (*Peter Tatchell*)

The cucumber for the Pan Books demo was made in the office. I have a feeling Paul Bunting might have had something to do with it. I remember Denis Lemon was one of the people who was buggered with it, had it poked into his bottom at one point in the demonstration. That was quite a fun demonstration and I remember that the transsexual group were particularly keen to be properly represented there. I don't blame them because the book is unspeakable about transsexuality. Some people said, oh no, this is a lesbian and gay event and they were saying, but we are deeply offended. (*Nettie Pollard*)

Pan Books were rather less accommodating than W. H. Allen had been. Ralph Vernon-Hunt, the Managing Director, sent for the police and refused to meet a delegation or to answer any letters on the book. A GLF leaflet called him a 'lovable old publisher who stands to make a mint of money out of libels on nice people' and put out another leaflet saying:

> Oh sister! Oh brother! Don't trust this book. Don't let your kids think it's right. Don't let your granny have it . . . You might be a homosexual girl, or the parent of one. This is what you will read in this Pan book: that you are to be reckoned a prostitute and that if you find someone to love, you will 'betray and deceive each other with monotonous regularity' . . . you might now be a thalidomide child old enough to read this Pan book, or the parent of one. This is what you read: 'the sight of a dozen or so bright healthy youngsters playing in a schoolyard, cheerfully flipping their flippers, totally unaware that all children aren't that way, is hard to take. Some day they will have to leave their special school and face a world full of arms and legs.' Are they performing seals – are we – Pan books? You might be a homosexual guy, or the parent of one. This is what you read in the Pan book: that you 'thrive on danger', that you 'rarely know the names' of those you love, that 'random and reckless selection of partners' is your trademark, that 'mutilation, castration and death' are 'sadly all part of the homosexual game'.

The leaflet went on to urge readers to action. 'Well, you say, what can I do about it? Tell people. Warn them off it. Try MPs and the usual channels. Write to yours. We cannot, on this leaflet, suggest that you take more positive action. Unfortunately. That is your own decision. It depends on how much you care. We care.'

Another ground-breaking action that Autumn had a more sombre tone. Understanding of the Nazi role in exterminating gays as well as Jews and other 'racial undesirables' in their concentration camps was around within GLF from a very early stage. One of the earliest versions distributed of the Demands contained a poetic statement on the back which ended 'In the name of the tens of thousands who wore the badge of homosexuality in the gas chambers and concentration camps, who have no children to remember and whom your histories forget, we demand honour, identity and liberation.' It was therefore not surprising that GLF should propose to join in the national commemoration of the dead of the Second World War on Remembrance Sunday 1971 and to begin the ceremony, carried on to this day by other lesbian and gay groups, of laying a wreath at the Cenotaph after the march past of service veterans.

On the day, some fifteen members of GLF wearing pink triangles – at that time an unusual symbol and not widely known – bore a wreath to the Cenotaph with a card inscribed with a variation on the above wording: 'In Memory/of the countless thousands of homosexuals branded with the pink triangle/of homosexuality who died in the gas chambers and in the concentration camps of Europe/who have no children to remember them and your histories forget/We Remember/The Gay Liberation Front.' The delegation were told by police that they must remove their badges as they were 'too political'. Unusually for GLF, they complied in order to be allowed to lay the wreath, but within minutes staff from the Department of Environment, in charge of the event, tore up the label. Another was made but this was torn off within the hour and replaced with one saying 'honoured remembrance on behalf of HMS Hull'. People from GLF noted that members of the Campaign for Homosexual Equality who had been expected to turn up failed to show, probably in fear of GLF's usual belligerence towards any form of authority. Ironically, within a couple of years the responsibility of organizing the annual ceremony was taken up by them.

But at least one GLF person had not put up lightly with such interference. As Alan Wakeman partially related in *Come Together* 11 (he noted with resigned annoyance that despite the pious disclaimer that no article had been censored, his had been cut by over half), he had been arrested in a similar but less public incident.

> The day before Remembrance Sunday last year, I was walking past Westminster Abbey . . . In the gardens of the Abbey a field of remembrance crosses had been set out. Many of these were for specific named groups and the field did its job – that is, it set me remembering. I thought in particular of the thousands of homosexuals who were interned and executed by the Nazis. No one knows exactly

how many – because no one has ever bothered to count. Like the Jews, they were made to wear special identifying marks . . . On this particular November Saturday, thinking about all these things, I was moved to buy a cross with a poppy on it, like the hundreds of others that had been set down. If I had a pink triangle, I would have put that on it, but this was a spontaneous act and all I had with me to identify the cross with those it specially commemorated was a GLF badge. I fixed this to it and put it in the ground.

He was subsequently challenged by a young policeman who, when Alan took out a notebook to take his details, arrested him and took him back to the station. The case ended up with Alan convicted of a minor public order offence on entirely fictional evidence, although, as he remembers, the young copper had the grace to be somewhat ashamed at having to go through with giving false evidence in cold blood as a result of his momentary loss of temper.

Following the highly successful disruption of the Miss World competition in 1970, it was inevitable that Women's Liberation would make another attempt on the following year's competition. After their involvement in GLF's Operation Rupert and GLF's support of their Wimpy Houses actions, it was a natural move for GLF to get heavily involved. John Chesterman remembers liaising with a woman called Stephanie and others over a plan to link hands and surround the Hall. Many GLF people took part and a women's liberation newsletter shortly afterwards contained a letter from someone commenting on how well organized the GLF people had been, even bringing their own loudhailer. Bette Bourne is well remembered as playing the compere, Dirty Dick.

> The Miss World protest was a joint action with the Women's Liberation movement. There were possibly two hundred or more people involved. The contrast between the protesters and the audience was a cultural chasm miles wide. There we were in our countercultural hippie garb and street theatre fancy dress. There they were with high society people wearing diamond tiaras, mink furs and tuxedos. We aimed to ridicule the whole Miss World event. One guy was dragged up as Miss Ulster, swathed in bloody bandages. Others were attired in parodies of Miss World outfits like Miss Used, Miss Conceived and Miss Treated. They paraded on an alternative catwalk outside the main entrance of the hall.

The Miss World contestants arrived in a bus at the side of the hall. We had scouts all around the building to alert everyone to their arrival. As soon as the signal was given, the main body of protesters moved to surround the bus. The contestants had to wait for police reinforcements to arrive to drag us out of the way and make a corridor to let them pass. One group did try to break the television cables which relayed the event to outside broadcast units, but because of the previous year's disruption [a BBC van had been blown up] there were a lot of plainclothes police officers and people were quickly pounced on.

When the contest was over the audience came down the main staircase to the foyer, which was surrounded by people banging on the plate glass windows, to the point where they looked like they were going to break. I can still vividly remember the trembling, shocked looks on the faces of these wealthy prestigious people as they came down to the foyer expecting to be able to go to their cars and instead facing a sea of protesters who had completely blocked the exits. For the next hour there was a running battle with the police as they tried to clear us out of the way and get the guests out of the hall. (*Peter Tatchell*)

Julia L remembers a woman called Jenny being held by police against a wall and Steven Bradbury, one of the new style of radical drag queens then emerging, being arrested. But overall there were few arrests in comparison to the level of disruption.

Many of the protesters treated taunting the police as a game, pushing them to their limit and then melting away only to reappear elsewhere. But there were a few people present who were aware that it was a dangerous one and becoming increasingly so. The area was crawling with plainclothes and Special Branch, in hopes of catching the terrorists responsible for the previous year's bomb. There are tales of being followed away from the scene by mysterious and threatening men, of walking faster to get into a well-lit area. John Chesterman felt that this mystery was quite something 'until just afterwards I met someone who'd just been released from prison after trying to burn down the Imperial War Museum, which made me feel like I'd really just been at a party in comparison'.

Apart from these set-piece demonstrations there were also many other events going on for GLF. There was another London think-in in October to consider strategies to deal with the large meetings and high turnover of new members, a special Gay Day at the Labour Party Conference in conjunction with Brighton GLF, a series of Street Theatre appearances at various Magistrates Courts in support of people arrested at the Festival of Light, the Skegness and Holloway Prison actions, support for abortion and anti-internment marches through London, a Politics of Psychology conference at which GLF spoke, street selling of *Come Together* and the founding of the first local London GLF group in Camden.

In one week in December 1971, someone involved in GLF had the following choices:

On Thursday 9th, they could go to Media Workshop (where people were discussing their recent roasting over political censorship), the International Liaison Group which corresponded with and supported gay revolutionary groups throughout the world, the Jewish Research Group which was planning their first seminar, or the newly formed Camden GLF, who promised that tonight they would 'help liberate the Balls Pond Road'. Given that this is a street in Islington and Hackney, the label of 'Camden' was clearly a loose one and more about where they met than who they aimed to attract.

On the Friday, they could have an early start at 10 a.m. to support a trial at Bow Street related to the Festival of Light Trafalgar Square arrests. At 12.30 they would have to nip down to St James tube to penetrate the portals of Pan Books with the giant papier mache cucumber. That evening they could trek out to Penge for the Communes Group at Tony Salvis and David McLellan's house. If they were women (including transsexuals), they could go to the increasingly separatist Women's Group meeting or anyone could attend awareness groups across London. If none of these attracted you, then help was needed with selling *Come Together* 10 in London pubs and clubs.

Saturday was a quiet day; just a GLF jumble sale in All Saints Hall, Powis Square, to raise funds for the hire of the Hall. But on Sunday there was the Church Group and Agape Feast, the Dance Group arranging the next benefit bash, the TV/TS Group, the Counter-Psychiatry Group still hanging out together at Ivor Street (Jeffrey and Micky's house) and a final planning meeting for the big children's Christmas party.

Monday was an exciting and packed calendar. First of all there was a Jill Tweedie article in the *Guardian* about sex roles which made much play of the philosophies of GLF as recently published in their Manifesto and carried a photo of Paul Theobald, Barbara Klecki and others at the Bow Street 'Miss Trial' demonstration. You could read it while sitting through the continuing trial at Bow Street or the new one of Alan Wakeman for planting a pink triangle cross in a Garden of Remembrance. The Youth and Education Group met, as did the Action Group and the Premises Group, which was seeking a new and larger office and home for GLF London. Last and most certainly not least, there was the office collective meeting to sort out the ever-increasing bureaucratic needs of the organization and the running of the office as smoothly as possible.

Tuesday there was a demonstration at the trial of those arrested at the Chepstow sit-in (see next chapter) and, if you were a group representative, the co-ordinating committee to plan the agenda for the general meeting. Wednesday morning was now the deadline for information for the weekly newsletter, a combination of listings and gossip put together by the office collective and cranked out by hand in time for distribution at the general meeting over at Notting Hill by 7.30 p.m. that evening. The pace was extreme and more than enough to distract most people from the growing problems that were shortly to precipitate splits.

Chapter thirteen

A Pint of Crème de Menthe

ALTHOUGH Notting Hill was a tolerant community, there was one place where GLF found constant conflict – in the pubs. This was largely a matter of homophobia combined with the unnerving GLF tendency to descend *en masse* after a meeting and kiss and hug over a half pint. Many of the local 'straight' pubs were happy to accept small groups and there was a certain level of integration from day to day for those who lived locally, including transsexuals and drag queens; but the local police, already notorious for their poor handling of the racial situation, swiftly took against the weekly influxes of hippie perverts from all over London and discouraged publicans from serving them.

This only increased the nervousness of the existing local gay pubs, serving the 'scene' crowd of respectable, closeted gays, who did not want to attract police attention and were horrified by the new style of homosexual in their midst. 'I remember being barred from the Champion, which was a gay pub, just for hugging my boyfriend. You couldn't show any human affection, not even in a gay pub' (*Paul Theobald*). The Champion, to this day a well-known gay pub on Notting Hill Gate, was particularly antagonistic but this was less of an irritation because it was too far from the meetings for most people. The nearer pubs, Henekeys and the Colville on Portobello Road and the Chepstow in Chepstow Road, were swiftly seen as a problem. By September, in the middle of the Festival of Light campaign, they were refusing to serve anyone with a GLF badge. After the meeting of 22 September, those attempting to drink in the Chepstow were met by a police cordon. The barman of another local pub refusing to serve them, the Artesian, let it be known to GLF supporters that the police had visited and threatened the publican with opposition to renewal of their license if they continued to serve GLF people. Four publicans independently met and made a pact not to serve GLF.

The *Morning Advertiser*, the newspaper of the licensed victuallers trade, reported on the issue in a way which encapsulates the prejudice of the time: 'The GLF, an organization of homosexuals, mean to plague public houses "to exercise their rights as citizens to purchase drinks in pubs of their own choosing". Licensees are up in arms about the threat. One said that he had to refuse admission to the "gay people" when they descended on his pub en masse.' The chairman of the St Marylebone branch of the Licensed Victuallers Association said 'This is a trend that is likely to snowball. The GLF have already started pestering pubs in the Portobello Road area. Now I understand they are moving towards the West End.' A policeman warned 'Certain sections of these people have been using premises at Notting Hill for regular meetings. They usually go for a drink in a pub afterwards. They are anxious to initiate any form of action to get publicity.' According to a licensee, 'these people are not just homosexuals. They include a lot of hippies, tearaways and drug addicts . . . many of them contend that they want to be allowed to kiss and cuddle in public . . . they are liable to do all sorts of things in dark corners.' The licensees were incensed by the lack of support from their brewery, which had 'laughed it off' when they complained about the influx of gay custom.

GLF people appearing on a Thames TV programme, *Today* (presumably about the Festival of Light) made a public fuss and obtained a pledge (unfulfilled) from Lord Longford to investigate. But again on the following Tuesday, a number of GLF people making exploratory visits to various pubs in advance of the Wednesday meeting were refused service. The next night at the general meeting it was decided to mount a full-scale campaign. Although the right to drink might seem less vital than some other issues that GLF covered, its refusal was the sort of small everyday indignity that really rankled. Some of the publicans, prior to refusing service, had also raised their prices to GLF people. It held echoes of 1960s demonstrations in many English towns against racial discrimination by pubs refusing to serve black people or overcharging them, which some GLF people had been involved in. In some way, it became a symbol of every piece of petty anti-gay behaviour and also a stand-off with the local police; if they were able to harass GLF out of the pubs, they might seek to expel them from the area altogether.

For all these reasons and more, the pub campaign of Autumn 1971 took on a symbolic importance. It was meticulously planned by a group of people including Martin Corbett and Phil Powell, a college lecturer and previously a straight left ally of Aubrey and David in the Vietnam war campaign who had become one of the earliest 'effeminists', remembered by several people for his political one-upmanship in wearing a working-class charlady outfit when chairing the meeting instead of the glamorous 1930s drag favoured by others. 'A few months after GLF started, he came out and then he joined the frock brigade and got rather aggressive about it. He used to threaten people before they could object! He was good at organizing things like the pub demonstrations. The *Come Together* article on pubs, "A pint of creme de menthe" was probably his' (*Aubrey Walter*). The pub campaign documents have survived in almost their entirety and so the story is told through them and through witnesses; although sometimes repetitive, the documents give a very good idea of how a serious campaign to change this kind of behaviour should still be mounted.

First, there was a leaflet to local people asking for support:

To the people of Notting Hill:
At last, during the Notting Hill People's Carnival, we felt what it was like to be part of a community. We danced, sang and got high together, and it felt good. Did you notice if the man or woman standing next to you was Black or Gay or Greek, and if you did, did it make any difference. No. We just got it together and had a good time; Notting Hill is now a true community.
During the Carnival, you probably went to a pub for a drink. We, as Gays, couldn't go into at least three pubs in our community, Henekeys, the Colville and the Champion. We have been banned because we're gay, openly gay. END WHITE MALE CHAUVINISTIC PREFERENCES NOW! Let's keep our 'People's Carnival' spirit alive. Help us by boycotting these three pubs until they lift their ban. Then, we can all drink, get high and have fun together as people should.
Who knows, soon you may need our help as we now ask for yours.
Love, *ALL POWER TO THE PEOPLE!*
Gay Liberation Front

Then there was a leaflet distributed in other gay venues during the following week:

[First side]
PISSED OFF
WE'RE PISSED OFF BEING OVERCHARGED, HERDED TOGETHER IN A SMALL NUMBER OF OVERCROWDED GAY GHETTO PUBS AND COFFEE BARS WHICH EXPLOIT GAYS AND GIVE LITTLE IN RETURN – no holding hands, no close dancing and behave or you're out
• WE'RE PISSED OFF being barred for expressing our sexuality
• WE'RE PISSED OFF being beaten, and hustled and pushed around on the streets for simply being ourselves, gay,
• AND, ABOVE ALL, WE'RE PISSED OFF with not being allowed to talk as we want, be what we are, act as we want
• YOU KNOW THAT HOMOSEXUALS ARE DENIED FULL CITIZEN'S RIGHTS and it's getting worse not better
SO, WE'RE DOING SOMETHING ABOUT IT – THAT'S WHY WE'RE TOGETHER
And that's why, next Wednesday, we're going to some Notting Hill pubs that the police and landlords have barred us from
WE'RE GOING TO *DEMAND* FROM LANDLORDS AND POLICE EQUAL RIGHTS FOR ALL OUR HOMOSEXUAL BROTHERS AND SISTERS – the right to drink where we please
If you think our problems are your problems – join us
7.30pm, next Wednesday, All Saints Church Hall, Powis Gardens, Notting Hill

[Second side]
GLF is a lot of different people from different places with different ideas.
That's why some of us turn you off sometimes.
BUT – we have the one thing in common that really matters – our homosexuality – that's why we ask you to join us.
Join us this Wednesday – in a place where gay people are getting together as people and not as consumers. Are you gay during licensing hours only?
Come and see what it's all about. Get us to listen to you.
We must learn from each other to work out a better style of life.
In GLF we are developing real relationships, real warmth, real love.

The politics is only one aspect of a way of life that is allowing gay people to stand up to say and mean and *feel* that *Gay is Good.*
Gay Liberation Front/5 Caledonian Road/[phone number]
Meetings Wednesdays, 7:30 All Saints Church Hall, Powis Gardens, W11
GAY IS GOOD

GLF scrupulously notified the police and breweries of their intentions; this was no zap, but was intended to be a calculated and blatant show of strength:

To: Superintendent, Notting Hill police
Copies: Commissioner of Metropolitan Police
       Press
Re: harassment of gay people in and around Notting Hill pubs
The members of the Gay Liberation Front intend, on Wed, October 6, evening to exercise their right as citizens to purchase drinks in pubs of their own choosing
We shall respond passively to any hindrance or violence, whether by publicans or police. Any assaults that occur will be on us not by us.
We will not be dissuaded by any means that are available to you from our purpose of securing the right to equal treatment whilst wearing a badge that expresses our identity as people
We may, as we see fit, file a complaint relating to police threats to publicans who serve people wearing GLF badges, which complaint would be backed by signed affidavits.

A similar statement was sent to Notting Hill area public houses and relevant breweries. Finally and unusually for GLF, they made a very strong attempt to attract the press to witness their demonstration:

Press statement, October 5th
Police harassment of Gay Liberation Front
    On Wednesday, October 6th, 300 or more members of Gay Liberation Front are prepared to be arrested, if necessary, to secure the right to drink at pubs of their own choosing. They are pissed off at the continual harassment which has prevented them from exercising that right.
    After a meeting of GLF at All Saints Hall, Powis

Gardens, W11 on Wednesday Sep 22nd, members went to the Chepstow public house in Chepstow Rd, where they had been warmly received by the landlord and his wife on the two previous Wednesdays

They found the entrance barred by a large number of policemen, some apparently drawn from other areas of London. In the road outside were a black maria and various other police vehicles. The police informed us that they had been called as the landlord no longer wanted to receive our custom.

On going to The Artesian (corner of Chepstow Road and Talbot Road) we were told by a barman that *we could only be served if we removed our badges* as THE POLICE HAD TOLD THE MANAGER THAT RENEWAL OF HIS LICENSE WOULD BE OPPOSED IF HE SERVED GLF CUSTOMERS and that THE SAME THREAT HAD BEEN MADE TO OTHER PUBLICANS IN THE AREA.

Members then visited other pubs, including the Colville, the Alma, and the Duke of Norfolk, in all of which we were refused service.

This harassment by police of GLF was raised by one of us on the Thames TV programme 'Today' (Friday 24 Sep) during which Lord Longford offered to go with us to the pubs in question.

After considerable evasion LORD LONGFORD HAS NOW AGREED TO MEET A REPRESENTATIVE OF GLF TODAY (Tues 5th) WITH A VIEW TO ARRANGING THIS VISIT. WE EXPECT LORD LONGFORD TO FULFIL HIS PUBLICLY STATED PROMISE AND TO BE WITH US ON WEDNESDAY NIGHT

Scotland Yard has demanded a transcript of the television programme

This act seems particularly significant in view of the brutal police behaviour towards GLF demonstrators when they arrested several of them in Trafalgar Square and Hyde Park on Saturday, Sep 25, during the Festival of Light. So violent and brutal were the police that a number of Festival of Light supporters have offered to testify in our defence and to pay our fines. The events were reported in the Sunday Times

As a non-violent organization, GLF particularly resents the statement by a police inspector, reported in the Sunday Times (26th) and witnessed by several of us, that he knew 'the GLF is connected with the Angry Brigade'. This

accusation has no possible basis in fact; but it is one that
the police seem to be using against an ever increasing
number of groups, in order to give an air of legitimacy to
what is a crude attempt at the repression of various
legitimate minority groups.
It is impossible to view the events of the past fortnight
without reaching the conclusion that the police are
mounting a campaign against GLF members, with the
object of driving them back into the ghetto.

Just in case the real press did not turn out, John Chesterman
and others arranged for 'GLF TV' to be in attendance, with lots of
impressive looking lights. They also made sure that plenty of
photographers from the underground press would be there to
signal to the police and landlords that their actions were being
watched and recorded. Then, after the meeting on 6 October, they
set out on a novel pub crawl.

A leaflet had been given out to all attending that evening's
meeting:

THE RIGHT TO DRINK WHERE WE CHOOSE
After this evening's meeting we propose to go to a local
pub, to make a small and modest demand – to buy a drink
The pub chosen is The Colville: ripped us off for a few
weeks (bitter at 20p a pint) then threw us out
The Colville represents many pubs in the area
We do not intend to be denied our right to drink where we
choose, and we will use all passive means to gain that
right . . .
IT MAY BE NECESSARY FOR LARGE NUMBERS OF US TO BE
ARRESTED IN THIS STRUGGLE TO SECURE A BASIC RIGHT HELD
BY EVERY OTHER CITIZEN
The police would prefer to arrest people out of sight, when
we are in ones or twos. Whether you are prepared to be
arrested or not, stay with the main group. If you want to
leave, go with a group and get out of the area quickly
BUT THERE IS NO NEED TO GET PARANOID: the police cannot
touch our minds, because we are right and we know where
it's at. In the end we cannot lose and they know that . . .
A) For those who are prepared to be arrested
(1) We will go as a body to the Colville (see map) –
everyone wearing badges
If you are admitted and served – enjoy it!

If you are admitted and refused service – sit down
If you are not admitted – sit down outside
Being passive doesn't mean that we have to keep silent –
but let's *test* the Colville first, and then get a little noisy, in
our own style
(2) Under no circumstances should you push past police or
landlord to gain entry (technical assault)
The landlord has the right to evict you using 'all reasonable
force'; if you resist, it's technical assault
BUT IT IS NOT AN OFFENCE TO REMAIN PASSIVE AND HAVE TO BE
CARRIED OUT WHETHER BY LANDLORD OR POLICE
Outside the pub the landlord has no right to touch you;
tactically we recommend non-retaliation to any assault
Outside, if the police demand you move, remain passively,
preferably sitting (makes it more difficult to invent an
assault charge) till arrested
(3) Before you leave here
   – give your name and address to the relevant convenor
   – leave and stay with people you trust
(4) If you are arrested
   – shout out your name
   – don't talk to the police
   – don't sweat: we love you and there are lots of people
   working to get you out
   – ask for your phone call, and call the number to be
   announced (write it on your wrist)
   USE your phone call: give as many names of others who
   have been arrested – especially those who are less likely
   to be known . . .

The Chepstow was the first sit-down demonstration I'd
been on for GLF. Local pubs were refusing to serve people
wearing GLF badges and we decided we would all go into
the pubs and if they refused to serve us we would just sit
down and refuse to leave. The first one, the Colville, we got
served in. They just gave in immediately and started serving
us. Everyone was very determined and efficient beforehand,
we had taken the names of everyone prepared to be
arrested – the assumption was that people would be
arrested but it was only a civil offence and it wasn't really
likely. They took the names of people who would stand

bail and I felt nervous so I put my name down for bail and
so did Micky Burbidge rather than be demonstrators.

There were quite a lot of us . . . Not everyone went on
after the meeting. We went into the Chepstow and were
refused a drink and people started to sit down. Somebody
made an announcement about what we were doing,
because obviously there were some regulars there, it was a
gay pub and I'm sure there was a leaflet explaining what
we were doing, which I thought was really important. We
had observers from the National Council for Civil Liberties
there. It was very well organized, I don't know why. It was
a really exciting atmosphere and a very nice feeling
between everybody and there were a lot of women there. A
lot of people, like me, sat down when they'd said they
weren't going to, when we saw everyone else do it we
thought we should, because it would make it harder.

Eventually the police turned up – they took ages and ages
and we were sitting there for half an hour. First of all they
said 'Come along now, ladies and gentlemen, time to leave'
and by then there were all these photographers and they
didn't really want to put a foot wrong. The media were
there. Eventually they had to ask each individual person if
they would leave, so they had to ask about sixty people
'Are you prepared to leave?' and they would go 'No!' or
'Gay Is Angry, Gay Is Good!' or some such answer, and
then they could be removed. I noticed that everybody was
being a little bit too cooperative so when they came to me I
went utterly and totally limp because it is much harder to
remove someone if they're being completely limp than if
not. So they had to make the most enormous effort, it took
two officers eventually to dump me in the street but they
were being very gentle because they knew the media were
there.

People were taken out of the back entrance and some of
them did just walk back in the front and start again. I was
one of the last to go out, so I didn't have the opportunity. It
was a very successful action and it worked. (*Nettie Pollard*)

I remember, I had been in a pub sit-in in Leicester in the
sixties, we would go in and be joined by a black friend and
then the landlord would try and get rid of us and we would

sit in. I remember the police being pretty rough about that, the way they threw us out. My memory of the GLF action, the way I expressed it at the time, was that they picked us up as if we were porcelain, and they sort of stacked us on the pavement outside, but it was always two of them and more if you struggled. But most of us didn't struggle, we had decided to be peaceful and we were picked up, carried out and stacked on the pavement outside. (*Mary McIntosh*)

The law of the day made it very difficult for police to deal with demonstrators on private property; each person had to be separately approached and asked to leave, which was time-consuming. And since it was only a civil offence and not an obstruction of the highway, there were no charges. The demonstration received considerable coverage in the local, London and national press and produced immediate results. Courage Brewery issued a statement denying that they had supported discrimination; the local police denied undue pressure on landlords; and by Friday evening you could get a drink in any pub in Notting Hill wearing the gay badge of your choice. Only at the Chepstow itself did trouble start up again a few weeks later, against the wishes of the brewery itself, because of the strong anti-gay prejudice of the landlord's wife. GLF took a dignified view that there was little they could do about 'one nasty and rather pathetic person' (*Come Together* 10) and rested content with their very public victory for the right of homosexuals to drink in peace without being ripped off.

Chapter fourteen

Armed Love

Brothers and sisters, what are your real desires?
–Angry Brigade Communiqué 8

RELATIONS between GLF and the agents of social control
– police, courts and secret services – were both adversarial and
complex. As a self-proclaimed revolutionary movement, GLF identified with and broadly supported many other groups which used
varying levels of violence to further the revolution, and was seen by
agents of the state as part of the same range of extra-parliamentary
opposition. Though there were many members who were themselves broadly law abiding and pacific, they would at the least unite
behind any person seen as persecuted by the state and many would
go further in their practical support for revolutionary change.
Others, while doing little practical, would talk up a storm in order
to enhance their revolutionary credentials.

It is important to remember that GLF flourished in an
atmosphere when many in the counterculture and the left thought
that some sort of social Armageddon really was just around the
corner and acted accordingly. The embarrassment of remembering
these utopian hopes means that many people rewrote their history
in the late 1970s and Thatcherite 1980s and the issues are seldom
recalled by many who were there. Inevitably, this has been a
difficult area for chroniclers of GLF, who have previously been
people who were not only there but closely involved in the
arguments around political direction. There was also an immensely
strong (and entirely sensible) taboo within the counterculture
about speaking out on illegal or politically sensitive matters to the
broader public, which still operates to some extent. The memories
of various people who, metaphorically speaking, played with fire
and got their fingers burnt still reverberate.

One of the least discussed issues is the extent to which people, even on the fringes of the counterculture, were drawn into criminal activity. At the mildest end this was smoking dope, which almost everyone in GLF did at some time, and taking acid, which was at least as common as the use of Ecstasy on the London gay scene now and infinitely stronger in its quality than most modern acid. Almost half of the people interviewed for this book discussed some form of illicit activity, on or off the record – Post Office and cheque fraud being the most common after drugs, but also car theft, burglary, dealing, organized prostitution and conspiracy to do a wide variety of interesting and illegal acts. But these were not (except for a very small group) professional criminals; they were more like children playing at being naughty, assuming that this was what everyone did and you had to do it to look cool.

> I had a woman friend who lived in Parsons Green . . . I went round one afternoon and we were talking and playing classical music when I heard someone moving about upstairs . . . it turned out she was hiding [someone] on the run from police for Angry Brigade related offences . . . that sort of thing used to happen all the time, it was just something you took in your stride. (*Simon Watney*)

> There was a bunch of people who did some fairly criminal things, they were into cars. There was one night when somebody in a stolen car went sailing down Park Lane with a policeman across the bonnet, she got arrested. They were a gang, run by David Martin who later became quite a celebrity as a jewel thief in drag. I had a very short relationship with David. One night, I was at home with Michael in Ladbroke Crescent when we saw a report on Police Five about the theft of a red BMW. BMWs were the big status symbol car at the time, quite new and distinctive. And then this woman turned up at the door with a white BMW! We told her to go away. The police did find the red BMW wherever it had been put and they towed it away to the police pound. It had incriminating evidence in it somewhere, so she went into the pound and stole it back again even though they had let the tyres down. (*Carl Hill*)

Forgery and deception were talents that could be put to good use in some of the more innocent GLF actions, such as the disruption of the Festival of Light. However, in the hysterical atmosphere engendered by the frequent bombings and security service paranoia of the early 1970s, it was common for GLF people to cause more havoc than they expected with very little means. The spray painting of the Stock Exchange, covered in chapter ten, is an example of this.

> I remember sending a fake bomb to the *Daily Mail* once with some other people. I got an *Anarchists Cookbook* from Compendium and used the inner tube from a vacuum flask and other things in a biscuit tin. One woman, who was in drag, and I gave it to a taxi driver to take to the *Daily Mail*. Another woman was in a phone box outside the *Mail* and when the taxi delivered it, she phoned a warning to the police. Then somebody else phoned a different police station and alleged that there were people impersonating police officers in the *Mail* building. It caused absolute havoc but of course it never made it into the press. (*Carl Hill*)

Given these activities, it is hardly surprising that both revolutionary movements and the security services saw GLF as a target, fuelling the paranoia that was common in such groups.

> There were some GLF people involved with other, more revolutionary left-wing groups. A few were apparently approached to join the Angry Brigade on the grounds that as gays we were used to living a double life and therefore supposedly well suited to secretive clandestine political activity. I was approached by an Irish guy who asked me if I was willing to do 'some work' for Ireland. I presumed he was talking about support and surveillance work for the IRA. I declined. (*Peter Tatchell*)

> I was involved in a lot of causes, I always seemed to have friends in prison who I had to visit, especially Holloway, which used to have a really unpleasant charged atmosphere before they rebuilt it. I remember visiting the women arrested for the Angry Brigade there. They [the Angry Brigade] were the most incompetent bunch of terrorists I've ever met. The establishment was terrified and most of it never even got into the papers. The Special Branch really did think that street revolution might happen, which it eventually did in Eastern Europe and it nearly had in Paris in '68, which was why the state was so paranoid.

Everything runs on the consent of the people, even prisons run on the consent of the prisoners. (*John Chesterman*)

There was a GLF social event fairly early on that got raided for drugs – it was just a form of intimidation. They took names and addresses and it gave rise to a paranoia that was at least partly justified. Some people did allege that there was police infiltration, but I remember somebody suggesting that John Lindsay must be a police plant because he was South African. Michael Mason was supposed to be one too because he looked straight. People were also paranoid about heterosexuals in GLF – somebody once told Mick Belsten that I was straight. At one point Aubrey suggested that only people who were in encounter groups should be in GLF, because the others must have something to hide if they weren't in them. Some of the encounter groups could get very intense.
(*Tony Halliday*)

Everyone used revolutionary rhetoric. We all knew people involved in direct action and theft and things like that, it seemed normal at the time. There were police informers, I experienced one who tried to ask too many questions about drugs and the Steering Committee exposed him. There was a lot of paranoia about infiltration. We were convinced that the phones were tapped and that we were all liable to be raided. (*Jeffrey Weeks*)

Sometimes the police would come to the main meetings in plain clothes, so the zaps were often not discussed there and you wouldn't know what was happening until it did. There were police spies – one of them almost got to be Treasurer once. People assumed that the office phone was tapped after a while. Sometimes the police seemed to know in advance what was happening, for instance at the first wreath laying at the Cenotaph, and they assumed that was how the police would have heard. (*Michael Brown*)

The police often sent women officers along to GLF, who stood out like a sore thumb because they weren't feminists and they asked the wrong sort of questions. People would just take them to one side and ask them to go away. But it did make people paranoid about things like smoking dope.
(*John Chesterman*)

In some respects, however, the paranoia was entirely justified.

I was completely naive about that. Because I began with a sort of British public schoolboy's assumption that the secret services know their place and anyway, even if they don't know their place they are totally incompetent, there's nothing they could ever manage to do. Some of my school friends went into the secret service, I should know. Not that I know them any more, of course, but they did. So whenever people would say things like, 'Do remember the Special Branch will be present in our meetings' I used to think, what does it matter if they are?

I didn't realize just how paranoid those services were, I just didn't know. I did discover as a result of this that there was a file on me in the Secret Service, because one of my schoolfriends who'd gone into the Secret Service, he didn't tell me, but he told a friend. He said 'Guess what, I was going through our files and I pulled out one on Andrew' and that can only have been as a result of the Gay Liberation Front, so there's personal testimony that they did compile dossiers on us.

I thought some people enjoyed the air of being hunted by the state. I had enough trouble understanding all the gender politics, the sexual politics, all of which was entirely new to me, so when it came to the relatively conventional left-wing politics, or the very extreme politics, it was completely beyond me. I think it was so far beyond me that nobody ever bothered me with it, nobody ever asked me to take part in anything remotely like that. I'm surprised that anybody should have a story of being approached about the IRA there, simply because we thought of the IRA as being violently opposed to queers.

There was a funny attitude amongst people in authority then, it was a period when, not long before GLF started, William Rees-Mogg who became my editor at *The Times* and the Archbishop of Canterbury or something had a meeting with Mick Jagger, who arrived by helicopter. The idea was that the establishment should have a conversation with the young, as represented by Mick Jagger. It was a very odd period when all over the place in authority there were people who felt a tug towards this anarchy or flower power or GLF or any of these things and so occasionally you might find anywhere someone like a magistrate who really secretly thought it all rather fun and quite good. There were far more of those people around in establishment circles then than there ever are now, it's a much more poisonous attitude in the ruling class now than it was then. (*Andrew Lumsden*)

The security services were wrong in thinking that any of the traditional leftist groups might be interested in colonizing GLF. Most of them took one look at the anarchic, challenging, chaotic structure and fled.

The left wouldn't touch GLF with a barge pole, except for the Angry Brigade people. We were approached to get involved in a 'gay wing' of that – but the respectable Marxists didn't want to know us for the first couple of years at least. The left were into everybody else's meetings. Just before GLF started, we went to a Maoist meeting on women at the LSE which was led by a man, Harpul Brah, who was giving us a lecture on women's rights. But they only began to relate to GLF when it had become calm and almost reformist. (*David Fernbach*)

The birth and first year of GLF coincided with the flourishing of the only remotely successful British anarchist revolutionary group, the Angry Brigade. This was a considerably more genteel (though it would have been deeply insulted to have been called so) British relation of the Red Brigades in Italy or the Red Army Faction in Germany. It tended on the whole to bomb property rather than people, and to defraud Post Offices rather than doing armed robberies of banks. Even this was far too much excitement for the Special Branch and the British media, who soon transformed the Angry Brigade in the public mind into a cross between mass murderers and master criminals with close links to the IRA, Basque terrorists and anyone else that would put the wind up the Establishment. Worst of all, the organization demonstrated a certain sense of humour and an uncanny ability to penetrate and bomb a wide range of targets, from Home Secretary Robert Carr's kitchen and Scotland Yard's computer room to the Post Office Tower and fashion boutique Biba (after which they issued a communiqué paraphrasing Bob Dylan on consumerism).

The hunt for the Angry Brigade became a total obsession for the Special Branch. In a sinister backdrop to a beautiful sunny summer full of successful demonstrations and actions for women's liberation and gay liberation, they launched a series of random raids based upon following a trail through people's address books and telephone taps which, given the amount of political liaison going on between the organizations, inevitably led to a lot of GLF people. For many who were not particularly involved in anything relevant, this was an exciting and slightly frightening confirmation of their underground status and another illustration of the oppressive nature of the state. But eventually, as political debates about the direction of GLF and its relation to the left grew throughout 1971, the paranoia it engendered became a major contribution to the explosive arguments that blew the core of the organization apart.

> I think there was an atmosphere of paranoia because so many people had been raided. Really, I can't think who wasn't raided. They used to take away address books, rather like with gays in the military now. They used to go through the address book and then everybody got raided in turn, so you knew that if you had been telephoning a house that's been raided and that the house that had been raided had got your address in their address book, then it was very likely that you would get raided yourself. I can't remember how many people within GLF itself had been raided, certainly Agitprop was raided many, many times, which Andy Elsmore was obviously involved in. And lots of people were raided in the Gate and it was an association with GLF because the meetings were being held there. (*Angie Weir*)

The reason [the police] went into places like the Women's Liberation Workshop was that [someone] grassed to the police about it. At a very early stage, before I was involved with the Women's Liberation Workshop, she had gone to the police because she found some harmless tract, probably some Maoist literature because they did get involved – but she thought it was illegal – she was very naive and she went to the police. And I don't think they did anything about that, but she certainly alerted them to the existence of it. It was a stupid thing to do. The connection was then that the women at the collective at Grosvenor Avenue (who were friendly with Angie) were closely related to the Women's Liberation Workshop, so it's not that it was completely paranoid, but I felt that by behaving in the way they did, essentially David and Aubrey gave credence to the whole thing rather than combating it and I felt and still feel that that is what they should have done. (*Elizabeth Wilson*)

The Angry Brigade was a very amateur organization. We and Mick Belsten and others were very anti the Angry Brigade and wanted to block them from taking over GLF. At the time I thought this was very wrong, to use gay people as tools for another agenda. For the Angry Brigade, the main thing was the class struggle. I was against terrorism, because by its nature it's a clandestine act and can't be discussed or be democratic. It was unfair and elitist, some people playing at being the vanguard and using others as troops on the front line. (*Aubrey Walter*)

Tensions simmered throughout the summer and were brought sharply to a head by, as is often the case, a very small and otherwise insignificant issue. The Media Workshop, who had practical control of *Come Together* under the eye of the general meeting, were presented with an article called 'Towards A Revolutionary GLF' by Andy Elsmore of Agitprop. The piece, now apparently lost in its original form, placed GLF within a revolutionary framework with a much stronger socialist interpretation and class analysis than usual and suggested that GLF should play a much more active part in the struggle against the whole system rather than prioritizing sexism and homophobia. It was deeply critical of the shortcomings of GLF while somewhat skating over those of the revolutionary left and was easily interpretable as a plea to GLF to get more involved in revolutionary action – which was taken by some as code for the Angry Brigade. Whatever the reality of the situation, there are several people who remember that Andy identified very publicly with the Angry Brigade. 'I think Andy wanted to pose as Angry Brigade. I don't think he was anywhere really but he thought it was tremendous to be associated with it' (*Elizabeth Wilson*).

Barbara and I were invited to become involved in something more radical, quite loudly, by Andy Elsmore. He said 'Do you want to join the Angry Brigade' on the top of a bus, with other people listening and I thought 'You asshole.' I think I looked out the window. They were such assholes, so stupid about it and I thought, 'These guys are going to get busted' and of course they were. They were all middle-class and as middle-class people are wont to do in Europe and America, while the working-class people are too busy earning a crust of bread the middle-class people go out and bomb. (*Carla Toney*)

I do not think that anyone at Agitprop had any connection with the Angry Brigade: had there been even the remotest evidence that they had, it would have been very much in the interests of the police to arrest someone from the collective as it would have lent credibility to their activities. Police attention directed at Agitprop was clearly intended to spread paranoia amongst the extra-parliamentary left in general and, to judge by what happened in GLF, it was not ineffective in that respect. (*Tony Halliday*)

The Media Workshop had carried information relating to support for people arrested for bombings in the past and articles advocating a revolutionary struggle, without any problems. As one in *Come Together* 8 said, 'Repression doesn't mean that they're getting stronger – it means that we are. The rulers have nowhere to go. No future . . . and now they are more frightened than ever . . . when they can't use sexism and racialism then force is the only thing they can use. And we must go on getting stronger, go on fighting . . . because we have no choice but to fight for our liberation. And as our critique of the system is total so must our choice of weapons be . . . ARMED LOVE.' The collective had also refused to print articles that they disapproved of and cut others, but many other members were not aware of this.

The row over 'Towards A Revolutionary GLF' was part of the sundering of a cohesive grouping. The cohesiveness was always to some extent a myth, but the meetings had given us a sort of community. (*Jeffrey Weeks*)

I and others went along to a meeting of the collective at Mick Belsten's place about it. It wasn't a very good article, but it became a *casus belli* over the control of *Come Together* – people in the collective were starting to control what went in and what didn't, particularly Aubrey and Phil

Powell. Mick himself wasn't very hard line on it. Elizabeth was with me and we sat and argued till dawn. Sarah Grimes and I were the only ones who stayed to the end. We were attacked for just turning up to the one meeting, but Sarah was a regular member of the collective and was on our side. What I felt was happening was that one group with rather Maoist notions was attempting to impose an identity on GLF, to purify the movement. (*Tony Halliday*)

[Andy] wasn't some outside political infiltrator, he was part of GLF and so were the other people who were involved in the article and defending it, but that was an argument used against it. It was threatening in some way to some of the Media Collective. There was a move from some people in that group to 'lead' a mass movement, courting the apolitical queens and putting them against the intellectuals. There was some fallout amongst the women too – some women thought that the way men had handled the issue was wrong. There were no women amongst the group of people who were in favour of suppressing the article and on the other side, some were socialists and supported it, some were anti-censorship on principle and some just objected to male control.

My memory is that we thought the collective were being undemocratic and high-handed. One of us was on it and was completely over-ruled and we then sent some more people to the meeting. The collective had no basis beyond those who got together to do the paper, so there was no special status, and turning down an article was something that hadn't been done before. We thought there was a lot wrong with the article, it needed rewriting, you wouldn't necessarily agree with it but this amounted to censorship. And there was a meeting at our house where we heard what had been going on and planned what to do next, but we were outmanoeuvred. That was the first time that David and Aubrey and people started calling us male-identified and saying we had no right to speak on behalf of women. Which I didn't particularly want to do, I didn't have that kind of attitude, but it really developed our sense of being women.

The ridiculous thing was, we were being called not feminist and accused of putting class politics first and not being properly into sexual politics, because it was being made into an either/or. I think they probably did think that GLF was being infiltrated by the straight left, but that was a bit ridiculous in the sense that none of us were in organizations. We had started that move towards women's liberation and so we started meeting the straight left in that context, but at Skegness we had opposed the Maoists. We didn't know much about the difference, we were opposing that kind of left attempt to control the women's movement, we were very much autonomous. (*Mary McIntosh*)

David and Aubrey believed in a revolutionary sexual politics. I think they thought that that was the important issue. They in terms of tactics and strategy were more concerned with appealing to the gay community and making a politics which was acceptable and accessible to the gay community . . . I suppose our line was . . . a radical alliance of the oppressed and creating new cultures and seizing power and using it in a totally different way. So both projects saw themselves as radical. The arguments were extremely interesting and some time they'll have to be raised again. Looking back, obviously there was lots of fighting and splits and that was bad but the issues were discussed at a more informed theoretical level, and the debate wasn't organized particularly around personalities although different people held different positions. I think many of these issues are long-term and we have to continue to think about them.

I think there were two central issues, the gender issue of the relationship of lesbians to gay men and gay women to the women's movement, and the other was socialism against civil rights politics, though we didn't really discuss it in terms of rights, it was quite clear that it was referring to the age of consent. In a way the most interesting debate was about whether a radical or revolutionary, as they would see it, sexual politics had any relationship to a revolutionary socialist politics or not. So it wasn't reformism against revolution, or direct action against lobbying or anything like that. (*Angie Weir*)

I do feel that they [David and Aubrey] were rather manipulative in using the Angry Brigade stuff. I think that people like Carla – with Americans, however left-wing they feel they are, that generation, they were tremendously anti-Communist. That was the mindset . . . I felt there really was a blind spot, Communism was just evil and Carla got into that . . . but to be charitable I can understand in retrospect that there was a legitimate cause for anxiety if GLF was to be seen as very close to the Angry Brigade, because it wasn't really. It wasn't at all. It was simply that people who were in GLF happened to get caught up in the trial and so on. (*Elizabeth Wilson*)

The arguments reverberated for weeks in the general meeting. Firstly, the article itself was reworked after its initial rejection with the help of others and resubmitted; it was rejected again by Media Workshop at the heated meeting in Barnes remembered above. The dissidents then duplicated the second draft and circulated it for discussion at a general meeting, along with a list of what they perceived as Media Workshop objections and a plea against political censorship. This was discussed a fortnight later after further leafleting from various people, including a perceptive plea by Bob Mellors for self-criticism throughout the organization. It is obvious from the documents that Tony Halliday is right in seeing the issue as a *casus belli*, an excuse to break the power of Media Workshop alongside a hidden power struggle over the direction of the organization as a whole. The article was never published in *Come Together*, but after the next issue, number 10, the magazine was never produced by Media Workshop again but handed from one group to another for special issues, destroying any chance of a central identity or editorial control.

With the issues still fresh in everybody's minds, and after an almost interminable series of raids upon women's liberationist and gay liberationist households and arrests of the former, the Special Branch finally made up their minds on 11 November, two days after searching the Women's Liberation Workshop with an explosives warrant, to arrest someone from GLF. Given the connections with women's liberation and the pattern of raids, the person they chose was no surprise.

I was having a nap after work . . . There was a knock at the door and I sort of heard this knock and Elizabeth or Tony actually shouted, 'There's somebody come to see you' so I wandered down, half undressed and met Inspector Long charging up the stairs with several members of the Special Branch and dogs and God knows what. And they searched the house and I thought, we all thought, it was just another search but then they said, 'One other thing – you're coming with us' and I was carted off to Albany Street. Then I was taken to Tottenham Court Road and then to Holloway. I was very pleased to go to Holloway because it was very tiring being questioned in the police stations, it was extraordinarily uncomfortable and the food, such as you get, is so disgusting it's unbelievable. And when I got to Holloway, the reception wing was the old wing in which they held the suffragettes when they were on hunger strike, so I thought that was rather good. (*Angie Weir*)

It wasn't long afterwards that Angela did get arrested, but the reason that happened was because they blew up the GPO tower. The explosion actually woke us up and we said 'Oh God, whatever's that?' And there was another bomb in Holloway and that was when they decided they were going to have to round up somebody. So after that I guess that a lot of my energy went towards organizing [her defence] . . . It was a strange period. It was a weird contrast with the [more jokey] GLF trials. I think that was why I felt rather annoyed with people like Carla, I felt they didn't really understand the seriousness of it. And of course I think, suspect that some of the people who did get convicted didn't understand the seriousness of it either.

   In a way the whole thing was rather odd because it wasn't like the Baader-Meinhof group, nobody ever killed anybody or kidnapped anybody. I suppose in a way it contributed to a changed climate, it sort of spoilt the fun of GLF because even if people felt paranoid about the Angry Brigade and just wanted to be shot of them, which I think at one level is understandable, it somehow spoilt the fun and everything was grimmer after that. Not just for me, for everybody, it must have affected . . . I think that was a kind of sea change in British politics in a sense, everybody became aware of the Special Branch and MI5 and everything after that. It was an important moment. (*Elizabeth Wilson*)

I was in prison from November until some time in January, so it was a couple of months. And then I had to go and there was an enormous fuss about giving anybody bail and there were very stringent bail conditions, I've forgotten how much money I was worth, quite a lot I think, sureties of twenty and thirty thousand, and I had to live with my parents in Basingstoke and had to sign on at the police station about three times a day, just to control my behaviour. It got farcical because the trial went on so long and those of us who were on bail all made applications to go on holiday, so I made an application to go down to Brighton and after a lot of fuss they agreed that I could go so long as I signed on at a police station in Hove. And the first time I got there, I went up to the sergeant at the counter and gave my name and said that I'd got to sign on three times a day. I was playing tennis and I went up to the counter wearing shorts and he leaned over the counter and said, 'What can I do for you, sonny?' so I said , 'My name's Angie Weir and I've got to sign on' and he wouldn't believe me, I had to make him ring up the Special Branch, it was all a great fuss. (*Angie Weir*)

The trial, which took place during the entire latter half of 1972, was largely suppressed in the press although monitored by the counterculture and underground. The defendants became collectively known as the Stoke Newington Eight, after the area in which most of them had been arrested.

People in GLF were enormously supportive and that was really nice and heartening. I think people were quite shocked really. I had lots of letters and the sense that one was supported by a whole group of people. And during the trial really quite large numbers of people came forward and gave evidence. I had witnesses from GLF, Denis Lemon, Andrew Lumsden, Michael James, quite a few. It was interesting because it was probably one of the first times that out gay politics were mentioned at the Old Bailey and the judge was trying to be helpful in the summing up about it. (*Angie Weir*)

I suppose that was the end of my relationship with GLF. In a way, I don't know how much I had in common with people around the trial but there wasn't any alternative but to be involved in that . . . I think they [the police] were disgusting because they never treated us as badly as they did Grosvenor Avenue because it was all a nice middle-class

home and they could relate to that, they were always quite polite and I can remember them going through some photographs and one of them was a girlfriend of mine and they were sniggering over that and saying, oh, she's a good looker, isn't she? But that was the extent of it really. They never took up the carpets, which is a standard thing, whereas Grosvenor Avenue just got turned over time and time again, they just thought they were the scum of the earth . . . Agitprop got done over time and time again, I don't think I've got much to grumble about compared with what happened to other people, let alone what's happened to Irish people and so on, it was all fairly benign.
(*Elizabeth Wilson*)

GLF didn't support terrorism but there was enormous solidarity with Angela, especially amongst the women. She came from women's liberation as a straight delegate. She was fairly butch at the time, a strong socialist . . . She came from a very working-class background. She was short and shy but quite tough and she went through that trouble very well. I remember being very shocked when I heard she'd been arrested and was at Albany Street Police Station. She was probably pretty shocked too. It was no secret that those people all hung out together. Eventually people were prosecuted and some of them were found guilty and some of them weren't. She wasn't, as we know.

After Angela was arrested I felt one should show complete solidarity with her because she was being attacked by the state, never mind whether you thought bombs were a good idea or whether she was innocent, it's still what I would say today. I went out one night, two actually, doing flyposting about the trial of the Stoke Newington Eight with Tony Halliday, who used to live with Elizabeth and Angela, and another woman, Jenny. It was my car we were using, it was suitable because it was a scruffy estate car and you could get paste and posters and brushes in the back, the kind of things you used . . . We did it, I'm afraid to say, in a very amateurish way.

For a start we went into the City of London and we put these very provocative posters up. One of the things the Angry Brigade did was bombing the kitchen of Robert Carr who was the Home Secretary, and these posters had two

little pictures, one next to the other, one was a picture of
Robert Carr's bombed kitchen and one was a small child in
a derelict kitchen and said 'A bomb devastates a cabinet
member's kitchen – damage repaired in six hours', and the
other said ' poverty and squalor – can this damage ever be
repaired? Support the Angry Brigade'. It was actually a
good poster making a good point. But it was pretty
provocative! Some of them said things like 'Defend The
Stoke Newington Eight' and 'They Are Innocent', which
was much more acceptable. So we went round putting
these exceedingly provocative posters on places like the Old
Bailey and the Stock Exchange. It's not entirely surprising
that the police noticed, they weren't exactly derelict
hoardings that we were putting them on.

We were cruising round and eventually we stopped and
bought some chips and then unfortunately the police
arrived. So I started off in racing car mode, whizzed off and
they had a road block, but there was room to get through it
and so I got through it. They were pretty annoyed and
went chasing us. Then I came to some traffic lights and
they were red and I thought, 'No. I will definitely be
committing an offence if I go through these and it's not
worth it, I'd better stop.' So I stopped and we got arrested
of course. And we didn't end up charged, which I certainly
would if I had gone through it. Anyhow, they took us in
the back of this police car and it was funny really, they
were saying things like 'Where does the GLF get its funding
from, it's obviously heavily funded?' and we said 'Oh, we
just hand a hat round at the end of the meetings.' And they
said 'Nonsense!' It was actually quite funny. Then we got
to a police station and they took all our names. Jenny for
some reason didn't give her middle name and said did we
think it mattered, and they came back and asked her about
it and she admitted it, because she had previous
convictions. I didn't have any but they took it all very
seriously, and they did the nasty policeman, nice policeman
act with one of them demanding to know what we were
doing, who our connections were and so on and the nice
one saying would you like a cup of tea, have a chocolate
biscuit, 'The other guy gets a bit fraught, I'm afraid, but
why don't you just have a chat to me.'

We couldn't believe it, really. So when we didn't have anything to say to them, we didn't maintain our right to silence but didn't really say anything of any substance. I talked to them endlessly about GLF and the meetings, completely innocuous stuff. But it was this complete paranoia that GLF was somehow a terrorist organization. There may have been people in GLF who were sympathetic to terrorism. Some people were. There was also paranoia within GLF, that's true. But hardly anyone who was associated with that particular group of people was actually within GLF. A lot of them were lesbians and of course Andy Elsmore got arrested eventually, I was forgetting that. But to be fair, a lot of people were extremely unwise and it was very badly organized. The very fact that I was absolutely nothing to do with it at all and yet I know rather a lot says it all, doesn't it? (*Nettie Pollard*)

Although GLF stood firmly by Angie, visiting her down in Basingstoke and providing several incontrovertible witnesses who effectively demolished the already very weak prosecution case against her, the events had a strong effect upon the group and some members.

I left GLF because I was becoming in danger of being arrested for things that I didn't do. Photographs of people had been taken by the police, there was a high level of paranoia because some people were suspected of being involved in much more violent political action outside the Gay Liberation Front . . . people did say 'Ask Carla' a lot and I was a public speaker. At the Festival of Light demonstration in Trafalgar Square, I was the only GLF woman arrested. Mary O'Shea heard a senior officer point at me and say 'Get that one.' I was aware that my profile was high, I think Angela had been arrested by then and I was very scared. I was not involved in anything violent, but I was nervous of being accused of it so I disappeared for a while. Our phone was tapped for years after that. I used to pick it up sometimes and go straight through to a police station. (*Carla Toney*)

Angie, along with some of the other defendants, was eventually found not guilty after what was at that time the longest criminal trial in British history. Andy Elsmore was later charged with conspiracy to procure guns, and eventually the police persecution of the collective forced the bookshop to close and hand over their East London premises to a radical drag commune, Bethnal Rouge. But the events left the whole of GLF with a legacy of paranoia and an assumption, often but not always justified, that they were being watched by agents of the state.

> Bethnal Rouge is where I realized that everybody's address book was kept in a communal plastic bag because there was this idea that we were going to get raided and so were our associates and we were very moral about it. We would leave the dope lying around but not the address books, which were kept by the kitchen window so that you could run out onto the flat roof and throw it away if you had to. We wouldn't incriminate anybody else for what we were doing. It was after the Angry Brigade trial and Stuart had been saying all through 1972 that this was important, we were alone and unique and if the agents of the state wanted to get us that was okay, but why should we tell them about others? We knew that everybody's phone was tapped. I got shot at in 1973 in the Bayswater Road after coming out of Louise's, a gay club in Soho. I was tripping off my box but the gun was real and the shots were real and I thought it was Special Branch trying to kill me. Really, it was horrific. And after I'd given him a blow job, too. (*Julian Hows*)

Chapter fifteen

Sitting There Feeling Superior

*The whole experience was so novel at first that people were
prepared to undergo radical changes in their way of thought and
listen to what other people had to say. As it expanded and
became more structured, people's background allegiances loomed
larger again.* –David Fernbach

AS 1971 drew to a close, many of the central politicized
figures within GLF began to focus more on their differences than
on what held the Front together.

> For me personally, what began to emerge as one of the
> significant divisions in 1971 was in the ranks of those who
> regarded themselves as the real radicals, the real
> revolutionaries, which was between those who were much
> more interested in trying to put gay liberation into a
> socialist perspective and those who, we thought at the time,
> wanted to emphasize lifestyle shifts and became represented
> by the radical feminists, the queens who were into
> communal living and changing their head and
> experimenting with drugs. Now there wasn't a hard and
> fast division between those, because even the staidest
> socialists were part of the drugs culture and certainly
> wanted to change our thinking about sexuality and so on.
> But round about the *Manifesto* and debates over that, it
> became really divisive and by 1972 they were really tearing
> each other apart, the radical wing was tearing itself apart.
> (*Jeffrey Weeks*)

> The tensions were there from summer 1971 onwards;
> I remember trying to get people to confront the issues.

The row about involving straights wasn't divisive, it was worked through and dealt with. There was a strain between the developing ideology and a sense of personal liberation. 'Gay Is Proud' really meant something concrete. Having gone through personal liberation, we all tried to find the roots of our oppression – and there were too many answers. The dyed-in-the-wool Marxists tried to fit it into that, the women's liberationists fitted it into sexism, which was a much more fruitful strand. The counterculture and the anarchists produced the radfem version of sexism, which was extraordinarily vibrant as male expression, but very sexist in itself. The main division was between the radfems (who supported the women) and the others. Most sisters didn't agree with them, but the office collective and some other people were very practical and managerial compared to the others. They wanted a managing structure and their formalism put a lot of people off. I never got centrally involved in the fights. (*Michael Mason*)

But for many members of GLF who were less a part of the inner ideological circles, life continued through the winter of 1971–72 much as before. There were more groups, including local ones, to choose from and the majority of demonstrations seemed to concern supporting the people arrested at the big set-piece actions of the autumn; but the office sent out the newsletter, the meetings continued to debate issues and the fame of GLF continued to spread. And as it did, increasingly GLF London people travelled out to spread the word to other towns which did not yet have their own GLF group.

One day there was a phone call from the Winchester teacher training college socialist union – would we send a guest speaker to their monthly meeting? And I happened to be in the office, so I took the call and I said yes. Then I asked various people and it seemed like a lot of people were interested and in the end six of us went including Albert Smith, a young cockney who was my boyfriend at the time. I had some money so I hired a transit van and organized the trip. On the way down we discussed how to deal with their expectations and we collectively decided that if they had arranged the hall, as we expected, to divide us from them, we would initially accept that and take it in turns to introduce ourselves as individuals and then whoever was the last to speak would say 'We don't like the way you've laid out this room, we want the whole room divided into small equal groups and one of us will go into each group.' There weren't any women with us, there were very few women in the office, although up to a third of meetings could be women.

Anyway we had a nice time on the way down and we stopped for a picnic – in those days being out with a bunch of gay people, not in a gay venue and not out hunting for a partner, was so revolutionary that it was enjoyable just as an experience. We arrived and were shown into the hall and the person who came to meet us told us various things. He said first of all 'I have to tell you that usually we're lucky to get twenty people turn up to our monthly meetings, but we've had to take the main hall as the whole school's turned up, and that's just because we put "Speakers from GLF" on the board.' We thought that was pretty interesting and secondly, he said 'I also have to tell you that at our induction lecture, the Principal of the College said "Anybody found to be homosexual will be expelled immediately"' and the entire intake of trainee teachers had listened to that without protest. But obviously, they'd talked about it afterwards amongst themselves, but you can imagine the effect that had on the gay men and women there. If they hadn't been in the closet before, they certainly were after it.

So then we were led into the hall and there was this crowd, I can visualize it, of more than 250 people and it was clear they were agog – what was going to walk into the room? And in walked this curious assemblage – a bit of rough trade, a long-haired hippie, two or three very conventional-looking civil servants in suits, a cross-section of humanity, and as we had expected they had separated us from them, we were on a platform with a table, chairs, decanter of water, glasses . . .

The six of us sat in a row and I was on the extreme right next to Albert and the man at the other end spoke first. He said . . . that he did not represent the Gay Liberation Front but that we were all individuals who were a part of the Gay Liberation Front, that the Gay Liberation Front was not an organization, it was a movement – we agreed whoever got up first would say that. And then the next person got up and introduced himself.

I was getting very hot under the collar. I had been observing the audience while the first man was speaking and I was getting mad at what I saw – people sitting there feeling superior to us, that they were wonderful broad-minded people to come and actually listen to this bunch of perverts . . . So as it went along the row of speakers I was getting more and more angry and in those days I had a technique for dealing with tension and stress which was that I would embroider things. So as it was a while before I would speak, I got out my embroidery and sat on this platform in front of hundreds of people and tried to embroider. I can remember trying to concentrate on each stitch and stay calm.

Of course, with hindsight I can look back and see, what could have been more guaranteed to freak them out? But I promise you, at the time I was using embroidery as a kind of meditation and I was in a fairly disturbed psychotic state just then, because that same year I had dropped out of my· job, become diabetic, become vegetarian, taken LSD, joined GLF . . . I was in a pretty amazing state. Embroidery was the only thing I could do that kept me calm. In meetings, on the tube, in public places, calmly, one stitch at a time . . .

But by the time it got to my turn I was in a rage. Albert, I remember was wonderful. He got up and in his matter-of-fact cockney way said 'Well, I'm from Willesden and I'm gay and I've always known that and I can't see that it's such a big deal', and then looked at me. I got up and said 'My name is Alan Wakeman and I have to tell you I find you people outrageous. You're all sitting there feeling so fucking superior. You think you've come here to give us your support because we're poor things and need your support. Well let me tell you, we didn't come down here to get your support. We came down here to tell you how screwed up you are! And how much you need to change.' And at this point the whole room came alive . . .

Of course, this led seamlessly into 'And furthermore, we don't accept the way you've laid this room out. I mean, why are we up here when you're down there, what is this meant to imply? We require you all to rearrange the room and we're going to come down among you and if you don't like it then you'll just have to lump it, because what we want is small discussion groups.' So we all got up and went down and there was a lot of shifting around of chairs and things and eventually each one of us found ourselves in a group . . . and the groups were a bit like GLF discussion groups; people produced prejudices, we challenged them, they said sorry and we went on to the next prejudice.

One of the important things that GLF were doing at that time was having creative groups to brainstorm about a particular thing, and one evening in my flat we'd had a brainstorm about new gay badges and had come up with a sheet of paper badges. I had taken the sheet with us . . . We got them to duplicate the sheet during the meeting and the badges were cut out and – I can't remember how we managed for pins, we must have done something . . . At the end of the small groups, we got back onto the stage again and related what had happened in our groups. It was a bit unfair as we were taking back the power, but anyway we did, and announced that we had brought these badges and that if everybody was genuine in what they'd said in the groups, that they really wanted to support us, then they wouldn't mind, would they, wearing a gay badge for twenty-four hours as a gesture of protest against the Principal who'd said that anybody found to be gay would be expelled. 'If you all wear a gay badge, he can't expel all of you', and to our astonishment, the whole meeting agreed to do that. We waited by the door and they each took one and so the entire meeting went out wearing gay badges.

The way the meeting ended was interesting too because at the end about thirty people were left sitting in their seats who said, 'How do we join the Gay Liberation Front?' and we said, 'You don't have to do anything, just call a meeting, start.' I remember noticing that the people who stayed behind at the end and came out to us – men and women in about equal proportions – were the people who'd hardly spoken at all in the meeting. They'd sat there petrified and silent and they were also the ones who had found it hardest, and many of them had refused, to wear the gay badges. The ones who weren't gay didn't find it difficult to do that as a gesture of solidarity but the ones who were gay found it impossible. And then we all got in the transit van and went back home. And the next thing we heard was that there was a Winchester GLF group, formed that night . . . I think it must be the case that the teachers training college was never the same again. (*Alan Wakeman*)

GLF was too hot not to cool down. It had a natural life-span and any attempt to keep it going would have been a failure. As I remember it, it was David and Aubrey who thought that the all-London meetings should come to an end and that there should be local groups instead of the all-London ones. It was them who started the Camden group. I thought of it as right, that the weekly meetings had an element of clockwork about them and it wasn't remotely as it had been when the first meetings were held . . . week after week, people were effervescent with things they could contribute or suggest, or set up a group, but it was growing repetitive by the time the Camden suggestion came up. (*Andrew Lumsden*)

Aubrey's recollection is that it was Bob Mellors who first suggested starting a local GLF group in North London, to get round the increasing problems of the gigantic, faction-ridden all-London meetings in All Saints. 'When Bob Mellors formed Camden GLF we went with him to Foresters Hall in Kentish Town. We were fed up with the big meetings and Powis Square was too far away. They would split into little groups for discussion at every meeting and we would escape to the kitchen and make tea.' The group soon became a microcosm of the main GLF, with its own newspaper now that Media Workshop was in disarray, and with many of the debates about sexism and socialism.

Inevitably, the success of Camden (which attracted many of the earliest central male figures) led to further local groups around London. 'The regions of London were pretty evident from early on. Notting Hill had the hippies, North London the students, West London the scene people and East and South London also had different characters' (*David Fernbach*). West London GLF rapidly became associated with running the dances and South London went in for local politics and large membership drives, while East was more working-class and social in character in its early days.

Camden GLF continued to do a variety of political action and invented one particular form of what would now be called 'outreach' which has become legendary. 'We were part of the tea trolley action. The original idea was rather Maoist, serving the people – we felt that these were poor oppressed queens forced to cottage who needed a cup of tea' (*Aubrey Walter*). A group of men from Camden GLF (the group was heavily though not entirely male dominated) took a tea trolley up onto Hampstead Heath, a notorious North London cruising ground, and tried to engage the men cruising with cups of tea, chat and paper sales.

Although patronizing in its original intent, the basic idea of going out to where people were was sound. The experience was a formative one for a number of GLF men, who soon came to realize that their assumptions were naive, that many men went to the Heath out of choice. As Mike Rhodes, who later helped with much of the early work on AIDS in London through London Lesbian and Gay Switchboard and other groups, put it in *Come Together* 13, the Camden-organized issue, 'I found that I had been thinking in terms of us (GLF) and them (cruisers) and then I caught myself in the role of missionary. Spreading the "good word" about liberation. It was only when I left our group and started cruising myself that I could stop thinking in terms of categories of "us and them" and start relating honestly.' Twenty years later, this experience was echoed by the first cruising project from Gay Men Fighting AIDS to do safer sex work on the Heath – a project which centrally involved a number of other ex-GLF men including Julian Hows and Michael Mason.

The locality groups were not the only type now springing up. Following in the wake of the women, other groups with particular concerns or oppressions began to meet together.

> The first gay Jewish Group came about at a GLF meeting. I was sat with someone who was an Orthodox Jew and in the closet. People were talking about having a religious group and assuming that it would be about Christianity. Some of the leftist GLFers sometimes made some anti-Semitic remarks, which was not uncommon, and criticized Jews. The other man stood up and said 'What about Jews?' and this brought the usual comments, which I protested about. Someone said 'Well, have your own group' and the other man said 'We will, then' and I agreed and so it started. It lasted eighteen months or so with speakers and discussions, before other people took it over and it turned into what is still the Jewish Gay Group. It was formed to campaign both in GLF and in the larger society. I remember doing a radio interview in the early '70s for London Radio on Judaism and homosexuality for it. (*Michael Brown*)

New members were still arriving, bringing new views and fresh ideas, including some very young people.

> I arrived at the basement of 5 Caledonian Road and became part of that mad circus and was treated with the correct amount of decorum and wonderment by most of the people there, Cloud Downey and various others who were sweet to me like maiden aunts, because I was fifteen going on sixteen. When anybody else under twenty walked into the room, they sort of made sure that the kindergarten was in one corner, 'Oh, you must talk to Julian.' So I had long afternoons in the GLF office necking with older teenagers, with a matronly aunt in the corner, which was quite sweet. (*Julian Hows*)

GLF was now firmly at home in Notting Hill, where the weekly general meetings continued to be held. Members felt grateful for the support that they had received, both over the pub demonstrations and in the welcoming, cosmopolitan atmosphere. In the autumn Alan Wakeman suggested that they throw a Christmas Party for deprived children in the neighbourhood who wouldn't get a party otherwise. There was so much nodding and approval that he passed a hat round to get a party fund started. 'It came back to me with £55 in it, which is not bad going twenty-four years ago.'

> Afterwards about six or seven people came to me, including Graham Chapman of Monty Python. One of the others was Warren Haig. Jim Anderson of *Oz* was one and we had our meetings in the house where he lived with Germaine Greer at that time, near the church hall. She was to be seen coming and going and I was impressed by the company I was keeping. Jim Anderson was notorious at that stage because of the *Oz* trial and I was a fan of Germaine Greer . . .
> I volunteered to do the invitations. Graham Chapman said he'd do the conjurer, someone else, possibly David Seligman, said he'd organize a theatre troupe to come and do a little play and they were what led to trouble with the press. At that time I was part of a band called the Solid British Hat Band and they sang folk songs at the party. We gave away 200 invitations because that's what we could cater for, someone did food with party staples like jelly and

we went on having meetings once a week relentlessly until the party happened, and it was pretty chaotic.

One of the reasons it was chaotic was that nobody had wanted to take responsibility for keeping order or making sure that the kids didn't get out of hand. And since nobody was responsible for it, they did get out of hand. I think they probably had a great time but it wouldn't have been the kind of party I would have enjoyed because the rowdy kids basically took over and just spent time screaming and throwing things about, but it started with the show and the conjurer and the theatre group and so on. They had a great time and went home with their faces dirty and glowing.

All that needs saying because of what happened immediately after. The very next day, I was on the duty rota at Caledonian Road [the office] on a Sunday and everyone was in tears. There was a boy at the office who'd turned up the week before, having run away from his parents because he'd told them he was gay and they'd thrown him out of the house, so he'd come to London because he'd heard that there was the Gay Liberation Front in London and he'd turned up at Caledonian Road. There we were and what were we supposed to do? We weren't social workers. Somebody said, 'Oh, you can sleep at my house', and he just became a *de facto* member of the office collective.

He was at the party and unknown to us this journalist had turned up at the party and was going around charming people into talking about themselves, saying how great he thought it was what we were doing. Of course, he was from the *People* and the next morning there was this story which I think was on the front page. The young guy was 'outed', so was somebody who hadn't told their parents, and we were all in a state of shock because we'd come into the office with this afterglow of 'Wasn't that great!' and the kids had had a great time and it was all good PR. Their parents had been happy for them to be there, but of course subsequently they said 'We weren't told that it was a gay party, if we'd known we wouldn't have sent our children along, how dare they . . .' All of that came out afterwards, but at the time the kids had a great time and the parents had a great time. When they collected their kids from us, they saw perfectly well what kind of party it was.

The whole place was in a state of shock and we had an emergency meeting of the office collective. We made some decisions about dealing with the media and produced a list of instructions which was pasted up over the phone. It would have said something like, 'Don't assume somebody ringing is not a journalist looking for a story – don't assume that they are. Don't give out your name on the phone.' Basic instructions . . . we should have thought of all that before it happened.

But even that bad thing had a positive outcome which was totally unexpected, which was that the phone started ringing and by about midday of the Sunday of the *People* article, people were ringing saying 'I think it's really great what you did, throwing a party for kids, I just wanted you to know', and other people were saying 'How can I join the Gay Liberation Front, I read about you in the *People*', and in the end the number of phone calls that were from people who'd ignored what it said and simply picked up that this existed, outweighed the number ringing to abuse us. I remember thinking, weird old world, you think something's awful and it turns out all right.

There was an endless aftermath in the local papers, they tried to call us pederasts. Social workers claimed they would never have accepted the tickets if they'd known we were homosexuals, but I was forearmed with the knowledge of what had happened over the *People* and I didn't care. (*Alan Wakeman*)

The incident did make quite a splash in the press, mainly because the *People* claimed that children should not have been shown a theatre piece including ridicule of a police officer and violence towards him. GLF people responded, with perfect logic, that the most popular children's entertainment at straight-organized parties was Punch and Judy, which contained not only violence towards a policeman but also towards women.

One other seed was planted that winter which bore long-term fruit.

The project to start a newspaper began in the winter of 1971. I began then to feel that it ought to really happen. I remember the row about Media Workshop but I don't really connect the two. But there were also all the people who didn't live in London. It was all very well having a wonderful time in London but all round the country, they never knew anything that was happening. People had said to me a lot that the trouble with *Come Together*, much as they liked it, was that there was no certainty of publication. It was put together when people felt like putting it together and it wasn't remotely a newspaper, that wasn't it's purpose. It wasn't very together, after a while. Its pioneering capacity was wonderful, I loved it, that's why I could never dream of writing for it, I just felt too straight.

A lot of people felt something should be done, could be done, might be done. It was the mood of the moment. The only contribution towards it as an idea that mattered when Denis Lemon and I first discussed it was we both agreed that it should be something that came out on the dot. You knew when it would appear, it wouldn't want to take sides between all the different groups within the gay community, it would be open to people to write from any possible viewpoint. And it would have national distribution and it would have a cover price, so that it could if possible pay its way. There were no freesheets then. Those were the basics.

Which was by itself to stipulate a relatively straight way of doing thing, as we would have put it then. It was never intended to be instead of *Come Together* but some people saw it as an opposition because its basic idea was so different, it was meant to be something routine that came out, reliable. Nobody at GLF said to me they were interested in the idea when I brought it up except for Denis Lemon, that particular type of paper anyway. He said he thought that this was absolutely right and that he'd wanted to do that sort of paper. He was in the office collective and he'd been very much involved with the Festival of Light stuff. He was working in a record store at the time and as far as I knew, he had no higher education, had left school at sixteen or something. He always was very diffident, said he couldn't write, he knew nothing about journalism, was in no way qualified but he wanted to see it happen. He very quickly drew other people in. It only needed saying that it was now starting for other people to want to join in. But to begin with, there was only one other person who thought it was a good idea and that was Denis Lemon.
(*Andrew Lumsden*)

Chapter sixteen

Stepping off the Planet

These were the bravest people. –Andrew Lumsden on the queens

'PEOPLE packed in or lost their jobs and flats and banded together to create communes. We saw them as the logical outcome of following the *Manifesto*. They followed on from consciousness raising groups, which a lot of people were in. I was always too busy and too practical to get into them, Street Theatre Group was awareness raising enough for me, getting into drag and getting paranoid on the streets. Rehearsing and performing was CR of itself' (*Stuart Feather*). 'At Christmas 1971, at the big meeting Bette stood up and invited everyone who had nowhere to go to his house – and this was before the commune' (*Nettie Pollard*). 'The communes were part of the vast strain of trying to rebuild society from your inner self outwards' (*Tony Halliday*).

As the actions of GLF came to their peak, so did the wildest experiment of the organization – its communes. Communes were a way of living popular amongst many parts of the 1960s and 1970s counterculture, but GLF put its particular stamp upon them as it did upon much else. Communes were not simply very large flat-share arrangements, though that is what some of them eventually degenerated into; they were a conscious attempt to reject capitalist notions of property and patriarchal notions of the nuclear family, by sharing the lives and belongings of several people. As in a monastery, nothing was individually owned and everything was shared; in the most developed form of commune, this included total removal of privacy in order to break down the separate egos of the communards. In some this included removing the door of the toilet.

An article in *Come Together* 11, the second lesbian issue of January 1972, describes the early days of the Faraday Road commune (dealt with in more depth in the next chapter). Titled 'Fuck

The Family', it details a mixed-sex commune of six people who shared all their clothes, food and money. Regular consciousness-raising sessions ensured a brutal honesty; coupledom and factions were banished, supposedly, by an agreement that whenever two or more held a discussion it must be repeated to the others. Everyone ate in the same room, studied in the same room, slept and made love in the same room. Unsurprisingly, this meant that they felt they had abolished monogamy although they admitted that they were still having a little difficulty sorting out the housework. Even a previously separatist woman was said to enjoy cuddling the only man in the commune in bed. They admitted that all this was extremely difficult, but felt that it was worth it to be able to 'live our politics'.

But Faraday Road developed into one of the two most extreme communes within GLF – the other being that of the radical drag queens and friends in Colville Houses. There were several others of much milder political temperament.

> The Bounds Green commune came together in 1971, it was the first time I got to speak to Warren and David Fernbach. I went up to Warren because I was so impressed by him and he and David Fernbach were speaking together and they mentioned a suggestion about a commune and pointed out some people who were interested in it. And I spoke to them and we started the commune together . . . Noel and I started going round together and I was afraid it would be a problem to have somebody under age in the commune. There were two other communes I knew, one in Brixton and one in Notting Hill Gate. But I wasn't aware of any other lesbian and gay ones at that point.
>
> In Bounds Green we had a small living room with loads of mattresses and you had to step over everybody. It was very informal. The landlord was interested in amateur drama and wanted a couple of the young men from the group to act for him, he wanted them to pretend they were being spanked. One of us had an idea what was really going on and he went round and managed to get our rent reduced, though we never asked how! We had a rota for doing the dishes and cleaning but we ended up cooking almost in couples, which became an issue because Noel and I got a lot of hassle from people for being a couple. They were very critical of us for having a nuclear family set-up

but we didn't care, we just wanted to be together and that was that. We didn't feel apologetic about it. I didn't believe freedom meant not having anything but communal relationships.

We shared clothes and there was a lot of debate about the men having to wear whatever was available including women's clothes. If you didn't, you were hanging onto your male image and so forth. So there was a lot of cross-dressing but not drag, not full drag. We just put on a blouse or a skirt because it was around and occasionally we'd go out in public in it, but in those days unisex was becoming more fashionable and with the hippie thing of wearing flowing robes a skirt didn't seem to be like a skirt as such. We had weekly meetings about problems, mostly they were about sorting out the bills and who hadn't done their washing up and cleaning. The sharing ethic was very strong. People would move in with their suitcases and after a while they'd stop worrying about particular items and what was whose. It even got down to toothbrushes and I put my foot down at that point. I said, 'My toothbrush is mine and I'm not having twelve other people into it.'

The commune lasted for two years. We pooled our money and some were working and others signing on. Noel worked most of the time in a really straight job in architecture and it was a running joke because everybody else would be dressing in whatever they were dressing in and Noel would be popping off to work in his suit, looking exactly like everybody else on the street. Actually it had a certain amount of repercussions in his job, where you were expected to bring people home and he couldn't. Because he would have lost his job straight away, if they saw twelve guys and three women and this communal bedroom. We had several low key parties, they seemed low key to us because we were used to having about twelve people around playing loud music all the rest of the time, dropping acid because in those days acid was considered to be mind-expanding rather than just a silly game . . .

We had a very nebulous political concept. First of all it was simply trying to break down the norms of society and not living like a nuclear family . . . People had their own philosophies but we weren't collectively Marxists or anything like that. So we did sit around for a couple of meetings trying to talk about, what were the roles of women, what were the roles of men. I tried to initiate a discussion about race but as I was the only black present it didn't work very well. It was just me lecturing everybody and everybody, being very liberal and so on, they would just say yes to whatever I said and it didn't get anywhere. On the occasions that we did meet with particularly the Colville queens, we felt quite intimidated but admiring of them because they did seem to analyse everything. They would wear make-up, for example, and think of it as a political act, disrupting, and the people who wore make-up in our house wore make-up because it was pretty and they didn't give a damn about whether anybody was changing the world or changing sex roles and so forth.

In the commune Noel and I became a couple pretty soon. Everybody had either relationships with other people in the commune or steady girlfriends or boyfriends and it wasn't an issue, but when we went to Colville, people who were seen twice to be with the same person were criticized because we were getting into the nuclear family stuff. Most of the men in our group were fairly conventional in that sense and Danielle, who was the only woman by that time, had a steady girlfriend. She never dressed like what would be considered to be dykey and we all looked quite hippie, but not a bunch of queens in make-up. Except for Blossom.

We didn't have a television, deliberately. Partly because we felt that we'd all wind up watching it and be brainwashed. I think that was our only political act, not to be dominated by TV programmes which emotionally hit us. A lot of us had problems with our families and were running away, to be blunt, from family problems. We didn't bother much with newspapers, we read *IT*, *Oz* and the radical papers and we went to demonstrations which were fun, not for political reasons. We went along to the big GLF meetings. All of us flipped through the groups but none of us got involved with them for any considerable length of time. (*Ted Walker Brown*)

The issue of coupledom and monogamy was a constant argument within GLF and particularly within the communes, though with hindsight one of the members of Colvillia, Julian

Hows, admits that you were more likely to be hassled for being in an unbreakable couple if someone fancied you.

> There was a very strong movement against monogamy, couples were really uncool. Because everybody wanted to have sex with everybody! But politically, we were breaking up the nuclear family and we were not going to have any ersatz nuclear families and I can't bear gay weddings. I think it's disgusting! All these silly queens imitating their oppressors. Please, do something original, what is this contract, is this a business? It's like doing a deal with someone. I think it's really naff. Really naff. One of the great things in the commune was, it was so taboo because it was so fatal. I mean, I've got an eighteen-year relationship now and it's very different from living with a group of people. It's very powerful, but it's not good in a group. (*Bette Bourne*)

The commune in 7a Colville Houses, often called Colvillia, was the final glory of a floating group of people who started, relatively late for the GLF communes, in the early summer of 1972 in a rented house in Tulse Hill. The backwaters of Brixton soon proved rather less welcoming to unorthodox lifestyles than Notting Hill or Bounds Green. By sheer chance, the house happened to be by the gates of a school attended by one of the youngest people in GLF, who like the founders of GLF came with a track record in activism.

> A few months before, I'd been one of the leaders of a National Union of School Students demo. The NUSS was run by this cute politico. I had him. He was so bound up in really bad class politics and he wasn't very out. We closed down the school for a day and went on this march he'd organized. The night before the march, I'd been round to his flat . . . [for sex] and then on the march I'd gone up and he ignored me. I was very upset and hurt. The South London section of the march only got as far as County Hall. I was carrying a copy of *Lord Dismiss Us* by Simon Raven and wearing John Lennon glasses, a 'Free Angela Davis' badge and a GLF badge I'd picked up. I got pushed up from the crowd to speak on the platform and I encouraged them to sit in at ILEA in County Hall and got arrested by DI John Bateman for causing an affray or

something. They'd arrested me on a private road, so I refused to recognize their arrest and wouldn't tell them my name for six hours. So my mother had had acres of trouble with me. (*Julian Hows*)

It was a nice big house, it was well furnished and it had a big back garden. It seemed relatively private as well. We had no idea what we were taking on. In due course we moved in and people came to visit us. The trouble first started when we started to hang our washing out on the line. The neighbours saw pairs of tights and skirts and what is traditionally called women's clothing hanging on the line and they could see us in the garden in our make-up, because we were all really outrageous and used to paint our faces. That had been established well before the commune. We played it cool when we went to the estate agents because we wanted to get the place, but once we were in it anything went. The neighbours used to yell at us when we went in the garden, homophobic abuse, which was fine in itself. But then one of the local lads came round with a gun and started firing it through the window.

We went to the school play. They were doing this play and Julian told us about it and encouraged us to come and to dress up as much as we liked. So we went along and put on the most extraordinary things we could find. We were done up like opera singers, huge dresses and tiaras and furs and long gloves, dripping jewellery and one of the men who went was dressed as Princess Margaret. We walked in and the place was in uproar. They stopped the play eventually and asked us to leave because of the uproar. People were yelling at us and throwing things at us. I was very glad to get away, actually, it was very nasty. There were only four of us against all these South London mums and dads and the kids themselves could be really heavy. So after that I had nothing more to do with anything about the school. I didn't enjoy it at all and if I had my time over I would never do it now. But at the time I was all for it and thought it was a great idea.

And then someone got attacked with a milk bottle by a teenage boy. It got to the point where we were actually under siege. At one point we were piling up wardrobes against the front door. It was really frightening. And we weren't actually doing anything, we were just living our lives. We didn't have wild parties, people came and stayed overnight but it was never out of hand. It was like a barricade, people came to help us, Michael [James] became very important then and Bette was there, they were constant visitors. Nigel Kemp lived there, Ken, Richard at first, Alaric and me. (*Cloud Downey*)

I remember that the first occasions when the kids from the school came round, they were the younger kids and they came in to see the clothes and the make-up and whatever and just to find out who we were, to talk to us. I remember on one occasion they were trying to decide which of us was the most good-looking – all very relaxed. They were eight- or nine-year-olds and it was fine and we got on okay with them. But the next day their older brothers came round. There were about twenty fifteen- to seventeen-year-olds. The bell rang and I answered it. Naively (I was just nineteen), I just continued what we had been doing previously . . . I let them in to see our clothes and talk. I took them upstairs. Since there had been no trouble with the younger kids, I didn't think of danger. Nigel was downstairs in the kitchen.

After some talk, one of them said to me, 'You don't think I'm going to hit you with this milk bottle.' I felt strangely calm and I said something like 'I think it's quite possible but it seems completely irrelevant.' Somebody else spoke and I turned, which meant that when he hit me the bottle shattered on my forehead and cut the bridge of my nose. If I hadn't turned it might have cut my eyes. And then they all ran downstairs and vanished. I walked downstairs with blood pouring from my face to find the police in the open doorway.

There were two policemen and the first thing that one said was 'What were you doing to that boy to make him hit you?' I was absolutely outraged and the other policeman apologized. He started trying to persuade me to have an identity parade at the school to find the culprit . . . GLF theory at the time was that you shouldn't use oppressive state mechanisms such as the police and that the kids were only playing out their oppressive conditioning and therefore punishment through the state system would be counterproductive, so I refused. When they left I went to hospital . . . I must have gone back that night . . . I remember bricks coming in through the windows and glass falling, the curtains preventing it flying across the room . . . I decided I couldn't stay. (*Alaric Sumner*)

I went over to the Brixton commune when they were having trouble with the local schoolboys. I remember the day I went there and they came past and yelled 'Hello girls!' and we rushed out in our frocks, ran out of the house down the street after them, frightened the shit out of them and chased them back in the school yard, yelling 'Don't you give us any more fucking trouble', because they'd been as stroppy as they could be and it was getting out of hand. It was like a charge down the street. (*Bette Bourne*)

Kids were going round and throwing bricks through their windows and taunting them in the street and so on. And this was all happening in breaks and lunch hours. So I thought, as the vice head of one of the houses at the school and a school prefect, this is not on. I went to the deputy head and said this was not on. They were telling me that what pupils did outside of school, they had no control over and I said, 'That's not quite true is it? Because if it was the local shop that was getting it, you'd have two teachers posted outside.' He said 'Well, pupils below the sixth form aren't allowed outside the school gates during break,' and I said 'Yes, but we all know it goes on and when we've had trouble before, teachers would stand outside the chip shop or the newsagents or whatever.' He said, 'This is not a commercial establishment and they ought to get the police round.' He refused to put two people on the gate leading out to their house. So there was a bit of an uptight scene.

So I went round to see Cloud and Alaric Sumner and Ken, Richard and others. I got very upset that I couldn't do anything about it but they said, that's all right because we're going to do something about it. A few days later, a whole bevy of people came down and spent the night in the house and printed leaflets to distribute in the school the next day. I told them how to get into the school and where the headmaster's study was and all that. I spent the night before this event in a room with fifteen queens sleeping on sleeping bags on the floor and was told that I had to sleep on the sofa. This was their thing, because I was obviously jail bait. They were very, very sweet and it was 'Look, don't touch.' So I had to put up with the sight of Bette Bourne and Tim Clark fucking like bunny rabbits about three feet away, with me lying there like the virgin queen on a cut moquette sofa. Because they didn't want to take advantage of me. I thought, fuck that, Mary.

The next day we went into the playground and started handing out leaflets with all these demented queens. The police had arrived before that, though and I had decided, sod it, I was going to blow all these hypocritical queens that I'd had sex with, these teachers, I was going to tell the police. They came along and said,

'So, sonny, what are you doing with these people then?' And I said 'I'm one of them.'

'But aren't you a school pupil?' 'Yes, I'm a school pupil as well.'

'Well, what are you doing with these homosexuals?' 'There's more homosexuals in that fucking school than there are out here.'

'What do you mean?' 'I could tell you all their names' – and I went to pull out a list of all of them, because I'd written them all down and I was going to do what we'd now call outing, I thought, fuck that. And Michael James grabbed the piece of paper off me and ate it, while he was smiling at the police officer. He said to me 'That's not nice.'

So we went into the school and handed out all these leaflets and then in the best traditions of liberalism they said 'Perhaps you'd like to discuss this with the headmaster.' The kids were going mad. They herded all these queens into the administration block and put them downstairs. Now downstairs all there was was the caretaker and some medical rooms. Upstairs was the head's office and so on, the staff common room and so on. As a pupil you weren't allowed to walk up those stairs without being invited. I heard one of the schoolkeepers, who I'd knocked off once or twice at a cottage in Brixton, announce very loudly, I think so we could hear, 'So you want me to call the police?' I couldn't believe what they were doing, I told them but everybody didn't quite want to believe me, they thought I was just being an overexcited, hyperactive child.

So I walked out and found the headmaster and told him he was disgusting and that he ought to be ashamed of himself and that he was a bastard and various other things, that he was calling the police to these people and not actually going to talk to them at all, was he? We had a furious stand up row witnessed by lots of people and then of course the police arrived and escorted everybody off the premises. (*Julian Hows*)

The local newspaper, the *South London Press*, gave the incident extensive coverage and photographs in their next edition on 7 July 1972, estimating that thirty GLF men had taken part in the invasion of Tulse Hill Comprehensive and quoting the leaflet they had distributed:

We are gay men living in Athlone Road. We do, and dress, and have sex and are what we want to be, which is nice for us and doesn't affect you. We start no trouble, no arguments, no violence. Since we moved in, we've had shouts, bricks, two of us have been hit with bottles, most of the windows and the door have been broken in. We've also had a lot of support. We know a lot of you are on our side. We are not being driven out by a few confused uptight people trying to look big. From now on, any trouble and we'll answer back. We're not going to use the school, or the police. We don't believe in them any more than you do. We'll do it ourselves and there are a lot of us. We have a lot of friends. Today there are dozens, next time there'll be hundreds. We believe in talking, in friendship, in understanding each other and we'll talk anywhere – on your ground or ours. But we won't talk to those who attack us. We will attack back and there are a large number of us. We are very strong because we love each other.

The newspaper commented: 'The group was accompanied by 16 year old Julian Hows of Bonham Road, Brixton, who has been suspended from Tulse Hill School for "being rude to staff". They had also been asked to leave the school production of *Oliver* when they "arrived in gay garb".'

I was expelled for being a corrupting influence upon the younger pupils, that was the official phraseology, in a letter to my mother. I begged him to rescind his decision not to give me a reference for any school that had pupils in it under the age of sixteen. Because with the A levels I was doing, I needed a school and not a tech. So that was the end of my education, though in some ways it was really the beginning. (*Julian Hows*)

When we decided to leave Tulse Hill, we went up to Bette's to stay, and with other people around the Gate. And we realized that there was this big empty house opposite [42 Colville Terrace] that nobody seemed to know much about, a grand house with a flat roof and balconies. It had been bought by the Notting Hill Housing Trust who were going to convert it into flats for people on their waiting list, but they didn't have the money so it was just standing there for a long time. Tim Bolingbroke lived next door and Rex Lay and Gabrielle, so we went in. No gas, no electric, no water but we managed. That was one of the happiest periods of my life, in there. It was a much more bohemian neighbourhood. We had a few problems on the streets getting yelled at by drunks and kids but nobody threatened our home there.

Well, we were raided by the police because there was a very heavy drug usage going on, mostly cannabis and acid but there were one or two people using heroin as well. It was drugs all the time and parties, pretty wild ones. People would just turn up, we were a feature of the Gate, it wasn't just gay people. It was difficult for those of us who actually lived there to keep some sort of regular life. There were frequent attempts at eviction, but it took them a long time. We were barred at the Champion. I remember dancing on a table there once and being physically ejected – but we could go in Finch's on the Portobello Road, which wasn't even a gay pub, and drink quite happily there with no problem in whatever we wanted to wear and people would talk to us. It was interesting that it was actually the gay community, the men, who were against us. The customers were abusive to us in the Champion, they helped to throw us out. (*Cloud Downey*)

The commune – it was stressful. Talk about PC! The moral insistence upon revolutionary codes of behaviour was very interestingly extreme. It was fighting in a very fearsome and unstructured but dogmatic way to be free. There was certainly a lot of 'you ought to wear dresses, you ought to deconstruct your masculinity – and if you don't, you're an enemy of the revolution.' I find it very difficult to pin down exactly what my position was to that, because when I look back to it I seem to have floated around in relation to it all, taking sides by my actions but not inside. Obviously I was interested in the deconstruction of gender, obviously I was interested in the actions we were doing, but I certainly always felt that there was something oppressive about the way it was sometimes being done. And again, some of the drug stuff was quite insistent, that you ought to take it because this was the way to achieve understanding . . . Not everybody took acid when I was around, that was apparently later, but I remember the only time I took acid was a half tab. I can't say I was bullied into taking it, but there was a certain amount of pressure. I think encouraged is the word.

I remember walking around Notting Hill in frocks and make-up and people asking me questions about why I was dressed like that and having perfectly sensible conversations about it . . . I think the most self-expanding times were the times when I wore frocks alone, going to a demo or party and just doing my nail varnish on the tube. Because there was a period when I would always make it very obvious, explicit in that I would wear a beard or football boots. On one particular occasion I remember sitting on the tube doing my nail varnish on the way to a dance, it must have been a Hammersmith Town Hall one because it was the District Line, and people looking but not talking, not doing anything. (*Alaric Sumner*)

Wearing drag was easier for some of the men than others:

Mick Belsten I knew through Bette, and at a Hammersmith Town Hall dance we went together and did a grand entrance in beautiful evening dresses and Mick had these beautiful velvet roses in his hair and looked amazing. It was the first time I'd seen him in drag, he'd had a lot of problems with it, he supported it but he was very hesitant about doing it himself. And then this night, he did it and we became friends. He used to stay at Colville Terrace but he was more often to be found in Bette's flat, but then he

moved into Colville Houses . . . he got more and more into
drag and feminism, it was a big thing for him.
(*Cloud Downey*)

Crocheting – Robert started it and it was a form of therapy
for us, that it was calming. We made all our cushion covers
and bedspreads and I remember always taking a bag of
wool and crochet needles to do it on the tube.
(*Alaric Sumner*)

As a sizeable minority of GLF men moved towards radical
drag as a political expression, it became a point of controversy as
well as an acid test of commitment. 'The Marxists tried to get involved with the commune at one point, but they couldn't cope with
the drag. We were in it day and night by then' (*Stuart Feather*).
'Lots of men used acid to break down their egos and to get into
drag' (*Aubrey Walter*).

> Mick was the only one of us drag queens who'd had any
> political experience, he had a strong socialist background,
> came from the Bristol docks and was very well read. John
> Chesterman and I parted company over the drag and the
> feminist politics, he couldn't cope with them. Being a
> visibly out gay person, wearing badges and things like that
> were completely new. All that we did in the Colville
> commune was to take it that one step further and say that
> all men should wear a frock. We thought that it was the
> answer. It almost was. It still is.
>
> It was discovering a new world as you discovered your
> own personality. The atmosphere was exciting and the
> ideas flowed. We called the middle-class Marxists in their
> cosy flats in West Hampstead, like Phil Powell, Martini
> Mansions, that was our name for them. It was us, who they
> classed as theoretical communists, who were putting all our
> money in one teapot and sharing all our clothes and
> possessions whilst they considered themselves the practical.
> (*Stuart Feather*)

Though the radical feminist men were talked about as
being into personal liberation, they were actually quite
community oriented . . . The actions countered the political
posturing. (*Sarah Grimes*)

There were a number of strong friendships amongst the radical drag queens and the feminist lesbians and, given the way that their politics dragged them in opposite directions, it is ironic that some of the warmest feelings expressed in people's memories were between the lesbians and the queens. As one woman from Faraday Road now sees it, 'The men at Colville Terrace weren't dressing as they did to be like the old type of transvestites of the fifties. They had taken it to an outrageous extreme, just like we did, we didn't want to fit into any roles that society had put on us and neither did they' (*Julia L*).

The new lifestyle was very attractive to some of the other gay men.

> What was interesting me more and more was the 'rad fems'. I don't know where that label came from, I remember people using the phrase, but I never used such a phrase about myself. I didn't like those political categories and I didn't use them of myself or anybody else. To me, this was drag and nothing more complicated, except that it wasn't the sort I'd seen Danny La Rue do. There was no doubt in any spectator's mind, you could see this was a man, a youth, a boy who was wearing a mixture, very often, of men's and women's clothes. What attracted me was, I thought these were the bravest people. That's what delighted me and so I wanted to know more of it and more of them and take part in it more. But there was an obstacle and that was that I don't have any ability for drag at all. Absolutely no clothes sense! That made me a singularly awful representative of that sort of look.
> (*Andrew Lumsden*)

> I left home, packed my bags and disappeared off to Colville Terrace in which most of the Brixton queens had ended up. That was opposite where Bette lived and two doors from that was David Hockney's lover who used to invite us to tea and send up food parcels. I lived there but we were getting evicted by Notting Hill Housing Trust. We were well barricaded. That was the last place for a year and a half that I had my own bed, because in Colville Houses the beds were communal.
> Mick Belsten and I found the film studio, out on one of our little trolls looking for somewhere else to live. It was at

the end of Colville Houses, a cul-de-sac, and it was like the Secret Garden because at the end of the cul de sac was this long fence with ivy growing over it, it looked like the back garden of Westbourne Park Road. But there was a gate underneath all the ivy and if you pushed at it, you could walk into this film studio. And we squatted it.

You walked into an entrance hallway and to your left was a huge kitchen with a gas point and cupboards. And you opened a door from there into a room maybe sixty by twenty-five feet, an absolute hall, totally medieval. There was a little set of stairs which went off one side above the kitchen and hallway and to two little rooms, one of which had water and another inner room that was the water closet. And there was a gallery across the hall and right at one end, a wall about eight foot high with a six foot gap that was perfect as a wardrobe. And behind that a little lean-to.

Basically, we put twelve double mattresses around two sides of the wall. One wall had shelving with books and a stereo system and the fourth wall was overhung by the gallery. Lots of big orb lights hung from the ceiling, paper lanterns sprayed with sequins and hung with feather boas just suspended in space and lots of very cheap carpeting with deco rugs thrown on top. I lived there for about seven or eight months. As well as those who'd come from Colville Terrace, there were about a dozen other people who moved in as well over part of the time. (*Julian Hows*)

It took the queens three weeks with fabric and staple guns to transform the film studio into a bizarre palace, draped so that you couldn't hear the outside. They had a fabulous collection of frocks, kept communally so 'if you wanted to wear something special, you'd squirrel it away so that no one else would come down in the frock you wanted to wear that night' (*Michael James*).

I loved the commune, which I wasn't part of. It was like stepping off the planet. You went into a no-daylight zone where there were places to sleep strewn all over the floor, posters to do with pop groups, endless sounds always on, you were always offered dope or acid. The welcome was lovely. It was unstructured to a degree that was terrifying if you had led any kind of structured life and I think there were people who came and went very quickly, in about ten

minutes. None of the ordinary ways of coping seemed to be there. Somebody might be walking round without their clothes on, somebody else spending hours and hours making up. There was a wardrobe, a very large area for frocks and shoes and make-up and mirrors, people could spend hours in there sometimes. Somebody might be making love on one or another mattress, all in this twilight. Twilight gives the wrong impression, I remember colours. There were blues and golds, yellow, all under artificial light. Candles. Somebody stole the candles from the church, rather apologetically, one evening when there was no alternative and the vicar said, 'That's all right', when he was told – 'If you needed them, you needed them.'
(*Andrew Lumsden*)

Mick Belsten I thought was one of the most interesting people I met through GLF. He was quite a lot older than me, thirty-eight then and a very thoughtful sort of person. He was the first man I saw in bed with another man. We stayed over there once and it was all non-monogamy and moving around, the rules they had there. Everyone had sex with everyone else and it was him and Peter Bourne lying one on top of the other. I thought it was rather erotic, they were just kissing, they didn't really do anything but I thought it was rather wonderful. I remember he said to me he thought it was very very sad how many gay men don't take the opportunity of the fact of their homosexuality to think about being men. To never think about the implications of their homosexuality, which I thought was interesting and very true, a missed opportunity . . . It was a houseful of strong characters certainly and they weren't all the same, some of them had very strong egos.
(*Nettie Pollard*)

We had our routine, we knew that we had to earn our money so we had a stall Fridays and Saturdays. I didn't like doing the stall myself, Stuart loved doing it. It was bric-a-brac, bits and pieces, we used to sell stuff to Brian Ferry and Eno, we used to get their stiletto shoes for them and jackets. I didn't do the stall often, what I used to do was make sure – I was brought up in an Irish household and you've got to eat – these dizzy queens, dear, couldn't shop to save their lives, so I made sure we had food in. I went down with whoever was around and got our evening meal together, got our Sunday lunch, and the rest of the week more or less organized itself, but as long as we had food on the weekends. Then we'd all be back by about three on a Saturday, Roger [a friend of Stuart] ran baths for us from his boiler, he'd have upwards of ten to fifteen of us from two o'clock. I always went over for the last bath about eight o'clock. In between early tea and the last of us coming back from Rosie's [Roger] someone would have scored acid for us. On the odd occasion, there was no acid and we were out till midnight in Bette's van knocking on dealers' doors but we never had a Saturday without acid, we always got some eventually. At ten shillings, 50p a tab, it was a cheap weekend, pretty pictures and everything. Very economical.

We pooled all our money, it was put in a thirties teapot, but I've subsequently found out a lot of people took out far more than they ever put in and that's very distressing, but it's all past history now. I used to feel guilty about buying myself a chocolate rum truffle when I cashed my giro. That was my little treat for myself and then I'd give the money in. Other people were ripping us off left right and centre. So I guess it all had to fold up in the end, but it was magical. It was lovely but like everything else it had its peak and finished. (*Michael James*)

All the money went into an art deco teapot that I still have. I bought it in Maidstone Market by going up to Stuart Feather and saying 'I've just seen this Clarice Cliff teapot and it's got a chip in its spout, but it's only twenty-five pence.' . . . Stuart, when he decides to move into action, he's very fast. It was like something from Loony Tunes.

We were all getting money various ways. We were mainly on the dole and I, being still a youngster, had to go to the youth employment office in Shepherds Bush and register to be employed. I went down there in a frock. A very nice Grecian frock, boots from Granny Takes A Trip, red-hennaed hair, long cigarette holder and a gold lamé clutch purse. I thought, well, no-one's going to make me fucking work, dear. So I wandered down there, went in and nearly got mobbed by the sixteen-year-old Uxbridge boys. This man interviewed me and freaked out, got me to fill in a form and said I didn't ever have to come back. They gave me money over the counter and said I could just phone them in future and confirm I was still looking for work and they'd send the giro.

We hardly ever went to gay liberation meetings by then. What was the point of sitting in a meeting talking about gay liberation and thinking about doing things about gay liberation and planning things about gay liberation when you could sit in Colville Houses and actually live it? There was no point to meetings.

But we had Gay Days and marches. Coming through Colville Houses, on a Saturday it could be eighty to a hundred people passing through the house for a cup of coffee, a joint, a chat, another joint. Cream cakes, maybe a dance. Three or four of us would be sitting on the mattresses holding court for various groups or interests – look, it's automatic, my hands are automatically trying to roll joints as I talk about it! Stuart would be rolling one sort of joint, I'd be rolling another and then Chris S would decide, sod this, let's make the joint into the object, so he would make the joint a foot long, put the joint into a long roach which had pearls draped from it, or butterfly wings in wire and paper, or diamante or ostrich feathers. It was life as performance art and we were the performers.
(*Julian Hows*)

Drugs were central to the commune, especially acid – Microdots, Pyramids, Windowpanes, Scorpions, Crabs, Sugarcubes and something called Purple Haze which was reputed to have been brought over by the Grateful Dead. 'I never dropped acid till I'd got my make-up on' (*Michael James*).

We used to get flak on the streets. I remember one time, I was pushing a baby [from the commune] in a wheelchair down to the Market, someone asked me what I was doing and I said, 'I'm going to take [him] for a walk down Portobello', and some of the men started giving me flak and the women went, 'Leave him alone, he's got a baby with him, leave him alone', so the baby was my protection . . . it was just my turn to look after him for the day.

I remember one of my suggestions was that we should all be naked in the commune, to get used to each other's bodies. I think I just wanted to get them all stark naked.

And then I said 'I think we should have a Roman orgy', and Julian thought that was a wonderful idea and arranged it, with columns he'd found somewhere or the other, in some studio and drapes . . . he'd done this wonderful job of making a Roman setting and we did all end up having mad sex at one point or another. Some people sat about looking disapproving – people who were less confident about their sexuality.

I was constantly told off for bringing boys in – I thought this was what gay liberation was about. Mick Belsten said 'There's not one young boy that walks through that door that doesn't end up in your bed!' He was very angry. And I said 'Well, I hope it continues.' I was very interested in sex. I lived in the commune and kept the flat on, gave keys out to people who wanted to go there to be on their own. We shared all our money in a teapot, took out what we wanted. You never knew who was getting how much, you just took what you needed. It worked because people really did trust each other and everyone was, if you like, infatuated with each other, and some of that affection goes on to this day. But people moved on because it wasn't their scene, or people started to take the wrong drugs . . .

One of the nice things we did in the commune, we had a reading of *Lysistrata*, it was very funny. I was dying to do a bit of acting, I was 'We've got to act!' and Mick Belsten said 'Well, fucking well act then!' So I bought twelve copies of *Lysistrata* and we sat round. One of the women was called Joyce, she was about in her mid-seventies I suppose. She was here with her younger lover. She was a street woman. She took part in the reading as did Chris S who thought he was Marilyn Monroe, he really did think he was at one point, it was all the drugs . . . he read his part as Marilyn Monroe and everybody read their parts as what they wanted to be and it was just hilarious. This woman Joyce turned out to be a wonderful actress, a natural. I suppose I'd never thought of myself as someone who'd be able to organize a theatre group. I always thought that was a special skill, and then I met Hot Peaches in '76 and realized it was about being bossy and I was the bossiest queen, so I decided I should do something . . .

We were a tourist attraction and we hated it. They'd be down Portobello Road with their cameras and the more

they clicked the angrier we got. I had a stall on Portobello outside the Rising Sun. But we were deeply suspicious of breadheads, as we called them, people who ran around ripping GLF off. It seems like a long summer now . . .
(*Bette Bourne*)

One new addition to the commune at this time was Steven Bradbury, a young gay man from the Potteries who had come to London to work in a bank. Very much in the closet and on the scene, he ended up by chance in the Portobello Road branch of the Midland Bank, where the queens of Colvillia would take their giros. He remembered seeing these spectacularly dressed men in robes and make-up and envying their freedom and self-confidence. And one day, when he was feeling particularly fed up with the bank and the scene and life, in came the queens and while he was serving them the manager made an insulting remark about 'queers'. Without pausing, Steven closed his counter and walked round, out through the door and up the road, following the queens back to their commune, running away to join the circus. Steven died before he could contribute to this book, but Stuart Feather confirmed the tale. 'The story of Steven Bradbury and the bank is true. He left his timidity behind in the bank, too, when he put a frock on.'

The Colville commune also put together *Come Together* 15, the last but one issue, in early 1973. It is a microcosm of all that the commune stood for and includes a photograph of most of them. The whole of the SCUM Manifesto, which advocated violent revolution by women against men, was included, along with pieces on communal living, on sexism, on masculinity and queendom. Some, such as Michael James' 'Working Class War Baby', are autobiographical, and others, such as Julian Hows' 'Childhood, Ageism and the Ageing Pederast', are a mix of theories and observations. ('The gay teacher, even if he is a good fuck on the side, is totally supporting a system which is oppressive to children.') The introduction was written by Ramsay, one of the few black GLF people. In the commune's history, 'Happy Families', there is an invitation to visit them. 'Come up and see us sometime. We are squatting in a disused film studio with no bath but plenty of bubbles.'

It was totally last minute, totally! I wrote 'Working Class War Baby' within two or three minutes, or as long as it took me to sit down and type it straight out. All it got were punctuation and spelling corrections. Bill Halstead and

Mick Belsten wrote for it. I think Mick Belsten wrote the piece with the remark about bubbles although it sounds like a Julian line. (*Michael James*)

I had an article in it, it was SO bad . . . the picture was fabulous, though. I did it on this stand-up-and-beg Remington, everybody had to write and type their own articles. Mick Belsten did the big article with me and Stuart and whoever was there and stoned at the time. We did it because it was at that stage when things had fallen apart a bit and we thought it was our turn. (*Julian Hows*)

Chapter seventeen

Cottages and Haunted Houses

We wanted to be free and to trust but it doesn't work like that.
–Julia L

THERE is a line scribbled in the margin of the second page of *Come Together* 15 which says 'Happy Families don't SNAP!' But by the time it was written, GLF had well and truly broken apart. And it had been the actions of women from the other major politicized commune, that of Faraday Road, which had helped to bring it to a point where even the most obtuse had to recognize that GLF was no longer one happy family.

The first women's issue of *Come Together* has a range of photographs of prominent GLF women dressed as gangsters. They are women playing light-heartedly with their sexuality and roles, as well as making a serious point about it. The whole edition, while looking at issues specifically relating to women and lesbians, is undogmatic and inclusive in its style, accepting of diversity while critical of sexism and other problems within GLF.

But that issue was written in the early summer of the first year of GLF, while women were finding their voice within the organization. By the following year, they had found voices but were forced to face the fact that many of the men didn't want to listen and a growing number didn't care about what they were saying. And now, after the cataclysmic effect of the GLF lesbians' intervention at the Skegness Women's Liberation Conference, they had another home to go to.

As the women's movement developed more and more lesbians became involved, and eventually the lesbians in

GLF decided to work within the women's movement and also more straight women became lesbians . . . [In GLF] there was all sorts of chauvinism. I remember very clearly the night before I was arrested, chairing a meeting with Denis Lemon who did *Gay News* and he was actually very new, he'd just come along and not been very involved before, and every time there was a difficult bit of the meeting I remember him saying 'Look, just stand back and I'll deal with this', so those sort of attitudes were quite prevalent. (*Angie Weir*)

Some of the men made it intolerable for the women by the way that they behaved. People like Tony Salvis opposed moves by pro-feminist men to get the men to look at their chauvinism. (*Aubrey Walter*)

I sympathized with the complaints that the women were making within GLF. The meetings were dominated by a handful of very strong, self confident men . . . there was a more egalitarian spread between the women speakers, not one or two who dominated in the way that a handful of men did.

Quite a lot of the men in GLF made a conscious attempt to give women space and keep their own contributions brief, [but] there was a group of GLF men who were not consciously misogynistic but tended to neglect or overlook lesbian issues and perspectives. They were very reluctant to take on board the critique of sexism that GLF was developing. They saw the gay struggle as distinct and separate from the women's struggle. It was their refusal to acknowledge the links between patriarchy and homophobia that got on the nerves of a lot of the women and some of us men too. They had a very shallow law reform, civil rights agenda. (*Peter Tatchell*)

GLF's success and public profile meant that every gay organization had achieved a large increase in membership during 1971. But many men with a CHE-type agenda of single issue activism found that they preferred to work in GLF because of its greater attachment to those aspects of the counterculture that they found attractive. Basically, CHE was not by and large the place for dope and rock 'n' roll. These men came increasingly into conflict, not only with the women but also with the radical feminist men;

but it was the two groups of men who had the social training to fight it out in the meetings.

There had also been something of a quiet power struggle in the women's group of GLF. The socialist feminist politics of the earlier leading women, such as Mary McIntosh and Elizabeth Wilson, had been to some extent superseded by the radical feminist politics of the women who identified with the Faraday Road commune. The arguments over Media Workshop had caused rifts and then Angie's arrest and defence took up much of the former group's energies. 'Then there was a split between Angie Weir and our house, because they'd gone off in one direction and this separatist movement grew and grew. It became quite nasty because nobody was allowed to disagree' (*Julia L*).

The second women's edition of *Come Together*, number 11, was produced at Faraday Road and shows the totally different flavour of their politics. It contains a number of articles (from both sexes) that assume women should work separately from men, and one called 'Why I Cannot Work In The Gay Movement'. A letter from four Faraday Road women announces the Women's Think-In on 29 January and another article suggests a 'gay women's centre'. One dissenting piece from Street Theatre, while full of self-criticism, defends radical drag and questions the women–good, men–bad analysis which was emerging.

The Faraday Road commune which produced this edition had evolved over time from a mixed sex and sexuality group into a lesbian separatist one, based on the experiences of the women involved. 'During the early stages there were two straight men there, one of them called Tom and very sexist and another, Bob Weaver, who later came out as well. They didn't mix with the commune and kept to their own room' (*Tony Halliday*). One founding member of the commune, who was there through all the changes, now takes a more jaundiced though possibly more accurate view of communal life than the rosy memories of Colvillia in the previous chapter.

> I heard about these short life houses . . . I was put on a list, which was short because nobody knew about it. There was the Festival of Light and all the theatre groups in London got involved. I was sent by my group, which was mixed and not gay, to meet the women's theatre group at what turned out to be Angie Weir's house . . . I went down into the basement of this house and looked around and went

'Oh!' I ended up sitting next to Caroline Thompson and her girlfriend Lorna and we were chatting, and they said they hadn't got anywhere to live so I said 'I've got some space, come and live in my house.' So this gay couple moved in. And that was the beginning of the end really.

Caroline and Lorna moved into the house and I met their friends and one thing led to another. The politics started and the men were slowly forced out of the house. Straight men in this house! It was silly really and very stressed. Other women moved in and poor old Alan was the last to go, a friend of mine . . . And then gay men moved in. That was okay. Richard Dipple, Aubrey used to visit and various other people. At that point it was gay fellowship, we are one, we are united. There's that dreadful article about where we share socks and T-shirts and all the rest of it. And meanwhile I was the only person who was working in the house, the only one who ever did, and I continued to work the whole time I was in the house. How I ever did it I don't know, because we were stoned out of our heads at night. I'd be home an hour and I'd be smashed.

It was the most haunted house you've ever been in. The first time I went in was with Caroline Thompson and there was an atmosphere. Down in the basement, she was one side of the room and I was the other. She said, 'Stop tapping my shoulder' and I said, 'But I'm not.' Now that should have been a warning to us, but it wasn't. The house had belonged to some old girls, everything was original including the wiring. How it didn't catch on fire I'll never know. There was no hot water so we fitted our own geysers, learnt how to do it ourselves and it was all quite exciting.

It was all one big happy family and lots of gay politics and sharing and men and women coming round. The doorbell would go, October would walk in in her school uniform straight from school. Everybody was welcome, we had women's meetings there, gay men's meetings, you name it. Slowly the word spread and so many people stayed, all over the place. And we had the ghost . . . People would be in the darkroom and their cigarette would be thrown on the floor. It was eerie.

So more and more people would come round, Rachel and Edie. There was Rachel, six foot three in a tight red dress with shoulders like a lumberjack, huge Adam's apple, thick pebble glasses and 'Hi, I'm Rachel.' Oh, okay. Everybody was welcome. Then there was Bobbi who we thought was a woman, turned out to be a man who'd had breasts implanted and then he had them cut off. It was all terribly matter of fact and if there was anybody weird in the neighbourhood, gay, transsexual, whatever, they were down our house. More and more people.

We tried encounter groups and therapy groups. One day this woman called Sandy came in, six foot, huge, very powerful woman. Said she was having a bad time. Somebody suggested rebirth, we were into rebirth at that time, so anyway it ended up with us chasing her round the house, her naked under a fur coat turned inside out, screaming 'I want to be reborn!' And then she went through the downstairs floorboards, I'll never forget it. We had to pull her out. She was hysterical, 'I need birth!' screaming at the top of her voice. God knows what the neighbours thought was going on.

The gay men lived in a commune down the road in Colville Houses and it was this huge old film studio with beds neatly in rows. And at the end, all the frocks hanging up. Frocks, not dresses, mind you. We used to go in there and they used to visit us and we all went to gay liberation meetings and down Portobello Road, us with our trilby hats and stetsons on in jackets and them in their dresses, hand in hand, stretching across Portobello Road, the brothers and sisters and men dressed up as Marlene Dietrich and all. There was a local witch who joined in, Lyndsay, who cast spells for people who were arrested. She cast my spell.

There was a huge split between the men and women. The house ended up just as women. Richard moved out. Mad Lizzie, Sapphire, Lorna, Caroline, Barbara, me, Lynn, there were lots of us. We were still together as a household, we had a lounge and a huge bedroom where women could stay, everything was free love and everything else, you can use your imagination. Of course relationships started happening and splitting up and the dramas were out of this world. Everything was analysed in full . . . people came from all over the country and then another women's house set up in Kilburn. You could pick up the phone and get them without having to dial a number, we were convinced that we were tapped, everyone was paranoid. You'd dial another number and still get the women's house. It was outrageous.

We'd have group sessions where we would all join together and become one. Someone would lie down and then you'd all touch that person, to give them spiritual healing and uplift. Except if somebody fancied that person, the touching became very sensual. It was all a big fraud. Meanwhile we were having seances. They got quite intense. We had one and the goldfish in the tank went onto its side and stayed there for the whole seance and then afterwards it was all right again. We got in touch with women from Venus at that point, who'd landed in Wales.

It was all very intense and spiritual and sexual. Then every Saturday we'd go to the Crown and Woolpack disco in Islington, drink as much as we could as fast as we could. It was run by two huge women who were together and some other women from East London who were a bit rough. We weren't into violence. You'd be up there, it was the first real gay women's pub disco, we wouldn't go into the Gateways because it wasn't politically right on. Barbara Klecki and people had been thrown out for leafleting. So we had our own place. Well, talk about politically right on. Pissed as puddings and the fights! I remember I was talking to somebody once and they went 'Duck!' and a record hit the wall just above our heads and we carried on. Then somebody would say, 'Quickly, help, there's someone cut their wrist in the toilet!' and we'd say 'Oh dear, who is it this time?'

We were going to change the world, we really believed it. I think a lot of it did change, a lot of political viewpoints and sexual viewpoints. In the house, everything was very intense and incredibly traumatic. And there was acid. I would never take it because I don't like things that make me hallucinate. So four women went into one room for their first experience, they cut a tab of acid into four pieces and came out with new feelings and messages about sexuality. We would play music, we had a banjo and we'd all sit together and make music in the evening, we were all musicians at heart and we all had the ability. So we'd be sitting there stoned making this hideous row, singing and playing. Awful. But it was really amazing, man, and we were really into it and we could dig each other's vibrations.

And nobody should be jealous and nobody should be monogamous, so of course as soon as somebody became slightly monogamous and then they went off with somebody else, there would be a jealous tantrum so we'd all have to talk about it all night. And we talked about it around seven nights a week. Week after week. Endless, stoned. Then of course we'd all go off to Hackney and somebody would meet somebody else and there'd be more rows the next day because it's politically right on to be with whoever you want and if you want to, you should do it. Unless it happened to you, do you know what I mean? What we believed and how we coped with it were two very different things. We wanted to be free and to trust, but it doesn't work like that. We didn't realize it at the time.

Then slowly but surely there was this period when everything seemed to break up and some of the women in the house suddenly went into a total extreme of separatism. That was it, men – don't need them, don't want them, rabbits can have babies by themselves so we can, basically. Separatism reared its ugly head very fast, at a great rate. It was like this huge enveloping bubble that spread round the house. Meanwhile one woman said she had become pregnant and had never fucked anybody. I don't know if people believed it or not, I think we wanted to. (*Julia L*)

One of the women became pregnant. I went into the toilet and found 'Immaculate Conception' written on the toilet wall, and the line was that this was an immaculate conception because she couldn't remember having been with a man. It was an insane place, Faraday Road, and of course I didn't toe the line because I wasn't a separatist. Richard Dipple lived there for a while in the commune but they threw him out because one of the women decided he was trying to seduce them. I tell you, this was the last thing on Richard's mind. (*Carla Toney*)

There were in-house arguments because people were starting to vary in their politics. I taught boys and girls, and my cat was a boy cat, much to everybody's horror. Splits started happening because we had this separatist idealism but I couldn't live with it because (a) I liked my father,

(b) I had a cat and (c) I taught boys. The other house went separatist too so we had this separatist clique. A friend of mine came round and brought me a Christmas tree and they wouldn't let him in, they had to open the basement door and bring it in. Some of us were having a very hard time, but we were still together. Gay men were shunned, ordinary men didn't exist. It ended up with some of us moving and one woman wanted a child and she'd worked out how to have a female child, separatist and so forth, and what happened was, of course, she had a boy child and then it all changed. That was a bit of a hoot . . .

I remember one day sitting in bed and the door opened and everybody piled in because of my politics, they didn't agree with them. Shouting and screaming, real mob handed but I was quite a strong personality and I wouldn't budge. And also my name was on the rent book. I will always remember my boy cat sitting on my lap looking at them. I wouldn't answer. 'You're doing this, you're manipulating that' which I probably was. At that age and with several strong personalities in one house, you don't know how to handle it.

The whole atmosphere was terribly political. Leaving GLF – I don't think it's completely fair to say it was mainly Faraday Road, a lot of it was that at first gay liberation was marvellous and then a lot of the women wanted to find their own identity and they were young women. They wanted to find their own identity and not be driven by the gay men's needs, sexually and politically. I think separatism had already crept in a bit, so there were a group of women who were part and parcel of the move, but there were lots of other women there who went along with it quite happily. I remember all the women getting up and walking out, I don't think I was concentrating at that point, and suddenly there was an exodus. (*Julia L*)

That night I was there. I went with all the other women to a pub near All Saints Hall and the women got quite emotional and were saying things like, the men didn't care about them, all they cared about was cottaging and cruising. It was the radical feminist type women rather than the socialist feminist type women. It was Faraday Road and the women who hung about with them. I don't really remember specifically who it was but it was a general feeling. Frankie was another who was saying it. People like Mary and Elizabeth were still around but I don't remember them being there that night. I think they may not have been. There were quite a lot of women there, about forty or fifty, but obviously they had come in strength in order to walk out. And then we went in and it was the ordinary part of the meeting, and then one of the women got up and said why the women were going to leave.

It was at that point that I was a bit shocked because I could see relief on some of the men's faces. The ones who were saying things like, 'The women ought to be given all of the money', I just thought, you know, it's a way of getting rid of us, isn't it, so they can just be on their own. Several men were saying from the audience, 'Give them the money, we loathsome men should . . . pay them to go away.' I was a lot more impressed by the men who were very upset about it and wanted us to stay but perhaps respected the decision. Some of the men did try and remonstrate with us. Eventually it was agreed that the women should be given half the money and they all went out and about two or three of us were left in there. I had mixed feelings because I really thought that I ought to walk out with everyone and I had also felt that I wanted to stay because it was clear that women were still welcome there.

Blossom [a man from Bounds Green commune] came up to me and went something like, 'I'm so glad that you're still with us love', and I thought, well, I don't know if I am after that. Because I was fairly shocked by the attitude of some of the men. Because I'd actually thought they were much less sexist than men elsewhere and I felt that the women were perhaps over-reacting and yet I did see that reaction in quite a few of them and that made me more worried than I had been before. (*Nettie Pollard*)

Not all the women, especially the bisexual and heterosexual ones, were so sure of the move. 'It was the women splitting that killed it off – it was fashionable to be a separatist. I thought it was boring – you don't fight sexism by walking away from it. The men were sexist, but not that sexist. There was a paranoiac atmosphere' (*Sue Winter*). Some lesbians also felt the move to be false and were suspicious of the motives of the men supporting it.

There was a lot of tokenism about women really, and that was all a bit spurious in a way. Some of the men were very supportive but there was a level of hostility underlying it all in the case of some men – not all by any means. I think in the end they [David and Aubrey] made this totally disingenuous argument. The feminist line was that women should meet separately, that women should not meet within GLF but separately, period. That was their radical feminist line . . . Some men were on the side of the women. I don't have any quarrel with Bette Bourne or Stuart, they were a bit more clued up, but I think David and Aubrey mobilized a latent misogyny, a kind of rank and file and it was all very plausible. As far as I'm concerned it would be wrong to say that we got fed up and decided to go. I feel we were pushed out and manipulated into going. I didn't feel like we had a choice. I didn't have anything to do with the second women's *Come Together*, I think it was very much Faraday Road. (*Elizabeth Wilson*)

I was at the meeting where the women split, not long after I arrived. Men were always in charge, grabbing the mike and it was very hard for women to get heard. The women were pissed off and they had a clearer political vision and had done a lot more groundwork than many of the men. The women were very diverse, from straight women through bisexual hippie chicks to butch dykes, all kinds of them, but they were joined together by being patronized and having to fight for any space. And by and large they were excluded from the mass sex that the men were having, which acted as a bond. (*Tim Clark*)

I wanted the women to stay in GLF but I understood and accepted why they had to leave. I didn't agree with breaking GLF up into local groups although perhaps it was an inevitable development. I feared decentralization would fragment the energies of GLF. We were at the cutting edge of a new and revolutionary movement. There were not sufficient activists with enough energy . . . When the women left I had the feeling that GLF had begun to die as well . . . Of course, not all the women left GLF.
(*Peter Tatchell*)

When the women had left – the women had been saying that they couldn't stand it for a long time before, so it wasn't precisely a shock. But it was disgraceful that the women said they had had enough. Probably if I had a clear chronological memory I might think it was the moment that GLF ceased in its first form. It was done most courteously, they were extremely polite, they just said, 'We can't cope with the way things are going on.' It was pleasantly said, it wasn't a slanging match in any way that I recall. There was rather a stunned silence.
(*Andrew Lumsden*)

I wasn't part of the group of women that left, but everything went wrong after that. Some men got very misogynistic at the meetings and the women had met in the pub and discussed leaving earlier. Four or five of us stayed and the rest, thirty or so, walked out. I was very upset. After that, gay women's lib used to meet at the Angel, but nothing much came of it and I continued to go to GLF.
(*Nettie Pollard*)

Nettie was not alone in this. Although the general meetings from here on were very male dominated, the working groups and projects continued to be mixed to some degree and there was still collaboration on specific issues. 'The women's walk-out was largely symbolic. Lots of the centrally involved women continued to work with us' (*Jeffrey Weeks*). But it was now easier for the men who wanted to, to ignore both women and sexism as an issue; the impetus of much of GLF's theoretical basis, of what distinguished it from the rest of the movement, had gone.

By the time I was acquitted, the general meetings had ceased and it had sort of split up into local GLFs. I largely went into the women's movement. In a sense there wasn't a gay politics for women at that time. Lesbians were going into the women's movement, I don't think any lesbians went into gay things for a bit. It wasn't a conscious departure, it was just that if you were a lesbian, that's what you did. And of course there was the whole development of radical feminism, which some lesbians were quite involved with although I was never involved in that and didn't really support it. The women's group at Faraday Road, they were into an intense sort of lived radical feminism, though radical feminism was very associated with lesbianism in a way that I think, how shall I say, rather undermined lesbian sexuality. (*Angie Weir*)

But it is very easy, with hindsight, to dismiss the split as motivated by an extreme form of feminist politics which has subsequently been largely repudiated. What should be remembered was that those politics came out of a more than justified anger at the way that women were still treated in an organization which claimed to have an understanding of, and opposition to, sexism.

What caused trouble between the men and women was that so many of the men wanted to talk about cottaging in the meetings . . . I can't remember details but it was a frequent subject and women resented so much time spent on it . . . They tried to tokenize me. I was asked to speak on television and places and I asked for other women to come along too and they wouldn't let them so I refused. 'Want A Token Sister?' [*Come Together* 10] was written after I was invited to represent the women in the Gay Liberation Front on television and I did not wish to be the only woman, the only spokeswoman to represent all the views. I said I wanted other women and I was told it wasn't appropriate so I chose not to – I thought, they wanted a token woman, there were to be a number of men and one woman.
(*Carla Toney*)

'Want A Token Sister, Mister?' is a highly articulate, angry polemic which any lesbian who has been used as a 'trusty' to validate a group of gay men who want to feel politically correct can relate to, and is as true at the end of the 1990s as it was at the start of the 1970s.

Drag, however radical, increasingly fuelled the anger of many GLF women who saw it not as men breaking down their own inhibitions and machismo, but as a guying of traditional womanhood.

I remember being somewhere at a GLF do, with what would have been called heavy women, and it had become an issue of what the queens were doing about dragging up and how they were portraying women. There was a lot of queens where it was very much a political issue, a statement . . . it was something like 'Hey Big Spender' [and one queen] had this white dress on with two slits up the side and he had no knickers on and he was showing it all. Hazel and her girlfriend went upset and had a physical fight . . . went up onto the stage and I felt quite cut because these women were my pals. And yet I . . . felt they had a right to get up there because they had to recognize that this was camp, it was gay men camping it up, whatever they were wearing, they weren't pretending to be women, they were wearing garments that people associated with women. The women had trousers on, I really went into one and Hazel never really did forgive me. (*Harry Beck*)

Radical drag didn't start out as a problem for most of the women; we had been pro it as a political move, but it started to get very problematical. I remember one Ball where some men were wearing what felt like very mocking radical drag and others were doing a striptease. None of it had been thought through. Carla got very angry at them. (*Mary McIntosh*)

I don't know what was the most significant thing. I think the women in GLF then did feel very odd about drag and it was a problem, and men used to say to us, 'Why don't you get into drag', without realizing that it's not the same. I think there was some recognition that traditional drag might be offensive to women. There were all these efforts to have radical drag, so they would dress up in all these horrible old clothes. I remember Phil Powell in a headscarf and he looked like Ena Sharples. (*Elizabeth Wilson*)

Drag or transvestism as an issue was always clearly separated from transsexuality in the minds of most GLF women. Indeed, for much of the life of the GLF women's group, transsexuals were welcomed by many lesbians and seen as less problematic politically than straight transvestites.

I got involved in the TV/TS group of GLF. That was a rather odd thing. We'd made ourselves available for straight transvestites and it wasn't really our thing at all, we were into gender confusion and sexuality, not into passing as women, but we felt we had a bit of a duty to welcome them into GLF. I got involved because I knew a transsexual really well. It was a real eye-opener because I rapidly discovered that they were into something totally different. I ended up going to their conferences and then realized that I was there as a voyeur, it wasn't my thing, I was a fraud and there for the wrong reasons. But there were big clashes between the trannies and the men from GLF. We never found a bridge, many of them were heterosexual anyway, the transvestites. The transsexuals believed they were women, some of them went to the women's group like Rachel who went to Holland and Carol. (*Cloud Downey*)

There was lots of discussion on whether pre-operative transsexuals should be able to go to the women's group. They were never banned and some did go. The main thing is that virtually everybody who was transsexual in GLF was male-to-female, in fact I can't think specifically of anyone who identified the other way around although I can think of someone I thought was, but wasn't out. In later GLF there was a transsexual group and some came then, but at the early meetings there weren't. Claudia was the first one, quite mad but in a queeny way. Then there was Bobbi who tended not to wear skirts and dresses. She was wearing silver boots and black trousers and going to the women's group, and I thought I wonder if Bobbi thinks that he/she is wearing women's clothes. In a way he didn't look any different from male clothes.

The problem about transsexuals was twofold. One, that transsexuality wasn't particularly well known at the time and a lot of people didn't believe it existed, and that maybe these people were gay men who weren't particularly well adjusted because of the way that straight society looked at them. And there was the problem that they wanted to join the women's group and the women's group was based on common experience and often talked about things like childhood experiences. And I felt extremely torn on the subject myself because I felt that transsexuals were perfectly valid, and didn't feel that they should be excluded, but at the same time I realized that their history wasn't entirely the same as women.

There was a time in the later era when Faraday Road was going when there might be ten transsexuals and about twelve women and it became like a mixed group because . . . there were people in the very early stages as far as any change they might be wanting to go through. Some of the women felt that these people had very male attitudes and were very patronizing to women and trying to steal women's oppression while not giving up their prick power. There was a great deal of feeling of that. And certainly a lot of them weren't particularly aware from the feminist point of view, so they may have reflected male attitudes that they'd been brought up with . . . I don't think there was any time when transsexuals were utterly banned from the women's group.

I remember Rachel and Edith coming who were a married couple, Rachel being biologically male at the time – that was fairly late on . . . we had a women's think-in at All Saints Hall on a Saturday and there was a lot of discussion as to whether Rachel, who I think was the only transsexual there, should be allowed in, with people saying 'Really, I'm not having that man in here' and 'This man's trying to take over women's space.' I remember he had on purple corduroy jeans with tights and women's shoes, some sort of blouse, and this was raging on in the hall and then suddenly this drunken man who'd seen people coming in started lurching around in the hall and saying 'What's that man doing here?' And the women at that point said 'That's not a man, that's a woman, now get out.' I thought that was a nice bit of solidarity, for the women to say, we think we'll have our differences to ourselves but if a straight man comes in we're not taking it from him. (*Nettie Pollard*)

The women's think-in was the one advertised in *Come Together* 11 and was the occasion on which most of the women agreed to formally walk out of GLF at a general meeting.

It was obvious after that meeting that the women were going to leave. I mean, they really did believe that the men were just into power and that really because GLF wanted to change the world that if the world was run by those men they didn't really think they would be any better off. That may or may not have been ultimately true but the thing was, GLF wasn't really going to change the world, I didn't think it was. I think it had a fantastically big effect, actually, even now, but the world's a little bit harder to change than that. It's not being run by radical feminist gay men with those ideals of society.

GLF was like a comet – it wasn't going to continue. At the beginning, what we had in common was much more important than all the differences between men and women, between socialists and radical feminists and everything else – people who were interested in cottaging and people who weren't, people who wanted to concentrate on women's issues and people who didn't, there was an enormous difference . . . By the time that initial excitement of being together and coming out had finished, we were all thinking about different things. People wanted to do different projects and go in different directions . . . It would have been nice if it could have continued like that because it was so exciting, but I think in a way that just was the nature of it, that it couldn't. And therefore I don't think it was that significant that the women left, I think it was a symptom of the fact that GLF was dying rather than the cause of it. (*Nettie Pollard*)

A note circulated at the following general meeting shows that the meeting of 9 February, while chaotic, had made a clear commitment to give the women leaving half the funds of the organization, some £260. No clearer indication of the attitude of the majority of men remaining in the organization can be given than the fact that this money was never handed over because the treasurer, Michel, was adamantly opposed to it; and that this never became an issue for the group as a whole and was a surprise to many who were told of it twenty-five years later. Lesbian feminism was out of sight and rapidly out of mind for them, but this did not signal any period of cosy *rapprochement* for the many gay men and fewer lesbians who were left – because its replacement, radical feminism, was driven by the queens. And however feminist the queens might consider their politics, they were men who had no intention of leaving quietly and nowhere else to go even if they had.

The GLF banner just before confiscation by the police, 25 September 1971 (© Martin Corbett)

centre: Action at its most direct – Pan was asked for a lot of refunds, thanks to GLF

below: Stickers for Reuben's book, October 1971

PAN BOOKS LTD., 22, TOTHILL ST., LONDON S.W.1.

IN VIEW OF CERTAIN CRITICISMS OF DR. DAVID REUBEN'S BOOK 'EVERYTHING YOU WANTED TO KNOW ABOUT SEX', PAN BOOKS LTD. UNDERTAKE TO REFUND IN FULL THE RETAIL PRICE, PLUS POSTAGE, IF YOU ARE NOT FULLY SATISFIED AND IF YOU GIVE YOUR REASONS.
PLEASE FILL IN THIS FORM AND RETURN IT, TOGETHER WITH THE BOOK, TO THE ABOVE ADDRESS.

YOUR NAME AND ADDRESS:

DANGER
THIS BOOK IS POISON
'Everything You Wanted To Know About Sex'
by "Doctor" David Reuben
IS INACCURATE HYSTERICAL & DANGEROUS

WARNING

THIS BOOK DOES NOT REPRESENT THE MAJORITY OF MEDICAL & PSYCHIATRIC OPINION

above: Denis Lemon and a fourteen-foot cucumber, Pan Books HQ,
10 December 1971 *(© Jeff Katz)*

below: GLF protest at Pan Books HQ *(© Jeff Katz)*

left: GLF lesbians tell
Time Out to
stop patronizing
them,
19 February 1972
(© Pennie Smith)

below: GLF at the
Roundhouse,
19 February 1972 –
women and men
together despite the
walkout
(© Pennie Smith)

above: The queens take a stroll, 27 June 1972 – Mike Rhodes, John Church, Cloud Downey, Michael James, Alaric Sumner

above right: Michael James and friends play hide and seek with the police at Picadilly Circus, 27 June 1972

right: Michael James, Mick Belsten and the GLF chorus line reclaim Trafalgar Square, 27 June 1972

right: Gathering at the Embankment on 1 July 1972 – Michael Mason, sporting a *Gay News* boater, reads *Come Together*

below: Getting to be a habit – nun (probably Chris Blaby) at first Pride rally, 1972

above: Good, Proud, but too nice a day to be Angry – the first Pride rally,
1 July 1972

below: The kissing game, Hyde Park Gay Day after the march, 1 July 1972

The Special Branch object to being photographed –
Angry Brigade proceedings, 1972

Chapter eighteen

Pride and Prejudice

Fascists in frocks. –variously attributed to David Seligman or
Denis Lemon
It was a social comedy more than anything else.
–John Chesterman

THERE were three major splits within GLF between
summer 1971 and summer 1972, each of which was interwoven
with the various personalities involved. First, there were the
socialist revolutionaries versus those who put sexism and sexuality
first; then the radical lesbian feminists against male chauvinists;
and finally, the radical feminist men versus single-issue gay civil
rights activists. Each of these polarities left a lot of bewildered
people milling around in the middle and led to lots of accusations
of elitism, vanguardism and any other -ism you could think of, in
general meetings which more and more became a forum for a
limited number of egos and the loudest voices until they were
finally abandoned.

> I got quite disillusioned with that and also I didn't see
> myself as a very articulate person, and talking in those
> meetings was quite an effort at times. You usually had these
> people who every meeting after meeting, they were glib,
> they were educated, there was one or two queens, the
> middle-class queens, who would take it over and the
> working-class queens couldn't get a word in edgeways.
> Because they didn't know how to speak, they didn't have
> that confidence . . . that was a drag. (*Harry Beck*)

It is important to note that quite a few women did not
'leave' on 9 February, including some of those who had been central; but with two of the strongest, Angie and Elizabeth, taken up
with the Stoke Newington Eight trial (as those accused of Angry

Brigade offences had become known) it was easier to dismiss those who remained. As proof of the continued collaboration, just ten days after the split GLF lesbians and gay men together supported women's liberation in their disruption of a *Time Out* conference on 'Freedom And Responsibility In The Media' at the Roundhouse in Camden Town, mainly in protest at *Time Out*'s sexism.

Shortly after the split, there was a national think-in at Lancaster University. Many women in other groups around the country wanted to discuss the London walk-out, but it was not the only London-inspired row simmering there; the two sides from the first split (socialism versus anti-sexism) were sounding the first notes of the third, loudest and longest argument that London GLF was to face. It is ironic that, while they started the debate, these early and rather academic protagonists were soon sidelined by the two groups they were speaking about.

Like many other GLF arguments, this one can be traced through pamphlets. The first, titled 'Gay Activism and Gay Liberation: a message to gay brothers' was written by Aubrey Walter and David Fernbach for the Lancaster think-in. It totally supports the women's walk-out, to the extent that it only addresses men and assumes that GLF is now a male organization. It reiterates the sexual politics of the *Manifesto* and describes the two possible paths of gay politics; gay liberation or gay activism:

> Gay activism is when gay males seek their full share of male privilege: . . . social equality for male homosexuals within a society based on male supremacy . . . In their eyes, a gay male is simply a man who likes sex with men, and where they're at in their heads is very visible from a look at their literature, full of bulging cocks, motorbikes and muscles, exactly the symbols of male supremacy and the oppression of women, supporting the gender-role system that is the basis of their own oppression . . . Gay liberation is not particularly interested in legal reforms, or even in acceptance by the straight world as a legitimate minority. Gay liberation sees the very existence of 'gay' and 'straight' people as the symptom of something very wrong. We don't think we can be liberated until men and women in general relate to each other as people on all levels . . . in fact we see all aspects of liberation as intimately bound up together; the thrusting straight man is part of the general problem,

the receptivity of women and gay males is part of the
general solution.

The pamphlet went on to say that gay liberationist activities
should be directed into building this new lifestyle rather than
formal organization to achieve civil rights, and to predict that the
departure of 'the women' would make it more likely that men
would choose the gay activist option. Accurate as this was, the
pamphlet's assumptions attracted an immediate rebuttal by four
other people from London GLF who still believed in a mixed-sex,
diverse organization – Jeffrey Weeks, Mary McIntosh, Nettie
Pollard and Paul Bunting. Their much shorter contribution,
'Radical Feminism And The Gay Movement', began by agreeing
with much of the criticism of reform-based gay activism, but adds:

> However, there are two issues on which we strongly
> disagree:
> 1. False Polarisation: The authors suggest that gay activism
> and 'gay liberation' (as they define them) are the only
> possible strategies for a gay movement. Gay liberation is
> then assumed to be the same as radical feminism. This we
> dispute . . . radical feminists are only a minority of the
> organized women's movement in this country, including the
> gay women's movement. There are many who believe that
> the solution to the oppression of women and gay people
> cannot be achieved only through a direct attack on male
> supremacy . . . What is needed is a fuller analysis of the
> relation between gender oppression and other forms of
> economic, political, social and ideological oppression. But
> it is not enough to make a facile equation of all oppressed
> groups with our own oppression . . . Street Theatre and
> new life styles have a valuable function but cannot change
> society on their own.
> 2. Women: Who are 'THE women' with whom the authors
> claim to be so close? Is it not an aspect of this same sexist
> culture for MEN to thus define the position of women? . . .
> If gay men wish to align themselves with the women's
> movement, they must relate to real women – in all their
> variety – and not to their fantasies of what women are . . .
> why should women be necessarily limited to their old
> receptive (equals passive) role? . . . LOVE AND STRUGGLE'

The leaflet from the four of us . . . it was just after the time when the women had mostly walked out . . . it seemed to us that David and Aubrey were claiming all sorts of positions that were completely beside the point, but basically what they were doing was trying to get support from the likes of Bette and it was an anti-intellectual, anti-politico sort of populist stance that they were taking and I guess that radical feminism would have been one of those forms of populism. They saw us as being male identified. [Did she feel affronted about this, given that she was a woman and the radfems weren't?] Yes, exactly! (*Mary McIntosh*)

The radical feminists never called themselves that, it was an external label. David Fernbach, I think, thought it up. The others were a set of groups really, there were a group of them into direct action, overlapping groups, and by this time the lesbian/gay split had taken place too. There were those like David and Aubrey who had a theoretical Marxist background, especially David with the *New Left Review*, but who were influenced by some of the early radical feminist stuff, and they had this odd flirtation with the rad fems and even started to get into frocks as I remember. That group focused around Media Workshop and *Come Together* for a long time. Then there were others like me who had a sort of loyalty to the Labour movement and had come through the Labour Party, but were dissatisfied with all that and not sure where we would place ourselves but regarded ourselves as leftist, some like me were a bit theoretical in our positions, and then there were a whole host of others. (*Jeffrey Weeks*)

The alliance between some of the intellectuals and the radical feminist communards did not last. 'Richard Dipple and I wrote a long leaflet eventually, called "Why we refuse to join the frock brigade". It had become a tyranny' (*Aubrey Walter*).

David Fernbach, with the benefit of a couple of years hindsight, put the basic conflict well in a pamphlet for the Gay Culture Series, *The Rise And Fall Of The Gay Liberation Front*. He said that the 'liberation' in Gay Liberation Front was essentially ambiguous. Liberation could mean the collective, political liberation of changing social structures. Alternatively, it could mean just changing oneself and leaving social structures alone. 'As GLF developed, the emphasis of liberation gradually shifted in meaning from the collective to the individual. Its name was originally coined by analogy with the National Liberation Fronts of countries such as Vietnam, but at a later stage it was possible for many people in GLF to use "liberation" in the sense of "are you liberated?"'

> A very substantial number of people in GLF weren't in either camp. They recognized that there were good things about both approaches . . . The radical feminist approach was that for men to don drag and live in communes was the route to gay liberation. Most of us had some sympathy with that position but felt it wasn't sufficient. It wasn't possible, in our view, for lesbian and gay people to completely withdraw from society into some sort of gay utopia . . . Those who primarily focused on a civil rights agenda or were involved from a radical leftist perspective tended to be very wary or even disparaging of the alternative lifestyle strategy. Those committed to homosexual equality and with no agenda beyond the removal of discrimination were happy to conform to straight expectations. They were not comfortable with challenging traditional masculinity, nor did they see it as a desirable political objective. (*Peter Tatchell*)

The aftermath of the earlier arguments involving *Come Together* also exploded in the spring of 1972. In the wake of intense criticism, Media Workshop had ceased to operate as the organizing group for the magazine. This had been no problem for Issue 11, which had been done by previous agreement by the Faraday Road commune. But as the months wore on and no new issue seemed forthcoming, a small group of GLF men took it upon themselves to get an Issue 12 together without the precaution of getting a mandate from the increasingly fractious general meeting.

As a copy of the news-sheet put it:

> Media Workshop dissolved itself and explained the reasons to a general meeting, at the same time pointing out why no issue had appeared since November. Since that time no new Media Workshop was formed and the meetings for Come Together 12 were not advertised or known to the majority of GLF members. Since GLF formed there has never been at any time the suggestion that CT was a monthly paper, it being more important for people to get to know each other

and to raise their consciousnesses within Media Workshop, than to produce a paper on a straight commercial basis of one issue per month, or whatever. The last think-in at LSE voted to stop issue 12 and to refuse to pay for publication out of GLF funds, as it was felt that the issue was not one which reflected the whole of GLF thinking. As it was published despite the wishes of the majority it now appears that anyone with sufficient capital can publish anything they wish, and pass it off as a GLF publication despite the protests of the majority of members.

I was very involved in *Come Together* 12. It wasn't a pilot for *Gay News*, though lots of people said it was at the time. There weren't any rules about *Come Together*, anybody could do it. Media Workshop, that was Mick Belsten's gang. It hadn't come out for a long time and we had the materials so we just got it together. I didn't understand the etiquette of it all, we put people's names in if they'd worked on it because that's what I thought you were supposed to do when you were publishing something. (*Martin Corbett*)

It is hardly surprising that people considered the issue to be a pilot for the proposed new newspaper, *Gay News*, which was attracting a certain amount of suspicion for its practical and businesslike stance. Two of the central figures in both were the same, Martin Corbett and David Seligman, both members of the office collective and very much seen as coming from the 'gay activist' perspective. The issue itself is also visibly a shift towards activism, containing much more on rights and traditional types of organizing, along with a large interview on the forthcoming *Gay News*. Unusually, it names almost all the contributors, which was often held to be a sign of ego-tripping, though a great help to later research. But there are also two of the best and most perceptive articles ever printed in any *Come Together*: a reprint of Rachel Pollak's 'The Twilight World Of The Heterosexual', originally published in *Ink*, and the previously banned 'Shirley Temple Knows'.

Rachel Pollak was a leading transsexual within GLF who has since become an acclaimed science fiction author. Her piece reverses hetero and homo prejudices and portrays the former as a sick minority, more to be pitied than condemned, involving strange rituals and hormonal imbalances. It formed the basis for many similar exercises by gay activists over the coming years. 'Shirley Temple Knows', an impressionistic piece written anonymously by Rex Lay, which had been suppressed by a majority decision of Media Workshop for both political and legal reasons, is one of the best pieces of writing about gay male sexuality that I know. It intercuts between a graphic account of a day in a cottage and a Mills and Boon style romance, but makes the former seem more romantic in its outlawry than the latter, ending 'Under the noses of the straights, in the middle of their palace, we make love.' Martin Corbett, in his usual practical manner, says that it was included simply because it was sitting in the *Come Together* file and nobody realized that it was controversial.

The row about Come *Together* 12 was taken to a special think-in at the London School of Economics eventually, for which the newsletter printed the following plea. 'We would like to object to the assertion in last week's newssheet that we have all been "ripped off" by David Seligman and Martin Corbett. Martin and David accepted any and all contributions which they received, and anyone who came along to help was welcome to participate. At one point there were about 20 people in the office working on CT12, plus all the contributors to be taken into account . . .', signed by eight people including David McLellan and Andy Elsmore.

At the base of this argument was concern about the growing power of the office collective who, with the growth of local groups and the atrophy of the general meetings, were assuming an increasingly central importance. As so often happens with volunteer-based organizations, power was reverting to those who were prepared to spend all day doing the menial office tasks which kept the information flowing.

> I was involved in the office collective. I used to make the tea at the meetings, which we sold for a shilling a cup. We used to make enough to run the office for the week. We also got money from selling badges and by collections and discos. The rent was a fiver and the rest went on the newsletter and stationery. We used to use an old Gestetner hand-cranked duplicator. When we started, we shared the basement with some elderly ladies who mailed out *Peace News* from there. I used to type the stuff for the newsletter. The office was basically used as a drop-in and social centre

by people. We got a few phone calls, but there wasn't a lot to do. We drank a lot of tea. Coffee was too expensive! (*Martin Corbett*)

It was absolutely chaotic, there was supposed to be two people on duty but they often failed to turn up, but there would be others like me who weren't on the rota but would be there. I always used to dress up for it. We made cups of tea and chatted to people, there was a lot going on but it never felt like it. Anybody would come in, often with horrendous problems, and we would try to help. What kind of job we made of it I don't know. We tried to get systems going. I never really knew who the office collective were because every time you would go to a meeting there would be different people involved, and then there would be rows about who was in the collective but just didn't come to meetings. (*Cloud Downey*)

I remember spending a lot of time in the office with Martin Corbett and Max and anybody who happened to turn up, answering the phones and some sort of office work, I don't remember. People answered letters and sat round and chatted and discussed the finer points of revolutionary theory. (*Alaric Sumner*)

The office, in the basement of Housmans Bookshop in Kings Cross, was tiny, ten feet by four feet nine inches, and meetings often spilled out into the general basement. Files were kept there for correspondence to each working group, general letters and phone calls answered, sales of badges and pamphlets organized and so on. A news-sheet for October 1973 gives an account of a typical Friday in the office during the later days of GLF.

ARRIVED LATE. Ten past ten – three people already here – they'd broken in when I didn't arrive at ten. However they had cleaned up and hadn't opened the mail so I was not too annoyed. About seven letters – four straightforward, asking for details about Gay Lib. One from a guy asking for a list of contact addresses, one from Australia GLF asking for a thousand manifestos and describing their group's activities – very interesting. The other letter was a long one from someone criticising an article in Come Together 14. Got people in office to answer straightforward letter and contact address one; we suggested that he join local group and also suggested 'Gay News'; other letters to put in files for groups to consider – more people arrived in outer office, big make up and hair dressing scene going on there. Two visitors arrived looking for crash pads – fixed up – several phone calls looking for info – fixed up groups for dance – got out letraset and knocked up hand bill for dance – several more phone calls – one from a hung up school teacher in Surrey who had taken several days to get it together to ring and then was all the time nervous in case his landlady returned – referred him to Icebreakers – Maurice arrived to take over – I went to printers and got hand bills printed, arrived back and found action group was assembled. Left and went to awareness group.

Given the anarchic and anti-organizational attitude of GLF, it is hardly surprising that there were constant problems in the office with theft and people generally taking advantage. 'There was constant ripping off within the office collective. The treasurer was caught fiddling and stuff often disappeared' (*Micky Burbidge*). Many people were more or less disdainful of the type of work involved. 'Most people didn't want to run the office, but they did want it to be there. It did attract a certain type of fairly organized person, as in any organization' (*David Fernbach*). 'The central office collective . . . was a bunch of sad bastards who had decided they had to go somewhere to do things' (*Julian Hows*).

Given that the two types of people who hung around the office in the spring and summer of 1972 were the gay male activists and the increasingly vocal radical feminist queens, conflict was inevitable. Following on rows in general meetings and groups about 'macho male' behaviour and attitudes, there was a blow-up at the office just before the first Pride march, as the news-sheet records:

Towards the end of last week and over the weekend there has been some conflict in GLF. This has centred around what would appear to be two viewpoints. The conflict arose when a group of gay men who see themselves as attempting to reject the privileges they retain as men even though they have come out as gay, reached the conclusion that the majority of men in GLF, even though they had come out as gay and were proud of it, had retained all the privileges they are allowed by society as men; the former group of people saw themselves as being mainly 'femme' people – though this was not defined, it was thought to mean that they were rejecting their male privileges by analysis of all these privileges, from wearing trousers, speech mannerisms to physical violence etc. and attempting to find ways whereby they could replace these with a truly gay life style. This group saw the other as being 'butch' – which was assumed to mean that they were not attempting to reject any of their male privileges; in the context of GLF, an organization which is attempting to develop a truly gay life style, rather than simply using parts of heterosexual life styles that more or less suit us, the femme men saw this as subverting GLF into becoming simply an organization of gay men who were not into changing their heads in any way whatsoever.

Well what happened: because the conflict was partly sparked off by the previous office collectives meeting, the femme men decided to try and change the offices appearance; they thought it reflected the attitude of male privilege that some of the office collective maintained; they got together some paint and on Saturday went in and painted the office in bright colours. They also reached the conclusion that it would be a good idea if they got into wearing dresses as one particular way of rejecting some of their male privileges; those who did not want to do this saw it as a rejection and complained about being 'forced to wear make-up and dresses' and that they had been 'thrown out' of the office.

These actions brought about a series of discussions on Saturday, Sunday and at the office collective meeting on Monday; while there was a lot of confusion, especially about 'labelling' people as butch and femme, about not attempting to listen to anyone else's viewpoint, about selfishness and not caring about people, and while no concrete agreements or conclusions were reached, it does seem that if people realise that they are not being rejected, and that the confusion resulted from the fact that nobody's view had been fully worked out and that we must all be open to criticism and change, then these events will be a positive benefit to GLF.

Repainting the office was something a group of us just decided to do. It was very dingy and it needed cheering up. We didn't even buy paint, we just got tins off anyone who had them and each took a bit of it, so it was really interesting because of all the people's different styles. It was completely organic, we just went in and did what we fancied. (*Cloud Downey*)

I have a feeling it happened more than once, that we were the first and that we were working in the office for the evening and decided to repaint it in psychedelic colours. And that there was no trouble that night. And then we came in the next day or two and they had painted over everything that we had done, because I remember being really pissed off that all that beautiful brightness and colour had just been covered in this puke single colour which made it look exactly like a tedious office . . . There was intense resentment of what we were doing at the time, wearing frocks and questioning gender roles, just as we resented intensely that they wouldn't understand what we were doing. How could they possibly not take part? Because we felt that we had the true GLF theory and with retrospect I'd still say that we did. That the motive of GLF was revolutionary not reformist. That the taking of the risk of self-transformation in the street, not knowing what on earth could happen, was part of it. The revolution starts with self-transformation. (*Alaric Sumner*)

The week of the first Pride was one of intense madness within GLF, a week when the newly styled (by others) radfems did a series of actions that caused huge rows within gay circles. This was at the height of the problems in the Athlone Road squat, just before the state of siege, and the queens must have been at the end of their tethers. In a state of mind best described as 'us against the world', they repainted the office and then moved on, fatally, to a free drinks party to launch the new feminist magazine *Spare Rib*.

That was when we went to the *Spare Rib* party afterwards, though we changed our dresses. I remember going to that and feeling very strongly about it. It was to do with class, *Spare Rib* was a very middle-class publication and we were terribly opposed to middle-class trendiness. Having said which, we were very trendy ourselves but we couldn't see that, we thought we were revolutionaries . . . Some people loved us and I remember dancing on the table, for some reason I was very into that in those days, and got very drunk on the free wine, and then rows started and we were ejected by force of numbers. And there were a lot of angry women . . . Alaric was there, Ken and others, I think Mike Rhodes was there but we were the only ones in drag. The *Gay News* people were there. Michael James and Denis Lemon, Martin Corbett . . . they never ever saw eye to eye. I remember Michael having long discussions with them at the commune about these political things. (*Cloud Downey*)

I remember walking across from the office across the Kings Cross area to The Place and walking in. I was told that the reason we were doing it was because they were advertising lipstick and things in this supposedly feminist magazine and therefore they were a cop-out and it was justifiable for men to go along and disrupt it. I don't remember any disruption or violence. I remember having a drink and standing around and it didn't seem to be a problem, there were people laughing and chatting and arguing excitedly, but I don't personally remember fighting or violence at all. (*Alaric Sumner*)

But violent disagreement there certainly was, and in front of the national media. The radfems argued, threw papers around and shouted 'Where's your head at?' at various straight but influential people and at the bewildered Spare Ribbers. People like Alan Brien, columnist with the *Sunday Times*, were quick to seize on the contradiction of feminist men telling women how they should behave, and to repeat the scorn of Denis Lemon and others, now associated with the new *Gay News* rather than with GLF, for the group they dubbed 'fascists in frocks'. It was the perfect chance for this group, many of whom had been in the despised office collective, to make the break with their origins and show the rest of the gay world, which was suspicious of the revolutionary GLF roots of *Gay News*, that they were all on the same side against this group of people who were characterized as 'letting the side down'.

I was with the drag queens when the time came that they fell out with *Gay News*. By then, *Gay News* seemed a thousand miles away. As a world it was all-consuming and anything else was impossible to attend to. So it was very remote when I learned what *Gay News* had said, repeating the remark of 'fascists in frocks' and so on. I disliked it when I learnt that the launch for *Spare Rib* had been demonstrated against. I don't know why it was done. I remember asking at the time 'Why have you done this?' As I understood it, they were saying, 'This is a middle-class device, this is a sell-out', but it felt to me that whatever they were wearing, men had gone and attacked something women were doing. That's how it felt from a distance.

 Gay News started because everyone was complaining that they didn't know what was going on, especially when there started to be a lot of different meetings. I thought, as someone who was working for *The Times*, that we ought to have a regular means of communication. *Come Together* was irregular. I thought the CHE subscription list was the key and I got on with them so they mailed out flyers. There were no freesheet newspapers then, so automatically we charged for it. Glenys Parry of CHE agreed to cooperate. We decided to call it *Gay News* because you couldn't be under any misapprehension about what it was. In those days the word 'gay' was still shocking. From the start it was non-party-political and not pro any one specific group, but a means of communication for all. (*Andrew Lumsden*)

There is no doubt that the coverage of GLF in the first few months of *Gay News* was adversarial and deeply hostile to the queens, and that to some extent they played into this. While *Gay News* might not be pro any one gay political group, it was repeatedly and openly hostile to radical drag and the communes. This increased the sense of 'us against the world' of the radfems as they were now generally known (though never self-labelled as such), and the communards in their turn attacked *Gay News* people, physically on occasions. It was the coverage in *Gay News* which produced the general consensus, lasting a generation, amongst more traditional gay activists that GLF was nothing but a bunch of hysterical queens and that it was people like that who were stopping respectable homosexuals from getting their rights.

 The birth of *Gay News*, though, should not be seen only in the light of their in-fighting with the queens. It was a brave and optimistic move which launched the most successful and, other than this, least sectarian lesbian and gay newspaper this country has ever seen. In their first issue they stated a policy of defiance to state censorship which was to be their hallmark. The trial of *International Times* for carrying gay personal ads had reached appeal stage at the House of Lords and been turned down there by four to one, with Lord Diplock dissenting, with the clear verdict on male homosexual behaviour: 'There is a material difference between behaviour exempted from criminal penalties and behaviour which is lawful in the full sense of the word.' *Gay News* promptly inserted a personal ads column entitled 'Love Knoweth No Laws' (a quotation from Chaucer) for which the founding collective each had to make up an ad, since they had not solicited any.

> The climax for me was the Gay Pride demo in '72 when there was a real tension between the radical fairies and the others who regarded themselves as revolutionaries. I had really fallen out with people like Bette Bourne and Stuart Feather and it was the worst sort of sectarianism. It cured me for life of sectarianism because it was like a religious divide. It wasn't just different nuances in a movement, it was like different groups with different access to the truth.
>
> But for me the crunch point was that Gay Pride march . . . There were lots of rows preceding it and there were lots of arguments on the march itself between those who were in radical drag and those who weren't. There were also rows between the radfems and the *Gay News* people. It was all very unhappy and gave people like myself a sense that the heart had gone out of it. There was no longer a Gay Liberation Front, gay liberation was becoming much more dispersed . . . which was the logic of the time but we resisted it. (*Jeffrey Weeks*)

The Pride march, the first in Britain, officially took place on Saturday 1 July 1972. In light of the many later moans about Pride losing its original political spirit in favour of celebration, it is enlightening to note that it was promoted strongly as a 'Carnival Parade'. It was attended by more than a thousand people and on the surface was harmonious; the separatist women returned with a banner 'Gay Women's Liberation' and all the local groups were present, although there was comment on how few people from CHE bothered to attend. The group marched from Trafalgar Square to Hyde Park, where they held a Gay Day, and photographs survive of the Street Theatre ball-throwing game in which Tony Salvis is kissing an unknown man while the young Julian Hows

looks on, days before his expulsion from Tulse Hill Comprehensive. Both *Gay News* and *Come Together* were on sale, as a photograph of Michael Mason promoting the one and reading the other
at an assembly point at the Embankment shows. But *Gay International News* painted a more honest picture:

> Gay Pride Week in London brought about an uneasy
> alliance between factions which have been in open conflict
> recently. The 'radical feminists' in glittering gender-fuck
> drag glared defiance at the 'straight' gays as they marched
> through London . . . or danced beside them at the ball the
> night before at Fulham Town Hall. At Hyde Park . . . they
> separated into groups to engage the straight tourists and
> sight-seers in their own forms of confrontation and
> dialogue. The lesbians too, for the first time since their
> break with the main organization, were marching with the
> GLF in splendid face paint.

It went on to describe the radfem actions of Pride Week,
including travelling the London Underground in drag offering
refreshments and conversation to other passengers, the office
invasion and the *Spare Rib* debacle, including a quote from Denis
Lemon that they were 'the Charles Mansons of GLF'. It ended
'Although both sides believe in the concept of homosexuals "coming
out", it is clearly on quite different terms. They are both taking up
intransigent attitudes and both are claiming that the others are
sabotaging the ideals of the Gay Liberation Front.'

The whole event had, however, been upstaged earlier in the
week by a pre-emptive strike by the queens which may have contributed to the irritation some felt about them on that day. Out of a
scheduled picket, a completely spontaneous march had evolved
which was, in effect, the genuine first Pride hike through central
London and was largely composed of radical drag queens with a
few rent boys in support.

> The march happened quite spontaneously. We were
> allocated a time slot with the Boilermakers Union to picket
> the American Embassy as part of Troops Out Of Vietnam
> . . . we decided to put our best frocks on for the Boiler-
> makers so we got there all glammed up and there was
> nothing going on. We stood around for a while and people
> joined us. We heard some music from Grosvenor Square
> itself so we went over to investigate. In the middle of

Grosvenor Square there's this memorial, I think to American soldiers who've died in both world wars, with very broad shallow steps and in front of that a huge paved area.

This American school orchestra was standing on these steps and playing. All the office workers and people were stood around the edge of this huge paved area. They were playing show tunes and bits and pieces, so Bette and I decided to have a waltz, or a quickstep or something, so we stepped into the dance floor area and danced around and were joined by other people and then we got the typists up for a dance and they loved it. They thought it was all part and parcel of the orchestra, with balloons and everything. Then the orchestra packed up in a fit of pique. They couldn't deal with it. That left us all high, so we decided to go down to Piccadilly to talk with the rent boys.

There were between twenty-five and thirty of us, all the local queens living in and around the Notting Hill commune, Colville Terrace. We were the only ones that had turned up. It was the general GLF turn on the picket line, but it was the queens that had turned up. I think we'd decided that we wanted to do it with the Boilermakers, actually, we wanted to meet them. Obvious, wasn't it? We freaked them out so much, they were invisible, dear. So then we all set off from Grosvenor Square, down through Bond Street, down Piccadilly, in all our finery and laughing and cavorting. We went down into the Underground and I think we did a couple of tours of the Underground with a couple of the boys standing there. Some more boys came from nowhere and were all standing round, they loved all this and the police appeared. (*Michael James*)

Mike Rhodes, who is now dead, used to tell people at London Lesbian and Gay Switchboard about how hilarious it was, with police chasing drag queens in and out of various tube exits.

So we all fled out of the Lower Regent Street end exit, hotly pursued by these two policemen. There was a big gang of us with rent boys now in tow, so we'd grown and also picked up other queens along Piccadilly, ambling around out for an afternoon or whatever. We fled down the steps and turned left sharply into the ICA, as if we'd disappeared off the face of the earth in seconds – the police were some yards behind us and by the time they'd got to the bottom of the steps we were nowhere in sight. The funny thing was, the ICA had an exhibition of revolutionary posters and as Stuart pointed out, we *were* the revolution, happening there and then.

So we had a cup of coffee and waited about three quarters of an hour and then we wandered out again and no one was around, so we went through the arch to cross over to Nelson's Column. A couple of people got up and of course there were tourists, it was a photo opportunity and we were sitting there posing and laughing and giggling. (*Michael James*)

A photograph shows Michael and Mick Belsten in possession of the plinth, a line of drag queens including Cloud Downey and Alaric Sumner doing the cancan behind them.

The police came over and said, where were we going? and we said, 'We're going to Hyde Park.' They said, which way were we going to Hyde Park? We said, 'Probably up Charing Cross Road and down Oxford Street' and they said 'Okay, we'll escort you.' So we had this amazing impromptu march. It was a few days before Pride . . . so off we marched . . . it all fizzled out in Hyde Park. (*Michael James*)

I remember getting ready at home and choosing an outfit for it with Richard. The thing in Piccadilly Circus, we were all in drag and it was a really humiliating thing to do to people, we actually went into the toilets and shouted about them being closet queens and all these frightened men ran out, because we were there in our cancan petticoats and stilettos, singing and doing the cancan. And encouraging people really loudly to leave the cottages and come out onto the streets. It's not the kind of thing I remember with pleasure, though at the time it seemed like enormous fun. It wouldn't be necessary now, anyway. We were always making statements, you see, we were doing what we felt was right for us and we believed in total outrageousness – the more you threatened the order of things, the more successful it was going to be. (*Cloud Downey*)

Chapter nineteen

Where's Your Head At?

Take A Deep Breath – The Pansies Are In Bloom –Michael James
placard, occasion unknown

BY the summer of 1972, GLF was regarded with a mixture
of affection and condescension by other, more reformist gay
groups, as an article by Bob Ardler in *Lunch*, the CHE magazine
shows.

> Salute to our sister GLF!
>
> *GLF is English.* Consider the words 'like', 'right', 'on',
> 'man', 'bad', 'scene', 'fuck', 'the' and 'pigs'. These GLFese
> words are all Anglo, and some of them are Saxon.
>
> *GLF is democratic.* Some meetings, for instance, are ruled
> with an iron hand (in a simply divine velvet glove) by this
> dreamy American [actually, Warren was Canadian] who
> disdains to join the so-called chairman and his clique of
> cringing fascists on the platform. Power to the people.
>
> *GLF goes its own sweet way.* As a matter of fact, it goes its
> own sweet several ways, one for each member. Everybody,
> especially Agitprop, tries to use it and exploit it. But its
> founders, in making it police-proof (no membership
> records, no ruling body) made it leader-proof also.
>
> *GLF is sublime.* A typical meeting will resolve:
>
> (a) To get into Policewomen's drag and have a gang bang
> outside Buck House during the changing of the guard.
>
> (b) To smash capitalism.
>
> (c) To crochet a new banner.
>
> *GLF has all sorts.* Political psychotics acting out their
> power dreams. Cynical little apoliticals there for the talent.
> Nice old dears there for the talent. Chicken-shit liberals
> from CHE raising points of order. Gay people seeking gay

society and desiring to bring fun and pride and dignity into gay life. Fuzz.

GLF is into solidarity. At every confrontation with the jackbooted oppressor (I refer to Sgt. G. Dixon, of Dock Green), you will see that banner with the camp device, which I would be glad to explain to you over tea and scones. GLF is not into solidarity with coarse workers who say eff off out of our picket line, we don't want no poofs here. GLF is sometimes into solidarity with CHE and sometimes not. (The two organizations have many members in common, how queer!)

GLF is a boys club. Denominational. Evangelical. Its meetings are revival meetings. Hallelujah, brothers and sisters. Its speeches are exhortations, they are testimonies, they are How I Was Saved, they are ego trips, they are Jesus trips, they are Speaking With Tongues. If your moral courage is flagging, go to GLF as well as CHE meetings. To stomach the squabbling, the yippier-than-thou-ism, the brother-you-sound-like-a-heretic-ism, you need to have a robust sense of humour or none at all, or to be stoned. But worth it if you can stand it.

For:

GLF has courage. Admitted that they would need more courage to do what they are doing if they were in Spain or China, South Africa or Uganda, Greece or Russia; or if they were ten years older or younger; or if the fascists Arran and Abse and 200 brave MPs hadn't changed the law; or if they had certain sensitive jobs – all admitted, GLF members risk (and get) imprisonment, sometimes deportation, they face prejudice and contempt and derision and hostility, and they damage their employability, in support of *our* cause.

GLF favours direct action. For temperamental reasons. Contrast their confrontations with the Gateways and the William – two utterly harmless little commercial concerns which give delight and hurt not: some crap about ghettos and exploitation and CHE's picketing of places that discriminate, and then only after every Machiavellian technique of middle-class intrigue had been tried and failed.

The confrontations with authority continued, though often without the mass support and organizational backup which had made them so successful the year before. A perfect illustration of this is the re-run of the pubs action in October 1972. This time around, it was against a gay pub and ended in arrests and no victory against the pub, although it is remembered with great fondness by those who were there and resulted in one of the more hilarious and better documented GLF trials using a Mackenzie lawyer.

> Being arrested in a pub demo was complete fun. It was wonderful. This particular incident was the Champion in Notting Hill Gate. It was a gay pub and always had been, but it was not very friendly anyway. They had a very hostile policy to anyone in drag and there were now a number of drag communes in Notting Hill Gate. So one day we went very obviously in drag to the Champion. It wasn't particularly a GLF enterprise, though we were all GLF people, but that was how GLF was – the Queering Committee didn't have to give you permission to do things. As far as I remember, some of us just agreed to go. (*Andrew Lumsden*)

> I went to the one at the Champion in 1972 which didn't work. It wasn't very well organized, my girlfriend Gaby and I were round at Colville Houses and some other women and we agreed to go, it wasn't organized and there were no big meetings by then. It was a more informal, anarchic way of doing it but we all knew each other by then which wasn't true before. Gaby went to a phone box and rang one of the radio stations and said there were two hundred angry homosexuals in drag descending on this pub, which wasn't true, and she said, 'No, but that's the way you get the media there.' They came.
> There were about twenty of us. We went and there was quite an aggressive atmosphere in the pub, quite a lot of the locals didn't like that they'd been invaded by GLFers. There were a lot of men in drag, more so than the previous time, and a lesser proportion of women. Eventually we were refused drinks and we sat on the floor, and also a lot of people there were saying 'You're just spoiling our fun and you're going to bring the police down on us – and why are you wearing those disgusting clothes anyhow?' Someone was in a wedding dress, Julian, he didn't get arrested. (*Nettie Pollard*)

Julian's memory is that the regulars hid him in a corner of the pub when police arrived and plied the seventeen-year-old with gins while asking him what it was all about.

So the police came and they were saying something about these people in drag and Gaby said 'Am I in drag?' and they stuttered. She was in purple loons and a tank top, nothing gender specific and they didn't know whether she was in drag or not or what to say. And they started dragging us out. The women were saying 'Come on, let's disperse now', and some of the men were getting angry at the way they were being pushed about and insulted by the police and they were hanging around and that's how arrests happen. If we had all just disappeared . . . it all happened afterwards outside. The police did provoke people and pretend they'd been hit. I remember thinking, oh no, come away, come away, but I don't blame them for being angry – but it wasn't a good idea, at the same time. (*Nettie Pollard*)

They called the police, the Champion. It was an unbelievable disgrace, this was about three years after Stonewall and here's a gay pub calling the police to throw out drag. We refused to go, so the police had to drag us out. My lover was Peter Reed and I saw what I thought was Peter being manhandled by some copper and I remember trying to tackle the copper, who punched me in the face. And they hauled us all off to the police station and the next day I went off to see a doctor to get a record of any abrasions on the face. I asked him if he'd write it all down in super medical language with technical descriptions, so it sounded absolutely terrifying. In fact it was just a slight graze and a bruise, nothing much. So when we appeared in court I could read out this terrifying medical statement as to what had happened.

We spent the night in the cells and I was rather disappointed the next day, because I was in a cell by myself, and several of the others including Richard Chappell were put into a kind of tank with various other people who were being held. And they claimed the next day that they'd all proceeded to have sex with the people in there. Well, people always did say that sort of thing so whether it happened I don't really know, perhaps it did. But I felt quite jealous the next day, because they'd all had this kind of orgy in Notting Hill Gate nick.

And Notting Hill Gate nick was greatly feared, it still had this reputation hanging over it from the race riots. I spent most of my time in my cell trying to see if you could hang yourself, because every now and again the newspapers would say that someone had hanged themselves in a police cell and I'd always wondered how they could possibly do it. You certainly couldn't do it in Notting Hill Gate police station, not the cell I was in. So if I ever read that someone had done so in there, I wouldn't believe it, on quite good grounds. I don't think any of us minded being banged up there at all, the whole thing was very entertaining.

And in due course we went off to Marylebone Magistrates Court and there, like all the trials that GLF ever got involved in, it was just a haze of frocks and hats and blowing soap bubbles in court, and my recollection is of the magistrates rather taking the side of these ludicrous prisoners. Perhaps we were quite a pleasant break in the routine. And the police always being hideously uncomfortable. Just hating it. It was an art form that had been developed before GLF, at things like the *Oz* trial and magistrates knew it was an art form. As soon as this kind of thing started, they knew exactly what was going on and just in due course bound people over and things like that. It was very unserious, the whole thing, and we all tended to use Mackenzie lawyers, so we could have even more people in drag and hats and things in the court.

Any of the drag queens were sensational as a Mackenzie, because with the drag queens who were involved in the communes – Michael [James] for instance was perfect, he had no respect for authority, a very fast wit. I think Michael was nearly always there. Stuart Feather would be very good. I did it on one occasion. It made an uproar in the court. I started off in awe of people like that, but by the time of the Champion incident I was used to it. If you live amongst people like that, it becomes the natural way of doing things and ceases to be startling. (*Andrew Lumsden*)

I went to the trial as well, which was fabulous. We caused complete havoc. At one point we were all dragged out of

court and out of the entire building, after lunch when we
were impossible to keep quiet. And we had all learned how
to go limp by then, and it was a very long way, right out of
the building. Ted Brown was there and made a good point
about it in relation to black people. At lunchtime, with all
of us in totally outrageous drag or disreputable dykes, we
went to this pub, an Irish pub, very ordinary, for a drink,
and I remember someone saying, rather depressed, 'I
wonder if we'll get served.' And we went in and they went
'What a lovely colourful group you are, come in', and they
were so nice to us and we thought, doesn't that say
something? They think we're adding to the colour of the
place and isn't it nice to have us, which was so different
from gay pubs who didn't want us. (*Nettie Pollard*)

The trial was also covered by Bob Sturgess of CHE, who
wrote it up for *Lunch*. He felt that 'after the lunch time drink-in . . .
spirits were high and only the nervous tic on the Magistrate's face
indicated that the party was not being enjoyed by all.' He cleared
the gallery after ten minutes due to hysterical giggles. 'After the
routine clutch of petty shoplifters, alcoholics and loiterers . . . it
was stimulating to see the dock suddenly fill with the five accused
from GLF. Richard Chappell wore an ankle-length black satin dress
with matching pill-box hat and net veil; Douglas MacDougall (of
the same address) wore a pink polka-dot dress and green glitter
round the eyes, while Peter Bourne (actor) wore, to great effect, a
red-patterned velvet dress.' All three were remanded to a later date
but a further two were proceeded with, 'Andrew Lumsden
(formerly of *The Times* and dressed most fetchingly in the fabric
equivalent of a Shirvan carpet) and his "affair" Peter Reed.'

The two of them asked for a Mackenzie, Michael James. 'It
was this friend who took upon himself, after the clearing of the
public gallery, to shout at the magistrate "You old queen, how
DARE you sit in judgement on us gays." Somewhat daunted by this
personal approach, the learned Magistrate no doubt felt that he
could best retain his grip on proceedings by adjourning them.' He
called Michael to his chambers, while the audience took the opportunity to have another argument with the police and be ejected
into the forecourt. A photographer had his film seized and exposed.
The CHE reporter was not impressed: 'As an ego-tripping piece of
vaudeville, the performance was hilarious; but it hardly presented
the gay movement in the best light and, from a public relations

standpoint, proved embarrassingly counter-productive . . .' However, all was redeemed by the brilliant way Andrew Lumsden conducted his defence. History does not record the exact length of the spoon with which Michael and the Magistrate handled each other at their interview, but the upshot was that Andrew stood firm on his rights and refused to re-enter the dock unless Michael was in there with him.

The landlord of the Champion appeared mild enough when he first entered the witness box, but Andrew quickly laid bare his underlying truculence and made entirely credible that he had said things like:

'You're revolting, you're not men . . . Get out of here . . . I won't serve you . . . I'd give anything to kick you lot in the face . . .'

'Or maybe', said Andrew to the Magistrate, 'it was in the behind. It was somewhere, at any rate . . .'

'Do you know what drag is?' Andrew asked the landlord.

'Yes, I do.'

At this point, Andrew got Michael to stand on the dock bench, his bare knees showing prominently under what, to the layman, appeared to be a white bed-sheet. Whereupon, Andrew directed the landlord's attention to this vision in white.

'Is that drag?'

'Yes' replied the landlord.

'Well, it's not. It's a kaftan. It's worn by male Arabs. That shows how little you know about drag, doesn't it?'

'Do we have to be dragged through all this?' asked the Magistrate wearily.

'Speak up!' said Andrew. 'I can't hear you.'

Andrew went on to greatly confuse a constable giving evidence against him.

'When the other defendant – '

'My lover, you mean?' interrupted Andrew.

'When the other defendant attempted to regain access into the pub, I barred his way, and he was very rude to me. 'You fucking big brute' he said to me – '

'You fucking big what?' asked the Magistrate.

'You fucking big brute, Sir.'

'You said that to him, you mean?' the Magistrate asked, a trifle nervously.

'No. He said that to me.'

'He said to you: "You big fucking brute?" Can I take it that – '

'No Sir. The "fucking" came first, if you follow my meaning.'

Renewed titters from the public gallery.

'SILENCE!' said the Magistrate . . .

The Magistrate made the mistake of trying to understand one witness in a frock. 'Do you always dress like this?' 'No, but we like to look nice when we go out' was the immediate answer. The article ended by condemning the general behaviour of the queens, while praising 'Andrew Lumsden's cultivated detachment and incisive rapier-like thrusts'. But in all the criticism of the queens in the 'straight gay' press, there was little consideration of why they should have felt it necessary to act against a gay pub in the first place.

The dislike between the queens and the mainstream gay scene was mutual.

> I went to the Boltons once or twice, I went down the Masquerade, I went to Louise's and did the Coleherne, but I was told, 'Well, it's full of scene queens, dear, they really don't know where things are at.' And on the few occasions I went to these places, I thought, well, actually Stuart, Michael, Bette, you're right. I don't need this. I don't need this degree of self-oppression, 'Oh, there's the new chicken in town – oh, she dresses a bit funny.' Why should I give up what I had to get into some quite seedy sexual alliance with somebody who's going to kick me out of bed, as they often did when I went to these places, at seven o'clock in the morning pretending they were straight again? And for an awful lot of people, that was what was going on. Even then, after gay liberation had happened, they were going to accept me for what I'd decided not to become, but not for what I was.
>
> The whole thing about the Boltons in 1972, 1973 was that upstairs was full of people who were not quite overt. They were overt, but they weren't. The rules were very definite. So you would have these two Spanish queens standing there flashing fans, or castanets of a Sunday lunchtime, with the queens standing at the back dropping their downers. But they knew their place, it was still a question of them knowing their place. And they thought we

were the sort of gay who didn't know their place. It was a question of the way the bar owner felt that you fitted in with the rest of the crowd . . . The way that the straight commercial scene reacted to us, it was a question of the vibes they thought they were getting from the other people in the places. They thought we were not prepared to play by the rules, so there were ripples. And because there were ripples, the owners thought 'these people are not safe'. (*Julian Hows*)

By the second half of 1972 GLF was in very rapid decline. It was no longer a cohesive movement, if it ever had been. It was no longer a single meeting place. Camden and other groups were meeting separately. There were many cohesive groups, but they were all going in different directions. There was a core of people in the office but that was itself an issue because many of us in the different groups felt that they were arrogating to themselves the idea that they were GLF. By and large these people were not the radicals, they were people who were doers and wanted something practical, which was fine, but I certainly regarded them as just one group amongst many and that's how I saw the gay movement developing, along a whole series of functional activities and running the phone was one aspect of that.

That overlapped of course with those who founded *Gay News*. There was an overlapping membership of the two groups and *Gay News* was seen, I saw it, as a useful development but also a pity because it was a bit too accommodating both to straight gays and to straight society. I think I've changed my mind on that but it was one of the issues at the time – was this de-radicalizing gay liberation? Many of us at the time felt it was. (*Jeffrey Weeks*)

Meanwhile, the queens were still on their voyage of self-discovery. The wearing of public drag acted for many of them as the same sort of liberation that early attenders at GLF had discovered at the meetings. Like Elizabeth Wilson and others before them, they had found their voices in this new world.

I remember the first night I went to the meeting in a dress. It was red. I put it on and walked across to the meeting, I was living very close by as I still do. I turned up at this

meeting and sat very quietly with my bag. I got a cigarette
out. And then I just said 'Well, I don't hear the women
saying much, and the queens', and there was a terrible
silence. And I went on and I said, 'I've been sitting here
listening to all this stuff and it doesn't seem very real to
me.' It was extraordinarily hard for me, because people
thought I was this dopey little queen who didn't know
anything. We all approached it from a very basic level of
what we saw. We hadn't read anything. It was very strong,
wearing a dress and all that, so I just carried on doing that.
Eventually we could be heard.

Being in a frock . . . we told ourselves we wanted to find
out a bit about how women felt. In a way it was superficial
but . . . it was quite strong. We got a lot of flak for it –
especially the more masculine, if you didn't have too much
of a beard line it was easier obviously. We were very keen
that people took us seriously. Some of the women
complained and said that they thought we were guying
them . . . Of course, my dark secret was that I looked very
butch and had been brought up in a very butch way, but
actually I wanted a husband. I was quite happy being
Arthur or Martha but I did prefer Martha, if you see what I
mean. That was my secret, which certain men knew about
obviously who'd been my lovers, so really I thought of
myself as a queen and not as a man. I went to the clubs in
tight jeans, very butch, never a hint, nails had to be cut the
right length, you had to be aware of the way you walked,
the way you sat down, everything. It was a wonderful relief
for me to come out as a femme.

We didn't take the label radfems. It got thrown at us one
night in an argument . . . 'You radical femme acid queens!'
. . . it was something from outside. We never used words
like that. We would say 'Get a frock on dear' whenever
they were ranting away . . . We may have looked fearless
but it was very, very frightening to do it . . . I've got to the
point now when I can go out and wander round in my fur
coat and my hat and I forget what I'm wearing.
(*Bette Bourne*)

By the autumn, London GLF had fallen apart. The central
London meetings ceased for a while and then reverted to monthly special ones. The only thing holding the whole organization

together was the weekly news-sheet put out by the office in Caledonian Road, which listed all the group meetings, special events and a bit of obscure gossip, usually detailing arguments over money or politics. As David Fernbach noted in his pamphlet the following year for the Gay Culture Series, most gay activists had gone into *Gay News* or civil rights work, and the sort of personal liberation being pursued by the radical feminists did not need an organizational framework. Local groups flourished, particularly those in Camden and Brixton, and the dances still went on courtesy of the West London Group and Gay Women's Liberation. Many people had begun to work within particular projects, such as Icebreakers, which had begun as GLF but taken on a life of their own and which are covered in the next chapter.

The only people left who regarded themselves as London GLF were the office and, to some extent, the queens. They were busy moving from Colville Terrace, where they fought bailiffs, to Colville Houses. Over the course of the autumn and winter there was very little action, as the Chronology shows. Apart from the Champion trial, the high spot was in November when Michael James, Tim Bolingbroke, Andrew Lumsden, Sarah Grimes, Tony Halliday and Denis Lemon buried their political differences to give evidence for Angie Weir in the Stoke Newington Eight trial at the Old Bailey. Their solid alibi evidence, alongside contradictory statements from handwriting experts, was a major contribution to her acquittal the following month. Peter Tatchell zapped a psychiatry conference, as told in chapter eight, and GLF women attended a national Women's Conference on Homosexuality in Manchester organized by the CHE women there.

In March, the communard queens moved into a new home:

> Bethnal Rouge came about through Andrew Lumsden, Richard Chappell and Steven Bradbury, who hung around together. The three of them got the building from Agitprop in the spring of 1973. Agitprop were giving up the lease on the building and wrote to various groups offering the premises. I brought the letter back to the commune and after we decided not to move there we passed it on to Andrew and Richard. The people who went to Bethnal Rouge included Steven, Matthew Dallaway, Michael Kennedy and Margaret. (*Stuart Feather*).

Agitprop had finally been forced out of business by constant police harassment; two of the commune there were on conspiracy to procure firearms charges while another two were facing severe opposition to their visa renewals.

February '73 my mother moved and I went down to help, left the commune for a month but before that, I don't know how, but *de rigeur* political correctness had crept in somehow, not overtly but subversively, and I felt I didn't have the freedom to wear trousers when I wanted to. I felt there were times when I didn't want to go out and be looked at by everyone in the street, I just wanted to slip out quietly. There were people who were giving us a hard time for doing that. The month away made my mind up that I was going to Amsterdam, and the following week I rang my friends in Amsterdam, and they had been asking me to go over for twelve months. The film studio was breaking up anyway and people were going off to Bethnal Rouge – it only lasted six months or so but there was lots of action packed into them. I didn't fancy the East End at all, I went down to look at it but it wasn't me. Andrew Lumsden and Stuart were very into it and Julian. Bette wasn't 'cos it was out of his direct sphere, and also Bette was a Hackney boy and the last thing he wanted to do was go back to Hackney, dear. (*Michael James*)

I wasn't at all a hippie. I wore a suit to work at *The Times* and the tradition was there that if you worked on a Saturday you were allowed to come in in a sports jacket and flannels, but every other day you had to wear a suit. I'd been wearing a suit more or less all my life. This was part of what was so entertaining later, when I came to love all the hippie side of GLF, because then I started to dress like that but continued to go to *The Times*, where everybody else was still in suits. Nobody said anything about me wearing a shoulder bag and beads and painted fingernails and turning up at *The Times*. And I was very bad at drag, I looked awful. I couldn't do make-up because I've always hated it, lotions and things, so it was an unvarnished face and I couldn't cope with the shoes. I had a moustache for a while and long hair and was very thin. I was wearing nail polish at *The Times* with male clothes. I remember the Chairman of Shell saying to me 'Where do you get your nail varnish?' during an interview with him. And then I left *The Times* after all and went to Bethnal Rouge and became the sort of person that Denis [Lemon] couldn't stand, one of the radical feminists.

It was a time when everybody exchanged helpful information about what was going on and somebody said, Agitprop were moving out of where they were in the East End and looking for people to take over the lease and wanted to choose who would take over. So we went and were interviewed. I remember nothing about the interview, I should imagine the way we looked was enough. Agitprop said we could have it.

I've never forgotten the Peanuts cartoons. The bathroom was filled with Peanuts cartoons from the *Observer*. It seemed rather endearing, this in the revolutionary Agitprop premises. They were rather large, we had a bookshop on the ground floor and the publishers were very easy going about supplying books on credit. We had a till by the door and we sold some, though it never made any particular profit. We were supposed to take it in turns to run the bookshop. We painted a mural at the far end of the ground floor and upstairs we turned the living room into the same as 7a – drapes and hangings everywhere, mattresses strewn around the floor and various people came to live there and visit. We used to go to a local pub which was staggered by these drag queens turning up, but it was a standard cockney pub, they had a piano and they liked to have a sing song and quite a lot of the people in the commune were very good at sing songs, so that made us reasonably popular and we spent quite a lot of dole money in there, so that was all right . . . We even took the door off the loo because we didn't believe in privacy, everything had to be done in public. I left eventually because of the heavy drug use there. Lots of heavy straight men began coming round.

I think it deserved just to dissipate, that it should do that, it wasn't an organization. People were always saying in the early meetings, someone could be relied upon to say, 'Can't we have a membership list or membership fees to raise money' or something like that. And week after week, somebody would leap to their feet and say 'This is not an organization, we don't want to be an institution of any sort', and so for me the great thing about GLF was that it dissolved gradually. So many things did come out of the ideas put forward, people concentrated on what suited them the most. (*Andrew Lumsden*)

I . . . was asked by Richard Chappell whether I thought it would be a good idea to open a bookshop in Bethnal Green. We moved in a little while after it had been set up. Bethnal Rouge was strange because it was this bookshop cum warehouse and you walked into a kitchen which went into open plan East End camp with a built-in bar in tacky plastic. The place had originally been owned by one of the Krays' bankers, who was serving twenty-five years in Maidstone, and Agitprop had been very nice to his wife, who they thought got a rough deal. It was the first house I ever lived in with a wall safe and we kept on looking at various places for hidden money, under the floorboards and so on.

I managed the Kentucky Fried Chicken shop in Bethnal Green Road under a false name. I went along for a part-time job and became the manager in weeks because it was two queens who were brothers who were running it and took a shine to me. So we managed it and the rest of the staff left because they couldn't cope with me, and the whole of Bethnal Rouge tried to manage it. We were making an awful lot of money because we were going across the road to Tesco's and buying cases of chicken, cutting them up and using Colonel Sanders name to pull the punters. And we got evicted from Bethnal Rouge and lived in Parfitt Street, in one of the few back-to-backs left in the East End. (*Julian Hows*)

In a Bethnal Rouge special issue of the news-sheet for 14–20 June 1973, there is a jokey diary which gives a flavour of life at Bethnal Rouge:

Doin' The Bethnal Rouge

6am we go to bed; except Nicole who gets up and Geoffrey who rises for his bath.

9am forget to put the dustbins out. Michael turns off central heating. Open door to sunroof – going to be blazing hot day.

10am 33 unknowns appear from bed for breakfast. Matthew makes station hotel breakfast for 85.

11am   Man turns on hot water system; Lydia looks for her giro; Andrew can't find his Wall Street Journal.

12am   forgotten to open the shop; huge queue outside – oh, they're waiting for bus. Lydia quieter.

1.00   cocktails and California beachwear on roof; social security visitor expected; gramophone red-hot.

2.00   shop opened; thermostat mad for 4th week: can only have hot water if central heating at full blast; fat visitor melts.

3.00   we've forgotten to buy the food for supper. Remember it's early closing.

4.00   Michael turns off central heating. Lydia turns off SS visitor.

5.00   everybody awake. Man puts on hot water & accordingly central heating.

5.30   the party continues. Somebody steals £50. Richard starts getting supper together from somewhere – Michael makes salad from unpaid bills.

6.00   cocktails on the sunroof. Someone steals £40 & the green shield stamps. Gramophone explodes.

7.00   guests arrive. Full meeting of commune efficiently deals in quarter of an hour with all practical and emotional problems.

8.00   do bookstall at GLF meeting. The men start thinking about sex. Central heating explodes. One million for supper.

10.00   somebody steals the furniture; we get thrown out of Tricky Dicky's disco.

12pm   somebody steals Bethnal Rouge; we go to sleep in the dustbins

And there was a small addendum in the following week's news-sheet:

8.00   Margaret also thinks about sex – then does the washing up.

In the same issue, there was a plea for help for the understaffed office. Caledonian Road staggered through the summer of 1973 with little support and an increasing workload as other groups outside London came to rely on it. There was a constant funding crisis due to fraud and mail theft, what the collective themselves referred to as 'general abuse of the building

by people who professed to be into GLF but who were only interested in dossing in the office, pushing dope and ripping off
anything they could get their hands on'. In June it began to charge
a nominal sum for the news-sheet and slowly the hours it was open
began to decrease and even these became more unreliable with
evening opening only one or two times a week. On Pride Day in
June 1973, there was a march followed by a coach to Birmingham
for a disco at the new community centre there. Bethnal Rouge held
a jumble sale instead.

Inevitably, there was a final row over the bones of GLF
between Bethnal Rouge and the office collective. It had been
preceded by a war of words and leaflets in the occasional all-
London meetings that were now being held at Conway Hall. The
office felt beleaguered and unloved despite all the hard work they
were doing, but others were angered by their protectiveness and
insularity. As a leaflet of August 1973 put it:

> Its happened again. The MEN have: formed a GROUP . . .
> took over the CAPITOL (our office) – started to make rules
> for others than themselves . . . printed PROPAGANDA on a
> newssheet . . . took complete control of PUBLIC property . . .
> THE SAME OLD RITUAL . . . wot next? Forms in triplicate,
> secretaries, candidates for parliament???? . . . The office
> collective say 'ALMOST' anyone can join. I don't want to
> 'join' anything, so apparently I can no longer use 'our'
> office . . . and of course ALL the GLF mail and expressed
> opinion is now to be answered by the MEN from the Stone
> Age, men who don't use their own minds, but copy all the
> mistakes MEN have made since the world began. I don't
> want to stop them using OUR office, but I and perhaps
> others expect to be able to use it as well without 'joining'
> anything.

After an inconclusive all-London meeting in September,
where a proposal to move the office to Bethnal Rouge was discussed, matters boiled over into direct action. 'We raided the office
because we couldn't get any sense out of them' (*Stuart Feather*).
Stuart, Richard Chappell, Julian Hows and Mary French were all
involved in the action and its later public defence. 'I remember
fighting with Julian Hows over a pile of *Manifesto*s. Julian lost'
(*David McLellan*).

One of the office people wrote up the conflict for the first
October newsletter.

And On The Third Day They Came

Last Wednesday morning, Stuart Feather, Richard and
half a dozen others arrived at the elegant and well appointed
5 Caledonian Road and loaded everything into a
truck, including the worldly possessions of some of the
members of the office collective, tore everything off the
walls and generally caused as much indigestion as can be
caused by that number of people at that time of the
morning. Cherubim, hearken unto your fairy godmother,
the place looked like Cinderella's coach at two after
midnight.

That, apart with getting foot and fist heavy with odd
peaceful people standing around or offering oral objection,
was what happened. Why is a much more difficult question
to answer. At the all London meeting at the Conway Hall
the previous evening the possibility of moving the office
from 5 Caledonian Road had been discussed, but naturally,
the all London meeting being the all London meeting, no
decision had been taken. And indeed, 5 Caledonian Road
does not exist only for the benefit of London, so
presumably the forty five other GLFs should have had some
say in the matter, but a small group of people in GLF have
got themselves so liberated that they have now gone a
complete circle and adopted the methods of our flat-footed
brothers. This incident is merely the cumulation of two
months of bickering, internecine warfare and general
nastiness which has driven people away from the meetings
at Conway Hall, wasted the efforts of the office collective
and of the Bethnal Rouge commune so that nothing has
been done to further the liberation of London at all, with
the exception of two demos. Well you may ask brothers,
where our communal head is at, I'll tell you – it's stuck
between our legs fist fucking.

In the middle of all this, why have an office at all? The
process of liberation is a long and painful one which never
finishes; there are people all over the country who are in
various stages of the process. They need pamphlets, badges,
information, contact, speakers, assurance and a voice to fill
fantasies while they wank off into a public telephone
booth. Laugh not, brother, for there go you. In addition, in
London, there needs to be somewhere where posters can be
made and stored, demos got together, and something done

about turning London on. Finally there needs to be
somewhere central for people all over the world to drop
into when they find themselves in this big wicked city.

By whom can this function be filled? Bethnal Rouge
commune is in London and has plenty of space; it has
someone there almost all the time and has gay people who
are trying to make a go of a totally new life style, needing
all the help from brothers and sisters which they can get
(Newsletter 14 June). On the other hand they are away
from the centre and difficult for strangers to get to, paying
a very heavy rent and rates, which makes them financially
insecure and most emotionally, so liberated that they can't
communicate with most of the human race, and most of
the human race can't communicate with them.
Unfortunately most gays are still members of the human
race; you must remain within shouting distance of those
you want to relate to. On the other hand, the office
collective has been able to answer all mail, provide a
reliable service as promised, pay off a lot of the debts, build
up a certain amount of confidence, and pay the rent. The
rent is low, the land-lords very co-operative (despite the
hassles our internal troubles give them), the number and
address known all over the world and the members of the
collective so unsure of their own liberation that nothing is
absolutely right. Now thanks to those mentioned at the
beginning the office is cleared of the detritus of the past and
ready for painting.

The feeling of the collective is that there is a function to
be performed at 5 Caledonian Road, and that it should be
continued with; they further feel that the heavy methods
used by some are contrary to the spirit and practice of GLF,
damaging both to individuals and the GLF as a whole.
They would like the matter discussed at the national get-
together in Brighton and some guidance given on the role,
if any, which other GLFs would like the office to perform,
what they would like it to be called, how and by whom
they would like it to be manned.

GLF has now reached the stage that it must move on into
new areas, it must change within itself to allow for a
greater number of people whose only thing in common is
that they feel put down. It must not put them down itself, it
must not become as small and destructive as the society

from which we are trying to escape, but unless it can turn outwards from itself, it will turn inwards upon itself and destroy itself. (*John Lindsay*)

Gay News covered the incident, remarking in passing that South London was now the only remaining effective GLF group in London. There was silence for a few months until February 1974 when the office collective, which had taken to referring to itself from the above incident as a general GLF resource and therefore not answerable to Londoners particularly, published 'The Last Newssheet':

> The office . . . will not exist after the 16th of February. At the last meeting of the office collective and the Gay Switchboard collective on Sunday 3rd February it was agreed that Gay Liberation Front would still operate as a mailing service address only but the info which it normally can relate by phone would be done by the switchboard . . . . the office collective decided to repaint the office to enable the switchboard to operate in more civilized surroundings. This is GLF's contribution towards the new Gay Switchboard.

It went on to give a financial statement and to say that profits from the badges and books they would still distribute by mail would go towards disco equipment for the new weekly discos run by the office at the Prince Albert pub nearby (now Central Station). It gave final listings for Icebreakers, Harrow Gay Unity, the TV/TS Group and the Women's, South London and West London discos. It was signed, 'Peace and love The winding up office collective.' And underneath, 'Excuse the typing but the typewriter is 100 years old. B.'

The badge and pamphlet sales were administered after this and into the 1990s by the GLF Information Service, who were three survivors of the office collective: Martin Corbett, David (Max) McLellan and Peter Madders. When stocks of the *Manifesto* finally ran out, they arranged for a reprint but cut out the section dealing with communes, on the grounds that they disagreed with it. It was a final act of revenge on what the 'straight gay' activists of the office saw as the foolish ideals that had poisoned GLF.

Chapter twenty

Go Your Own Way

It had achieved what it set out to do; dramatize, voice a change people felt in themselves, but saw nowhere reflected as yet. It was a play, and all the actors were amateurs except for one, and we finished our run – to terrific audiences – and then off we went to other engagements. It was a miracle play moving about the streets, which achieved miracles. –Andrew Lumsden

IF you see GLF as a dandelion which grew, flowered and then degenerated into a fluffy but insubstantial head full of seeds which were then blown by several gusts into new areas of the meadow, it is easy to understand the way in which it is connected to a whole host of major lesbian and gay initiatives of the 1970s, 1980s and even 1990s.

> The positive outcome of the break-up of central GLF was that a whole series of new initiatives emerged. GLF was a school for revolutionary activists. People came into the organization, developed a sense of self-confidence and pride and then were able to go on and do things they'd never dreamed were possible. It was a process of personal and collective empowerment. Nobody came into GLF and remained the same, everybody was changed by their involvement, mostly for the better. The GLF experience enabled a whole raft of people to found key community institutions like *Gay News*, Switchboard and Icebreakers. (*Peter Tatchell*)

The first of these was Icebreakers, the gay befriending service which lasted into the mid-1980s and acted as a politicized place for gay men to come out and learn about both the scene and activism. An offshoot of the Counter-Psychiatry Group, it started out mixed, but soon was for men. Its informal but politicized methods of bringing people out socially were often questioned by more conservative groups, but were highly effective in training the 1980s generation of gay male activists.

> Icebreakers turned out to be really important. It was a creature of its time based on the simple idea that people who were gay and afraid needed contact with other gays and not psychiatric help. The moment when Icebreakers emerged as an idea was when I went to the GLF office one evening and found that there were lots of people calling the phone number as their first point of contact, but that there was no care in the way people answered the phone to them. The attitude was 'Why should we bother with them if they're too afraid to express their sexuality', and sometimes they would even get abused. It filled me with horror that some people in GLF could not recognize the difficulties that they faced. Some people used to answer the phone with phrases like 'Poofs Anonymous' and of course, people often hung up on them. That's when I had the basic idea of having a different line and a different response, some time in 1972.
>
> Icebreakers often came under attack from Friend [a counselling offshoot of CHE] and others because we were not 'trained counsellors'. Antony Grey called us 'silly'. We were ideologically opposed to being professional or trained and we bent over backwards to just be ordinary people on the phones, but I can recognize now that some callers did need more professional help and Icebreakers couldn't admit it; but I'm glad that we did what we did because it was the right thing for most of the callers. I would just tend to take a more balanced view now. But Friend had a very strong emphasis on people having problems and having to be specially trained to deal with that. I remember that at an early planning meeting, we agreed that caller confidentiality would be total, that we wouldn't even discuss the calls amongst ourselves and David Hutter said 'But that would be half the fun!' (*Micky Burbidge*)

Icebreakers in its turn was responsible for a range of other groups founded later by men from it. The most notable of these was Gay's the Word, the first London gay activist bookshop which, although founded mainly by men, was one of the few influential gay agencies of the early 1980s to make a real stab at including lesbians and giving them their own space with a Lesbian Discussion Group through which many of us passed. GLF and Icebreaker people were also involved in the founding of First Out, the first London lesbian and gay cafe collective.

The next major offshoot was *Gay News*, whose chequered history is told in *Title Fight* by Andrew Lumsden and Gillian Hanscombe. It soon ceased to be a collective and spent many years under the editorship of Denis Lemon, undergoing a famous trial for blasphemy at the instigation of Mary Whitehouse and eventually collapsing under a combination of changing tastes it did not mirror and bad management. Within a year of its founding it had not only broken free of GLF but disowned it; in its first anniversary edition no mention was made of its roots and parentage. But it flourished for over a decade, producing a standard of intelligent gay reporting and excellent arts criticism which was generally unbiased by either partisan politics or advertisers. Its listings section was the information backbone of most of the gay switchboards around the country.

Some of the academics took their experiences back into academia and virtually founded a new branch of social studies. 'I became involved in the LSE Gay Culture Group, which met and did talks on Friday nights on gay history and theory . . . We published some pamphlets from that in 1972–73. David Starkey used to come to those meetings, as reactionary then as he is now actually and as sprightly then as he is now. He was always open about his gayness in that quirky individualistic way that he still has.' Jeffrey Weeks went on to be centrally involved in the Gay Marxist Group and Gay Left collective, which published an influential magazine during the late 1970s and early 1980s that sought to continue links between gay activism and the unaligned left.

> Icebreakers, Gay Left, Gay History Group, Switchboard, *Gay News*, Gay Marxist Group, Gay Research Group came from it. Everything I am now was shaped by those two years. I'm doing a research project on lesbian and gay attitudes to the family. In the sixties and early seventies, radicals were anti the family and that's reflected in the GLF *Manifesto* and a whole series of other things we said about the family. And we were looking for alternatives to the family. The commune movement was subconsciously an alternative way of living to the family. What I think has happened over the last two decades is that that hostility to

the family has gone and what people now talk about is
alternative families. So instead of the family and the rest –
those who weren't in a family – we now try to argue that
what we're living, in our different ways whether communal
or coupledom or whatever, are alternative families.

We're entering the discourse of the family and making
family a broader term than we used to think. I think today
people are talking, thinking and living in family type
relationships or aspiring to that sort of way of life and the
emphasis on partnership laws in many parts of Europe and
in Stonewall's campaign is part of that. What we were
doing in the early seventies was seeking validation of our
identity, of our sexual desires and increasingly as that has
been normalized and our sexual desires made almost
acceptable, to some extent, we've begun to argue for the
validation of our relationships, which I think is a different
part of the journey. (*Jeffrey Weeks*)

The most enduring organizational legacy of London GLF is
undoubtedly London Lesbian and Gay Switchboard. Founded
from the ashes of the office collective and with the twin parentage
of GLF and *Gay News* (who were sick of information calls to their
office), it still maintains the GLF structure of coordinating committee and working groups, though it has added company and
charitable status subsequently. Until 1994, it still worked out of the
same building in Kings Cross, although its overwhelming success
meant that it soon had to move out of the tiny basement office into
the upper floors. Uniquely amongst London gay voluntary groups,
it has its own freehold premises and over 100 volunteers operating
a twenty-four-hour service. Over the years, it has also acted as
something of a conciliator for old GLF people on it and still contains both someone who worked in the GLF office and at least one
radical gay communard.

Through the early AIDS work of London Lesbian and Gay
Switchboard, there is also a thread from GLF to the Terrence
Higgins Trust and other long-standing AIDS services. Switchboard
was the instigator of the first public meeting on AIDS in Britain,
and many of its volunteers deserted to either the Trust or the early
incarnations of the National AIDS Helpline as they realized the
seriousness of the threat facing their community. Other GLF people
such as Cloud Downey have also been central to the growth of the
self-help movement; Cloud was an early Chair of Body Positive and

founder of Positive Theatre, and many others are or have been volunteers in such groups.

Aubrey Walter and David Fernbach went on to create the first out gay publishing house in Britain, Gay Men's Press (later GMP), starting with Hans Heger's *The Men with the Pink Triangle* (on gays in the Nazi concentration camp system) in 1980. Their compilation of GLF articles *Come Together – the years of Gay Liberation 1970–73* with an historical introduction by Aubrey Walter is the only book previously published on GLF in Britain.

Some GLF people went into the theatre and were involved in the founding of both Gay Sweatshop and Bloolips, which Bette Bourne still runs. 'What came out of it all for me was Bloolips, which was a natural progression from Street Theatre, putting my politics on stage. We started off with a version of the Ugly Duckling and as we went on the ideas got more refined and we became more disciplined' (*Stuart Feather*). 'I went on after GLF to manage Hot Peaches for a while, when Bette was performing with them in Amsterdam, and then to get involved with Bloolips. I was tour manager and when Julian Hows dropped out of a European tour as a performer I went in his place' (*Paul Theobald*). Julian had not wanted to give up his job with London Underground, which he was eventually to leave in a blaze of publicity after he demanded the right to wear a uniform skirt without providing a certificate that he was undergoing gender counselling; on his last day, he wore it anyway and called every tabloid paper in the country to a photo-shoot.

> When it comes down to it, there is more to be learned from wearing a frock for a day than a suit for a lifetime. I still very much believe that. I still believe that the things people used to do, like asking people to wear a badge saying they were homosexual, whether they were gay or straight or whatever, just to wear that for a day and see the reaction they got, are still inestimable . . . it still sorts people out, doing that. (*Julian Hows*)

Some of the lesbians became involved with a variety of women's liberation groups in London, particularly the one in Radnor Terrace, Vauxhall, in *Spare Rib* and other publications.

> I think the first thing that happened after the trial was we got approached by Red Rag. I think one reason the *Morning Star* supported [the defendants] was Bea

Campbell, she got interested in it. I think Angela and I had written something before she got arrested or while she was on bail and that came to the attention of Red Rag and Bea, who had covered the trial, was involved with it, so we got involved with that. And then there were all those debates about lesbianism in the women's movement which got very exciting. (*Elizabeth Wilson*).

Looking further ahead, by the mid-1990s both of the major London-based general lesbian and gay rights organizations, Stonewall and OutRage!, had GLF people as their figureheads and within their volunteer bases. Peter Tatchell's knowledge of direct action has informed the tactics and targets of OutRage!, and Angela, at Stonewall, still works with the GLF Principles and Demands pinned up above her desk. 'It was like watching a caterpillar turning into a butterfly. Groups begat other groups – GLF to *Gay News* to Switchboard to THT. It was as if someone had said "Let a thousand pansies bloom – in the basement of the LSE"' (*Antony Grey*).

What it spawned was important – *Gay News* was a direct product, if a bone of contention – it was seen as exploiting people, because it was sold and not free. There were Icebreakers, Switchboard partly via *Gay News*, Sweatshop, First Out via Bruce Wood, OutRage! via Peter Tatchell and Stonewall has Angela Mason. When GLF vanished, many people got involved in other things but took the GLF view of life with them – it livened up CHE for a while! (*Michael Mason*). [Michael, of course, was also the founder of the first successful gay freesheet in Britain, *Capital Gay*.]

The repercussions of London GLF didn't only affect the gay movements on the mainland of Europe. 'Lewis Rabkin is in that photo (in *Come Together* 15), who went off and started gay liberation in Johannesburg. As far as I know, he was the first person to get black queens into the Royal Box at the Johannesburg Opera' (*Julian Hows*).

For many people in GLF, the enduring transformations were on a more personal level.

I was the dentist to lots of people in GLF as time went on. I already had a lot of gay patients at my practice in St Johns Wood and was making lots of money there. I moved to one in Tottenham which was a much more working-class area

and more GLF people came, looking very wild, the straight
Tottenham housewives were very thrown by them. I used to
kiss people goodbye on the lips at the door to the surgery
in my white coat, which amazed people in the waiting
room. I remember I caught myself doing an examination
one day wearing green nail varnish that I'd forgotten to
remove. I tried to bring GLF principles to bear on my
dentistry practice – it's all common stuff now, but it was
revolutionary then; telling people the pros and cons of
treatments and letting them make their own minds up,
offering different ways of treating them, demystifying stuff,
trying to be less hierarchical. I lost a few local patients that
way, I think they found it a bit bewildering.
(*Michael Brown*)

The early sexual politics of GLF, with their insistence on the
acceptability of polymorphous perversity and sexual diversity, unfortunately did not last even the life of the organization. 'I was in
the GLF office one day, answering the phone, and this woman I'd
been sleeping with rang me up to tell me she was pregnant by me. It
didn't go down very well in the office. I drifted out of GLF after I
started having affairs with women. There was never any open
denunciations of bisexuality, but there was a frostiness, especially
once I was living with Caroline' (*Tim Clark*). It is only in the 1990s
that some organizations have been able to loosen their prejudices
enough to accept people with a range of sexualities and to make the
kinds of alliances across the homo/hetero divide that marked out
early GLF.

Many people went on to non-gay organizations where they
now felt more able to be open about their sexuality, and slowly
many political parties and other causes became safer places for
lesbians and gay men.

I think everyone was a bit tired and a bit dispirited in a
way, but also perhaps more confident to move in different
ways and to other things. I mean, a lot of people who'd
really wanted to be involved in non-gay issues felt much
more confident after GLF. They had been out and gay or
out and lesbian and then would go off to International
Socialists, or environmental issues or whatever, CND.
Whatever it was, they didn't feel they were going to have to
hide themselves any more to be a part of things.
(*Nettie Pollard*)

Not everyone went on to a better life, and it is important to remember the price that some people paid for their involvement in GLF: prison sentences, disrupted lives, drug problems, loss of jobs and careers. Some people level stronger accusations, including founder Bob Mellors who is on record as saying that 'the activities of the Gay Liberation Front paved the way for AIDS'. But the consensus of most is that if GLF and groups like it had not blown gay oppression wide open, AIDS would still have spread through illicit sexual activities; and without the example of empowerment and self-help that was GLF, there would have been a far weaker gay community to act against AIDS in all those years before governments deigned to take any notice.

This book was only possible because GLF people were still around and involved in everything across the lesbian and gay world. Some of them first came together again to unveil a plaque at the London School of Economics for the twentieth anniversary of its founding, where Bob Mellors quoted Chairman Mao: 'A tiny spark can cause a prairie fire.' After this, a few of them started to look out for others and to begin discussing once again what had happened in GLF, how it related to modern lesbian and gay politics and the gulf between the two.

> It was extraordinary, so strange that so many people – I
> can't believe so many people are still around, I find it quite
> exciting because I thought it would be like my parents used
> to tell me, that after the war everyone was a Communist
> and then in ten or twenty years they all had a good job and
> were voting Conservative and you never heard from them
> again. And I thought, oh, they're all radical now because
> GLF was the in thing and the most radical thing happening
> that year – in five years' time they'll all be back in the closet
> and getting jobs in banks. But for many of us that hasn't
> actually happened. There are an awful lot of people I knew
> who were in GLF who have not gone on to have straight
> careers. Which I think is really nice, and it shows that GLF
> really was an agent for change. (*Nettie Pollard*)

Talking to GLF people as they came together for this book and for the Pride celebrations of 1995, where they appeared on stage and spoke of GLF in the twenty-fifth year of its founding, I found that they often had a very clear analysis of how GLF had fed into the intervening years and, in its way, been subverted into the gay consumer ethic.

GLF changed the face of this country. It made everyone aware very quickly – 'have a gay day', 'Gay Lib' and so on entered the language. We could be seen to stand up for our rights. And capitalism, in the shape of people like the breweries, found another market to exploit. Since GLF it's bloomed for gay pubs and clubs and it keeps on getting bigger. Everybody learnt to feel a lot more confident and we've still got the initiative, even though the eighties were a bad period. We felt like voices crying in the wilderness then. All the socialist ideas were buried and being gay was nothing but a part of consumer society. People were blinded to their rights being taken away, they were so enamoured of the glamour of consuming. (*Stuart Feather*)

But on the Pride main stage in 1995, the GLF people found that their message was once again clearly appreciated by the crowds. They recited GLF texts and slogans and, to their amazement, found themselves cheered to the echo by the crowd on lines like 'The nuclear family is not in the best interests of gays and women.' The Pride crowd is often criticized by people who see themselves as gay activists, because they are there to enjoy the festival; but GLF understood from the start the importance of Gay Days; and what is Pride if not the biggest Gay Day of the year? It was GLF, after all, who christened the first-ever Pride march a 'Carnival Parade'. In 1995 in Victoria Park, the scene of one of their best Gay Days more than two decades before, some thirty GLF lesbians, gay men, queens, bisexuals and transsexuals found themselves near to tears as the huge crowd yelled back their understanding and agreement. We cannot go back to 1970, and most of us would not want to, but the crowd's reaction made it clear that what was said then can still be heard today.

Appendix 1

Chronology

June 1969

22 Judy Garland dies in London.

27 Stonewall Bar in New York is raided and people being arrested riot. The riot spreads over the next three days.

July 1969

4 Lesbians and gay men walk out of a Mattachine Society New York meeting and walk over to the Alternative University in Greenwich Village, where they found what becomes the Gay Liberation Front.

Summer 1970

The USA resumes bombing of North Vietnam and state troopers shoot dead four anti-war protesters at Kent State University, Ohio.
The age of majority (for voting, etc.) is reduced in Britain from twenty-one to eighteen.
The Female Eunuch by Germaine Greer and *Sexual Politics* by Kate Millett published.
IBM invent the floppy disc for storing computer data.

July 1970

Antony Grey (Albany Trust) and others organize conference entitled 'Social Needs of the Homosexual'.

10 Retired policeman in Stoke Newington is bombed.

23 House of Commons evacuated after tear gas bombs are thrown from public gallery.

August 1970

'Lola' (The Kinks) rides high in the hit parade all month.

Huey Newton of the Black Panthers issues a statement supporting gay liberation.

18   London office of Iberia Airlines (Spain) bombed.

30   Commissioner of Metropolitan Police's home bombed – not reported in press.

September 1970

'Tears Of A Clown' (Smokey Robinson & The Miracles) is number one.

Letter printed in *Frendz* calling for gay heads to get together.

Aubrey Walter and Bob Mellors meet in New York at the Revolutionary People's Constitutional Convention.

5   Salvador Allende, Marxist, democratically elected President of Chile.

8   Attorney General's home in London is bombed and, again, unreported.

18   Jimi Hendrix dies of an overdose; the following month, Janis Joplin also dies of one.

2   Barclays Bank, Heathrow, bombed, as is Iberia Airlines in London and other major European cities.

October 1970

'Band Of Gold' (Freda Payne) is number one all month.

Time Out lists seven drag pubs in London – The Black Cap in Camden, the Royal Vauxhall Tavern in Vauxhall, The Bell at Kings Cross, The Duke of Fife in Upton Park, The City Arms in Poplar, The Great Northern Railway in Hornsey and the Windsor Castle in Maida Vale.

8   Second bombing of Attorney General's home.

9   Italian-state-owned buildings in London, Birmingham, Manchester and Paris bombed.

13   First London meeting of the Gay Liberation Front in a basement classroom of the LSE in Houghton Street, advertised by posters in the LSE. Nineteen people including one woman, Bev Jackson. Also David Fernbach, Aubrey Walter, Bob Mellors, Richard Dipple.

20   Second meeting attracts a few more people, mainly students who have seen notices in LSE. Those present agree to leaflet

West London gay pubs and areas, including cinemas showing *Boys in the Band*; brings hundreds more in during November.

24   Cleansing Department of Greenford Council bombed (during strike).

26   Barclays Bank, Stoke Newington, firebombed.

Keele University admin building firebombed.

31   *Time Out* reports that London Gay Liberation Front have invaded the *Sennet* office at the LSE, spraying slogans in response to an article on students and sex which denigrated women and 'queers'.

November 1970

'Voodoo Chile' (Jimi Hendrix Experience) reaches number one posthumously

Demands are formulated and circulated early this month.

International Times (*IT*) trial finishes this month; proprietors are given eighteen months suspended each and a total of £2,600 in fines. Appeal runs all the way through GLF, finally losing at House of Lords just before the first publication of *Gay News* in June 1972.

Meetings are now being attended by crowds of people and move to a larger room.

20   BBC van covering Miss World contest firebombed at 2.30 a.m. outside Albert Hall.

21   Women's Lib, including a number of lesbians later to join GLF, massively disrupt the Miss World competition.

24   Media Workshop, now meeting regularly, starts to compile the first edition of *Come Together*.

25   A meeting of over 200 people votes for the Louis Eakes case demo, acting on a suggestion from Antony Grey of the Albany Trust.

Yukio Mishima commits ritual suicide in Japan after leading a failed coup.

27   At Highbury Fields, between eighty (*The Times*) and 150 (*CT*) GLF supporters meet at 9 p.m. at the tube and walk across the Fields carrying torches. The Demands are read out to calls of 'Right On'.

28   *The Times* reports the demo, seen by one of their journalists, Andrew Lumsden, who then goes to GLF.

Time Out publishes a piece in their Agitprop section saying 'Gay Is Good'. 16 North Gower Street (Agitprop bookshop) is given as the address and the Demands are stated.

31   Media Workshop copies *Come Together* 1.

December 1970

Best-selling album of 1970 (and for almost the whole life of GLF) is *Bridge Over Troubled Water* (Simon & Garfunkel).

Performance, a film with Mick Jagger and Edward Fox featuring a blatant gay subtext, released to rows about censorship and/or the lack of it.

3   Spanish Embassy in London machine-gunned. Angry Brigade claim it and, by inference, Miss World, Barclays Banks and other bombings in Communiqué 1.

Industrial Relations Bill published.

4   First GLF dance at LSE in the St Clements building.

7   Power cuts throughout Britain due to a work-to-rule over Industrial Relations Bill.

8   First big demonstration against the Industrial Relations Bill. Department of Employment bombed the same night. Claimed by Angry Brigade.

9   Principles, drafted by David Fernbach, discussed and voted on.

12   *Time Out* finally lists Gay Liberation Wednesday meetings and says 200 people attend. They are being held in Room E108 in the basement of Clare Market LSE building. It also advertises the first dance at Kensington Town Hall with a cartoon.

13   GLF attend a countercultural event at the Roundhouse with cookies and cakes but decide not to demonstrate

22   First GLF Ball at Kensington Town Hall – 'GLF People's Dance', 750 people admitted and 500 turned away.

23   GLF moves to Camden Arts Lab at Robert Street, Camden while LSE closed over Christmas vacation.

Come Together 2 published this week, listing various groups.

27   The *People* covers the GLF Ball with photos and interviews.

30   The general meeting discusses a separate women's caucus for the first time; women start to meet as a subgroup.

Second year of Vietnam peace talks end in Paris with no progress.

January 1971

'My Sweet Lord' (George Harrison) makes number one.

Come Together 3 published at start of month.

Spectator carries an article on GLF written by Andrew Lumsden, after *The Times* refuses to print it.

4   Louis Wane Eakes, twenty-five, journalist of Highbury, remanded to 19 February on £100 bail on a charge of gross indecency with another man in Hyde Park bandstand.

8   *Watford Evening Echo* attacks GLF.

    Tupamaros guerrillas in Uruguay kidnap British ambassador.

9   Two bombs explode at Minister for Employment's home on the
    day of another demonstration against the Industrial Relations Bill.
    Claimed by Angry Brigade.

    Series of Special Branch raids on known leftists and anarchists
    throughout London begins, extending into the counterculture, gay
    and women's movements.

16 First think-in at LSE discusses tactics and the organization of
    GLF. Antony Grey's ideas for a more structured organization
    defeated due to a mistrust of the traditional gay reformist groups.

17 *Observer* article with photograph of *Come Together* sellers at a
    gay venue.

    Other groups are already said to exist in Manchester, Sheffield
    and Brighton. The Brighton group is founded by, among others,
    Simon Watney and Mark Rowlands.

    Agitprop bookshop commune's house in Muswell Hill raided and
    address book taken by Special Branch; one of the collective is
    Andy Elsmore of GLF.

19 Jake Prescott, sought by police in relation to the bombings,
    arrested in Notting Hill on a cheque charge; bailed to 3 February.

20 National postal workers strike in Britain until 8 March.

22 Police bust the GLF disco at Prince of Wales in Hampstead Road
    on a drugs warrant.

27 Michael Mason attends his first GLF meeting as a young
    Conservative and is horrified; he gets over it.

February 1971

'Your Song', Elton John's first success, enters hit parade.

Warhol exhibition opens at Tate Gallery, his first major exhibition
in London.

Come Together 4 published between 4 and 16 February.

GLF moves into the basement of 5 Caledonian Road (Housmans
Bookshop), beginning a twenty-three-year gay occupancy of the
site.

4   'Miss Trial' demonstration outside Bow Street Magistrates Court
    (in support of Women's Liberation people arrested in November
    at Miss World) is the first major public event for Street Theatre.

5   First British soldier killed on duty in Northern Ireland.

6   GLF has 'get together' in basement of Housmans.

7   Women finally get the vote in Switzerland.

8   First warning letter written by Counter-Psychiatry Group and sent to W. H. Allen, hardback publishers of Dr Reuben's book *Everything You Always Wanted To Know About Sex – but were afraid to ask.*

11   Jake Prescott rearrested and charged with the Miss World and other bombings.

       Miss World trial disrupted by police investigating bombings.

12   GLF visit W. H. Allen in Essex Street, Strand to protest about the Reuben book. A letter with 158 signatures is given in by the deputation. Covered by *Peace News*, *Guardian* and *Evening Standard*.

13   Leafleting against the Reuben book outside Foyles and W. H. Smiths in Notting Hill, Sloane Square, Earls Court.

15   Decimal currency introduced in Britain.

17   Meeting decides on retaliatory action against the Gateways for banning women wearing GLF badges.

20   GLF zap of the Gateways; thirteen arrested including two passers-by; Marshall Weekes later deported as a direct result. Covered in the *Guardian* on the following Monday.

       Emergency warning of nuclear attack broadcast in USA by mistake.

21   GLF people and placards attend the Industrial Relations Bill along with 125,000 others. *Guardian* gives them good coverage the following day: Placards read 'Homosexuals Oppose The Bill', 'Poof To The Bill' and 'Gay People Are On The March'.

26   GLF Dance at Kensington Town Hall with Ginger Johnson and Patto.

27   Communiqué Five from Angry Brigade points out they do not kill, only damage property, and draws attention to unreported attacks.

March 1971

'Hot Love' (T. Rex) is number one.

In France the Front Homosexuel d'Action Revolutionnaire (FHAR), GLF's sister organization, is founded after people visit London GLF. Organizations across Western Europe begin to spring up or radicalize.

6   Women's Liberation national demonstration marches from Hyde Park to Trafalgar Square.

7   Ian Purdie arrested and charged with Angry Brigade bombings.

18   Ford Motors bombed during strike.

       Britain sends 1,800 more troops to Northern Ireland.

29	Charles Manson and three others sentenced to death for the Sharon Tate murders in 1969.
31	William Calley sentenced to life imprisonment, later commuted to twenty years, in USA for the My Lai massacre in Vietnam.

April 1971

'Power To The People' (John Lennon and The Plastic Ono Band) in the hit parade.

Come Together 5 published after 7 April.

1	*Little Red Schoolbook* published in Britain and seized immediately by Scotland Yard's Obscene Publications Squad.
3	GLF book group meet at 'Blonds at 56 Doughty Street' to consider putting together a book in response to the offer from W. H. Allen.
7	Possibly the week in which meetings move from Room E71 at the LSE to Middle Earth, 43 King Street, Covent Garden.
9	*New Statesman* publishes article by Ian Harvey, leading member of CHE, attacking GLF.
11	Festival of Life, Alexandra Park. GLF Street Theatre perform a Liberation Ceremony in Berman's costumes. Easter Sunday.
12	*Guardian* carries very sympathetic article by Jill Tweedie, portraying GLF as healthier than the existing gay scene; written after meeting Andrew Lumsden at a dinner party.
17	Rehearsal for first Gay Day.
	Paul Temperton of CHE replies to the Jill Tweedie article in *Guardian*, criticizing GLF.
	Time Out publishes the GLF fist design badge.
19	Unseen, a Women's Liberation 'Vengeance Squad' hoist a bra on the London Weekend Television flagpole. 'Worthy of the Marines' comments one baffled security officer.
	British unemployment, at 3.4%, reaches highest levels since 1940.
22	Arson at Whitechapel Barclays Bank.
23	Leafleting in Earls Court (probably for the Gay Day).
25	First Gay Day in Holland Park – 'Homosexuals Come Out!' sticker printed and stuck all round central London.
	12,000 protesters against the Vietnam war are arrested over the coming week in the USA.
28	*The Times* receives letter bomb and note from Angry Brigade; all staff fingerprinted.
30	Dance at Camden Town Hall.

May 1971

'Knock Three Times' (Dawn) number one for almost the entire month.

Coordinating committee structure is established; planning reps from each group meet weekly to share info.

Come Together 6 published.

1   Biba, fashionable boutique, bombed in Kensington. Claimed for the Angry Brigade in Communiqué 8.

4   Bomb found on the underside of Lady Beaverbrook's car (Lord Beaverbrook owns the Express Newspapers).

6   First meeting of Communes Group.

8   GLF think-in – probably when the coordinating committee structure was decided.

14   GLF Party at Ivor Street, Jeffrey Weeks and Micky Burbidge's place, happily remembered by some as their first orgy.

16   Gay Day, site unknown.

22   Scotland Yard computer room bombed, also British Rail, Rolls Royce and Rover in Paris, claimed as collaboration between European groups including Angry Brigade. Agitprop immediately raided.

26   Metro trial starts, Notting Hill black activists charged following a police raid which turned into a fight.

29   GLF women's disco, basement of coffee bar, 470 Harrow Road, W9.

Time Out reports that schoolchildren in Barnet have formed the 'Slightly Angry Brigade', leaving stink bombs in trendy boutiques.

June 1971

Rehearsals at Cavendish Avenue for *Measure For Measure*.

6   *Measure for Measure* goes to Bath Festival; *Come Together* 7 states that it was two Street Theatre pieces on Liberation and the Trial scene from *Alice in Wonderland* – perhaps both?

11   Red Lesbian Brigade zap Stock Exchange; reported as major terrorist incident with security implications in *Evening News*.

12   Trafalgar Square rally for Angela Davis and all political prisoners.

16   Michael Mason's diary notes: 'Chair general meeting – moment of glory!'

19   First national GLF think-in at Leeds.

Street Theatre rehearse for the Harley Street demo.

Glastonbury Festival this weekend.

20	GLF London attends Traverse Trial in Edinburgh on homosexuality as witnesses/advocates.
22	*Oz* trial starts at the Old Bailey.
	Banner made at GLF office for Harley Street demo.
23	GLF disco at Middle Earth.
24	Aubrey Walter, Paul Theobald and others spray paint Harley Street.
25	Demo along Harley Street at lunchtime; leaflets, street theatre.
	Margaret Thatcher, Education Secretary, ends free milk for primary school children.
28	Three Black Panther supporters given suspended sentences at the Old Bailey and one acquitted for riotous assembly after fighting breaks out during a police raid on the Oval House in Kennington.
29	Lala in court – nobody can remember quite why.
	Little Red Schoolbook trial starts at Lambeth Magistrates Court.

July 1971

'Get It On' (T. Rex) at number one.

Come Together 7 published at the start of the month.

1	*Measure for Measure* abandoned – (at least, it's the last rehearsal noted).
	Publisher of *Little Red Schoolbook* found guilty and fined £50, book effectively banned.
	Agitprop reopens in Bethnal Green (248 Bethnal Green Road).
4	Freak Festival in Hyde Park.
9	British troops shoot dead two rioters in Derry; inquiry is refused.
	11 Gay Day in Victoria Park from 2.30 p.m. 'GLF teeshirts will be on sale by then. Please try and wear one.'
14	Metro Trial at Marylebone Magistrates Court.
16	Women's Liberation and Gay Liberation stage tenth and most successful sit-in and picket of Wimpy Houses to protest their policy of not serving unaccompanied women after midnight; more than 150 take part.
22	Ford's Managing Director bombed by Angry Brigade.
23	Dance at Hammersmith Town Hall.
28	Meetings move to All Saints Church Hall in Notting Hill Gate after King Street is put up for sale.
31	Secretary for Trade and Industry's home is bombed despite heavy security and claimed by Angry Brigade, Communiqué 11.

August 1971

'I'm Still Waiting' (Diana Ross) at number one.
Come Together 8 published.
Agitprop's new bookshop in Bethnal Green is raided early in the month and material taken.

15   Territorial Army centre in Holloway bombed after announcement that internment would start in Northern Ireland; claimed by Angry Brigade Moonlighters Cell. Series of raids in Islington that night, including on GLF members.

16   Agitprop raided again, this time with a warrant to search for explosives.

19   GLF marches down Fleet Street, leafleting and using newspaper hoardings as placards, to protest at media portrayal and stereotyping of gays.

20   North Sea oil and gas concessions first put up for auction by British government.

21   Jim Greenfield, Anna Mendelson, John Barker and Hilary Creek arrested at Amhurst Road. Stuart Christie and Chris Bott also arrested there later.

23   All above charged at Albany Street Police Station with offences relating to explosions and weapons.

28   Gay Day in Hyde Park followed by first march through London to Trafalgar Square, officially to protest the age of consent. Covered next day by *Sunday Times* ('nearly 500 people, banners, Nigerian drum band, men in drag, distributed leaflets'); *Time Out* says 1,000 people.

      After the rally in Trafalgar Square, about thirty GLF people are ejected from Jolyon's (Joe Lyons Tea House) on the Strand because manageress objects to two men in drag (Claudia and Malcolm).

September 1971

'Hey Girl Don't Bother Me' (The Tams) at number one.
GLF women attend Women's Lib social in Cambridge Circus.

9   Festival of Light starts with rally in Central Hall, massively disrupted by GLF-coordinated coalition of counterculture and liberation groups. Covered extensively in press the next day, especially the nuns who did the cancan.

      Attica Prison riots in New York leave forty-two dead including Black Panther prisoners.

22   After general meeting, large crowd attempts to go to the
      Chepstow; met by police cordon and van, informed that landlord
      does not want to serve them. Later refused service at Artesian
      (corner of Chepstow and Talbot Roads).

      House of Commons recalled for emergency debate on Northern
      Ireland.

24   GLF members appear on Thames TV *Today* programme.

      Despite police claims to have arrested all of the Angry Brigade,
      they bomb Albany Street Army Barracks.

25   Festival of Light culminating rally in Trafalgar Square only
      attracts 35,000 instead of the predicted 100,000: GLF and
      Women's Lib heavily outflanked by police and many arrested.
      Some continue to Festival of Light rally in Hyde Park, where Gay
      Day has been called for Speakers Corner. GLF banner featured in
      press photos but is confiscated by police as an offensive weapon
      and never seen again.

26   *Sunday Times* covers GLF arrests including the accusation from
      police that GLF are associated with the Angry Brigade.

      Benefit at Theatre Royal, Stratford East for a Premises Fund 'to
      find a social alternative to the pub/club scene'.

28   GLF visit several local pubs and are told that they will not be
      served.

October 1971

      'Maggie May' (Rod Stewart) at number one all month.

      Manifesto published this month.

      'Towards A Revolutionary GLF' submitted for publication,
      rejected by Media Workshop – subsequent row delays *Come
      Together* 10 until November.

2   Think-in at LSE.

4   Benefit concert for GLF at Seymour Halls.

5   Press statement released about pub demo, letters distributed to
      publicans and police.

6   After general meeting, 250 people go to the Colville where they
      have previously had problems. They are served (bright publican!).
      Then they go on to the Chepstow, where the landlord refuses to
      serve them. They occupy with a sit-in, forcing closure. Police take
      an hour to arrive and carry them out one by one. By Friday night,
      every pub in the area is serving people wearing GLF badges.

7   Britain sends another 1,500 troops to Northern Ireland.

8   Pan Books publish the paperback version of Reuben's book.

9   GLF London joins GLF Brighton in a Gay Day on the beach to coincide with the Labour Party conference.

11   Meeting in office discusses what to do about Pan Books and the Reuben book.

12   *Jesus Christ Superstar*, first major musical from Andrew Lloyd Webber and Tim Rice, receives premiere in New York.

16–17 Weekend: Women's Liberation National Coordinating Conference at Skegness. GLF women, told that they are a bourgeois deviation, seize the microphone and lead a grass roots revolt which changes the whole conference. Lesbianism suddenly on the agenda for feminists.

19   Jeff Marsh of GLF found not guilty of assault on a police officer at the *Oz* trial. GLF Street Theatre performed 'The Courtroom Charade' outside to passers-by. Several others found guilty including a woman accused of shouting, when an officer lifted her bodily to remove her, 'He's trying to get a free one up my arse.' The officer maintained he was embarrassed.

20   Angry Brigade claim bombing in Birmingham.

22   GLF think-in discusses strategies for dealing with the big meeting, new members, high turnover, etc.

       GLF Centenary Dance at Fulham Town Hall, 50p.

28   Parliament votes 356 to 244 for Britain to join the European Community; most Conservative MPs are in favour, most Labour MPs against.

30   Major demos against the Reuben book along Charing Cross Road.

       First Holloway Prison demo in support of women's liberation and Radical Alternatives To Prison, primarily about bad conditions and for Pauline Jones.

       Antony Grey establishes National Federation of Homophile Organizations with Arena Three, CHE, Integroup, North East Women's Group, SK Society, SMG and others from York, Nottingham and Manchester. GLF the only major player which rejects involvement. (NFHO collapses in 1972–73).

       Angry Brigade claims bombing of Post Office Tower, London.

3   Anti-Internment march through central London supported by GLF.

November 1971

'Sing A Song Of Freedom' (Cliff Richard) peaks at number thirteen.

Fifteen members of GLF lay wreath of carnations with pink triangle for first time at the Cenotaph on Remembrance Sunday; police try to keep them away and tell them to remove the pink triangles they are wearing because they are 'too political'.

5   Paul Temperton of CHE writes to Bob Mellors at the office asking GLF to stop publishing the addresses of CHE convenors and asking for 'a supply of your excellent warning stickers for the Reuben book'.

Three GLF members, Mark Roberts, Peter Wells and Alan Ellaway, arrested for obstruction after refusing to leave the Chepstow when landlord refused to serve anyone wearing a GLF badge; thirty members had gone to the pub after a 'Gay Fawkes' bonfire in Powis Square.

6   Bombings in several major European cities of British government targets in support of the arrested in 'Angry Brigade' investigation.

Miss World demo with full GLF participation in support of Women's Lib – try to hold hands round the Albert Hall.

9   Five policemen and one woman raid Women's Liberation Workshop with explosives warrant, but on blatant trawl for names and addresses.

10   GLF Street Theatre attends Bow Street Magistrates Court as 'Gerillah Theatre'.

Denis Lemon and Angie Weir chair general meeting.

11   Angie Weir arrested in raid on Haverstock Street and charged at Albany Street with conspiracy to cause explosions.

16   Demo in support of National Union of Students attended by GLF and banner.

17   Chris Allen charged with conspiracy to cause explosions after raid on house in Talbot Road, Notting Hill (charges later dropped for insufficient evidence).

19   Sisters disco, free to women, Kings Arms in Bishopsgate.

20   Abortion demo on International Abortion Day supported by GLF.

24   *Come Together* 10 published.

25   First meeting of Camden GLF at Foresters Hall, Highgate Road, NW5.

'Fed up with up-tight rip off clubs etc. The Alternative Scene has begun at the Kings Arms, 213 Bishopsgate 10p admission' (newsletter).

Harold Wilson, as Leader of the Opposition, produces plan to unify Ireland by 1986.

26   Pauline Conroy arrested on conspiracy to cause explosions after raid at Powis Square, Notting Hill (charges dropped before trial on insufficient evidence).

27   Politics of Psychology conference at LSE, a radical psychiatry event for 400 participants, has GLF speakers.

        Street selling of latest *Come Together*, which had just arrived in the office (done from 8 p.m., which strongly suggests selling in bars).

29   Henekey's demonstration defendants at Well Street Magistrates Court.

December 1971

'Jeepster' (T. Rex) is kept at number two all month by 'Ernie, The Fastest Milkman In The West' (Benny Hill).

Death toll in Northern Ireland for the year is 130 civilians and forty-three troops.

1   Trial of Ian Purdie and Jake Prescott on bombing charges ends. Purdie not guilty on all charges, Prescott guilty of conspiracy only, gets fifteen years.

9   Media Workshop in Barnes.

        International Liaison Group.

        Jewish Research Group.

        Camden GLF – 'help liberate the Balls Pond Road'.

10   10 a.m. Festival of Light defence support at Bow Street.

        12.30 p.m. Demonstration at Pan Books in Westminster with giant papier-mâché cucumber.

        Communes Group in Penge.

        Women's Group at Faraday Road.

        Awareness Groups throughout London.

        Street selling of *Come Together* 10.

11   GLF Jumble Sale at All Saints Hall, Powis Square.

12   Church Research Group and Agape Feast.

        Dance Group.

        TV/TS Group.

        Counter-Psychiatry Group at Ivor Street.

        Christmas Party Group – final meeting.

13   Tweedie article in *Guardian* on sex roles makes much mention of GLF and carries photo of Miss Trial demo in February.

        FoL defence 10 a.m. Bow Street.

        Remembrance Day defence for Alan Wakeman, Bow Street.

        Youth and Education Group.

        Action Group.

        Premises Group.

        Office collective meeting.

14 Chepstow defence, 10 a.m. Marylebone Magistrates Court.
    Coordinating committee.
15 Deadline for info for newsletter, done today for distribution at
    general meeting.
    General meeting, 7.30 p.m., All Saints, Powis Square.
17 Cosmic Carnival Weekend, dance at Seymour Hall.
    Festival of Light defence, 10 a.m., Marylebone Magistrates Court.
18 National think-in at LSE.
    Children's Party in Notting Hill Gate.
    Disco at General Picton in Caledonian Road, N1.
    Kate McLean arrested on charges of conspiracy to cause
    explosions.
22 News-sheet gives dope and acid market prices over Christmas;
    concludes 'Alcohol and other beverages at usual government
    controlled prices'.
23 Camden GLF Christmas Party.

January 1972

'I'd Like To Teach The World To Sing' (New Seekers) number one
all month.
The first computer game is invented some time this year.
Come Together 11 published, women's issue.

3   Committal proceedings for 'Stoke Newington Eight' trial, as the
    Angry Brigade defendants have become known.
9   British miners go on strike, threatening the nation's energy
    supplies, in response to Government industrial and pay policies.
12 Remembrance day defence at Bow Street.
14 Chepstow defence at Marylebone – Mark Roberts, Alan Ellaway.
15 Demonstration outside Holloway prison at which Julia L arrested.
17 Festival of Light defence at Marlborough Street.
19 Chepstow defence at Marylebone – Peter Wells.
20 Unemployment figures go over one million for the first time.
22 Britain, Denmark, Ireland and Norway join the European
    Community.
25 Reporting restrictions on Stoke Newington Eight Trial lifted and
    Angie Weir finally bailed on condition she leaves London for
    Basingstoke; those bailed are scattered to make defence
    consultation far more difficult.
29 Women's think-in at All Saints Hall, possibility of leaving is
    discussed.

30   British troops shoot dead thirteen civilians during an anti-internment march in Bogside, Derry. This becomes known as 'Bloody Sunday'.

31   NCCL begins campaign to collect information on police harassment of gays; GLF help to distribute 10,000 leaflets and questionnaires.

Torchlight vigil in Grosvenor Square for Angela Davis, US black activist, on the day her trial begins in US on terrorism-related charges.

February 1972

'Telegram Sam' (T. Rex) number one.

Camden GLF thrown out of William IV in latter part of month for leafleting.

Bloody Sunday March, in which thirteen coffins are delivered to Downing Street and there is a riot in Whitehall. Large GLF contingent marches from Hammersmith with banner.

9   Women walk out of GLF meeting and announce they will work separately in future.

Demonstrators burn down British embassy in Dublin.

11   David Fernbach and Aubrey Walter produce 'Gay Activism and Gay Liberation: a message to gay brothers' which is distributed at Lancaster think-in the next week.

18   National think-in at Lancaster University begins with disco.

19   National think-in discussions, including on the role of lesbians.

South London GLF recruiting demo.

'Freedom and Responsibility In The Media' conference at Roundhouse organized by *Time Out* and The Other Cinema, disrupted by Women's Liberation and GLF after women are ignored for the first half of the event. Women take over the platform and South London GLF Street Theatre break out the banners.

22   IRA bomb kills seven in Aldershot, where many British troops are stationed.

23   News-sheet reports big financial problems.

Agitprop raided for fourth time on an explosives warrant.

March 1972

'Without You' (Nilsson) number one.

Come Together 12 (the unauthorized version) published in latter half of month.

Winchester teacher training college trip.

Gay International News starts publication from a back room at 305 Portobello Road (*Frendz* offices).

3   West London GLF dance at Fulham Town Hall.

7   Union Tavern ejects South London GLF people for leafleting, in case the pub gets a name for being queer; landlord's son punched a GLF member the previous day for doing the same.

Meeting held to discuss *Gay News* – GLF people express fears that it will not be radical enough. Those involved in *Gay News* at this point are David Seligman, Suki Pitcher, Peter Reed, Denis Lemon, Sylvia Room, Andrew Lumsden and Martin Corbett.

9   Tim Bolingbroke Festival of Light appeal hearing at Newington Causeway.

11   GLF think-in on the future of central London and local GLF groups, LSE. Decision made to stop unauthorized publication of Issue 12 of *Come Together*, defied by office collective.

GLF banner taken to Arthur Blessit evangelical rally in Trafalgar Square.

19   Kilburn GLF founded. It joins South London, Notting Hill, West London, Camden, Harrow and Ealing as area groups.

21   Fifty members of GLF, organized by Camden, occupy *Time Out* offices to demand that gay ads be published and sexism within the personal ads reduced.

26   Anti-Internment League march.

27   Special meeting in office to decide what to do about Arthur Blessit.

30   Britain assumes direct rule over Northern Ireland.

April 1972

'Amazing Grace' (Royal Scots Dragoon Guards Band) number one all month.

Come Together 13 from Camden.

Camden GLF go up the Heath with the tea trolley.

All-London meetings suspended.

11   West London dance at Fulham Town Hall – benefit for Flaum family including Trevor, Paul Theobald's boyfriend, jailed in Italy for trial on drugs charges.

22   Gay Day at Keele University, Londoners attend.

May 1972

'Rocket Man' (Elton John) in charts.

Gay News originally scheduled to be published this month, but does not appear until June.

5–7   National *Come Together* at Birmingham University and Birmingham 's first GLF People's Dance at Digbeth Civic Hall on Saturday 6th.

6   Teach-in on homosexual liberation at LSE for people working in education and law, attended by about 100 people including a dozen heterosexuals and some CHE members.

12   West London dance at Fulham Town Hall.

14   Gay Day, Clapham Common.

Ulster Defence Association sets up Protestant no-go areas in Belfast.

17   Schools demo at County Hall by the Schools Action Union; Julian Hows arrested but not charged.

20   National Union of School Students launched to organize school students to claim their rights.

21   Gay Day, Waterlow Park.

28   Gay Days, Primrose Hill and Wimbledon Common.

30   Trial of Stoke Newington Eight begins in Number One Court at the Old Bailey. It becomes the longest criminal trial in British history.

June 1972

Exile on Main Street (Rolling Stones) is the top-selling LP.

Come Together 14, Youth Issue (perhaps) at end of May.

Evidence given at Stoke Newington Eight trial this month against Angie Weir thoroughly refuted in defence evidence in November.

Brixton commune at Athlone Road is founded and soon attracts hostility from neighbours and local schoolboys.

2–4   Bath Festival with Street Theatre group performing on Saturday.

4   Festival at Widcombe Manor, near Bath.

Gay Day, Finsbury Park.

11   Gay Day, Parliament Hill.

Angela Davis demo, Trafalgar Square.

13   Huge row at office collective meeting over feelings of exclusion by 'fems'.

14   *IT* loses appeal to House of Lords on 4–1 majority verdict (Lord Diplock dissenting), upholding conviction that gay advertisements were a conspiracy to corrupt public morals.

17   'Fems' repaint office in bright colours and change decor to make it less macho.

Five people arrested at Watergate apartments in Washington while trying to bug Democratic Party headquarters there.

18   Office discussions continue.

Gay Day, Alexandra Park.

Speakeasy with Jimmy Saville on homosexuality excludes GLF; other gay groups collude in this.

19   *Spare Rib* launch party at The Place, Euston, disrupted by GLF members; given heavy press coverage by *Sunday Times* and *Gay News*.

Gay News 1 published; carries criticism of the West London dances by David Seligman and a photo of Regents Park Gay Day. Ian Dunn of SMG refers to 'the old guard . . . delighted and yet bewildered at the great diversification in the gay world since GLF shattered the silence'.

There are twenty-nine GLF groups listed in *Gay News* 1 outside London and eight local ones in London, as well as subject/minority groups.

23   West London dance organized by Youth Group – *Time Out* reports that it was poorly attended.

24   First Gay Pride week starts, organized by GLF Youth and Education Group.

Fifty gays march from High Street Kensington to Earls Court ghetto pubs; thrown out of the Boltons and Coleherne and receive little support.

25   Gay Days, Waterlow Park and Battersea Park.

27   'Oscar Wilde demo by Street Theatre' followed by picket, as most weeks, of American Embassy. The queens arrive en masse, dance to a band of the US Marines and hold an impromptu march down to Piccadilly and Trafalgar Square, then on to Hyde Park.

July 1972

'Puppy Love' (Donny Osmond) number one all month.

1   Carnival Parade from Trafalgar Square to Hyde Park for a Gay Day. More than a thousand people attend including all factions, lesbians march under GLF Women's banner, thirty members of FHAR attend from France, hardly anyone from CHE. Heavily policed.

2   Gay Day, Primrose Hill.

5   Athlone Road commune invade boys school across the road to protest about attacks on their house. Police are called. Julian Hows subsequently expelled for assisting.

7   GLF Dance at Fulham Town Hall – Tony Reynolds arrested after local youths cause trouble and he challenges the police present for being friendly with the queerbashers. Also much friction between queens and *Gay News* sellers.

9   Gay Day at Bishops Park, Fulham.

16   Gay Day, Peckham Rye.

23   Gay Day, Turnham Green.

22   National dock strike begins.

August 1972

'School's Out' (Alice Cooper) at number one.

President Idi Amin of Uganda expels all Ugandan Asians; many with British passports settle in the UK.

September 1972

'Virginia Plain' is Roxy Music's first big hit.

Severe friction between London GLF and *Gay News* throughout this month – *Gay News* complains of refusal to provide information.

9   All London *Come Together* (renamed think-in) only gets attendance of 120 men, few women and starts two hours late. Report by Laurence Collinson in *Gay News* 7 is very critical of rows. Agrees to hold monthly all-London meetings.

16   Champion demo and arrests; twenty GLF people in drag, five arrested (Chappell, McDougall, Lumsden, Reed, Bourne) and held at the station for over three hours.

21   Internment without trial ends in Northern Ireland.

24   Gay Day in Victoria Park held by East London Gay Liberation Front, who distribute Demands.

October 1972

'John I'm Only Dancing' (David Bowie) in charts.

East London GLF sets up via Agitprop at 248 Bethnal Green Road.

19	Attempts are made to evict the squat at 42 Colville Terrace. Residents begin to search for new premises. Mick Belsten and Julian Hows find 7a Colville Houses, an old film studio.
21	European Community summit in Paris approves economic and monetary union by 1980.
24	Champion trial at Marylebone Magistrates Court. Lumsden and Reed fined £5 for threatening words and behaviour and bound over in sum of £20 for a year; twenty to thirty gays in gallery blowing bubbles and talking – gallery cleared after lunch.
28	All-London think-in at NW5, hosted by Camden.

November 1972

'My Ding-a-Ling' (Chuck Berry) is number one.

2	At Stoke Newington eight trial, Michael James, Tim Bolingbroke, Andrew Lumsden, Sarah Grimes, Denis Lemon give evidence for Angie Weir, corroborating her alibi of being on a GLF demo at Fleet Street on 19 August 1971 instead of an Angry Brigade trip to France to blow something up.
	Symposium on aversion therapy by London Medical Group (Christian medical group) with Prof. Hans Eysenck disrupted by Peter Tatchell who challenges them until they throw him out.
7	President Richard Nixon wins re-election in USA by a landslide of 520 to seventeen.
12	Cenotaph wreath laying ceremony successfully done by CHE.
15	People urged to attend picket of Old Bailey where Stoke Newington Eight trial is almost over.
	Financial statement from office collective shows that GLF has debts of £210 and cash of £10; the office is said to run on £40 a month now that a payphone has been installed.
18	Demo outside Holloway prison for Stoke Newington Eight defendants and others held there.
	GLF people in drag are attacked on Northern Line tube after GLF disco at Bull & Gate in Kentish Town, after a series of incidents at West London dances with skinheads.
19	First National Think-In on Jewish gays organized by the Jewish Homosexual Liaison Group.

December 1972

'Crocodile Rock' (Elton John) and 'Jean Genie' (David Bowie) in the charts.

467 killings attributed to troubles in Northern Ireland in the year.

6   Trial of Stoke Newington Eight ends. Angie Weir and three others acquitted. Four others sentenced to ten years for conspiracy to cause explosions. Jake Prescott's sentence reduced to ten years. Trial has lasted 111 days, a record for a criminal case.

20   Diplock Commission recommends suspension of trial by jury in Northern Ireland.

22   GLF Christmas Party at Lime Grove Baths, including a pantomime.

January 1973

'Blockbuster' (The Sweet) at number one.

Watergate trial opens in USA.

National Women's Conference on Homosexuality in Manchester coordinated by Liz Stanley and Glenys Parry, CHE, produces paper including dialogue with GLF women.

February 1973

Come Together 15 produced by Colville commune sometime this month.

March 1973

1   GLF commune takes over the old Agitprop offices in Bethnal Green, henceforward known as Bethnal Rouge.

3   Gay Marxist conference, Warwick University.

26   Noel Coward dies.

29   Last US troops leave Vietnam.

31   Ideal Homes Exhibition demo with GLF supporting Homeless Action Campaign.

April 1973

'Tie A Yellow Ribbon' (Dawn) at number one.

3   Squat at 44 Parkhill Rd forcibly evicted, sending Camden GLF scurrying for new meeting place; had been meeting there for past month due to lack of funds to hire hall. Meetings move to Malden Road.

6   Attempt to evict 7a Colville Houses ('Colvillia') foiled after forcible entry effected; report from queens claims 'hand to hand fighting in the Grand Salon'.

7   GLF Counter-Psychiatry Group zaps the conference of the British
        Psychological Society.
        CHE first national conference in Morecambe today and Sunday
        8th.

May 1973

46   National GLF conference/*Come Together* at Essex University,
        organized by Marion Prince.
22   Lord Lambton, Under Secretary for Defence, resigns after scandal
        involving sex workers and drugs.

June 1973

        'Walk On The Wild Side' (Lou Reed) in hit parade.
        Office starts to charge 1p for the newsletter.
13   After all-London meeting, forty people invade offices of Fleet
        Street papers and leaflet in-trays, toilets, etc.
        Pride Week events:
22   Bethnal Rouge benefit disco.
23   Disco from South London GLF.
24   Gay Day in Hyde Park.
25   Riverboat dance.
26   All-London meeting at Conway Hall followed by West London
        disco at Fulham Town Hall.
27   Open air disco at Clapham Common bandstand.
28   Meetings of local groups.
29   Demo at Fleet Street, leafleting and talking to the press.
30   Gay Pride Rally and picnic in Hyde Park; then coach to disco in
        Birmingham.
        Bethnal Rouge hold a jumble sale instead.

July 1973

        'I'm The Leader Of The Gang' (Gary Glitter) at number one.
        Come Together 16 is published, last issue printed.
        David McLellan, writing in the newsletter, points out that the
        office is now only open one or two evenings a week.

August 1973

Peter Tatchell attends World Youth Festival in East Germany, endorsed by all-London meeting as representative. His serious clash with the organizers and rest of the British student delegation after raising gay rights against their wishes makes the British press.

September 1973

Iceland threatens to break off diplomatic relations with Britain after shelling British trawlers in the 'Cod War'.

29   Meeting held at The Boltons to organize for a Switchboard, invitations sent by *Gay News* to fifteen groups and many individuals.

October 1973

3   All-London meeting discusses possibility of moving the office to Bethnal Rouge due to curtailed opening hours and lack of support.

4   *Gay News* 33 reports that the Caledonian Road Office has been invaded by 'Radical Gay Communards' from Bethnal Green. They are prevented after a fight from removing equipment but announce that the office has moved to Bethnal Rouge.

6   Second Middle Eastern War after Egypt and Syria attack Israel during Yom Kippur.

February 1974

Skirmish at Goldsmiths College GaySoc dance – Bethnal Rouge are invited and the queens turn up in drag. Group 4 security, hired by GaySoc, attack and expel the queens in drag. Steven Bradbury arrested.

4   GLF office collective publish 'The Last Newssheet' saying they will close on 16 February and operate a mailing service only selling info and badges. The office will be handed on to London Gay Switchboard collective after repainting as a present to Switchboard from the office collective. Money from sales and anything owed would go to disco equipment for the Friday night GLF discos held at the Prince Albert in Wharfedale Street, N1.

March 1974

GLF Think-In at University of Sussex hosted by Brighton GLF; Bethnal Rouge explain their action of previous October in raiding office.

Gay Liberation Front Manifesto – London 1971 *price 10p*

Introduction

Throughout recorded history, oppressed groups have organized to claim their rights and obtain their needs. Homosexuals, who have been oppressed by physical violence and by ideological and psychological attacks at every level of social interaction, are at last becoming angry.

To you, our gay sisters and brothers, we say that you are oppressed; we intend to show you examples of the hatred and fear with which straight society relegates us to the position and treatment of sub-humans, and to explain their basis. We will show you how we can use our righteous anger to uproot the present oppressive system with its decaying and constricting ideology, and how we, together with other oppressed groups, can start to form a new order, and a liberated life-style, from the alternatives which we offer.

HOW we're oppressed

Family

The oppression of gay people starts in the most basic unit of society, the family, consisting of the man in charge, a slave as his wife, and their children on whom they force themselves as the ideal models. The very form of the family works against homosexuality.

At some point nearly all gay people have found it difficult to cope with having the restricting images of man or woman pushed on them by their parents. It may have been from very early on, when the pressures to play with the 'right' toys, and thus prove boyishness or girlishness, drove against the child's inclinations. But for all of us this is certainly a problem by the time of adolescence, when we are expected to prove ourselves socially to our parents as members of the right sex (or to bring home a boy/girl friend) and to start being a 'real' (oppressive) young man or a 'real' (oppressed) young woman. The tensions can be very destructive.

The fact that gay people notice they are different from other men and women in the family situation, causes them to feel ashamed, guilty and failures. How many of us have really dared to be honest with our parents? How many of us have been thrown out of home? How many of us have been pressured into marriage, sent to psychiatrists, frightened into sexual inertia, ostracised, banned, emotionally destroyed – all by our parents?

School

Family experiences may differ widely, but in their education all children confront a common situation. Schools reflect the values of society in their formal academic curriculum, and reinforce them in their morality and discipline. Boys learn competitive, ego-building sports, and have more opportunity in science, whereas girls are given emphasis on domestic subjects, needlework, etc. Again, we gays were all forced into a rigid sex role which we did not want or need. It is quite common to discipline children for behaving in any way like the opposite sex; degrading titles like 'cissy' and 'tomboy' are widely used.

In the context of education, homosexuality is generally ignored, even where we know it exists, as in history and literature. Even sex education, which has been considered a new liberal dynamic of secondary schooling, proves to be little more than an extension of Christian morality. Homosexuality is again either ignored, or attacked with moralistic warnings and condemnations. The adolescent recognising his or her homosexuality might feel totally alone in the world, or a pathologically sick wreck.

Church

Formal religious education is still part of everyone's schooling, and our whole legal structure is supposedly based on Christianity, whose archaic and irrational teachings support the family and marriage as the only permitted condition for sex. Gay people have been attacked as abominable and sinful ever since the beginning of both Judaism and Christianity, and even if today the Church is playing down these strictures on homosexuality, its new ideology is that gay people are pathetic objects for sympathy.

The Media

The press, radio, television and advertising are used as reinforcements against us, and make possible the control of people's thoughts on an unprecedented scale. Entering everyone's home, affecting everyone's life, the media controllers, all representatives of the rich, male-controlled world, can exaggerate or suppress whatever information suits them.

Under different circumstances, the media might not be the weapon of a small minority. The present controllers are therefore dedicated defenders of things as they stand. Accordingly, the images of people which they transmit in their pictures and words do not subvert, but support society's image of 'normal' man and woman. It follows that we are characterised as scandalous, obscene perverts; as rampant, wild sex-monsters; as pathetic, doomed and compulsive degenerates; while the truth is blanketed under a conspiracy of silence.

Words

Anti-homosexual morality and ideology, at every level of society, manifest themselves in a special vocabulary for denigrating gay people. There is abuse like 'pansy', 'fairy', 'lesbo' to hurl at men and women who can't or won't fit stereotyped preconceptions. There are words like 'sick', 'bent' and 'neurotic' for destroying the credence of gay people. But there are no positive words. The ideological intent of our language makes it very clear that the generation of words and meanings is, at the moment, in the hands of the enemy. And that so many gay people pretend to be straight, and call each other 'butch dykes' or 'screaming queens', only makes that fact the more real.

The verbal attack on men and women who do not behave as they are supposed to, reflects the ideology of masculine superiority. A man who behaves like a woman is seen as losing something, and a woman who behaves like a man is put down for threatening men's enjoyment of their privileges.

Employment

If our upbringing so often produces guilt and shame, the experience of an adult gay person is oppressive in every aspect. In their work situation, gay people face the ordeal of spending up to fifty years of their lives confronted with the anti-homosexual hostility of their fellow employees.

A direct consequence of the fact that virtually all employers are highly privileged heterosexual men, is that there are some fields of work which are closed to gay people, and others which they feel some compulsion to enter. A result of this control for gay women is that they are perceived as a threat in the man's world. They have none of the sexual ties of dependence to men which make most women accept men as their 'superiors'. They are less likely to have the bind of children, and so there is nothing to stop them showing that they are as capable as any man, and thus deflating the man's ego, and exposing the myth that only men can cope with important jobs.

We are excluded from many jobs in high places where being married is the respectable guarantee, but being homosexual apparently makes us unstable, unreliable security risks. Neither, for example, are we allowed the job of teaching children, because we are all reckoned to be compulsive, child-molesting maniacs.

There are thousands of examples of people having lost their jobs due to it becoming known that they were gay, though employers usually contrive all manner of spurious 'reasons'.

There occurs, on the other hand, in certain jobs, such a concentration of gay people as to make an occupational ghetto. This happens, for women, in the forces, ambulance driving, and other uniformed occupations: and for men, in the fashion, entertainment and theatrical professions, all cases where the roles of 'man' and 'woman' can perhaps be underplayed or even reversed.

The Law

If you live in Scotland or Ireland; if you are under 21, or over 21 but having sex with someone under 21; if you are in the armed forces or the merchant navy; if you have sex with more than one person at the same time – and you are a gay male, you are breaking the law.

The 1967 Sexual Offences Act gave a limited licence to adult gay men. Common law however can restrict us from talking about and publicising both male and female homosexuality by classing it as 'immoral'. Beyond this there are a whole series of specific minor offences. Although 'the act' is not illegal, asking someone to go to bed with you can be classed as 'importuning for an immoral act', and kissing in public is classed as 'public indecency'.

Even if you do not get into any trouble, you will find yourself hampered by the application of the law in your efforts to set up home together, to raise children, and to express love as freely as straight people may do.

The practice of the police in 'enforcing' the law makes sure that cottagers and cruisers will be zealously hunted, while queer-bashers may be apprehended, half-heartedly, after the event.

Physical violence

On 25 September 1969, a man walked onto Wimbledon Common. We know the common to be a popular cruising ground, and believe the man to have been one of our gay brothers. Whether or not this is the case, the man was set upon by a group of youths from a nearby housing estate, and literally battered to death with clubs and boots. Afterwards, a boy from the same estate said: 'When you're hitting a queer, you don't think you're doing wrong. You think you're doing good. If you want money off a queer, you can get it off him – there's nothing to be scared of from the law, 'cause you know they won't go to the law'. (Sunday Times, 7/2/71)

Since that time, another man has been similarly murdered on Hampstead Heath. But murder is only the most extreme form of violence to which we are exposed, not having the effective means of protection. Most frequently we are 'rolled' for our money, or just beaten up; and this happens to butch-looking women in some districts.

Psychiatry

One way of oppressing people and preventing them getting too angry about it, is to convince them, and everyone else, that they are sick. There has hence arisen a body of psychiatric 'theory' and 'therapy' to deal with the 'problems' and 'treatment' of homosexuality.

Bearing in mind what we have so far described, it is quite understandable that gay people get depressed and paranoid; but it is also, of course, part of the scheme that gay people should retreat to psychiatrists in times of trouble.

Operating as they do on the basis of social convention and prejudice, NOT scientific truth, mainstream psychiatrists accept society's prevailing view that the male and female sex roles are 'good' and 'normal', and try to adjust people to them. If that fails, patients are told to 'accept themselves' as 'deviant'. For the psychiatrist to state that homosexuality was perfectly valid and satisfying, and that the hang-up was society's inability to accept that fact, would result in the loss of a large proportion of his patients.

Psychiatric 'treatment' can take the form either of mind-bending 'psychotherapy', or of aversion therapy which operates on the crude conditioning theory that if you hit a person hard enough, he'll do what you want. Another form of 'therapy' is chemically induced castration, and there is a further form of 'treatment' which consists in erasing part of the brain, with the intent (usually successful) of making the subject an asexual vegetable.

This 'therapy' is not the source of the psychiatrist's power, however. Their social power stems from the facile and dangerous arguments by which they contrive to justify the prejudice that homosexuality is bad or unfortunate, and to mount this fundamental attack upon our right to do as we think best. In this respect, there is little difference between the psychiatrist who says: 'From statistics we can show that homosexuality is connected with madness', and the one who says: 'Homosexuality is unfortunate because it is socially rejected'. The former is a dangerous idiot – he cannot see that it is society which drives gay people mad. The second is a pig because he does see this, but sides consciously with the oppressors.

That psychiatrists command such credence and such income is surprising if we remember the hysterical disagreements of theory and practice in their field, and the fact that in formulating their opinions, they rarely consult gay people. In fact, so far as is possible, they avoid talking to them at all, because they know that such confrontation would wreck their theories.

Self-oppression

The ultimate success of all forms of oppression is our self-oppression.

Self-oppression is achieved when the gay person has adopted and internalised straight people's definition of what is good and bad. Self-oppression is saying: 'When you come down to it, we are abnormal'. Or doing what you most need and want to do, but with a sense of shame and loathing, or in a state of disassociation, pretending it isn't happening; cruising or cottaging not because you enjoy it, but because you're afraid of anything less anonymous. Self-oppression is saying: 'I accept what I am', and meaning: 'I accept that what I am is second-best and rather pathetic'. Self-oppression is any other kind of apology: 'We've been living together for ten years and all our married friends know about us and think we're just the same as them'. Why? You're not.

Self-oppression is the dolly lesbian who says: 'I can't stand those butch types who look like truck drivers'; the virile gay man who shakes his head at the thought of 'those pathetic queens'. This is self-oppression because it's just another way of saying: 'I'm a nice normal gay, just like an attractive heterosexual'.

The ultimate in self-oppression is to avoid confronting straight society, and thereby provoking further hostility: Self-oppression is saying, and believing: 'I am not oppressed'.

WHY *we're oppressed*

Gay people are oppressed. As we've just shown, we face the prejudice, hostility and violence of straight society, and the opportunities open to us in work and leisure are restricted, compared with those of straight people. Shouldn't we demand reforms that will give us tolerance and equality? Certainly we should – in a liberal-democratic society, legal equality and protection from attack are the very least we should ask for. They are our civil rights.

But gay liberation does not just mean reforms. It means a revolutionary change in our whole society. Is this really necessary? Isn't it hard enough for us to win reforms within the present society, and how will we engage the support of straight people if we get ourselves branded as revolutionaries?

Reforms may make things better for a while: changes in the law can make straight people a little less hostile, a little more tolerant – but reform cannot change the deep-down attitude of straight people that homosexuality is at best inferior to their own way of life, at worst a sickening perversion. It will take more than reforms to change this attitude, because it is rooted in our society's most basic institution – the Patriarchal family.

We've all been brought up to believe that the family is the source of our happiness and comfort. But look at the family more closely. Within the small family unit, in which the dominant man and submissive woman bring up their children in their own image, all our attitudes towards sexuality are learned at a very early age. Almost before we can talk, certainly before we can think for ourselves, we are taught that there are certain attributes that are 'feminine' and others that are 'masculine' and that they are God-given and unchangeable. Beliefs learned so young are very hard to change; but in fact these are false beliefs. What we are taught about the differences between man and woman is propaganda, not truth.

The truth is that there are no proven systematic differences between male and female, apart from the obvious biological ones. Male and female genitals and reproductive systems are different, and so are certain other physical characteristics, but all differences of temperament, aptitudes and so on, are the result of upbringing and social pressures. They are not inborn.

Human beings could be much more various than our constricted patterns of 'masculine' and 'feminine' permit – we should be free to develop with greater individuality. But as things are at present, there are only these two stereotyped roles into which everyone is supposed to fit, and most people – including gay people too – are apt to be alarmed when they hear these stereotypes or gender roles attacked, fearing that children 'won't know how to grow up if they have no-one to identify with', or that 'everyone will be the same', i.e. that there will be either utter chaos or total conformity. There would in fact be a greater variety of models and more freedom for experimentation, but there is no reason to suppose this will lead to chaos.

By our very existence as gay people, we challenge these roles. It can easily be seen that homosexuals don't fit into the stereotypes of masculine and feminine, and this is one of the main reasons why we become the object of suspicion, since everyone is taught that these and only these two roles are appropriate.

Our entire system is built around the patriarchal family and its enshrinement of these masculine and feminine roles. Religion, popular morality, art, literature and sport all reinforce these stereotypes. In other words, this society is a sexist society, in which one's biological sex determines almost all of what one does and how one does it; a situation in which men are privileged, and women are mere adjuncts of men and objects for their use, both sexually and otherwise.

Since all children are taught so young that boys should be aggressive and adventurous, girls passive and pliant, most people do tend to behave in these ways as they get older, and to believe that other people should do so too.

So sexism does not just oppress gay people, but all women as well. It is assumed that because women bear children they should and must rear them, and be simultaneously excluded from all other spheres of achievement.

However, if the indoctrination of the small child with these attitudes is not always entirely successful (if it were, there would be no gay people for a start), the ideas taken in by the young child almost unconsciously must be reinforced in the older child and teenager by a consciously expressed male chauvinism: the ideological expression of masculine superiority. Male chauvinism is not hatred of women, but male chauvinists accept women only on the basis that they are in fact lesser beings. It is an expression of male power and male privilege, and while it's quite possible for a gay man to be a male chauvinist, his very existence does also challenge male chauvinism in so far as he rejects his male supremacist role over women, and perhaps particularly if he rejects 'masculine' qualities.

It is because of the patriarchal family that reforms are not enough. Freedom for gay people will never be permanently won until everyone is freed from sexist role-playing and the straight-jacket of sexist rules about our sexuality. And we will not be freed from these so long as each succeeding generation is brought up in the same old sexist way in the patriarchal family.

But why can't we just change the way in which children are brought up without attempting to transform the whole fabric of society?

Because sexism is not just an accident – it is an essential part of our present society, and cannot be changed without the whole society changing with it. In the first place, our society is dominated at every level by men, who have an interest in preserving the status quo; secondly, the present system of work and production depends on the existence of the patriarchal society. Conservative sociologists have pointed out that the small family unit of two parents and their children is essential in our contemporary advanced industrial family where work is minutely subdivided and highly regulated – in other words, for the majority very boring. A man would not work at the assembly line if he had no wife and family to support; he would not give himself fully to his work without the supportive and reassuring little group ready to follow him about and gear itself to his needs, to put up with his ill temper when he is frustrated or put down by the boss at work.

Were it not also for the captive wife, educated by advertising and everything she reads into believing that she needs ever more new goodies for the home, for her own beautification and for the children's well-being, our economic system could not function properly, depending as it does on people buying far more manufactured goods than they need. The housewife, obsessed with the ownership of as many material goods as possible, is the agent of this high level of spending. None of these goods will ever satisfy her, since there is always something better to be had, and the surplus of these pseudo 'necessities' goes hand in hand with the absence of genuinely necessary goods and services, such as adequate housing and schools.

The ethic and ideology of our culture has been conveniently summed up by the enemy. Here is a quotation, intended quite seriously, from an American psychiatric primer. The author, Dr. Fred Brown, states:

> Our values in Western civilisation are founded upon the sanctity of the family, the right to property, and the worthwhileness of 'getting ahead'. The family can be established only through heterosexual intercourse, and this gives the woman a high value [Note the way

in which woman is appraised as a form of property]. Property acquisition and worldly success are viewed as distinctly masculine aims. The individual who is outwardly masculine but appears to fall into the feminine class by reason . . . of his preference for other men denies these values of our civilisation. In denying them he belittles those goals which carry weight and much emotional colouring in our society and thereby earns the hostility of those to whom these values are of great importance.

We agree with his description of our society and its values – but we reach a different conclusion. We gay men and gay women do deny these values of our civilisation. We believe that work in an advanced industrial society could be organized on more humane lines, with each job more varied and more pleasurable, and that the way society is at present organized operates in the interests of a small ruling group of straight men who claim most of the status and money, and not in the interests of the people as a whole. We also believe that our economic resources could be used in a much more valuable and constructive way than they are at the moment – but that will not happen until the present pattern of male dominance in our society changes too.

That is why any reforms we might painfully extract from our rulers would only be fragile and vulnerable; that is why we, along with the women's movement, must fight for something more than reform. We must aim at the abolition of the family, so that the sexist, male supremacist system can no longer be nurtured there.

We can do it

Yet although this struggle will be hard, and our victories not easily won, we are not in fact being idealistic to aim at abolishing the family and the cultural distinctions between men and women. True, these have been with us throughout history, yet humanity is at last in a position where we can progress beyond this.

Only reactionaries and conservatives believe in the idea of 'natural man'. Just what is so different in human beings from the rest of the animal kingdom is their 'unnaturalness'. Civilisation is in fact our evolution away from the limitations of the natural environment and towards its ever more complex control. It is not 'natural' to travel in planes. It is not 'natural' to take medicines and perform operations. Clothing and shoes do not grow on trees. Animals do not cook their food. This evolution is made possible by the development of technology – i.e. all those tools and skills which help us to control the natural environment.

We have now reached a stage at which the human body itself, and even the reproduction of the species, is being 'unnaturally' interfered with (i.e. improved) by technology. Reproduction used to be left completely to the uncontrolled biological processes inherited from our animal ancestors, but modern science, by drastically lowering infant mortality, has made it unnecessary for women to have more than two or three babies, while contraceptives have made possible the conscious control of pregnancy and the freeing of sexuality from reproduction. Today, further advances are on the point of making it possible for women to be completely liberated from their biology by means of the development of artificial wombs. Women need no longer be burdened with the production of children as their main task in life, and need be still less in the future.

The present gender-role system of 'masculine' and 'feminine' is based on the way that reproduction was originally organized. Men's freedom from the prolonged physical burden of bearing children gave them a privileged position which was then reinforced by an ideology of male superiority. But technology has now advanced to a stage at which the gender-role system is no longer necessary.

However, social evolution does not automatically take place with the steady advance of technology. The gender-role system and the family unit built around it will not disappear just because they have ceased to be necessary. The sexist culture gives straight men privileges which, like those of any privileged class, will not be surrendered without a struggle, so that all of us who are oppressed by this culture (women and gay people), must band together to fight it. The end of the sexist culture and of the family will benefit all women, and all gay people. We must work together with women, since their oppression is our oppression, and by working together we can advance the day of our common liberation.

A new life-style

In the final section we shall outline some of the practical steps gay liberation will take to make this revolution. But linked with this struggle to change society there is an important aspect of gay liberation that we can begin to build here and now – a NEW, LIBERATED LIFE-STYLE which will anticipate, as far as possible, the free society of the future.

Gay shows the way. In some ways we are already more advanced than straight people. We are already outside the family and we have already, in part at least, rejected the 'masculine' or 'feminine' roles society has designed for us. In a society dominated by the sexist culture it is very difficult, if not impossible, for heterosexual men and women to escape their rigid gender-role structuring and the roles of oppressor and oppressed. But gay men don't need to oppress women in order to fulfil their own psycho-sexual needs, and gay women don't have to relate sexually to the male oppressor, so that at this moment in time, the freest and most equal relationships are most likely to be between homosexuals.

But because the sexist culture has oppressed and distorted our lives too, this is not always achieved. In our mistaken, placating efforts to be accepted and tolerated, we've too often submitted to the pressures to conform to the straight-jacket of society's rules and hang-ups about sex.

Particularly oppressive aspects of gay society are the Youth Cult, Butch and Femme role-playing, and Compulsive Monogamy.

THE YOUTH CULT. Straight women are the most exposed in our society to the commercially manipulated (because very profitable) cult of youth and 'beauty' – i.e. the conformity to an ideal of 'sexiness' and 'femininity' imposed from without, not chosen by women themselves. Women are encouraged to look into the mirror and love themselves because an obsession with clothes and cosmetics dulls their appreciation of where they're really at . . . until it's too late. The sight of an old woman bedizened with layers of make-up, her hair tortured into artificial turrets, provokes ridicule on all sides. Yet this grotesque denial of physical aging is merely the logical conclusion to the life of a woman who has been taught that her value lies primarily in her degree of sexual attractiveness.

Gay women, like straight men, are rather less into the compulsive search for youth, perhaps because part of their rebellion has been the rejection of themselves as sex objects – like men they see themselves as people; as subjects rather than objects. But gay men are very apt to fall victim to the cult of youth – those sexual parades in the 'glamorous' meat-rack bars of London and New York, those gay beaches of the South of France and Los Angeles haven't anything to do with liberation. Those are the hang-outs of the plastic gays who are obsessed with image and appearance. In love with their own bodies, these gay men dread the approach of age, because to be old is to be 'ugly', and with their youth they lose also the right to love and be loved, and are valued only if they can pay. This obsession with youth is destructive. We must all get away from the false commercial standards of 'beauty' imposed on us by movie moguls and advertising firms, because the youth/beauty hang-up sets us against one another in a frenzied competition for attention, and leads in the end to an obsession with self which is death to real affection or real sensual love. Some gay men have spent so much time staring at themselves in the mirror that they've become hypnotised by their own magnificence and have ended up by being unable to see anyone else.

BUTCH AND FEMME. Many gay men and women needlessly restrict their lives by compulsive role playing. They may restrict their own sexual behaviour by feeling that they must always take either a butch or a femme role, and worse, these roles are transposed to make even more distorting patterns in general social relationships. We gay men and women are outside the gender-role system anyway, and therefore it isn't surprising if some of us – of either sex – are more 'masculine' and others more 'feminine'. There is nothing wrong with this. What is bad is when gay people try to impose on themselves and on one another the masculine and feminine stereotypes of straight society, the butch seeking to expand his ego by dominating his/her partner's life and freedom, and the femme seeking protection by submitting to the butch. Butch really is bad – the oppression of others is an essential part of the masculine gender role. We must make gay men and women who lay claim to the privileges of straight males understand what they are doing; and those gay men and women who are caught up in the femme role must realise, as straight women increasingly do, that any security this brings is more than offset by their loss of freedom.

COMPULSIVE MONOGAMY. We do not deny that it is possible for gay couples as for some straight couples to live happily and constructively together. We question however as an ideal, the finding and settling down eternally with one 'right' partner. This is the blueprint of the straight world which gay people have taken over. It is inevitably a parody, since they haven't even the justification of straight couples – the need to provide a stable environment for their children (though in any case we believe that the suffocating small family unit is by no means the best atmosphere for bringing up children).

Monogamy is usually based on ownership – the woman sells her services to the man in return for security for herself and her children – and is entirely bound up in the man's idea of property; furthermore in our society the monogamous couple, with or without children, is an isolated, shut-in, up-tight unit, suspicious of and hostile to outsiders. And though we don't lay down rules or tell gay people how they should behave in bed or in their relationships, we do want them to question society's blueprint for the couple. The blueprint says 'we two against the world', and that can be protective and comforting. But it can also be suffocating, leading to neurotic dependence and underlying hostility, the emotional dishonesty of staying in the comfy safety of the home and garden, the security and narrowness of the life built for two, with the secret guilt of fancying someone else while remaining in thrall to the idea that true love lasts a lifetime – as though there were a ration of relationships, and to want more than one were greedy. Not that sexual fidelity is necessarily wrong; what is wrong is the inturned emotional exclusiveness of the couple which stunts the partners so they can no longer operate at all as independent beings in society. People need a variety of relationships in order to develop and grow, and to learn about other human beings.

It is especially important for gay people to stop copying straight – we are the ones who have the best opportunities to create a new life-style and if we don't, no one else will. Also, we need one another more than straight people do, because we are equals suffering under an insidious oppression from a society too primitive to come to terms with the freedom we represent. Singly, or isolated in couples, we are weak – the way society wants us to be. Society cannot put us down so easily if we fuse together. We have to get together, understand one another, live together.

Two ways we can do this are by developing consciousness raising groups and by gay communes.

Our gay communes and collectives must not be mere convenient living arrangements or worse, just extensions of the gay ghetto. They must be a focus of consciousness-raising (i.e. raising or increasing our awareness of our real oppression) and of gay liberation activity, a new focal point for members of the gay community. It won't be easy, because this society is hostile to communal living. And besides the practical hang-ups of finding money and a place large enough for a collective to live in, there are our own personal hang-ups: we have to change our attitudes to our personal property, to our lovers, to our day-to-day priorities in work and leisure, even to our need for privacy.

But victory will come. If we're convinced of the importance of the new life-style, we can be strong and we can win through.

The way forward

Aims

The long-term goal of the London Gay Liberation Front, which inevitably brings us into fundamental conflict with the institutionalised sexism of this society, is to rid society of the gender-role system which is at the root of our oppression. This can only be achieved by the abolition of the family as the unit in which children are brought up. We intend to work for the replacement of the family unit, with its rigid gender-role pattern, by new organic units such as the commune, where the development of children becomes the shared responsibility of a larger group of people who live together. Children must be liberated from the present condition of having their role in life defined by biological accident; the commune will ultimately provide a variety of gender-free models.

As we cannot carry out this revolutionary change alone, and as the abolition of the family and gender roles is also a necessary condition of women's liberation, we will work to form a strategic alliance with the women's liberation movement, aiming to develop our ideas and our practice in close inter-relation. In order to build this alliance, the brothers in gay liberation will have to be prepared to sacrifice that degree of male chauvinism and male privilege that they all still possess.

To achieve our long term goal will take many years, perhaps decades. But if at the moment the replacement of the family by a system of communes may seem a very long way ahead, we believe that, in the ever sharpening crisis of western society, the time may come quite suddenly when old institutions start to crack, and when people will have to seek new models. We intend to start working out our contribution to these new models now, by creating an alternative gay culture free from sexism, and by setting up gay communes. When our communes are firmly established, we plan to let children grow up in them.

Free our heads

The starting point of our liberation must be to rid ourselves of the oppression which lies in the head of every one of us. This means freeing our heads from self-oppression and male chauvinism, and no longer organizing our lives according to the patterns with which we are indoctrinated by straight society. It means that we must root out the idea that homosexuality is bad, sick or immoral, and develop a gay pride. In order to survive, most of us have either knuckled under or pretended that no oppression exists, and the result of this has been further to distort our heads. Within gay liberation, a number of consciousness-raising groups have already developed, in which we try to understand our oppression and learn new ways of thinking and behaving. The aim is to step outside the experience permitted by straight society, and to learn to love and trust one another. This is the precondition for acting and struggling together.

By freeing our heads we get the confidence to come out publicly and proudly as gay people, and to win over our gay brothers and sisters to the ideas of gay liberation.

Campaign

Before we can create the new society of the future, we have to defend our interests as gay people here and now against all forms of oppression and victimisation. We have therefore drawn up the following list of immediate demands.

• that all discrimination against gay people, male and female, by the law, by employers, and by society at large, should end.

• that all people who feel attracted to a member of their own sex be taught that such feelings are perfectly valid.

• that sex education in schools stop being exclusively heterosexual.

• that psychiatrists stop treating homosexuality as though it were a sickness, thereby giving gay people senseless guilt complexes.

• that gay people be as legally free to contact other gay people, through newspaper ads, on the streets and by any other means they may want as are heterosexuals, and that police harassment should cease right now.

• that employers should no longer be allowed to discriminate against anyone on account of their sexual preferences.

• that the age of consent for gay males be reduced to the same as for straight.

• that gay people be free to hold hands and kiss in public, as are heterosexuals.

London Gay Liberation Front has already been active in some of these areas, and plans to start activity soon in others. The GLF youth group is involved in working for a liberated sex education in schools, and for the lowering of the age of consent. The counter-psychiatry group is fighting against institutions and doctors who daily torture gay people with aversion therapy. The action group is coordinating activity against harassment and entrapment by queer-bashers and the police. GLF has held demonstrations against publishers and bookshops who distribute anti-gay literature. GLF holds regular gay-ins in the public parks to develop our solidarity as gay people, to encourage others to join us and to show that we will no longer allow ourselves to be confined to 'safe' ghetto areas. Our paper Come Together, our street theatre and other propaganda activities are designed primarily for gay people, but they are also aimed at winning support from our friends in the straight community, and at exposing and attacking our enemies. Within a few months of our existence we have confronted millions of straight people with our homosexuality; these people will find it increasingly difficult to 'protect' themselves and especially their children from our ideas.

We do not intend to ask for anything. We intend to stand firm and assert our basic rights. If this involves violence, it will not be we who initiate this, but those who attempt to stand in our way to freedom.

Gay Liberation Front, 5 Caledonian Road, London N1

This manifesto was produced collectively by the Manifesto Group of GLF. We recognize that it leaves many questions unanswered and open-ended but hope it will lead to the furtherance of a scientific analysis of sexism and our oppression as gay people.

Appendix 3

Badges and Symbols of London GLF

The first London GLF badge was the clenched white fist with a purple flower and white male/female symbols in the palm, with white lettering 'Gay Liberation Front' on a purple background, produced in December 1970 in London (*see fig. 1*). It is a copy of a Philadelphia GLF design; the town where Aubrey Walter and Bob Mellors met up on their travels. The fist was a popular sign of revolution. The thumb is outside the clenched fist, rather than within – what does this signify? Despite being unpopular enough to be replaced less than a year later, it has subsequently become the most enduring symbol of GLF to later gay activists. My mother's teddy bear has worn one since 1980.

The GLF formally adopted another design in late 1971 or early 1972, after they were at All Saints. It is first advertised in *Come Together* 11 of January 1972. This was designed by Alan Wakeman and won approval over several other suggestions. There are stories that one of these was a revival of the pink triangle, promoted by John Chesterman, Michael Brown and others (felt to be too self oppressive). Alan Wakeman remembers discussion about pink triangles being late on, but internal evidence from various issues of *Come Together* suggests that at least some people in GLF knew about the pink triangle before this debate.

The winning design was an adaptation of the astrological symbol for Jove, seen as being jovial or gay. A fist was added. The design was a conscious effort to get away from the sexual polarities of the signs for Mars and Venus – roughly, the arrow and cross symbols still used to indicate male and female – and to be less sexually stereotyped (*see fig. 2*). The badge was produced in a number of colours and Max McLellan has them all. However, it never caught on.

Alan Wakeman remembers 'There had been discussion about having our own badge, people thought that the purple design was too messy. I was astounded that we would have Venus and Mars on a gay badge, because they were the symbols not only for male and female but for war and sex. I thought that we needed a New Age symbol, which was what I designed. The decision on the new badge was taken at a full meeting at All Saints and several suggestions were made which I can't remember now, though I don't think the pink triangle was known about in GLF then. I talked about the design, which turned Jupiter into the GLF initials, and explained the symbols – that Mars was Martial and Venus was venereal, and Jupiter was jovial or in other words gay – and they burst into applause. Of course, when people saw it without any of the explanation they didn't understand it. It was seen as a bit of a mystery, which is why I regard it as rather a failure. Roger Baker referred to it as a "masterpiece of obscurity". Then a clenched fist got incorporated into it, a tiny one that most people didn't notice.'

Lesbians within GLF used the same badges, the first of which at least was clearly unisex. After the split from the men, South London Lesbian Liberation (based at Radnor Terrace Women's Centre in Vauxhall) decided to have their own badge. Lindsay Turner explained to the Lesbian Archive some years later, 'The badge was designed and drawn by one of the members of our group. We all decided that we thought three women's symbols was more appropriate to our (officially) non-couple politics than two.' The badge was redrawn a few years later and was popular throughout the 1970s and early 1980s in London (*see figs. 3 and 4*).

The Lambda was later adopted by the Gay Activists Alliance in the US and rapidly spread as a gay male sign to the UK. It was promoted as the Greek letter for a catalyst. *Gay International News* claimed it was also the Japanese sign for penetration.

The pink triangle was known within GLF but usually rejected for the reasons given above. It was, however, seen as suitable for the wreath laid at the Cenotaph in November 1971 (beginning a tradition carried on to this day by a variety of lesbian and gay activist groups), where it was reproduced in pink carnations.

There were a variety of different flags and banners used over the period of GLF. The two best known and most frequently photographed were a simple reproduction of the wording 'GAY LIBERATION FRONT' and the one with interlocking circles shown in several photographs, which was in purple, red and white. It is shown on the day it was seized by the police at the Festival of Light event in Hyde Park in September 1971 and later destroyed by them.

A new Gay Liberation Front banner, recreating the first of these, was reproduced for Pride 1995 using traditional materials and methods, i.e. two queens and a dyke, rather a lot of dope and some serious hand stitching.

Figure 1

Figure 2

Figure 3

Figure 4

Where Are They Now?

Harry Beck still lives in Notting Hill.

Mick Belsten eventually worked for *Gay Times*, where he founded the international news section, and died of an AIDS-related illness.

Tim Bolingbroke joined an ashram, went on pilgrimage and was last reported in San Francisco several years ago, where he was a volunteer for the Shanti Project.

Bette Bourne is, in the words of the song, still here; he founded Bloolips and works in New York and London as an actor, most recently as a remarkable Lady Bracknell.

Annie Brackx is a journalist and editor.

Nicholas Bramble went to the USA and is dead.

Michael Brown went on to help found the Jewish Aids Trust and is now retired.

Micky Burbidge is a senior official at the Department of the Environment and a housing expert.

Richard Chappell was killed by AIDS in 1992.

John Chesterman continued to be involved in and to record revolutionary activities and the counterculture and is now living in Hampstead.

John Church died in 1994.

Tim Clark became chief sub-editor of *Time Out*; is now at *Arena*.

Martin Corbett still has the same job he had in 1970. He is a Saint in the Order of Perpetual Indulgence and a member of OutRage!

Richard Dipple, co-founder of Gay Mens Press, died of an AIDS-related illness in 1991.

Cloud Downey lives in London and works in the theatre, having been Chair of Body Positive and founder of Positive Theatre.

Louis Eakes died of an AIDS-related illness in the early 1990s.

Andy Elsmore was murdered in the 1980s.

Stuart Feather still lives in Notting Hill, was an original member of Bloolips and is a painter.

David Fernbach works for the *New Left Review* and is a founder and publisher of Gay Men's Press.

Peter Flannery is dead.

Jim Fouratt still lives in New York, writes for the music press and stirs things up as well as he ever did.

Hugh Gaw went to Australia and became involved in the movement there.

Sarah Grimes is a printer living in London.

Warren Haig returned to Canada and was last seen 'in a business suit' in the early 1980s – Warren, where are you?

Tony Halliday has just completed his thesis on the history of art.

Bill Halstead lives in Spain.

Carl Hill lives in Hampstead.

Andrew Hodges is a writer.

Julian Hows went on to Bloolips, the Brixton Faeries, London Lesbian and Gay Switchboard, and is now a sexual health worker; julian@misscane.demon.co.uk.

David Hutter became an acclaimed artist and died in 1990.

Michael James (was Lynham) lives on the coast and ballroom dances.

Julia L is still a teacher in London.

Denis Lemon became sole proprietor of *Gay News* and died of an AIDS-related illness in 1994.

Andrew Lumsden became editor of *Gay News* eventually and is a painter and tour director.

Michael Mason is the founder and proprietor of Stonewall Press, publishers of *Capital Gay*.

Mary McIntosh is a senior lecturer in sociology at the University of Essex, teaching on disputes in feminist theory.

David (Max) McLellan still works at Housmans.

Bob Mellors lives in Poland.

Nettie Pollard works for Liberty and was a founder of Feminists Against Censorship.

Tony Reynolds worked for *Capital Gay* and died of an AIDS-related illness.

Tony Salvis is thought to be still in London.

David Seligman was for over a decade a mainstay of London Gay Switchboard.

Tarsus Sutton died in 1994 of a heart attack.

Peter Tatchell became a Labour candidate in Bermondsey, joined OutRage! and writes and speaks on lesbian and gay politics and sexual health.

Paul Theobald went to New York, cleaned up his act, helped with Gay Mens Health Crisis, came back to the UK and is still an AIDS activist.

Carla Toney (was Hughes) has twin children, teaches creative writing at Hackney College and is a freelance editor and writer.

Alan Wakeman still lives in Piccadilly and is a writer and translator, most recently of an acclaimed version of *The Little Prince*. His hair has stayed the same length.

Aubrey Walter is a founder and publisher of Gay Mens Press and Editions Aubrey Walter.

Simon Watney has stayed involved in lesbian and gay politics, focusing on AIDS and working as a critic and curator; he can often be found at The Fridge.

Jeffrey Weeks is Professor of Sociology and Head of School at South Bank University and the author of many books including *Coming Out*.

Angie Weir (now Mason) became a solicitor and Director of Stonewall, the lesbian and gay lobby group, and has a daughter.

Elizabeth Wilson is Professor of Sociology at the University of North London and an author on many topics, currently fashion, cities and bohemian life.

Jane Winter works in a human rights project in London.

Sue Winter is still totally committed to gay rights and available; she is Sister Immaculate Deception in the London Order of Perpetual Indulgence.

Many others I was not able to trace or speak to; and there are some who have new lives and would rather not be remembered here.

Appendix 5

Printed and Archival Sources

There is disgracefully little available on London GLF, which is why I started out on this project in the first place. The primary sources of information in this book were the tapes and notes of discussions with people who were in the London Gay Liberation Front. These remain with the author, and authorized versions of longer interviews as agreed with participants have been lodged with the Hall Carpenter Archives.

The Hall Carpenter Archives were invaluable. They contain the Chesterman collection, the James collection and a vast amount of related material in the CHE, Albany Society and other collections. They were also the source of copies of *Gay News*, *Come Together*, *OZ*, *IT*, *Frendz*, *Lunch* and other relevant publications. I cannot over-praise the archives, which are in the British Library of Political and Economic Science at the London School of Economics and are free to enter on a day pass, if you state your destination clearly at the entrance.

A number of GLF people also gave me access to material from their personal archives, including Jeffrey Weeks, Mary McIntosh, Max McLellan, Sarah Grimes, Angela Mason and Elizabeth Wilson, Simon Watney, Michael Mason, John Chesterman, Carl Hill and Alan Wakeman. Where these were donated to me, they have been passed on to the Hall Carpenter Archives. If you have any GLF materials, DON'T THROW THEM OUT – give them to the Hall Carpenter Archives if you don't want them.

The main book sources were: *Come Together*, a collection from the magazines with an introduction by Aubrey Walter (GMP, 1980) (until someone kind reprints the lot, this is invaluable); *Coming Out* by Jeffrey Weeks (Quartet, 1977); *Homosexuality: Power and Politics* by the Gay

Left Collective (Allison & Busby, 1980); and some chapters in: *Radical Records*, ed. Bob Cant & Susan Hemmings (Routledge, 1988); *Peers, Queers and Commons* by Stephen Jeffrey-Poulter (Routledge, 1991); *Quest for Justice* by Antony Grey (Sinclair-Stevenson, 1992); and for the US section: *Stonewall* by Martin Duberman (Dutton, 1993); and *Making History* by Eric Marcus (HarperCollins, 1992).

A number of (sadly, out of print) pamphlets were very useful. I hope that somebody reprints them soon: *Psychiatry and the Homosexual*, Gay Liberation Pamphlet 1 (1973); *With Downcast Gays* by Andrew Hodges and David Hutter (1974); *The Rise and Fall of GLF* by David Fernbach (Gay Culture Pamphlets, 1973); and, of course, the *Manifesto* (1971) which is included here at appendix two. Do not confuse the genuine article with the late 1970s reprint by the GLF Information Service, which omits sections on communal living and the destruction of the family.

Index of Names

Note: page references in italic indicate where a person is quoted in the text